Pensions in the Public Sector

Pension Research Council Publications

A list of recent books in the series appears at the back of this volume.

Pensions in the Public Sector

Edited by
Olivia S. Mitchell and Edwin C. Hustead

Pension Research Council
The Wharton School of the University of Pennsylvania

PENN

University of Pennsylvania Press

Philadelphia

10   9   8   7   6   5   4   3   2   1

Published by
University of Pennsylvania Press
Philadelphia, Pennsylvania 19104-4011

Library of Congress Cataloging-in-Publication Data

Pensions in the public sector / edited by Olivia S. Mitchell and
Edwin C. Hustead
    p.   cm. "Pension Research Council Publications"
Includes bibliographical records and index
ISBN 0-8122-3578-9 (alk. paper)
1. State governments—Officials and employees—Pensions—
United States.   2. Local officials and employees—Pensions—
United States.   3. United States—Officials and employees—
Pensions.   I. Mitchell, Olivia S.   II. Hustead, Edwin C., 1942–.
III. Wharton School. Pension Research Council.
JK791 .P45   2000
331.24/29135173.—dc21   00-059384

Contents

Preface

Public sector pensions are much in the news of late. Insolvent state employee retirement programs undermined national economic policy in Brazil during the late 1990s, leading to a currency devaluation and then regional economic collapse. Problems with public pension systems in China threaten not only the wellbeing of retirees but also the economy as a whole. And in many countries, well-meaning efforts to privatize government-run firms have foundered when it has been determined that acquiring these firms imposes huge unfunded pension liabilities on the new owners, resulting from many years of low contributions and feeble investment returns.

What can be done to help public sector pension plans perform more efficiently, and thereby enhance old-age security? This volume seeks to answer this question by taking stock of the public pension situation in North America, offering lessons and highlighting challenges these financial institutions will face in the next several decades. We show that, unlike in other countries, North American public pension systems are performing rather well. State and local plans in the United States have impressive levels of assets backing their liabilities, they provide reasonable replacement rates to retirees, and they invest in a manner not too different from that of private pension managers. The picture is almost as positive for public pensions in Canada, although portfolio restrictions have produced lower investment returns, and funding patterns are less robust. But our assessment is less positive for U.S. military pension systems and the pension system developed by the U.S. Congress for the nation's capital, Washington, D.C. Thus even within the continent, wide variations have resulted from different structures and regulatory regimes.

Our analysis shows that building and maintaining a successful public pension system requires careful attention to benefit and financing policy, strong funding and investment performance, and continuous oversight. The ways in which these factors interact are traced across a variety of institutional environments, each of which has generated its own pension system. Contributors to the volume illustrate the range of options as they vary across public sector groups, ranging from uniformed employees (police, firefighters), to teachers, legislators and judiciary, municipal and state employees, military personnel, and others. It is a pleasure to have assembled such an impressive set of specialists and experts to take a serious look at these important financial institutions, asking what they do well and what they could do better. We also seek to learn lessons for private pension plans, so as to help policymakers and practitioners with suggestions for future pension design.

Sponsorship for the research leading to this volume was generously provided by the Wharton School at the University of Pennsylvania, as well as the U.S. Department of Labor. In addition we thank our Senior Partners and Institutional Members of the Pension Research Council for continuing support and guidance. On behalf of the Pension Research Council at The Wharton School, I thank them and the many contributors whose participation made this volume feasible. I am pleased that the Pension Research Council continues its long-standing interest in public sector retirement offerings in sponsoring this volume. The book should be required reading for all managers and policymakers designing public—as well as private—pension systems in the years to come.

I
The Structure and Function of Public Pension Systems

Chapter 1
Public Sector Pension Plans
Lessons and Challenges for the Twenty-First Century

Edwin C. Hustead and Olivia S. Mitchell

Pension systems for government employees represent an important and influential segment of the pension market. In the United States, for example, pension plans for state and local employees include almost 13 million workers (Mitchell et al., this volume). Military retirement programs cover an additional 3 million personnel, and the federal government has several of its own plans adding almost another 3 million covered employees to the public pension fold (Hustead and Hustead, this volume). Public pensions are also widespread in Canada (Pozzebon, this volume). Not only are the numbers of included employees impressive: the financial clout wielded by these plans is also enormous. In the United States, state and local employee pensions controlled over $2.4 trillion in assets in 1998, while federal and military pension assets stood at almost $700 million.

With so many participants and so much money at stake, it is only reasonable that these financial institutions have come under scrutiny of late. How are public pension plans structured, in terms of their benefit promises and financing? How is the public pension asset pool invested, and what issues are influential in designing the investment practices and resulting returns? What risks do participants bear, in these plans, and which risks are explicitly or implicitly passed on to other stakeholders including taxpayers, when pension promises are made? In this volume we provide answers to these questions by offering an overview of the benefits, financing, governance structure, and challenges facing a wide range of public plans in North America. The analysts writing herein speak to public plan benefits specialists, as well as policymakers, pension plan participants, and taxpayers, and those from the private sector interested in lessons from the public plan arena. While our focus is mainly on the United States and Canada, the findings here should also be of keen interest to those in other countries, as well.

Several different types of plans are examined here, including pensions for employees of state governments, local governments, teachers, uniformed officers (police and firefighters), the armed forces, and federal civil servants. The analysis in each case focuses first on the structure of the plans themselves, and next asks how good a job are they doing for the stakeholders involved. The stakeholders in public plans include participants and taxpayers, who must in turn ask how well these plans are funded, how they are governed, and how pension assets are performing. We also discuss possible arenas in which the form and structure of the public plan environment could be improved, including changes in the regulatory and tax environment in which they operate. Because private sector pensions operate under a somewhat different legal setting from public plans, we seek to draw lessons for private pensions from the public experience, and vice versa. Finally, we identify several challenges for the future that confront public sector pension plans. Some of these are also relevant to the workforce as a whole, involving the fact of population and workforce aging, while others are more specific to public plans, pertaining to the special governance issues that arise when plan sponsors are operating in the interests of both plan participants and taxpayers. We conclude with an analysis of several interesting case studies, ranging from the special circumstances of the District of Columbia to the issues linking pension and state budgets as in New Jersey and Florida, and governance as practiced in Pennsylvania.

The Structure and Function of Public Pension Systems

Most public sector pensions in North America are of the defined benefit variety, as indicated by Mitchell et al. (this volume) who focus on state and local plans, by Hustead and Hustead (this volume) who examine military and civil servant plans, and by Pozzebon (this volume) who reviews the state of Canadian public employee pensions. Beyond this broad generalization, there is tremendous diversity, since different types of pension systems cover state and local governmental employees, federal workers, and members of the military. Further the plans differ, one from the other, in terms of their benefits, their contributions and financing arrangements, and their governance structure. For example, in the United States, about three-quarters of all state and local employees are included in the national social security system, implying that here the public employee pension may play a relatively smaller role in meeting retirement income needs, as compared to plans that have opted out of social security. Similarly, 40 percent of federal employees are currently not included in social security, though all federal employees hired after 1983 and all military personnel have been included in the national social security program. In the future, social security will probably be extended to cover all governmental employees, since virtually all plans to reform the U.S. social security system require coverage for all state and local employees, as is currently the case for private sector employees.

In the United States, public pension plans are often seen as paying rather generous benefits to retirees, particularly compared to those provided to their private sector counterparts. One way to judge this contention is to compare benefit formulas, where a "benefit multiplier" is applied to years of service times preretirement pay. Private sector retirement plans tend to provide a multiplier of less than 1.75 percent of pay, and use the retiree's final five-year average salary. By contrast, the majority of state and local plans that use this approach employ a multiplier of 1.75 percent or higher; the federal Civil Service Retirement System (CSRS) also uses a multiplier that averages over 1.75 percent. In addition, CSRS and over 60 percent of state and local plans base benefits on the highest three-year average pay. The relative advantage of governmental plans compared to private sector plans increases after retirement, inasmuch as many state and local plans, as well as the CSRS, index benefits to inflation. By contrast, few private sector plans have automatic indexing and some never increase benefits after retirement. Most private sector plans rely instead on ad hoc inflation adjustments, which typically make up for less than half of inflation.

On the other hand, these more generous public plan benefits are often "paid for" by higher employee contributions than is typically found among private sector employees. As we show below, public employee contributions average 5 percent of pay, with higher rates (6–7 percent) for plans covering teachers, police, and firefighters. By contrast, in the private sector, it is uncommon for participants to pay out of workers' pay, as is true in the military retirement systems. It must be recognized, of course, that the cost of retirement benefits is related to more than simply benefit levels and employee contributions. Investment performance also plays a role in influencing the cost per dollar of benefit. For example, the CSRS employer contribution per dollar of benefits is higher than that of most other plans because CSRS is invested in U.S. Treasury-backed securities expected to earn 7 percent a year. By contrast, in recent years, many state and local plans adopted investment policies similar to those of private sector pensions, with heavy weighting in equities. This change in investment policy, coupled with a strong stock market, has resulted in lower employer contributions.

An important new development that we highlight in this volume is that some government employers have begun to move gradually to a defined contribution approach, while others have adopted a hybrid approach. This development is being adopted by public sector employers to better meet the demographics of tomorrow's workforce, according to Eitelberg (this volume) and Fore (this volume). One of the first defined contribution plans in

North America for public employees was the U.S. Federal Employees Retirement System (FERS), a plan that covers federal employees hired after 1983. As is the case in many private sector pensions, FERS combines both a defined benefit and a defined contribution plan. Under this plan, the combined income from both plans plus social security is about the same as was payable under the precursor plan, CSRS, but the mix of benefits is much different. Short-service employees at young ages will do much better under the new plan, FERS, than they would have under the old plan, CSRS. But full-career employees retiring with unreduced benefits will do much better under CSRS than under FERS. In this way, the new model of public pension plans is seen by employers, and often by employees, as better adapted to the mobile, investment-oriented workforce of the twenty-first century.

Public Pension Plan Finances

Pension plans represent long-term contracts between employers and the plan participants, who give up current salary either directly through salary reduction or indirectly through foregone earnings. This is done in exchange for future retirement benefits payable by the pension plan. In the case of a defined benefit plan, the retirement promise is financed by contributions and returns on invested assets. Figuring out how much must be contributed, and how the assets should be invested, constitutes a major task of the public pension plan managers. In general, contributions must be determined based on plan obligations, which are in turn determined by actuaries who conduct valuations of the plan. Assumptions play a key role, including anticipated age, service, and compensation of the plan's membership with demographic assumptions related to mortality, disability, and probabilities of retirement, and with economic assumptions regarding wage increases, inflation, and projected rates of return on plan investments (Hustead, this volume). The resulting valuation gives employers a measure of the plan's long-term liabilities and the contributions required to finance the long-term liabilities in an orderly and systematic manner through time (Mitchell et al., this volume).

In practice, of course, public plans differ from one another in terms of the underlying assumptions they use, and actuaries also can select among a range of methods to determine the pension plan's liabilities. In addition, alternative methods may be employed to determine the value of plan assets available to fund the promised pension benefits; it is not uncommon for assets in public plans to be reported in such a way as to reduce the volatility of year-to-year market fluctuations. For all these reasons, the status of public plans is not always transparent or comparable across systems. Despite these caveats, it appears that in the United States at least, state and local plans hold pension assets equal to 88 percent of liabilities, with somewhat higher funding ratios among state and local employee plans (90 and 97 percent, respectively) as compared to systems covering teachers and public safety employees (82 and 88 percent respectively; Mitchell et al., this volume). This is an improvement in the funding ratios of most plans over the last generation. The strong performance of the stock market has contributed to the improvement in funding status, to some extent as a result of increasing equity investment. The "flow" funding ratio of 98 percent indicates that state and local employers have typically met their new pension obligations as they arise. By contrast, the federal government pension plans prove to be much less well funded. In particular, the CSRS fund is not fully financed and the military benefits are funded over a much longer period than common for state government plans. The combined unfunded liability of the military and civilian systems is estimated at over $1 trillion.

One reason that state and local pension systems can boast such a strong funding stance today is that many of these plans invested heavily in stocks during the 1980s and 1990s. This would not have happened given investment restrictions and practices in place during the 1960s: indeed, for years, many public plans were prohibited from investing in anything but government bonds. The practice of requiring public sector plans to either invest in, or avoid, certain types of holdings is a very old one, as illustrated by Clark et al. (this volume) in their analysis of the Navy pension plan. But, as Munnell and Sunden (this volume) show, state and local systems have been allowed to gradually move increasing fractions of their assets into stocks in the last four decades. Today public pensions hold only slightly less equity (59 percent) than do private pension funds (64 percent) with the balance made up of more bonds (35 percent versus 29 percent). U.S. state and local plans also have some international equity exposure (11 percent) though less than that of private funds (14 percent).

Holding stock has benefited many governmental plans, but some restrictions remain for public pension plan managers. For example, Canadian public plans are still restricted from holding any more than 20 percent of assets in non-Canadian assets (Pozzebon, this volume). And in some cases, U.S. public sector pensions still face restrictions in terms of maximum ceilings that can be held in certain forms (e.g., venture capital). Whether it is a good idea for public pension stakeholders to have massive amounts of equity in the pension portfolio is also a matter of extensive and ongoing debate. Peskin (this volume) argues that public plans' assets should be chosen to match liability streams more precisely, rather than simply be invested in equities to the extent they are. A contrary view is taken by Munnell and Sunden (this volume), who argue that public pension stakeholders are better served by taking advantage of the equity premium. While this debate is not resolved here, the lines are clearly drawn and the choices illuminated.

Having recognized that the investment mix is rather similar between

public and private pension systems, it is logical that public plan investment
returns should also track private plan returns. Of course, returns are also
influenced by investment and other expenses that must also be taken into
account in judging investment performance. In the public plans under study
here, we find that per member costs averaged $211 per member per year
across all plans but were only one-third that level in a dollar-weighted computation. This suggests that larger plans incur substantially lower expense
on an annual basis (Mitchell et al., this volume). Investment expenses computed as a fraction of system assets totaled 44 basis points but were only
27 basis points for the dollar-weighted total. Fees in this range are consistent with the lower end of institutional money management fees charged by
pension investment managers.

Governance and Regulation of Public Pension Plans

Governmental pension systems are generally managed by a board, with
the group size and composition varying widely but averaging around eight
members. We find that the majority of the members is appointed by politicians or serves ex officio; sometimes board members may be elected by
plan participants. In general, these pension boards are directly charged with
pension investment decisions (88 percent), most are directly responsible
for benefits (71 percent), and most (84 percent) bear responsibility for asset allocation and actuarial assumptions needed to determine plan funding
and contribution obligations (Mitchell et al., this volume). An interesting
insight into how a specific board works appears in Brosius's (this volume)
evaluation of the board structure, duties and responsibilities for the Pennsylvania State Employees Retirement System. A different perspective on governance structure, of the federal retirement systems including the Federal
Thrift Retirement Investment Board, is examined by Hustead and Hustead
(this volume).

Federal regulation of governmental retirement plans has important similarities with the private sector but also many differences. Crane (this volume) highlights key differences including exemption from financial oversight by the Internal Revenue Service and from insurance charges (and
coverage) by the Pension Benefit Guaranty Corporation. Useem and Hess
(this volume) link board structure with public plan investment policy. They
find that retirement systems differ greatly in terms of their use of in-house
versus external money managers, the extent to which boards oversee investment strategy, and the resultant investment performance of public plan
assets.

Looking Ahead

Looking across the many different public sector pension systems that have flourished in North America over the last few decades, several messages become clear. Although there are many types of benefit formulas, the main model for public sector pension provision has been the defined benefit plan. However, the status quo is changing in the face of workforce and other pressures. By comparison, private sector pensions have been subject to similar workplace pressures for a generation, and many private employers have already made the transition to hybrid or defined contribution plans, well ahead of the public sector developments.

Public pension plan benefit offerings have also been seen as relatively generous in the past, as compared to private pensions, but some of this apparent generosity is attributable to the fact that governmental participants were often not covered by social security in the past. If social security coverage were to be mandated for the remainder of public sector employees, it is likely that benefit and contribution rules will conform more closely to offerings in the private sector.

Regarding plan financing, most public pension plans today require contributions from both employers and employees, and most plans are relatively well funded, albeit with equities making up some 60 percent of the assets. In the face of this trend, some investment experts argue that pensions are investing too much in equities as compared to their pension liability structure. On the other hand, this investment mix is the result of public pension plan governance structures, which are quite diverse and generally involve politicians as well as plan members. It is interesting that virtually the same investment asset mix has emerged in the private sector, where the pension governance structure is based on fiduciary law embodied in the Employee Retirement Income Security Act of 1974 (ERISA). Part of the reason that investment practices appear so similar is, no doubt, that public plans are increasingly being held to the same performance standards as private investment managers. Another reason is that public sector investors have been attracted with high market rates of return and little apparent risk over the last twenty years. In many ways, public pension plans have benefited from shifts in investment practices, greater competition in investment practices, and increased transparency in reporting and disclosure that have today become the norm in private pension practice.

Our review of the public pension arena at the threshold of the twenty-first century finds a generally robust, well-funded, and reasonably well managed pension environment. Notwithstanding this positive assessment, many challenges remain for the future. The aging and more mobile workforce will exacerbate pressures to make changes such as replacing defined benefit plans with hybrid or defined contribution plans. It would also be painful if there were a substantial and long-term economic downturn. Pension funding ratios are quite healthy at present, but this is partly a result of strong stock returns—which may not persist in the future. In order to spread this risk of possible market downturn, public employers may feel the need to move to defined contribution, or perhaps hybrid, plans that shift capital market risk to participants. Bryan (this volume) has shown how a state budget crisis can influence public pension financing decisions; whether state budgetary fiscal problems might translate into pension problems on a broader scale remains to be seen. Finally, an important challenge will arise as the nation's social security system is reformed. Broader integration and design issues would be raised for most public—and indeed private—pension plans if the nation's "first-pillar" of old-age support were altered fundamentally.

References

Brosius, John. This volume. "Pension Governance in the Pennsylvania State Employees' Retirement System."

Bryan, Tom. This volume. "The New Jersey Pension System."

Clark, Robert L., Lee A. Craig, and Jack W. Wilson. This volume. "The Life and Times of a Public Sector Pension Plan Before Social Security: The U.S. Navy Pension Plan in the Nineteenth Century."

Crane, Roderick B. This volume. "Regulation and Taxation of Public Plans: A History of Increasing Federal Influence."

Eitelberg, Cathie. This volume. "Public Pension Design and Responses to a Changing Workforce."

Fore, Douglas. This volume. "Going Private in the Public Sector: The Transition from Defined Benefit to Defined Contribution Pension Plans."

Hustead, Edwin C. This volume. "Determining the Cost of Public Pension Plans."

Hustead, Edwin C. This volume. "Public Pensions in Washington, D.C."

Hustead, Edwin C. and Toni Hustead. This volume. "Federal Civilian and Military Retirement Systems."

Mitchell, Olivia S. and David McCarthy. 1999. "The Structure and Performance of State and Local Pension Plans." Pension Research Council, The Wharton School, Philadelphia.

Mitchell, Olivia S., David McCarthy, Stanley C. Wisniewski, and Paul Zorn. This volume. "Developments in State and Local Pension Plans."

Munnell, Alicia H. and Annika Sundén. This volume. "Investment Practices of State and Local Pension Funds: Implications for Social Security Reform."

Peskin, Michael. This volume. "Asset Liability Management in the Public Sector."

Pozzebon, Silvana. This volume. "Canadian Public Sector Employee Pension Plans."

Steffen, Karen. This volume. "State Employee Pension Plans."

Trager, Kenneth, James Francis, and Kevin SigRist. This volume. "Florida's Public Pension Reform Debate: A Discussion of the Issues and Estimates of the Option Costs."

Useem, Michael and David Hess. This volume. "Governance and Investments of Public Pensions."

Chapter 2
Developments in State and Local Pension Plans

Olivia S. Mitchell, David McCarthy,
Stanley C. Wisniewski, and Paul Zorn

In this chapter we explore aspects of the history, financing, benefit structure, and governance of pension plans covering state and local government
employees in the United States. State and local pension plans cover a wide
range of employees including uniformed workers (firefighters and police),
teachers, members of the judiciary, and other members of state governments and local municipalities. These plans are the subject of much interest
because they are so large—they cover close to 13 million employees, pay
benefits to more than 5 million beneficiaries, and control $2.4 trillion in in-
vested plan assets.[1] And as we show in this chapter, these plans are extremely
diverse in terms of design, investment policy, and governance, in large part
because of their different histories and constituencies. Yet despite the differences across plans, they all face some similar challenges and opportunities
in the years to come.

In order to understand how these state and local plans work, it is useful
to recall that public sector pension plans in the United States tend to be
of the defined benefit (DB) variety. This means that retiring vested employees receive a specified retirement benefit throughout the course of their retirement that depends on age, years of service, and salary.[2] In the case of
DB plans, required contributions are typically based on actuarial valuations,
and investments are managed by financial experts selected by the pension
board. By contrast, in the private sector, many people are covered by defined contribution (DC) plans where the amounts contributed to the plan
are specified, but not the benefit payouts.[3] In the DC case, plan participants
generally decide where to direct their investments, given a set of options
established by the employer. Retirement benefits are then paid from the
contributions and investment income that accumulate in the participants'

accounts. If the funds in the accounts are not sufficient to pay benefits over the course of retirement, retirees must turn to other sources.[4]

Despite the large size and impact of public pensions, there remains much to learn about how these institutions function. Although the federal Employee Retirement Income Security Act of 1974 (ERISA) requires private pensions to furnish periodic and standardized reports to plan participants and the U.S. Department of Labor (McGill et al. 1997), state and local retirement plans are exempt from ERISA's reporting requirements. However, to comply with generally accepted accounting principles, state and local governments are bound to financial measurement and reporting requirements established by the Governmental Accounting Standards Board (GASB). For state and local retirement plans (and their sponsoring governments) the GASB's standards establish a uniform format for reporting financial information.

In order to explore key aspects of these pension systems for the present study, this chapter relies on several different sources including Bureau of Labor Statistics surveys on state and local pension plans (BLS, various years), Census of Government reports, and the PENDAT surveys conducted by the Public Pension Coordinating Council (hereafter PPCC; see Zorn 1997). These data, taken together, afford a useful set of insights into this important pension domain.

In the discussion that follows, we first offer a brief history of retirement systems in the public sector. We then proceed to describe and assess four aspects of public pension plan structure: their benefit provisions, their governance structure, how they are financed, and their investment behavior and performance. In doing so we seek to offer a better understanding of the way public pension plans work, and also to illuminate some of the challenges and opportunities facing public pension plans over the next several decades.

An Overview of State and Local Retirement Systems[5]

The first municipal retirement system in the United States was established in 1857, to provide lump sum benefits for New York City policemen injured in the line of duty. In 1878, this plan was revised to provide retirement benefits of one-half of final pay, for policemen completing twenty-one years of service. Over the next fifty years, numerous other state and local jurisdictions established retirement plans throughout the United States. But it was not until after the Social Security Act was passed in 1935 that public pension plan growth began in earnest.

The 1930–50 period. Between 1931 and 1950, half of the largest state and local plans in the country were established (U.S. Congress 1978). Initially, many of these plans provided two-part retirement benefits: one paid by the employer, based on the employee's salary and years of service at retirement, and a second resulting from annuitizing the employee's accumulated contributions. Often the employee's contributions were determined so that the total cost of the retirement benefit was allocated evenly between the employee and the employer.

In some instances, the employer's portion of the benefit simply matched the annuity provided by the employee's accumulated contributions. However, in order for employees of different ages and genders to receive adequate benefits on retirement, different employee contribution rates were required, and the plans became quite complex to administer. Consequently, many plans later changed their designs to provide for a pension based solely on age and years of service at retirement. Although employee contributions were still required, the amount of the retirement benefit no longer depended on the employee's accumulated contributions (Bleakney 1972).

When social security was first enacted in 1935, this federal old-age program intentionally excluded state and local government employees from coverage. This was mainly due to constitutional issues concerning the federal government's right to tax state and local governments. In 1950, however, Congress amended the Social Security Act to allow states to voluntarily provide social security coverage for their employees, when a state entered into an agreement with the Social Security Administration. In 1986, Congress mandated Medicare coverage for state and local employees hired after March 31, 1986 (IRS 1997). More recently, Congress has discussed mandating social security coverage for all newly hired state and local workers; whether this will actually mitigate social security's long-run financial problems is subject to debate (SSAC 1996).

The 1950–80 period. Congress's decision to provide states with the option to become included in social security resulted in many changes to state and local plan design during the 1950s; in fact, during this period more than one-third of the nation's largest public sector pensions were changed (U.S. Congress 1978). Initially, many of the plans joining social security developed a split-benefit formula, with a lower unit benefit percentage applied to the first $4,200 of final average salary and a higher percentage applied to the amount over $4,200. (The figure of $4,200 represented the social security covered earnings ceiling at the time.) Nevertheless, many of these same plans returned to a single benefit percentage in the 1980s, after it became clear that the split-benefit formula was difficult to administer and resulted in lower proportional benefits to lower-paid workers.

The 1960s and 1970s saw substantial consolidation among public pensions in the U.S. This occurred as pensions sought to take advantage of scale economies and upgrade their technologies. During this period, many of the larger pension systems succeeded in bringing smaller plans under their coverage. Consolidation proved not to be a panacea, however, and it continued

TABLE 1. Changes in State and Local Pension Systems, 1986–97

	1986–87			1996–97		
	State	Local	Total	State	Local	Total
Number of systems[1]	201	2,213	2,414	212	2,052	2,264
Number of members[1]						
Active members (M)	9.2	1.5	10.7	11.2	1.6	12.8
Inactive members (M)	1.0	0.1	1.1	2.3	0.1	2.4
Retirees and beneficiaries (M)	3.0	0.7	3.7	4.3	1.0	5.3
Total members (M)	*13.2*	*2.3*	*15.5*	*17.8*	*2.7*	*20.5*
Ratio of active to retired members	3.1	2.1	2.9	2.6	1.6	2.4
Receipts[1]						
Employee contributions ($B)	9.4	1.8	11.2	17.4	3.4	20.8
Government contributions ($B)	23.3	7.1	30.4	37.1	7.8	44.9
Earnings on investment ($B)	45.0	12.7	57.7	133.9	25.1	159.0
Total receipts ($B)	*77.7*	*21.6*	*99.3*	*188.4*	*36.3*	*224.7*
% from employee contributions	12.1	8.3	11.3	9.2	9.4	9.3
% from government contributions	30.0	32.9	30.6	19.7	21.5	20.0
% from investment earnings	57.9	58.8	58.1	71.1	69.1	70.8
Total investments ($B)[2]			530.1			2,094.1

Sources:
[1] U.S. Bureau of the Census, Census of Governments (specified years).
[2] Board of Governors of the Federal Reserve System (1999).
Values for total investments are not comparable with the values for contributions and earnings on investment due to differences in the methods used to collect the data by the different sources.

to be complex to manage benefits for multiple and divergent employee groups that often had very distinct plan provisions and separate valuations (U.S. Congress 1978).

The period from 1980 to the present. The 1980s saw many state legislatures seeking to expand the investment options available to state and local retirement plans. One way this occurred was with the substitution of a general standard of prudence for more restrictive "legal lists." Prior to 1980, public plan investments were typically limited to certain types of securities, approved by the state legislature, from which public pension plans were allowed to choose. The movement to the prudence standard permitted the public funds to hold a larger percentage of assets in equities (usually in domestic stocks), and it positioned many systems to take advantage of the unprecedented stock market returns experienced over the next decade. The income from these investments, coupled with actuarially sound employer and employee contributions, has resulted in strong funding levels for many state and local systems today.

To illustrate some of the dramatic changes experienced by state and local pension plans over the recent past, data on system membership, receipts, and total investments are provided in Table 1 for 1987 and 1997. One important change evidenced over this period pertains to the substantial increases in both system receipts and total investments. Across all state and local systems combined, total receipts more than doubled from $99B in 1987 to $225B in 1997. Most of this increase was attributable to investment earnings, which almost tripled from $58B to $159B over the period. These earnings, combined with employer and employee contributions, quadrupled total system assets and resulted in an aggregate public pension pool of over $2 trillion in 1997. In defined benefit plans, which are the majority of state and local pensions, investment earnings in excess of the actuarial funding assumptions generally reduce employer contributions (Hustead this volume).[6]

Other changes in state and local retirement systems in the last decade are also illustrated in Table 1. Although the overall number of systems declined slightly from 2,414 to 2,264, the total number of active members grew almost 20 percent, from 10.7M to 12.8M people. The retiree/beneficiary population grew even faster (some 43 percent), from 3.7M to 5.3M. Consequently, the ratio of active members to retirees fell from 2.9 to 2.4 for the combined systems (and from 2.1 to 1.6 in local systems alone). In the absence of substantial investment reserves, this decline would likely have put upward pressure on employer contributions, since retiree benefits were rising relative to active member payrolls.

Types of State and Local Retirement Systems

Public sector retirement systems can be categorized according to many dimensions including the type of benefit provided, the type of employees covered, the type of administrative jurisdiction, the number of contributing employers, the size of the plan, and the like. Here we have chosen to focus mainly on the differences and similarities among systems categorized by type of covered employees and administrative jurisdiction.

One reason why pension plans differ is that they cover employees with different employment characteristics. For instance, because police work and fire fighting are physically demanding occupations, retirement benefits for public safety workers typically allow retirement at earlier ages, in part to maintain a younger workforce. Consequently, the retirement benefits available to police and firefighters are usually different from those provided to teachers or to general employees. Social security coverage also affects benefit offerings. Plans whose workers are not covered by social security often provide higher retirement benefits to mitigate the lack of social security income in retirement. Since fewer teachers and public safety workers are in-cluded in social security than other workers, this also affects the benefits they are provided.[7]

Retirement systems also differ by administrative jurisdiction, with large state-level plans often having different characteristics than plans offered by small localities. This is often the result of the different political environments in which the systems operate, as well as the number of members covered by the system. System size may affect the resources available to the system for operations. Larger systems tend to have larger staffs. Larger systems also tend to have a larger amount of assets to invest and greater potential for portfolio diversification, which in turn may afford them greater flexibility in selecting investments and greater leverage in negotiations with investment managers.

Membership and Coverage in State and Local Pensions

To better understand what groups of workers are covered by public plans, Table 2 indicates system membership by plan type.[8] These data are based on the PPCC's 1997 survey of state and local retirement plans covering 11 mil-lion active members, and 4 million retirees and beneficiaries. Most active members (6 million or 57 percent) were covered by state-administered re-tirement systems, approximately one-third (3 million or 29 percent) were in systems specifically for teachers or school employees, one-tenth (1 mil-lion) were in locally administered systems primarily serving general employ-ees, and the remaining active members (327 thousand, or about 3 percent) were in systems specifically for public safety employees (i.e., police and fire-fighters). Similar breakdowns apply for the retiree/beneficiary breakdowns. Of the 4 million retirees and beneficiaries covered by plans surveyed, 2 mil-lion (56 percent) were in state-administered systems, 1 million (27 percent) were in systems for teachers and school employees, 466 thousand (11 per-cent) were in general local systems, and the remaining 168 thousand (4 per-cent) were in public safety systems. The ratio of active to retired members in Table 2 is lower, on average, for systems that cover only local employees (2.4 active/retired), than for statewide systems (2.7 active/retired). Further-more, the active/retired ratio for teacher and school employees is somewhat higher than the average (3.0), and for public safety employees it is lower than average (1.9).

Eligibility and Benefit Provisions in Public Pension Plans

The primary goal of a retirement system is to provide retirement benefits in a cost-effective manner, which, when combined with social security (if available) and personal savings, result in benefits that sustain the retiree's

TABLE 2. State and Local Government Membership by Plan Type, 1996

	State employee systems	Teacher and school employee systems	Police and firefighter systems	Local employee systems	All systems
Number of systems	68	31	35	127	261
Number of plans	72	40	126	140	378
Number of participants					
Active members (M)	6.320	3.276	0.327	1.105	11.028
Retirees and					
beneficiaries (M)	2.349	1.109	0.168	0.466	4.092
Total (M)	*8.669*	*4.385*	*0.495*	*1.571*	*15.120*
Average active members per					
plan (000)	87.8	81.9	2.6	7.9	57.9
Ratio of active to retired					
members	2.7	3.0	1.9	2.4	2.7

Source: Authors' tabulations from PPCC, PENDAT Database, 1997.
Means weighted by number of members.

standard of living through retirement. As noted earlier, almost all state and local retirement plans are of the defined benefit variety (BLS 1994). Consequently, the differences in benefits paid by state and local government systems are mainly a function of the specific details of the defined benefit plans.

Eligibility. Several key design features of public pension plans are indicated in Table 3, along with comparable evidence, where available, for private sector pensions. Most public sector employees tend to be included in their pension plan at hire, whereas private sector employees must generally meet an age and/or service requirement in order to be covered by their plans. Becoming legally entitled to a benefit typically occurs at a discrete time after a specific period of service, with cliff vesting the norm in both public and private retirement systems. But public sector workers take longer on average to vest, with 43 percent having to work ten years before becoming legally entitled to a benefit. By contrast their private sector counterparts typically vest after five years (or at seven years if the employer uses a graded vesting rule).

There are, of course, important differences in eligibility rules for pensions covering teachers, police and firefighters, and general employees. Members of teacher retirement systems often vest in their benefits after five or ten years of service, although in a few instances the vesting period is as low as three years, and in two cases the consolidated state systems offer immediate vesting. Vesting requirements for police and firefighters vary widely, from a low of three years to a high of twenty. Among general plans covering all

TABLE 3. Comparing Public and Private Defined Benefit Pension Plan Design Features

	Public (1994)	Private (1995)
1. Participation: minimum age or service or both (%)	[1]	69
2. Cliff vesting (%)	100	96
At any age		
<5 years	5	[2]
5 years	47	87
6–9 years	5	[2]
10 years	43	6
>10 years	[2]	[2]
Other	[2]	3
3. Early retirement permitted (%)	87	96
Eligibility based on		
Service (S) alone	23	7
Age (A) alone	0	5
A55+S10	8	31
A+S other	61	53
4. Normal retirement (%)		
Service alone	43	6
S30	29	5
Age alone:	5	40
A62	[2]	3
Age+Service:	40	
A55+S30	11	3
A62+S10	5	9
5. Benefit formulas (%)		
Dollar amount basis	[2]	23
Earnings basis	99	69
Career	[2]	11
Terminal		58
Five years used	20	78
Three years used	61	17
Other	18	15
Other basis	[2]	2
Percent of pay per year of service	78	37
<1.25	6	12
1.25–1.74	24	18
1.75–2.00	6	3
2.00+	43	4
Other	0	[2]
6. Prevalence of postretirement increases (%)		
Automatic	45	3

Sources: Adapted from Mitchell and McCarthy (1999); uses BLS (1995) for 1994 public plan data and BLS (1996) for 1995 private plan data.
[1] Not reported in BLS (1995).
[2] Less than 0.5%.

state and local workers, vesting periods are five or ten years, although a few systems use intermediate periods (seven or eight years; Zorn 1999).

Many plans also permit "purchase of service" credit, a concept that refers to the opportunity for public employees to purchase credit for past service under the plan. Without these arrangements, an individual who frequently changes jobs might work under several retirement plans over the course of his or her career without becoming vested. These provisions differ widely from one state to another, however, with regard to the types and prices of service that can be purchased, maximum amounts, and the payment options available.

Retirement benefits. Turning to DB benefit formulas, Table 3 shows that final average earnings play a central role in the pension formulas of state and local pension plans. By contrast, almost a quarter of the private pension plans use a flat dollar formula, mainly found in manufacturing union-negotiated plans. Public sector pension benefit formulas often use the last three years of an employee's pay to determine the benefit amount (61 percent), while private plans more commonly use five years or an even longer period (such as career average) to determine the fraction of pay used in the benefit formula (78 percent).

Another aspect of public pension plans is that a higher benefit multiplier tends to be applied per year of service than in private plans. Table 3 shows that 43 percent of public plans use a benefit multiplier giving more than 2 percent of pay per year of service, while only 4 percent of private sector plans accumulate benefits at this rate. Other studies have also pointed to the relatively larger benefits paid by public plans. Comparisons based on income replacement rates furnished by the BLS indicate that, at the turn of the decade, lower-tenured public sector retirees received benefits about 50 percent greater than their private sector counterparts (BLS 1989, 1992). The same studies reported that higher-seniority workers in the public sector received a replacement rate half to two-thirds greater at the same pay and service levels than in the private sector. It is not known whether these relative benefit levels changed more recently, since BLS no longer provides these comparative tabulations.

However, these comparisons do not take into account the fact that state and local employees contribute approximately one-third of the total contributions made to their defined benefit plans, while private sector employees typically make no direct contributions to their DB plans. Given that public sector employees typically pay a significant portion of the cost of the DB benefits they receive, it is not unreasonable that their benefits would be higher than in the private sector, all else held equal.[9] Furthermore, the studies referenced above do not include benefits received from defined contribution plans. Since many private sector employers supplement DB benefits with benefits provided through defined contribution plans, a significant

TABLE 4. State and Local Government Benefits Design Features by Plan Type,
1996

	State employee systems	Teacher and school employee systems	Police and firefighter systems	Local employee systems	All systems
Average annual unit benefit (% of pay/year)					
Covered by social security	1.67	1.89	2.26	1.72	1.74
Not covered by social security	1.90	2.02	2.30	2.24	1.99
Average accrued 30-year benefit (% of final pay)					
Covered by social security	51.2	57.7	66.6	57.3	53.5
Not covered by social security	57.1	61.9	70.1	69.1	60.3
Form of benefit (% of plans providing)					
Straight-life annuity	87	95	67	78	78
Joint and survivor annuity	84	95	81	87	86
Joint and 50% survivor	79	95	64	80	76
Joint and 100% survivor	69	85	64	69	69
Joint and survivor "pop-up"	57	76	30	26	38

Source: Authors' tabulations from PPCC, PENDAT Database, 1997. See Zorn (1997).
Means weighted by number of members.

portion of the private sector retirement benefit is not included in the comparison made from the BLS data (Zorn 1995).

Another explanation for the difference in benefit accrual levels between public and private pension plans is that approximately one-quarter of public employees are not covered by social security (U.S. House Ways and Means 1998).[10] As noted above, retirement plans whose employees are not covered by social security often provide higher retirement benefits to partially offset the lack of social security benefits. This pattern varies by employee groups, as indicated in Table 4.

Lack of social security coverage for some public sector workers may also explain why postretirement increases are more prevalent in the public than in the private sector; fully 45 percent of these plans offered a form of automatic indexation (although it appears that few had full inflation indexation). Automatic indexation is rare in the private sector, although augmentation of pensions at the discretion of the trustees is often seen.

Disability benefits. Among public plans, 91 percent had disability retirement provisions in 1994, as compared with only 73 percent of private plans in 1995. Almost half (42 percent) of public plans allowed workers to retire with unreduced normal benefits compared with fewer (29 percent) of private plans. Qualifying age and service conditions for disability retirement also tend to be less restrictive in the public sector (BLS 1994, 1995). This may be because disability is often covered through long-term disability (LTD) plans in the private sector, rather than through the pension plan, which is more common in the public sector.

Retirement Benefits Provided to Employee Groups

There is substantial variation in the retirement benefits provided by plans to different employee groups. This variation is a result of a combination of factors, including the different types of work performed and changes in the overall environment in which the plans developed. As a result of this variation, it is difficult to define a "typical" retirement benefit. Nevertheless, it is instructive to compare the general features of these plans.

Teacher plans. Among teachers' plans, the retirement benefit formula is usually a single-rate unit benefit, that is, the same benefit multiplier is applied to all years of service under the plan. As shown in Table 4, the unit benefit multiplier averaged 1.89 percent for employees covered by social security and 2.02 percent for employees not covered by social security. The accrued benefit after thirty years of service averaged 57.7 percent of final average salary for employees covered by social security, and 61.9 percent for those not covered. Final average salary is usually based on the highest three or five years of service, with the highest three years being predominant.

Many of the teacher systems offer an early retirement option under which employees can retire before reaching the age and service requirements for unreduced benefits (Wisniewski 1999). Generally, this option is available after twenty years of service; many teacher systems allow retirement at age 55 after completion of twenty-five years of service. In almost all cases, the benefit is reduced to reflect the full actuarial cost of early retirement, although two-thirds allow unreduced benefits to be paid at age 60, once the employee has vested in the benefit. A large fraction of the teacher systems also offers automatic postretirement cost-of-living adjustments (COLAs) to protect retirement earnings from inflation, although COLA formulas vary. For example, the Wisconsin Retirement System provides supplemental cost-of-living increases when investment earnings exceed the actuarially assumed rate (Wisniewski 1999). In other cases, employees lacking social security coverage are more likely to have automatic cost-of-living adjustments.

Public safety plans. For police and firefighters, retirement benefit formulas also vary, often linked to the plan's vesting requirements. Typically systems that require twenty years of service for vesting purposes have benefit formulas that specify a flat percent of final average salary to be paid at retirement (often 50 percent). Systems that allow vesting after five or ten years have unit benefit formulas that use either a single-rate or variable-rate multipliers for each year of service. Under a variable-rate formula, different benefit accumulation rates apply to different years of service. For example, under a variable rate formula, a member may accumulate a retirement benefit of 2.0 percent for the first ten years of service, and 1.75 percent thereafter (or vice versa). Variable-rate formulas are often used in situations where members are not covered under social security.

The unit benefit multiplier for police and firefighters covered by social security averages 2.26 percent, and 2.30 percent for those not covered. Accrued benefits after thirty years of service average 66.6 percent of final average salary for those covered by social security, and 70.1 percent for those not covered. Final average salary is often based on the highest three years of service; however, in some cases it is tied to the employee's final salary or the salary attached to a certain rank. Few of the systems offer an early retirement option, but unreduced retirement benefits are frequently available at age 50 or 55, after twenty years of service; in addition, unreduced benefits may be available at any age after twenty-five years of service. Most police and firefighter plans (80 percent) offer postretirement cost-of-living adjustments (Zorn 1999).

General employee plans. Turning to general public employee plans, age and service requirements for retirement are similar to those for teachers, with many systems offering unreduced retirement benefits at age 55, with twenty-five or thirty years of service, and retirement at age 60 or 62 upon vesting. As with teacher systems, single-rate benefit formulas are often used. Benefit formulas use a unit benefit multiplier averaging 1.72 percent for employees covered by social security and 2.24 percent for those not covered. The accrued benefit after thirty years of service averaged 57.3 percent of final average salary for those covered by social security, and 69.1 percent for those not covered. Final average salary is typically based on the highest three or five years of service (Zorn 1999). Many systems covering general local employees offer an early retirement option available at ages 50 or 55 with ten to twenty years of service. In almost all cases, the benefit is reduced for early retirement but, in some instances, does not reflect the full actuarial cost. Approximately 80 percent of the systems offer postretirement cost-of-living adjustments (Zorn 1999).

Changes over time. By comparing these pension characteristics with those reported in earlier studies, some changes can be discerned in the way pension plans have designed their benefit structures over time. First, there appears to be a significant movement away from integration of benefits with social security, a trend perceived among both public and private pensions. The proportion of public plans with a benefit formula integrated with social security decreased from 10 percent to 4 percent between 1992 and 1994; for private plans this proportion decreased from 63 percent to 51 percent between 1989 and 1995 (BLS 1989, 1995). While no single explanation for this trend is available, it may be that increased uncertainty about the social security system has led employers to curtail the risk that might be associated with unanticipated changes in the old-age benefits provided by the government. Second, the prevalence of the "age 55/service 10" (A55/S10)combination for early retirement appears to have decreased over time, in favor of combinations with less service (in 1989, fully 43 percent of private plans used A55/S10 and 9 percent A55/S5, compared with 31 percent and 21 percent, respectively, in private plans for 1995; BLS 1989, 1995). Third, pensions in the public sector uniformly base benefits on earnings rather than on a flat dollar amount, whereas almost a fifth of the corporate plans use flat dollar formulas.

Paying for Public Pensions

The promise of paying a pension benefit establishes an obligation on the part of the employer, which is usually financed by employer and/or employee contributions as well as income earned on invested assets. Determining how much to contribute, and how to invest the assets, are key responsibilities of the pension plan's board and staff. To assist in carrying out these responsibilities, retirement plans often hire actuaries, investment consultants, and other specialized professionals.

Actuarial valuations and assumptions. In order to measure plan obligations and determine the contributions necessary to systematically prefund benefits over time, pension plans hire actuaries to conduct valuations of the plan. The actuaries combine information about past and anticipated age, service, and compensation of the plan's membership with demographic assumptions related to mortality, disability, and probabilities of retirement, and with economic assumptions regarding wage increases and long-term rates of return on plan investments (Hustead this volume). The resulting valuation gives employers a measure of the plan's long-term liabilities and the contributions required to fund those liabilities in a systematic manner over time. Actuarial assumptions regarding inflation, wage increases, and investment returns are key elements in the valuation of plan liabilities. For example, assumed rates of return that are higher than can be sustained over time will, all else held equal, result in higher long-term plan costs, since the calculated employer contributions (and related investment earnings) will be less than would otherwise be the case.

For plans surveyed by the PPCC (Zorn 1999), the average assumed rate of return was 7.8 percent, with marginally higher rates assumed by systems serving state employees and teachers (8.0 percent for both groups) and the same or slightly lower rates for systems serving public safety and general local employees (7.8 and 7.7 percent respectively; see Table 5). Assumptions related to wage increases (including inflation and step/merit increases)

TABLE 5. State and Local Government Retirement System Funding, 1996

	State employee systems	Teacher and school employee systems	Police and firefighter systems	Local employee systems	All systems
Assumptions					
Actuarial assumed rate of return	8.0	8.0	7.8	7.7	7.8
Actuarial assumed wage increase	5.9	6.4	5.9	5.7	5.9
Actuarial assumed rate of inflation	4.5	4.5	4.4	4.4	4.4
Valuations					
Actuarial accrued liability ($B)	605.8	436.6	85.6	117.6	1,245.6
Actuarial value of assets ($B)	545.8	358.0	74.9	113.5	1,092.2
Ratio of assets to liabilities (%)	90.1	82.0	87.5	96.5	88.2
Other magnitudes					
Amortization of unfunded liability (years)	25.4	26.1	22.1	20.9	22.9
Employer contributions as percentage of payroll*	9.16	9.30	16.02	9.54	9.52
Member contributions as percentage of payroll*	4.39	6.08	7.02	5.32	5.09
Total additions ($B)	109.4	68.7	3.2	14.1	195.4
Member contributions	8.7	6.2	0.2	1.4	16.5
Employer contributions	17.4	8.7	0.6	2.7	29.4
Investment income	83.3	53.8	2.4	10.0	149.5
Notes					
Member contributions (%)	8	9	6	10	8
Employer contributions (%)	16	13	19	19	15
Investment income (%)	76	78	75	71	77

Source: Authors' tabulations from PPCC, PENDAT Database, 1997. See Zorn (1997).
Means weighted by payroll.

varied more across groups. The average assumption for all respondents was 5.9 percent, compared with 6.4 percent for systems covering teachers and 5.7 percent for those covering general employees. However, the assumptions regarding inflation were very similar across the covered groups, averaging 4.4 percent overall and only marginally higher assumptions among systems serving state employees and teachers.

Assets, liabilities, and plan funding. Actuaries calculate the plan's accrued liability in order to measure the long-term cost of retirement benefits and develop a systematic approach for funding the benefits over time. Different actuarial methods can be used to calculate the liability, depending on the funding pattern appropriate to the needs of the plan. Approximately two thirds of state and local plans surveyed by the PPCC use the entry age actuarial cost method, which calculates employer contributions as a level percent of payroll over time (McGill et al. 1997). This approach tends to stabilize pension contributions for long-term budgeting purposes.

Actuaries also determine the value of public pension assets accumulated to pay retiree benefits. The difference between the actuarial value of assets and the actuarial accrued liability is referred to as the "unfunded actuarial accrued liability," and it is amortized through contributions over time — typically twenty to thirty years. The actuarial value of assets is often determined in a manner that smoothes year-to-year market fluctuations over a three or five-year averaging period. This dampens the impact of short-term investment volatility on the measure of plan assets and tends to stabilize contributions.

Since actuarial methods and assumptions vary among the plans, so will the resulting asset/liability measures. This means that funding comparisons across plans are not strictly comparable (since all plans do not apply the same actuarial method and set of assumptions), but each plan's reported asset/liability measures reflect the methods and assumptions actually used to fund that plan.[11] With this caveat in mind, Table 5 shows that the actuarial accrued liability totaled close to $1.3 trillion across the entire set of plans responding to the PPCC survey in 1997, with approximately $1.1 trillion in assets available to fund the liability (Zorn 1999). Overall, the financial assets as well as liabilities of the systems serving state employees and teachers were substantially larger than those serving public safety and general local employees, since the state and teacher systems cover substantially more employees.

One measure that is often used to examine progress made in funding a retirement system is the "funding ratio," calculated by dividing the actuarial value of assets by actuarial accrued liabilities. Although this may be an imperfect measure of year-to-year progress made toward system funding, due to changes over time in the underlying assumptions and methods of measuring plan assets and/or plan liabilities, it is often used as a summary measure of funded status. Table 5 shows that the overall public plan funding ratio in 1996 was estimated at 88 percent for survey respondents; state and general local employee plans had somewhat higher funding ratios (90.1 percent and 96.5 percent, respectively) than did systems covering teachers and public safety employees (82.0 percent and 87.5 percent, respectively). Table 5 also indicates that the average period for amortizing the unfunded actuarial accrued liability was approximately twenty-three years.

TABLE 6. Changes in Average and Median Financial Status of State and Local
Pension Plans, 1992–96

	1992		1996		#Matched cases
	Average	Median	Average	Median	
Assets and liabilities ($000)					
Pension plan assets[1]	3,043,038	381,348	4,318,185	562,873	222
Pension plan liabilities[2]	3,657,065	472,916	4,954,381	679,507	222
Total underfunding	614,027	36,862	636,196	39,533	222
Stock funding ratio (%)					
Assets/liabilities ($-wtd)	83	87	87	91	222
Contributions ($000)					
Req. employer contributions	99,420	13,115	105,168	14,580	211
Actual contributions	138,959	18,531	162,846	20,930	211
Employer	88,866	12,454	102,662	14,580	211
Employee	50,093	4,553	60,184	5,316	211
Flow funding ratio (%)					
Required/actual contributions	95	100	98	100	211
Benefit payments ($000)					
Total benefit payments	161,547	12,485	204,289	18,048	135
Retirement	141,363	10,540	177,823	12,623	135
Disability	11,884	954	16,047	1,333	135
Survivors	6,361	823	8,086	971	135
Lump sum	1,940	0	2,333	0	135

	$-wtd.	Median
Per active participant ($000)		
Actuarial value of assets	165	116
Actuarial accrued liability	211	148
Contributions	5.5	3.4

Source: Authors' tabulations from PPCC, PENDAT Database (1995 and 1997). See Zorn (1997).
[1] Measured as the actuarial value of plan assets.
[2] Measured as the actuarial accrued liability.

More detail on public pension plans' financial status appears in Table 6. Here we provide average and median information for the public pension plans responding to the PPCC surveys in both 1992 and 1996; these are the for "matched cases" in the two years, a comparison that facilitates an assessment of the direction of change.[12] The data show that median funding ratios went from 87 percent to 91 percent between 1992 and 1996, and a similar pattern applies to the mean. In 1996, the average public pension plan reported actuarially-based assets of $4.32 billion and an average reported liability of $4.95 billion, for an average actuarial unfunded liability of about $630 million per plan. On an active participant basis, the median dollar-weighted value of assets per participant in 1996 was $116,000 with $148,000 in accrued liabilities.

In addition to the stock funding measures, we also report a "flow" funding measure in Table 6. This gauges the extent to which employer contributions in a given year cover the amounts necessary to systematically fund the plan. It is interesting that the average flow funding rate in 1996 stood at 98 percent and the median at 100 percent, indicating that public employers typically met their new pension obligations as they arose. The 1996 figures are not strictly comparable with those from 1992, since the GASB changed the way in which required contributions were reported during this time. Also the actuarial value of assets is often determined in a manner that smoothes year-to-year fluctuations, so increases in market value over time might not be fully reflected in the 1996 reported actuarial value of assets controlled by these public pension plans. These changes probably account for some of the observed discrepancy between stock and flow finding patterns between 1992 and 1996.

Employer and employee contributions. Employer contributions to public sector DB pension plans are based on actuarial valuations: generally a portion of the contribution covers the "normal cost" of funding benefits accrued to members in the current year, and another portion amortizes the unfunded liability. In the PENDAT plans surveyed, this unfunded liability is usually amortized over periods from twenty to thirty years. As shown in Table 5, employer contributions, including both the normal cost and amortization of the unfunded accrued liability, average 9.5 percent of payroll for the PENDAT respondents, with public safety system contributions exceeding contributions for the other groups of employees (this reflects the earlier retirement ages among uniformed officers). On average, employer contributions to state systems are the lowest.

Public employee retirement systems are typically contributory, that is, they require contributions by their members. Often these contributions are "picked-up" under section 414(h)(2) of the Internal Revenue Code, effectively making them pretax contributions by the employees. In this instance, they are different from private-sector defined benefit plans, under which employee contributions are made after taxes. This may be one of the reasons why private sector defined benefit plans are typically noncontributory. In the PENDAT survey, employee contributions range from 4 to 6 percent of the employees pay, and average 5.09 percent. Employee contributions are generally higher for plans covering teachers and police and firefighters (6.08 percent and 7.02 percent, respectively). Employee contributions in plans covering state employees averaged the lowest at 4.39 percent.

Public Pension Plan Investments and Performance

Asset allocation policy plays a key role in determining investment returns in a pension system. Before the early 1980s, state and local retirement systems held most of their assets in fixed-income securities, earning relatively low rates of return. This was often because their asset allocation choices were restricted by "legal lists," which specified the general types of investments that could be made and the maximum percent of assets that could be held in certain types of securities. For example, many legal lists limited the maximum percent of assets held in common stock to 30 percent or less.

During the 1980s, many legal lists were replaced by "prudent person" rules allowing investments in a wide mix of securities, as long as standards of prudence and diversification were met. Although long established in common law, the prudent person concept was codified with the passage of the Employee Retirement Income Security Act of 1974. Earlier concern about risk, a reason often given for the legal list restrictions, yielded to a desire to participate in the higher rates of return from equities and other investments.

Public pension plan asset allocation. During the 1990s, equities came to play a much more important role in the portfolios of state and local retirement systems. Table 7 shows that over 40 percent of public plan portfolios is now invested in domestic equities, with systems covering teachers investing slightly more (45 percent) and systems covering public safety employees investing slightly less (42 percent; Zorn 1999). The major difference in asset allocation across the plans covering the different employee groups pertains to investments in real estate and international securities. While systems covering state employees and teachers invested 16 percent and 14 percent of their portfolios, respectively, in these two major classes of investments, systems covering public safety and general local employees invested, respectively, only 7 percent and 9 percent. System size may play a role in explaining this difference. Systems covering state employees and teachers tend to be large systems, with sufficient assets to diversify their portfolios and sufficient resources to monitor complex investments.

Our comparison of investment patterns across public and private pension plans indicates that these differences have narrowed over time, comparing the public and private pension arena (Table 8). Among the top 1,000 pension systems, around half of the total assets (or more) are held in equities today, over one-third in bonds, and the rest in real estate, cash, and other forms of investments (Anand 1999). Overall, public pensions still do tend to hold somewhat less equity (59 percent) than do private funds (64 percent), and slightly more bonds (35 percent versus 29 percent). The international equity exposure of public funds (11 percent) is also lower than that of private funds (14 percent). Other holdings (real estate, cash) prove relatively similar.

TABLE 7. State and Local Government Pension Investments, 1996

	State employee systems	Teacher and school employee systems	Police and firefighter systems	Local employee systems	All systems
Percentage of total investments					
Short term	3.1	3.1	7.3	4.6	4.4
Domestic stocks	41.7	44.5	42.0	43.0	42.7
Domestic bonds	35.9	34.1	41.8	40.9	38.8
Real estate mortgages	0.4	1.6	0.2	0.7	0.7
Real estate equities	2.4	2.1	1.3	1.5	1.8
International equities	10.0	8.1	4.8	5.3	6.9
International fixed-income	2.9	1.9	0.7	1.3	1.7
Other	3.6	4.6	1.9	2.7	3.0
Total investments ($B)	545.8	358.0	74.9	113.5	1,092.2
Investment returns					
Rate of return 1996	13.9	13.5	13.4	13.7	1376
Exp. 1-year return given allocation*	11.7	12.3	11.5	11.7	11.8
5 annualized rate of return (1991–96)	11.5	11.0	10.6	11.5	11.3

Source: Authors' tabulations from PPCC, PENDAT Database, 1997. See Zorn (1997).
*Calculated using benchmark investment returns for the various asset classes.

Despite these similarities, it remains the fact that some state and local pension system investments are constrained within certain investment categories, facing prohibitions against purchasing certain types of investments and enjoinders to invest in some specific holdings (Mitchell and McCarthy 1999). For instance, 19 percent of the funds in the PENDAT sample face constitutional restrictions on investments; and 12 percent are or have been prohibited from making certain investments (usually in South Africa, Northern Ireland, or countries that did not follow MacBride principles). Other times there are mandates *favoring* certain investments: for example, 4 percent of the plans must direct a certain percentage of their plan investments to in-state holdings. In addition, many other funds have internal policy limitations on asset allocations, or other statutory limits on asset allocations (see Table 9). The extent to which such asset restrictions influence investment policy and investment returns as well as investment risk is an extremely important and complex issue (Mitchell and Hsin 1997a, 1997b; Munnell and Sunden this volume; Useem and Hess this volume).

Investment income and return. Tables 7 and 8 indicate rates of return earned by state and local pension investments, as reflected by the PPCC survey respondents. On average, the investments earned a 13.66 percent return in 1996, higher than the 11.77 percent expected return calculated using the

TABLE 8. Pension Plan Assets and Investment Performance, various years

I. Public vs. private plan assets (%)	Public systems[1]	Private plans[1]
Equities	*58.6*	*63.7*
U.S.	46.7	46.7
Foreign	11.2	14.2
Other	0.7	2.8
Bonds	*34.8*	*28.9*
U.S.	31.9	27.1
Foreign	2.1	1.7
Other	0.8	0.1
Real Estate	3.3	3.3
Cash	2.1	2.1
Other	6.6	2.0

II. Trends in public plan asset mix[2] (%)	Year						
	1950	1960	1970	1980	1989	1992	1996
Corporate equities	0	3	17	22	40	42	50
Corporate bonds	12	36	58	48	27	21	21
U.S. government securities	51	30	11	20	27	28	16
Other	37	31	14	10	6	9	13

III. Public plan investment performance	Year	Funds[3]	Index[4]	Number of plans
Return on assets (%)	1996	13.7	21.3	200
	1995	19.6	35.0	200
	1994	1.5	-0.1	213
	1993	11.8	10.7	213
	1992	9.3	8.2	213

Source: Adapted from Mitchell and McCarthy (1999).
[1] Anand (1999).
[2] Authors' calculations based on Mitchell and Carr (1992) and Zorn (1997).
[3] Authors' calculations based on Zorn (1997).
[4] CRSP Value-weighted NYSE/NASDAQ stock index including all distributions.

systems' asset allocations and benchmark returns earned on the major security classes. However, another study (Nofsinger 1998) compared public pension plan returns to a composite market index and concluded that public plans tend to underperform the market. Further study of this issue would be fruitful, but in any event the fact that public pension investment income contributes substantially to plan funding is not in dispute.[13]

TABLE 9. Investment Restrictions among Public Pension Systems, 1996

	Percent having ($-wtd.)	N	Percent having (plan-wtd.)	N
Statutory asset limits by type[1]				
Cap on bonds	15	260	4	261
Cap on bonds as percentage of issuer	6	260	7	261
Cap on real estate	29	260	18	261
Cap on foreign invst.	29	260	16	261
Cap on stock	39	260	25	261
Asset caps for those with statutory limits[2]				
Bonds: max % of portfolio	46	11	40	11
Max bond as % of Issuer	6	17	6	17
Real estate: max % of portfolio	13	46	9	46
Foreign invst.: max % of portfolio	11	43	10	43
Stock: max % of portfolio	54	65	59	65

Source: Adapted from Mitchell and McCarthy (1999).
[1] Statutory limits given in state constitution or state regulation.
[2] Some plans subject to statutory investment limits do not report actual fractional limits.

One of the driving forces behind state and local governments' success in funding retirement benefits has been the high returns earned in financial markets, especially domestic equities. State and local plans have been able to capture these returns largely as a result of the changes made to their asset allocations over the past two decades. Table 8 indicates the dramatic time series change in public plans' asset mix: as recently as 1989, they held the majority of their portfolios in corporate and government bonds, and prior to 1960 they held virtually no equities at all.

Returns on U.S. equities are often thought to be more volatile than returns on bonds, so the fact that public plans hold a higher proportion of bonds would be seen as reducing the volatility of public sector pension fund investment returns. But because equities have historically performed better than bonds, holding more bonds produces lower returns for public plans. This is seen clearly in the last panel of Table 8, which reports public pension fund returns over the period 1993–96 (for the PENDAT sample), as compared with a value-weighted market index over the same time period.[14]

The evidence in Table 8 shows that public plan returns are less volatile than market returns, outperforming the stock market in poor years and underperforming it in good years. It should be noted that these two return patterns are not strictly comparable, inasmuch as the underlying risks in the two portfolios are different. That is, a market basket of stocks would be anticipated to perform significantly better than public portfolios in good equity years and worse in poor equity years, because public plans hold a sub-

TABLE 10. Public Pension Plan Reported Expenses and Turnover, 1997

	$-weighted	System-weighted	Number of plans
Administrative expenses[1]	$78	$211	221
Investment expenses[2]	0.27%	0.44%	155[4]
Stock turnover[3]	38%		67

Source: Adapted from Mitchell and McCarthy (1999).
[1]Calculated per member (including active, retired, and disabled members).
[2]Calculated as % of fair market value of system assets at 31 December 1996.
[3]Turnover defined as the smaller of annual stock purchases and sales divided by the average portfolio value over 1996. Authors' calculations based on PENDAT Database (Zorn 1997).
[4]Statistically significant differences were found between funds reporting investment expenses and those not reporting; those not reporting were smaller (p < 0.05) and earned lower returns (p < 0.005).

stantial fraction of assets in bonds. Unfortunately, the database we use does not report investment returns for specific assets held by public plans. To the extent that private pensions also hold more equity than do public funds, one could also anticipate that private pensions will experience higher returns and higher volatility. It is not entirely clear why corporate stockholders should be less risk-averse than state taxpayers, and indeed with the growth of stockholding in the U.S. economy, it is likely that these two groups will overlap more considerably in the future.

The final investment-related question we consider focuses on public plan expenses and turnover in plan portfolios. This is important because higher returns can be eroded over time by high expenses, and all public plan stakeholders would likely benefit from paying close attention to the administrative costs of managing the plans. Unfortunately it is difficult to obtain data on expenses for the entire range of public plans; there was substantial nonresponse among respondents surveyed by Zorn (1997) on this question, suggesting that those who did reply may be nonrepresentative in some way. Our analysis of the 221 systems offering information on administrative expenses shows that these reported costs averaged $211 per member per year on a per member basis but one-third of that level in the dollar-weighted computation; hence larger plans incur substantially lower expenses (Table 10). Turning to reported investment expenses, these are computed as a fraction of system assets (year-end), and here too, it must be noted that only 155 of the full set of 379 plans responded to this question in the survey. For those reporting, average investment expenses totaled 44 basis points in 1996, which falls to only 27 basis points if dollar-weighted. Again, the larger funds prove to have lower expense ratios than smaller funds. Both results are compatible with previous studies showing scale economies in pension fund administration (Mitchell 1998), and these investment charge figures are consistent with the lower end of institutional money management fees charged by pension investment managers. Finally, Table 10 indicates how much turnover the public plans' stock portfolio experienced on an annual basis, for the sixty-seven funds that answered this question in the survey. Turnover is defined as the lesser of annual purchases or sales divided by the average amount in the portfolio over the year. This is an important number because some have argued that high turnover in pension fund stock portfolios result in high brokerage and investment commissions. These turnover figures (38 percent) are lower than reported by public funds in earlier years (McCarthy and Turner 1992) but the substantial nonreporting must lead one to question whether these results are generalizable.

Public Pension Governance and Structure

Over time policymakers have become increasingly interested in how public pension plans are governed, mainly because they are responsible for so many participants and such a large pool of investment funds. Generally, state and local retirement systems are overseen by a retirement board that has authority for making decisions related to investments, actuarial valuations, system operations, and in some instances the benefits provided by the plan. Day-to-day administration is usually conducted either by the retirement system's staff or by staff of the government sponsoring the system.

Governance and administration. A perusal of Tables 11 and 12 reveals that state and local pension plans in the United States are managed by a pension board of trustees, a group that typically bears responsibility for investment policy and often for asset allocation. The number of board members ranges from one to two dozen, but the typical board is usually formed by eight people, with most of the board members appointed by politicians or serving ex officio.[15] The average number of board members is higher for systems serving state employees and teachers (9.2 and 10, respectively) than for systems serving public safety and general local employees (7.5 and 7.6, respectively). It is interesting to note that board composition also varies with the type of covered employees. As shown in Table 12, systems serving teachers and public safety employees have a somewhat higher percent of elected members and lower percent of appointed members than do systems serving state or local general employees.

Typically, day-to-day system administration is done by staff under the supervision of the system's executive director or plan administrator. Many systems hire an executive who reports directly to the board. Some smaller systems established by a single governmental employer are administered by employees in the employer's finance or human resources department. Generally, staff sizes vary with the number of covered members and the services provided. Data provided by the PPCC survey shows staff sizes ranging from a

TABLE 11. Public Pension Plan Governance and Structure, 1996

	Mean	Median	Number of Plans
I. Board size and composition			
Number of board members	8.3	8	244
% appointed and ex officio	62	60	231
% elected by members	35	40	224
II. Board responsibilities (% responsible for)			
Investment	88		244
Benefits	71		244
Assumptions	89		244
Asset allocation	84		228
III. Constraints on board behavior (% subject to)			
Prudent Man limitation	88		236
Ethics standards written	66		233
State legal list	29		238
Constitutional restrictions on investment	19		225
Own investment prohibitions	12		235
In-state investment requirements	4		233
State insurance law	3		235
IV. Public pension board oversight (% requiring)			
Actuarial valuation annually	100		364
Annual audit	99		252
Independent investment performance audits	86		231

Source: Adapted from Mitchell and McCarthy (1999).

single individual working part time to administer a small local plan, to over 200 people for plans covering several hundred thousand members. While staff size averaged 53.6 for all respondents, systems covering state employees and teachers had much larger staffs on average (120.5 and 111.4 respectively) than systems covering public safety and general local employees (7.0 and 11.0 respectively). This is mainly due to the fact that systems serving state employees and teachers tend to have many more members than systems covering public safety and local employees.

When staff size is examined in relation to the number of active members served by the plan, the results suggest economies of scale in system administration. Table 12 shows that the typical public pension system has around 2.6 staff members per 1,000 active members, with systems covering state employees and teachers averaging 1.5 each, compared with systems covering public safety and local government employees (5.0 and 2.8, respectively). Since state and teacher systems have substantially more members than sys-

TABLE 12. Public Pension Plan Governance and Structure by Plan Type, 1996

	State employee systems	Teacher and school employee systems	Police and firefighter systems	Local employee systems	All systems
Average board size (N)	9.24	10.03	7.50	7.55	8.31
Appointed (%)	47	40	39	50	46
Elected (%)	31	43	45	32	35
Ex officio (%)	18	16	13	15	16
Other (%)	4	1	3	3	3
Staff size (N)	120.5	111.4	7.0	11.0	53.6
Staff per 1,000 active members	1.5	1.5	5.0	2.8	2.6

Source: Authors' tabulations from PPCC, PENDAT Database, 1997. See Zorn (1997).

tems covering public safety and local employees, it is likely that their lower staffing ratios reflect economies of scale.

The vast majority of retirement boards have the responsibility for overseeing pension investments. As such, board members are acting as fiduciaries and required to use their best judgment to ensure that future funds are available to pay plan benefits. In the private sector, corporate pension fiduciaries are regulated by the Employee Retirement Income Security Act of 1974; this law requires private pension funds to be invested using the "care, skill, and diligence" of a prudent individual acting "solely in the interest" of plan participants. While state and local pension plans are exempt from the fiduciary language of ERISA, it is interesting to that the same or very similar language has been adopted in most public plans (88 percent). Somewhat less prevalent are written ethical standards for public board members, with only two-thirds of all public plans requiring these. This approach seeks to limit potential conflicts of interest with regard to public pension boards, and has been championed by the California Public Employee Retirement System (CalPERS) in recent years. In addition virtually all reporting plans have annual actuarial valuations and are subject to annual actuarial audits, and some 86 percent are subject to independent investment audits. These reporting and disclosure requirements contribute to a more transparent public pension environment for all concerned stakeholders.

Conclusion

We conclude that state and local government pension plans have been generally successful in providing adequate and secure retirement benefits in ways that substantially reduce their long-term costs. Most benefits are provided through defined benefit plans, paid over the life of the retiree, that do not vary with fluctuations in the financial markets. In many instances, the benefits are also indexed to inflation. In addition, most of the plans are well funded, with investment income accounting for over two-thirds of plan receipts, thereby reducing required contributions. We have also shown that public plan assets are relatively diversified, especially as compared to the past. And compared to the private sector, public plans tend to have relatively smoother investment performance patterns, mainly attributable to their larger share in bonds and smaller equity holdings.

These signs of pension system maturity are strongly positive predictors for the future. Nevertheless, state and local plans will face challenges over the next several decades. The baby boom aging process suggests that public employers will face a burst of retirements within the next ten to fifteen years. Another potential pressure results from fiscal stress, which can undermine efforts to fully fund accumulating promises (Mitchell and Smith 1994). As long as economic conditions remain favorable, there appears to be little to worry about, but an economic downturn can reduce funding in a variety of ways. Additionally, if capital market returns are highly correlated with state and local tax revenues, funding problems could be exacerbated in an economic downturn. More research is required on this potential linkage.

Another development pertains to public employee and employer interest in defined contribution plans. Some states have adopted defined contribution plans, including the State Employees Retirement System of Nebraska, the Teachers' Defined Contribution Plan of West Virginia, and Michigan's State Employee plan for workers newly hired in 1997 and thereafter (Fore this volume). Whether others will follow depends in large part on cost and political considerations, including how state and local budgets are faring, and whether employee unions see them with favor.

These factors suggest some pressures for change. For example, to protect public plans from political pressures resulting from fiscal stress, the National Conference of Commissioners on Uniform State Laws has recently proposed that all states adopt a uniform set of laws related to public pension plan investments. This Management of Public Employee Retirement Systems Act (MPERSA) is intended to modernize investment decisionmaking in public pensions (Wisniewski 1999). Whether it will eventually be adopted by state legislatures remains to be seen.

In addition, demographic and economic pressures are also affecting plan design. In order to keep experienced, long-term employees on staff, some public employers have modified their retirement plans in ways that encourage employees to remain in service beyond their normal retirement date. These deferred retirement option plans (DROPs) reward employees who postpone their retirement by providing a partial lump-sum distribution when they finally leave employment (Eitelberg this volume). Additionally, concern over pension portability arising from the debate over defined contribution plans has lead some public retirement systems to adopt "hybrid plans" combining features from both defined benefit and defined contribution plans. Undoubtedly, plan design will continue to evolve over the next several decades, as state and local pension systems in the United States continue to evolve with the changing environment.

Notes

1. Active and retired participant data refer to 1997 and are taken from Zorn (1999); asset information for 1998 is from Anand (1999).

2. Some public sector plans are of the defined contribution variety as we note below.

3. For a discussion of pension plan types, see McGill et al. (1996)

4. For early discussion of public pension plans see Bleakney (1972), Inman (1982), and Phillips (1992); more recent analyses include Mitchell and Carr (1996), Hsin and Mitchell (1994, 1996, 1997), and Mitchell and Smith (1994).

5. This section draws on Zorn (1999).

6. Total investment earnings amounted to more then $780B over the entire 1987–97 period (not shown in Table 1).

7. For an analysis of teacher retirement systems see Wisniewski (1999).

8. These statistics are compiled from the Public Pension Coordinating Council's 1997 PENDAT Database (Zorn 1997). This survey covered plans employing more than 80 percent of active state and local system members.

9. The precise split between the employer and employee contribution amount is less consequential for eventual benefit amounts than is the overall cost of the plan. But here, too, it is difficult to compare public and private plan costs, since the rising value of private sector pensions due to good stock market performance has permitted many private employers to take "contribution holidays" from their pensions, for more than a decade. For further detail on employer costs for employee compensation see BLS (1999).

10. Perhaps as a result, only 4 percent of public plans have benefits "formally" integrated with social security payments; more than half of private plans do (many others have informal integration arrangements).

11. Prior to June 15, 1996, the Governmental Accounting Standards Board required public plans to disclose the pension benefit obligation (PBO), a measure of the actuarial accrued liability based on the projected unit credit actuarial method, in the notes to their financial statements. This was reported in addition to the actuarial accrued liability determined under the actuarial method actually used to calculate the plan's liabilities and required contributions. The purpose of disclosing the PBO was to provide a more consistent measure with which to compare funding progress across public plans. In 1996, GASB (1996) eliminated the PBO disclosure requirement after substantial debate, on the grounds that it did not substantially clarify funded status and was possibly responsible for a reduction in employer contributions for some plans. Currently, GASB provides for the use of any one of the following actuarial cost methods: entry age, frozen entry age, attained age, frozen attained age, projected unit credit, and aggregate actuarial cost. With the spread of GASB reporting among retirement systems, the PBO statistic has been deemphasized or dropped entirely from public employee pension system annual financial reports.

12. This is derived from the 1995 and 1997 PENDAT surveys (Zorn 1997).

13. See Munnell and Sunden (this volume) and Useem and Hess (this volume) for further discussion on this point.

14. In examining this table, readers should note that the comparison is between a group of funds (with a diversified asset mix, including stocks and bonds) and a stock index (including only stocks). Thus, the fact that the funds underperformed the index in 1995 and 1996 is not an indication of investment mismanagement but rather the result of holding a diversified portfolio.

15. Some systems, such as the Florida Retirement System and the Iowa Public Employee Retirement System operates without a board of trustees, relying instead on authority vested in a senior official of the sponsoring agency (Wisniewski 1999).

References

Anand, Vineeta. 1999. "Defined Benefit Assets Surge 20.3 percent." *Pensions and Investments* (March 22): 1.

Bleakney, Thomas P. 1972. *Retirement Systems for Public Employees.* Pension Research Council. Homewood, Ill.: Irwin.

Board of Governors of the Federal Reserve System. 1999. *Flow of Funds Accounts of the United States, Annual Flows and Outstandings, 1982–1990.* Washington, D.C.: Board of Governors.

Braden, Bradley R. and Stephanie Hyland. 1995. "Cost of Employee Compensation in the Public and Private Sectors." *Employee Benefits Survey: A BLS Reader.* U.S. Department of Labor, BLS, February.

Bureau of Labor Statistics (BLS), U.S. Department of Labor. 1989. *Employee Benefits in Medium and Large Firms, 1989.* Washington, D.C.: U.S. GPO.

———. 1992. *Employee Benefits in State and Local Governments, 1992.* Washington, D.C.: U.S. GPO.

———. 1994. *Employee Benefits in State and Local Governments, 1994.* Washington, D.C.: U.S. GPO.

———. 1995. *Employee Benefits in Medium and Large Private Establishments, 1995.* Washington, D.C.: U.S. GPO.

———. 1999. *Employer Costs for Employee Compensation Summary.* <www.bls.gov/news.release/ecec.news.html>

Eitelberg, Cathie. This volume. "Public Pensioin Design and Responses to a Changing Workforce."

Fore, Douglas. This volume. "Going Private in the Public Sector: The Transition from Defined Benefit to Defined Contribution Pension Plans."

Government Accounting Standards Board (GASB). 1996. *Statement No. 25: Financial Reporting for Defined Benefit Plans and Note Disclosures for Defined Contribution Plans.* Hartford, Conn.: GASB.

Greenwich Associates. 1998. "What Now?" *Greenwich Report* (Greenwich, Conn.), March.

Hsin, Ping-Lung and Olivia S. Mitchell. 1994. "The Political Economy of Public Sector Pensions: Pension Funding Patterns, Governance Structures, and Fiscal Stress." *Revista de Analysis Economico* (July).

———. 1996. "Managing Public Sector Pensions." In *Pensions for the Twenty-First Century,* ed. Sylvester J. Schieber and John Shoven. New York: Twentieth Century Fund.

———. 1997. "Public Pension Plan Efficiency." In *Positioning Pensions for the Twenty-*

First Century, ed. Michael S. Gordon, Olivia S. Mitchell, and Marc Twinney. Pension Research Council. Philadelphia: University of Pennsylvania Press. 187–208.

Hustead, Edwin C. This volume. "Determining the Cost of Public Pension Plans."

Inman, Robert P. 1982. "Public Employee Pensions and the Local Labor Budget." *Journal of Public Economics* 19: 49–71.

Internal Revenue Service (IRS), U.S. Department of the Treasury. 1997. *Federal-State Reference Guide: Social Security Coverage and FICA Reporting by State and Local Government Employers.* Washington, D.C.: Internal Revenue Service.

McCarthy, David M. and John A. Turner. 1992. "Stock Turnover and Private Pension Portfolios." *Trends in Pensions 1992.* U.S. Department of Labor. Washington, D.C.: U.S. GPO. 543–76

McGill, Dan M., Kyle N. Brown, John J. Haley, and Sylvester J. Schieber, eds. 1996. *Fundamentals of Private Pensions.* 7th ed. Pension Research Council. Philadelphia: University of Pennsylvania Press.

Mitchell, Olivia S. 1998. "Administrative Costs in Public and Private Pension Systems." In *Privatizing Social Security,* ed Martin Feldstein. NBER. Chicago: University of Chicago Press.

Mitchell, Olivia S. and Roderick M. Carr. 1996. "State and Local Pension Plans." In *Handbook of Employee Benefits,* ed. Jerry S. Rosenbloom. Chicago: Irwin. 1207–22.

Mitchell, Olivia S. and Ping-Lung Hsin. 1997a. "Managing Public Sector Pensions." In *Public Policy Toward Pensions,* ed. Sylvester J. Schieber and John B. Shoven. Twentieth Century Fund. Cambridge, Mass.: MIT Press. 247–266.

———. 1997b. "Public Sector Pension Governance and Performance." In *The Economics of Pensions: Principles, Policies, and International Experience,* ed. Salvador Valdés-Prieto. Cambridge: Cambridge University Press. 92–126.

Mitchell, Olivia S. and David McCarthy. 1999. "The Structure and Performance of State and Local Pension Plans." Pension Research Council Working Paper, Philadelphia: Wharton School.

Mitchell, Olivia S., Robert J. Myers, and Howard Young, eds. 1999. *Prospects for Social Security Reform.* Pension Research Council. Philadelphia: University of Pennsylvania Press.

Mitchell, Olivia S. and Robert S. Smith. 1994. "Pension Funding in the Public Sector." *Review of Economics and Statistics* 126, 2 (May): 278–90.

Munnell, Alicia H. and Annika Sundén. This volume. "Investment Practices of State and Local Pension Funds: Implications for Social Security Reform."

Nofsinger, John R. 1998. "Why Targeted Investing Does Not Make Sense." *Financial Management* 27, 3 (Autumn): 87–96.

Pensions and Investments. 1999. January 25: 74.

Phillips, Kristen. 1992. "State and Local Government Pension Benefits." In *Trends in Pensions 1992,* ed. John A. Turner and L. Dailey. Washington, D.C.: U.S. GPO. 341–492.

Social Security Advisory Council (SSAC). 1996. *Final Report.* <www.ssa.gov>.

U.S. Bureau of the Census, Census of Governments. 1987, 1992. *Employee Retirement Systems of State and Local Governments.* Washington, D.C.: U.S. Department of Commerce.

———. 1999. *Employee Retirement Systems of State and Local Governments.* <www.census.gov/govs/www/per.html>

U.S. Congress, House Committee on Education and Labor, 1978. *Pension Task Force Report on Public Employee Retirement Systems.* 95th Cong., 2d sess. Washington, D.C.: U.S. GPO.

U.S. Congress, House Ways and Means Committee. 1998. *Green Book.* Washington, D.C.: U.S. GPO.

Useem, Michael and David Hess. This volume. "Governance and Investment of Public Pensions."

Wisniewski, Stanley. 1999. "Salient Features of Large Public Employee Retirement Systems with a Focus on Education Employees." Pension Research Council Working Paper. Philadelphia: Wharton School.

Zorn, Paul. 1995. "Comparing Retirement Benefits Provided by Private Firms and State and Local Governments." *Research Bulletin* (Government Finance Officers Association), January.

———. 1999. "Local Government Employee Pension Plans." Pension Research Council Working Paper. Philadelphia: Wharton School.

———. 1997. *Survey of State and Local Government Employee Retirement Systems.* Chicago: Public Pension Coordinating Council, c/o Government Finance Officers Association.

Chapter 3
State Employee Pension Plans

Karen Steffen

This chapter explores and evaluates key characteristics of the major state retirement systems in the United States. Our goal is to offer comparisons of public and private plans with regard to history, structures, and essential features.[1]

U.S. Public and Private Retirement Programs
Since World War II

Pensions in the United States began as a personnel tool to recruit and retain employees. State and local pension programs began prior to World War II, during which time many pension programs were based on defined contribution features. However, low investment returns during the first half of this century were followed by high inflation after retirement, impelling many public pensions to move to the defined benefit form. Private sector plans were uncommon until World War II, when they began to be used to attract employees during a time of tight labor markets, wage controls and a strong union influence.

In the private sector, defined benefit (DB) plans[2] remained the norm until the 1980s, when three major changes in the pension environment made defined contribution (DC) plans more attractive than DB plans. One factor was the 1974 Employee Retirement Income Security Act (ERISA), which established complex regulations for private employer retirement programs. By contrast, public plans remained exempt from many of the ERISA changes to the IRS tax code, in particular, regarding funding rules (Crane this volume). Additional changes to ERISA rules in subsequent years made the private pension regulatory environment even more complex. The second factor was booming stock markets, which over the last two decades produced significant investment gains in pension systems. ERISA funding rules have restricted the extent to which private employers can make tax-deductible contributions to their DB pensions, leading employers to seek other ways to provide additional benefits and to receive relief from some of the more complex ERISA requirements. The third factor was a change in the degree to which corporate America adopted a paternalistic approach to employees. Corporate downsizing, increased labor mobility, and the end of lifetime jobs meant that pensions were no longer seen as a deterrent to turnover, but rather as more of a tax-deferred saving device. The paternalism of the old DB plan began to give way to the flexibility of the DC pension (Sass 1997).

These developments, and particularly the burgeoning stock market, boosted the growth of so-called 401(k) plans in the private sector. Public employers could not offer these plans after 1986, but they were permitted to offer regular 401(a) DB pensions. In addition, teacher systems may have 403(b) plans as well; these are tax-sheltered annuity plans, not available to private sector employees. Public employees may also be eligible for deferred compensation programs under Section 457 of the IRS Code.

Public and Private Pension Plans Today

Over the late 1990's, few private sector employers have established a traditional defined benefit plan; newer companies tend to have a 401(k) plan as their sole pension if they offer a plan at all. Older large private employers tend to have both a traditional, noncontributory defined benefit program, and also a 401(k) plan for employee contributions and voluntary supplemental retirement savings. In addition, a pension program known as a "cash balance" plan is being adopted by many private sector employers (Rappaport et al. 1997). By contrast, most state and local retirement systems still maintain a traditional defined benefit plan as their primary pension plan. Nevertheless, there are some signs of change here too. Recently a few systems have made the transition to a defined contribution plan, or have added defined contribution features to their existing defined benefit program (Fore this volume).

An important difference between private and public retirement programs today pertains to who pays for the plan. In the public sector, employees usually are required to contribute toward their DB retirement programs, generally on a pretax basis (under IRS Code 414[h]), whereas in the private sector DB plans are rarely contributory. By contrast, DC plans are more similar across public and private sectors in that both allow pretax contributions, though the circumstances differ somewhat. For private employees, 401(k) rules allow workers to contribute if they choose to do so on a pretax basis. In the public sector, regulations are somewhat different. IRS Section 414(h) permits employee contributions to be "picked up" by the employer and treated as employer contributions for federal tax purposes, but if they are, the employee no longer has the choice of either receiving the amounts directly or as a pretax contribution to the plan. Therefore, all picked-up contributions must be mandatory and of the same amount for all employees. In this way, employee contributions are treated differently for private and public DC plans.

As a result of the different employee contribution rules in public plans, a number of issues arise regarding equity, refund payments, and loss of accrued benefits that tend not to arise in the private plan arena. For instance, public plans often require employee contributions of at least 25 percent, but usually less than 50 percent, of total contributions. Many systems initially required a 50–50 cost split and paid benefits based on accumulated employee contributions matched with employer funds.[3] As benefit improvements were given retroactively, employer contributions tended to rise. Of course, recent market gains have cut employers' actuarially computed contribution rates and it remains to be seen whether these gains are reflected only in employer rates (as losses usually are), or whether employee rates are permitted to fall as well. Most public systems have employee contributions rates fixed by state statute which cannot be changed except by legislation.[4]

Private and public plan sector plans also differ in terms of their ability to change and terminate existing pension programs. ERISA and IRS rules require private sector employers to guarantee that no employee will lose any *already earned* benefit entitlement, but an employer is permitted to modify or terminate *future* accruals to both current and new employees. By contrast, in the public arena, it is much more difficult—if not impossible—to change future benefit accruals for existing employees. Thus if changes in a public retirement program are desired, it might be necessary to permit all current employees to remain under the current program, and then to apply the changes in plan design solely to new hires. This commonly leads to two-tier plans within the same employer group, a rare occurrence in the private sector.

Another key difference lies in the authority of the fiduciary group that administers plans across the two sectors. Private sector employers are comparatively free to make system changes as long as the proposed change meets ERISA and IRS requirements. If the plan is subject to collective bargaining, the union must also be permitted to bargain over changes. Private employees often have little voice regarding a change in their pension structure. By contrast, in a governmental plan, changes must generally be approved by a legislative group, and changes are subject to public disclosures, hearings, and discussions that accompany the political process. In addition, unions frequently play a role. For instance, there are thirteen states where only some employees have bargaining rights, and fourteen states where no bargaining rights exist; in others, retirement benefits may or may not be included in the bargaining process. But even when unions do not directly negotiate over pensions, these groups can be quite vocal in supporting or opposing pro-

TABLE 1. Key Differences Between Public and Private Retirement Programs

Features	Private plans	Public plans
Type of main program	Combined defined contribution and defined benefit	Defined benefit
Employee contributions		
To primary program	No	Yes
Mandatory	No	Yes
To supplemental program	Yes	Yes
Pretax basis	Yes	Yes
Covered under ERISA provisions	Yes	Only a few
IRS funding and deductibility concerns	Yes	No
Plan provisions	Legal document prepared by attorneys	Contained in legislative statutes
Contributions are expressed as	Dollar amounts	Percentage of payroll
Advanced funding of future benefits	ERISA required	by state provisions by state provisions
COLA provisions	Rare or ad hoc	Common, may be automatic

Source: Author's compilation.

posed legislation affecting retirement benefits and pension funding. Table 1 briefly summarizes several of the key differences between private and public sector retirement programs.

Benefit Features of Public Pension Plans

Despite these differences across public and private sector pension plans, the plans do share some key attributes. Most importantly, fundamental funding and design principles apply to all pension systems. Specifically, the cash flowing into a pension program must come from one of three sources: (1) contributions, (2) other new money coming in, and (3) net investment returns on assets invested in financial securities. This relationship may be summarized as $C + I = B + E$, where C refers to employee and employer contributions and other sources of noninvestment income, I refers to investment income, B refers to benefit payments, and E refers to fund expenses. Irrespective of what type of program is set up, this fundamental formula cannot be changed. Another way of looking at it is that all monies coming into the program must eventually be accounted for, and all monies to be paid by a retirement program must arise from some source.

What makes retirement programs much different from other entitlement programs or benefits is the considerable length of time between when the funds are deposited into the account, and when the benefits are actually paid out. For a new employee at age 25, benefits earned based on a year of service now will not be eligible for payment for up to forty years into the future at age 65. Then if annual pension payments are made, it may be another twenty years or more before the pension system is no longer obligated to make any further payments to the employee or beneficiary. Thus, the average time horizon for an employee entering a retirement program is generally at least twenty and often sixty or more years. This period is substantially longer than the commonly expected "long-term" horizon found, say, in the area of investments.

Core Benefits

Most benefit obligations promised to members of state retirement systems are associated with what are known as "core benefits." These refer to the benefit payable at the *normal* retirement age, covering work during a lifetime career with the covered employer group. This normal benefit is usually the reference for other benefit types, including the early and deferred benefits, as well as disability, survivor, and postretirement benefits.

Normal benefits. As outlined by Mitchell et al. (this volume), public plan retirement ages tend to be much younger than age 65; in fact, the public sector "normal" retirement age is usually age 60 or 62. The age 65 benchmark has been considered the "normal" retirement age for workers covered by social security though it was raised for baby boomers under the 1983 amendments. Public plans also tend to provide full "unreduced" benefits based on service or a combination of age plus service, such that the public employee may receive full, unreduced retirement benefits after thirty years of service, for example, regardless of age (or even as low as after twenty years of service in some plans; see Mitchell et al. this volume).

A typical benefit formula for normal retirement might equal a member's number of years of service times his or her final average salary, times a benefit percentage factor. For example, the Pennsylvania Employee Retirement System provides 2 percent per year of service, such that a member with thirty years of service and a final average salary of $45,000 would be entitled to a normal retirement benefit of 60 percent of $45,000, or $27,000. Over time, the percentage factor for public sector plans has risen; thus a 1.5 percent factor was common twenty years ago, but is rare today. Higher factors are generally found in public systems where members are not covered by social security; some 25 percent of all public plan members today are in this group. In the public sector, integrated benefit formulas are rare.[5]

Another factor important in computing normal retirement benefits is the averaging period used to determine the salary base to which the percentage factor is applied. Until recently, the most commonly used period was the highest five-year average. This is still the most common averaging period found in private sector plans. Recent benefit improvements in the public sector plans now have almost half of the public plans using a three year average period and less than a fifth using a five-year period (State of Wisconsin 1996). Some public safety plans base benefits on the final salary without averaging.[6] The shorter the period, the more likely a final retirement benefit will replace net preretirement income; that is, a benefit equal to 50 percent of average salary provides less than half of the final salary. Since salaries usually rise over the worklife, a shorter averaging period increases benefits. In addition, the shorter the period, the more likely an opportunity for antiselection arises. This happens when an employee artificially boosts compensation for the period of time just prior to retirement by working extra hours, taking on extra duties, etc. This "salary spiking" issue is of concern when determining the financial cost of providing benefits.

Early benefits. Once the base formula for the normal retirement benefit has been established, a member can often elect to retire earlier, but perhaps with a financial penalty. This early benefit tends to be reduced to account for the fact that the benefit will be paid to the member over a longer period of time, since payments are starting before the normal retirement age. If the reduction equals the increase in value for the earlier commencement of the benefit payments, the reduction is said to be "actuarially equivalent." Many private plans still require "full" actuarial reduction for early retirement benefits, while others have adopted a step reduction, such as 5 percent for the first five years of early retirement and 8 percent thereafter. If these reductions track the true actuarial reduction benefits are not subsidized; however smaller reductions create subsidized early retirement benefits. Public sector plans often provide subsidized early retirement benefit amounts.

Maximum benefits. Public plans may have maximum benefit limitations regarding the amount of the benefit to be accrued when expressed as a percentage of the final average salary. For example, a plan may pay "full unreduced" benefits after thirty years of service, but may prohibit the accrual of additional benefit credits after thirty years. In such plans, the only increase for the member's continued employment would be due to the increase in the average final salary due to pay increases. Such maximum benefit limitations are common in public safety plans, where unreduced benefits are seen as encouraging earlier retirement in light of the substantial physical demands for this type of work. It is interesting that some plans continue to collect employee contributions from members even after they reach the maximum benefit ceiling as a condition of continued employment.

Post-retirement benefit adjustments. Once retirement occurs and benefits have begun, they may be changed in recognition of changes in the cost of living.

Referred to as COLAs, or cost-of-living adjustments, the yearly increases are usually fixed, such as two percent per year, or may be tied to an outside index such as the Consumer Price Index. Regular increases are one option, but many only give "ad-hoc" increases made when a system can afford to pay for the increased benefits. Nearly all state-level public plans have either automatic or ad hoc COLAs, whereas less than half of private plans offer such benefits at all and those that are offered are almost all ad hoc in nature (Mitchell et al. this volume). The high cost of automatic COLAs, coupled with employer concerns regarding their ability to consistently provide such increases on an affordable basis, makes some public systems avoid what may appear to be a desirable plan feature.

For this reason, some plans undertake occasional benefit improvements to restore all or a portion of the lost economic value of the benefit due to inflation. Over time, members retired the longest will have lost the most purchasing power; these members also tend to be the oldest and therefore the least expensive candidates for a benefit increase. For this reason, when a system has a limited budget to improve benefits, a "restoration" COLA is often popular. There is also a new type of COLA adjustment, called the "excess interest" COLA. It occurs only periodically as with the ad hoc increases, but it is based on a fixed formula and is then guaranteed to be paid as long as the formula produces an amount in excess of certain criteria. Another alternative is illustrated by the Washington State Retirement System, which recently adopted a "gain-sharing" COLA. Here excess investment returns were split, providing both increased COLA benefits to retired members and also reducing the period over which the unfunded pension liability is amortized.

Noncore Benefits

The core benefits discussed above typically cost over three-quarters of the benefit budget, but several other types of benefits provided by state retirement systems are also worth mentioning.

Deferred vested benefits. Most retirement systems offer some benefits to employees who no longer work for the employer, but have earned enough credits to receive a retirement benefit. This is known as a deferred or a vested retirement benefit. ERISA requires private pension plans to provide vested retirement benefits after a minimum of five years, and there is no way for an employee to forfeit the vested earned benefit. Public plans differ in two critical ways when providing for benefits to vested members. One is that the vesting schedule, which indicates how many years of service the participant needs to be fully vested, can be much longer, taking as long as ten years. Older uniformed systems may even require full career service, such as twenty years, not granting any retirement benefit for termination prior to that time. Second, public employees leaving employment may elect to forfeit earned benefit rights by withdrawing their contributions when they leave, a practice known as a "refund." Sometimes a provision may be made for the member to restore his lost accrued benefit by repaying the refund amount with interest if he or she subsequently becomes reemployed and covered by the same retirement system.

Depending on the age and years of service of the member at the time of termination, the value of the accrued vested benefit in current dollars (the present value of the deferred benefit) may be less than the total dollars, plus interest, contributed by the member prior to termination of employment. Thus, any employer dollars contributed while the member was working may not necessarily add to the value of that particular member's earned benefit, but may be assigned to other members for purposes of benefit payments. This practice of benefit assignment within a DB plan gives rise to substantial misunderstanding in the public arena, and provides some impetus for the current trend toward DC plans in the public sector.

Death benefits. Nearly all state retirement systems provide for some type of benefit upon death while in active service. This benefit often takes the form of the benefit the member's spouse or beneficiary might have received had the member retired just prior to death. This is similar to the ERISA/REA (Retirement Equity Act) required benefits for private plans.

Disability benefits. Many, but not all, public plans provide retirement benefits payable if the member is disabled and no longer able to continue working. These disability benefits are usually related to the normal accrued retirement benefit, but can use a lower benefit percentage factor in computing the benefit, say 1.50 percent when the normal formula uses 2 percent. Some systems actually provide a subsidized benefit to disabled members, at least over the period that the member would have otherwise been working. In practice, disability benefits are often geared to replace some fraction of a member's income (e.g., 60 percent of average compensation) or provide a benefit equal to what the member would have earned had employment continued and the member had earned the full number of years of service to the normal retirement age. Some public systems have recently contemplated eliminating the disability benefit from their retirement system, instead providing this form of insurance outside the system. The financial impact of this can vary by system and may depend on whether or not the retirement agency is able to administer the program (deciding who qualifies for and meets the definitions of disablement to receive the benefit). Outsourcing the benefit determination process may occur with a third-party administrator, where the retirement system continues to pay benefits. This approach keeps disability benefit financing within the system but reduces the sometimes-difficult fiduciary issues that arise when reviewing individual situations.

Disability benefits are usually coordinated with worker's compensation and social security payments, in both the public and private sectors. Duty-related benefits may not require a service requirement, but non-duty related benefits may require five or ten years of employment, as well as satisfaction of the definition of disablement. The definition of disablement can vary, from disablement from any type of gainful employment to only disablement from the employee's own occupation. More disability benefits are paid to public safety officers than to other public employees. One reason may be the hazardous nature of the job, plus some duty-disability benefits payable to public safety members may be excludable from those individuals' taxable federal income. This may lead to an incentive to provide benefits under the disability rules rather than as a normal service retirement.

Optional forms of payments. Regular retirement benefits are usually payable as a monthly annuity, starting at retirement and stopping upon the member's death with no further payments to be made, regardless if death occurs one month or thirty years after retirement. Optional forms of payment are frequently available, usually set to be actuarially equivalent to the system's regular retirement benefit. Unisex factors are required by law, and simplified factors that reflect the overall actuarial values may be used. The monthly amount for an optional benefit is generally lower than for the regular benefit, to account for the financial impact of potentially greater total benefit payments paid by the retirement system due to the option's features. With the exception of the pop-up joint and survivor options, all options are found in both the private and the public sector.

Guaranteed payments. This form of benefit affords some type of guarantee to the member that a minimum number of benefit payments will be made; the larger the guarantee, the greater the reduction from the regular form of payment. There are two common types of guarantees: a period certain, and a refund annuity. Turning first to the *period certain* form, this ensures that a total number of benefit payments is guaranteed, regardless of when the member dies. If the member dies before all guaranteed payments have been made, the same monthly benefit amount will continue to a beneficiary until all guaranteed payments have been made to the member prior to death, or subsequently to the beneficiary. If the member lives beyond the guaranteed period, the monthly benefit payments usually continue until death.[7]

The *refund annuity* form is found in contributory retirement plans, and it guarantees that a member's accumulated contributions are repaid with interest, determined at time of retirement. The difference, if any, between the benefits paid and the guaranteed amount, is payable upon the member's death, either as a lump sum or as continued monthly payments to a beneficiary. When the total benefit payments equals the accumulated contributions with interest, the form is known as the refund annuity; this feature may be built into the normal form of payment for some public contributory plans and ensures that the amount payable upon death is an employer paid death benefit, rather than an optional form of payment with a reduced benefit. By contrast, if the employee-purchased portion (the annuity portion) of the sum of the total benefit payments is guaranteed to equal the accumulated contributions with interest, the form is known as the *modified refund annuity* form of payment.

Continuation to a survivor. These options ensure that if a named beneficiary is still living upon a member's death, the reduced benefit (or a portion of it) is paid to the beneficiary for the remainder of the beneficiary's lifetime. The beneficiary may be limited to only the spouse. This form of payment is called a *joint and survivor* form of payment, with the portion of the continuation commonly included in the name, such as a joint and 50 percent survivor option. A less common form of payment reduces upon the first death of either the member or the beneficiary. A different form, called the *joint and survivor with pop-up,* has become popular of late in public retirement plans. This is a variation of the joint and survivor form of payment. Under the pop-up option, if the beneficiary dies before the member, the member's benefit payment pops up to what it would have been had the member not elected the joint and survivor feature. Under the normal joint and survivor option, the member elects a reduced monthly benefit in order to provide protection to a beneficiary. When the beneficiary dies before the member, the protection is of no further value, yet the member's benefit is still reduced. In a sense, the member has paid for something that will not be received. Under the pop-up version, the member's benefit is restored once the protection is no longer needed. The reduction for the joint and survivor with pop-up option is greater than for the normal joint and survivor option, again to cover the financial cost of providing additional benefits. In a few systems, the benefit pops up upon divorce as well as upon the beneficiary's death. One variant found in the public sector (but rarely in the private sector) permits a retiree to direct survivor benefits to a new beneficiary upon remarriage.

Level income option. This option allows a member who retires prior to the normal social security age (SSA) to receive retirement benefits that are modified so that the combined income from the retirement system and from social security remains level throughout the member's lifetime. This means the pension system's payments are higher before social security payments begin, and they fall after social security begins. Depending on the retirement and the estimated social security benefit payment, it is possible that no retirement benefits would be payable after social security begins. Although the theory is that the member's income stream will be level, often it proves not to be in practice. This is because social security, and often the pension system as well, makes postretirement adjustments that upset the original "leveling out" feature of this option. This option is sometimes combined with the features of a guaranteed payment or a continuation to survivor form of payment. It may be feasible, within certain tax limitations, to provide a similar modified payment stream that is not dependent on expected social security payments.

DROP plans. "Deferred retirement option plans," or DROPs, refer to a public plan feature where members are allowed to effectively begin receiving retirement payments while remaining on the job.[8] These plans originated in fire and police plans where members could retire with full benefits at a comparatively young age, say after twenty years of service. Many cities could not afford to lose the experience and training of these seasoned officers and used the DROP programs to entice members to continue working.

These plans are relatively new and raise many concerns that include tax consequences to the member, benefit limitations under Section 415, and higher marginal tax rates that may apply to the pension payments. Benefit consultants tend to recommend that a private letter ruling be requested from the IRS before implementing any specific DROP plan. The DROP option is especially attractive if the system provides for no additional accruals after twenty years of service, and they provide public employers with the ability to predict with more accuracy future employment vacancies. Under a DROP plan, a member who would otherwise be eligible to retire and commence benefit payments, instead "freezes" the amount of retirement benefit payable and then continues to work in active employment. The benefit payments that would have been made instead accumulate in a tax-qualified fund accumulating interest (and sometimes additional member contributions). At actual retirement, the previously frozen monthly benefit payments are then paid to the member rather than to the accumulated fund account, and the member receives the accumulated fund balance as a lump-sum payment. Members like the advantages of receiving the lump sum payment at time of retirement. When a member elects to participate in the DROP, for purposes of the retirement plan, she or he is considered to have retired. But for all other employment purposes the member continues working and receiving a salary and full nonretirement benefits. The amount of the member's monthly retirement payment is frozen based on final compensation and service credits determined as of the date the DROP option is elected. The member continues to work while the DROP is in effect, but the continued employment has no effect on the amount of the member's retirement benefit.

At first glance it may appear that no financial cost is associated with this type of plan, since the system would have been making the payments had the member actually retired from service, the cost could range from no cost to 1 percent or more of pay. A number of different features and issues can affect whether this option is actually cost-neutral for the public system. In addition to the benefit features mentioned above, other factors affecting whether to offer a DROP include its impact on member beneficiaries, the desire to have members continue working longer, the complexity of the program, and whether other benefit improvements are more desirable.

Postretirement health benefit plans. Few public plans provide postretirement health benefits, but several have set up financial systems where some type of benefit is available to offset the cost of the insurance premiums for retired members. For example, both Wisconsin and Idaho provide for unused sick leave to be credited to an account at retirement, which is then used to pay for the employee's health premiums after retirement. However, once the account is depleted, the member must make premium payments from another source—usually from the monthly retirement benefit payment.

Reemployment after retirement. Many public sector retirement systems terminate or stop making payments to retired members if they return to work after retirement. Returning to work within the same retirement program may occur in the public sector for several reasons. First, government workers may have an experience base, which makes them more attractive to call back rather than hiring a new employee. Second, public members can retire earlier than private sector employees, so there is a greater potential for reentry into the workforce.

Portability. The concept of portable benefits has become an attractive goal for both private and public plans, and the advent of individual retirement accounts (IRAs) has greatly enhanced the portability of DC benefits. However, in the DB arena, few private sector plan participants can shift their assets or benefits across plans. By contrast, public sector plans have made some progress in permitting DB plan mobility.

One reason that portability has been seen as a problem in DB plans has to do with the benefit formula: vested accrued benefits depend on the final average salary at the time of termination, yet if an employee moves around and has several accrued DB benefits, the total of all vested benefits is much less than if the benefits had all been earned under one system (Fore, this volume). If true DB portability were to occur, the final average salary used for all vested benefits would have to be based on the final compensation at the last employer, which in turn boosts the value of the vested benefits left with the prior employers. A method of approaching this problem in the public sector is permitting employees to purchase "service credits" as they enter a new system, thus raising benefits payable by the new employer. This provision may require a mobile public sector employee to deposit employee contributions (or both employee and employer contributions) that the new system would have made on behalf of the member for the period of time the service was earned with the prior employer. Less often, a public plan allows service to be purchased based on employment with a previous *nongovernmental* employer; such purchases not directly related to prior service are called "permissive service credits."

Even with these "past contributions," it is unlikely the additional contributions will be sufficient to cover the increased value of the benefits because most members do not make such contributions unless it is to their financial advantage to do so. Also, because of the generous early retirement provisions in public plans, additional years of "purchased" service increase, not only the amount of the benefit to be paid, but the value of the entire early retirement benefit. Thus, the true cost to the system for the purchase of additional service needs to cover both the cost of the increased benefit directly attributable to the additional service and the cost of paying the benefit accrued without the additional service at an earlier age. This type of portability of benefits in the public sector is most commonly found among teacher plans on a state plan basis and plans within a local area. For instance, the Washington State Retirement Systems provide portability of service credits for determining retirement eligibility but not for benefit amounts between the major city retirement systems within the state.

The Legal Basis of Public Retirement Systems

A public plan is established and modified through the legislating body and approved, if necessary, by the executive. For a state retirement system, this is the state legislature and governor. The retirement plan documents, which contain all the provisions of the program, are included in complete detail within the state's legal statutes. The pension program is usually implemented and administered by a public agency and governing board.

Federal constraints: ERISA. Compared to private plans, fewer limitations are placed on public plans.[9] Except for the IRS qualification rules, members of public plans were exempted from the legal protection afforded to private plans under ERISA. Much of this relates back to the constitutional issue of states' rights and the ability of the federal government to place limits or restrictions on a state's activities. At the time ERISA was drafted, it was uncertain as to what impact the new law would have on public plans. The main concern for a state retirement system is to be able to retain its qualified plan status under the IRS code.[10] Without the qualification status, both the employer and the employee could incur undesirable tax liabilities. General nondiscrimination requirements has limited some plan design features, where it may be of interest to provide a higher or special benefit to only a selected group of employees such as judges or legislators. As long as no discrimination (higher benefits) is made toward the highly compensated groups, there are not many restrictions as to the ability to provide different benefits to, say, teachers, than to general government employees.

Federal constraints: contract rights. While public plan members may not have the rigorously defined protection of ERISA rules, the courts have served to define a much higher degree of protection in certain states. Commonly referred to as the contract rights protection, several state supreme courts have ruled that, due to a federal constitutional standard relating to contracts, the public employer is prevented from modifying the pension promise. Approximately half of the states have either a state constitutional provision or a statutory provision describing this contract right, or have past court cases that have inferred the existence of a contract with respect to the retirement program, and thus coverage under the U.S. Constitution. In the remaining states, the characterization of the pension benefits right as a contract is not well defined, or may have been rejected.

It should be noted that the promise is what cannot be modified or diminished. This means any employee hired under a retirement program has the right to earn benefits under the promise for as long as his/her employment continues. Clause 1, Article 1, Section 10 of the U.S. Constitution limits certain state powers; among these, the section provides: "No state shall . . . pass any . . . law impairing the obligation of contracts." Retirement system benefits have been interpreted as being under this contract concept. Thus, if any significant changes are to occur in a public pension plan, they usually result in a new layer of benefits applicable only to new hires, or to existing employees solely on a voluntary basis. Generally, "significant change" is interpreted to mean any reduction in future accruals, elimination of optional forms or otherwise to modify existing benefits rights without an offsetting comparable advantage.

In 1995, the Retirement Board of the Kentucky Employees Retirement System sued to try to force the General Assembly to mandate the amount of the state's contribution to the plan, and to set the contribution rate as recommended by the board based on an actuarial valuation. Their case was based on the impairment of contract theory. The Kentucky Supreme Court rejected the position that the budget bill adopted and set by the state impaired the members' benefit rights. The court acknowledged that the members had a contractual right to the benefits they were promised upon retirement, but there had been no showing that the benefits promised would be infringed by the General Assembly's failure to adopt the board's contribution recommendations.

Federal constraints: excess benefit plans. Public plans are restricted as to the size of the benefit payable by the plan, by the IRS maximum benefit limits under Code Section 415. Public plans have always had special Section 415 provisions that differed from those applied to private plans. Except in a few situations, the limitations allow higher benefits than what the private sector plans can provide. The Small Business Job Protection Act of 1996 permitted for the first time, a public agency to pay benefits in excess of the 415 limits by establishing an "excess benefit plan." Private sector employers have had this ability for quite some time.

The former Section 415 limits of 100 percent of the three-year average compensation were eliminated for public plans in the same act. Now, only the §415 limitations for defined benefit plans remain. The maximum permitted annual benefit for 1999 is $130,000 at age 62, an amount unlikely to impact very many government-paid employees. The dollar limitation does reduce for earlier retirement ages, but the most common group that used to bump into the limitation was the public safety group, where full unreduced retirement is available as early as age 45 under a 20-year and out provision.[11]

However, after 1996, no reduction is made in the $130,000 limitation for public safety members, regardless of age. But some public plans found that the §415 limits would not permit them to provide the full benefit required under their plan provisions (state statutes), and sought federal relief which was granted by permitting public plans to elect a special grandfather provision, protecting benefits for current members, but only if they applied the lower private sector §415 limits to all new hires in the governmental plan.

Public policy influence. The political atmosphere in which governmental plans operate is another aspect of plan design that private plans rarely deal with. As with any legislative process, a well-informed group of individuals can propose and promote changes in public retirement policies, which may or may not lead to change.

Sometimes proposed changes in the public sector come from special interest groups rather than as a suggestion or recommendation from the administrative staff or the retirement board. On the other hand, the retirement board may not be in a position to recommend any changes unless they are administrative in nature. In that case, the larger issue of plan design and adequacy is left to the legislative change process. It is for this reason that many plan changes are backed by special lobbying groups, often representing employees or retirees, which results in the plan design evolving based on employee requests rather than from employer needs. This rarely occurs in the private sector, except for negotiated plans.

Of course, as with private sector plans, changes usually come with an associated price tag. Employer groups or the states themselves may not be in a position to accept the financial cost of the proposed changes. Any increase in benefits will lead to a corresponding increase in costs because of the formula introduced above, namely, $C + I = B + E$. Higher benefits increase contributions. This is sometimes overlooked when what may seem like a reasonable but small adjustment to the system at present, can later result in a significant increase in costs over the long term for all future employees. This is particularly of concern in the DB arena for two reasons. In a defined benefit plan, an increase in contributions impacts not only the current fiscal budget but all future years' budgets as well. This long-term impact can sometimes be overlooked or given less weight, with elected officials who do not look much farther than the end of their term or the next election. And where private plan sponsors can change their minds if finances are lacking to support increased benefits, public plans rarely can reduce benefits. And because increased pension spending must come from constituent tax dollars, solving pension problems by raising contributions is generally seen as a result to be avoided if possible.

Public Pension Plan Administration

Public retirement programs are administered via governmental agencies that are typically independent of other agencies. The fiduciary responsibility for the program's administration is held by a board. The board is made up of elected, appointed and ex-officio members, and it manages the retirement program (see Useem and Hess this volume). The board usually has control over the investment policy and the actuarial assumptions. It hires the executive director, and perhaps other key staff, who in turn manages the agency staff that performs the tasks needed to administer the retirement benefits. The board may establish rules for the administration and operations of the retirement system, will approve all expenditures of the system, and have reports prepared and submitted to meet legal and other requirements. The retirement board is also the body that selects consultants and retirement staff. These include investment advisors and managers, legal and actuarial professionals, and medical advisors to assist in determining disability benefits. There have been some recent concerns expressed over real or perceived conflicts between retirement board members and vendors working for the system. Some states have implemented very strict rules on what board members and staff members may be able to accept in the form of meals and travel or other gifts from both existing and potential vendors. On the reverse side, some board members have solicited political contributions from vendors, implying support may be withheld to continue the vendor relationship, if contributions are not made.

Public Pension Plan Funding

Sources of income. Public retirement systems are financed by employer and employee contributions. As mentioned earlier, it is rare for employees to contribute to a private sector defined benefit plan, but in a state plan, the state may contribute not only for its own employees, but may also make a contribution toward the benefits of other non-state employees such as teachers. In that situation, the teachers' benefits may be supported from their contributions, the school district's contributions to the state retirement system, and the state's contributions to the retirement system. Public sector plan contributions are usually expressed as a percentage of salary rather than as a dollar amount, as is usual in private pension plans.

Governmental Accounting Standards Board (GASB) rules require an actuarial valuation of public pension funding status every two years, after which required contribution targets are set as either a fixed rate or a variable rate, based on the results of the actuarial valuation. When a system has both fixed benefits (a defined benefit program) and fixed contribution rates, the flexibility and recognition of experience fluctuations from year to year is usually absorbed by varying the length of time needed to pay for the benefit obligations. Employee contribution rates are fixed or may be tied to the employer contribution rate.

In addition to contributions, some public pension plans receive income from fees or earmarked levies. For example, judges' retirement benefits may be funded by a portion of the court filing fees. Some firefighter programs receive a portion of their income from fire insurance premiums received by the state. In such cases, income expressed as a percentage of salary is not a reliable measurement, as the source of those funds is not related to employee salaries.

Funding methods and assumptions. An actuarial valuation is performed to determine the funding adequacy of a defined benefit retirement program. In a defined contribution plan, the benefits are dependent on the contributions and the investment income, so there is no need to determine funding adequacy (in a DC program funding is the contribution; for more detail see Hustead this volume).

For a defined benefit program, the sponsor needs to be sure that the contributions and investment income will be sufficient to pay the benefits that have been promised. If this year's contributions exceed the benefits and expenses for this year, then the excess contributions can be retained in the plan's fund for future benefit payments. If no excess occurs and the cash inflow is only sufficient to cover the cash outgo, then the plan is said to be funded on a "pay-as-you-go basis." If an excess occurs and is invested, then additional income is derived from assets through investment return. If the excess contributions are computed to be sufficient to create enough assets to provide for benefits in the future, then the plan is advance funded. Nearly all public retirement programs are advance funded. However, a few supplemental benefits may be funded on a pay-as-you-go basis. Private plans under ERISA are required to be advance funded.

The most common advance funding method used in state retirement programs is the "entry age cost method."[12] Under this method, the actuarial present value of the projected benefits of each individual included in the valuation is allocated as a level percentage of the individual's projected compensation between entry age and assumed exit. The portion of this actuarial present value allocated to a valuation year is called the "normal cost." The portion of this actuarial present value not provided for at a valuation date by the sum of (a) the actuarial value of the assets and (b) the actuarial present value of future normal costs, is called the "unfunded actuarial liability." The unfunded actuarial liability is amortized as a level percentage of the projected salaries of present and future members of the system. Under this method, contributions expressed as a percentage of salary, are expected to remain stable over time, from one generation of taxpayers to another. PENDAT (1997) reports that 63 percent of the reporting public plans used the entry age cost method.

When both benefits and contribution rates are fixed, the entry age cost method allows for the experience fluctuations to be reflected in the amortization period required to fund the unfunded actuarial liability. Another cost method, the "aggregate cost method," allocates the present value of benefits not already funded by the current actuarial assets, over the expected working lives of the active members, which is usually between ten and fifteen years. Under this method, the contribution rates vary, reflecting the experience of the system since the last valuation. Another method used less in the public than in the private sector, is the "projected unit credit method." Under this funding method, the projected benefit is allocated to each valuation year by a consistent formula. Under this method the experience gains and losses reduce the unfunded actuarial liability.

Actuarial assumptions are used to project the value of benefits that will be paid in the future to active members upon their retirement, as well as how long the benefits currently being paid to retired members will continue. The economic assumptions regarding the future investment income and future salary increases can produce the greatest variation in results. The assumptions related to the movement of employees in and out of the system, the demographic assumptions, are dependent on the particular system and will not be based on as much subjectivity as are the economic assumptions. Usually, an actuarial valuation makes no projection of benefits for future employees, but focuses on the liabilities associated only with the current employees and annuitants. Those employees are assumed to then terminate employment, retire, die, or become disabled. In addition, the actuary must assume at what rate the members' salaries will increase, what postretirement increases to benefits will be, if any, and perhaps the probabilities of marriage or having dependent children. All of these assumptions are common in a private pension plan valuation as well as a public plan valuation.

One assumption related to a contributory plan is the probability a terminating member will elect a refund of his or her contributions, and thereby forfeit any rights to any accrued retirement benefits. Since private plans are not contributory, this assumption is somewhat unique to public plans. If a private sector plan did require employee contributions, ERISA requirement would guarantee some minimal employer paid benefit payment.

Another assumption more commonly found for public than for private plans has to do with the expanded retirement assumption. Since public plans often provide unreduced benefits at more than one retirement age, or offer subsidized early retirement benefits at younger ages, there may be more than one retirement age at which a member can be expected to retire. A greater degree of flexibility and variation in the retirement patterns is experienced in the public sector. The private sector does not see as much of this, as their reduced benefits may be closer to the actuarial equivalent of the benefit paid at the normal retirement age.

The economic assumptions, the future rate of investment earnings and the expected salary increases for both individual members and the total covered payroll of the system have an important impact on the valuation of the costs and liabilities for a system. Assumptions should not be considered independently of each other, but viewed together as a group. The interrelationship of assumptions should be consistent, particularly with respect to economic assumptions. ERISA and professional standards require all actuaries to use assumptions that are reasonable and which represent the actuary's best estimate of anticipated experience.

Accounting disclosures—GASB requirements. For fiscal years beginning after mid-1996, new GASB reporting standards have been required for defined benefit pension plans reporting and disclosures. Statement no. 25 establishes standards for the measurement, recognition and display of pension expenditure/expense and related liabilities, assets, note disclosure, and, if applicable, required supplementary information in the financial reports of state and local governmental employers.

The requirements for Statement no. 25 include certain supplementary information to the financial statements regarding the funding of the pension plan. These include a schedule of funding progress, and a schedule of employer contributions. The schedule of funding progress compares the amount of unfunded actuarial liability (UAL) from year to year, and measures the progress of the employer's contributions in reducing this amount. Under most acceptable funding methods there is a UAL, however, under the aggregate actuarial cost method there is no UAL and a schedule of funding progress is not needed. The required schedule of employer contributions compares the employer contributions required based on the actuarial required contribution, or ARC, with employer contributions actually made.

GASB Statement No. 27 is effective for fiscal years beginning after mid-1997, and it is required for pension accounting by state and local governmental employers. The disclosures include the measurement of an annual pension cost (APC). The APC is equal to the employer's annual required contributions (ARCs), as actuarially determined by the funding methods and assumptions for pension benefits used for GASB purposes and an adjustment to account for prior year contributions. If the employer is required to make a contribution (APC) and does not make a contribution equal to the APC, then a net pension obligation (NPO) account is established and the computation of the APC reflects adjustments made to the NPO account, as well as the ARC. For GASB purposes, the ARC must be calculated based on certain parameters required for disclosure purposes. The acceptable actuarial funding methods under these parameters all require the retirement benefits to be funded by the time a member exits the retirement program. Actual employer contributions based on a plan's funding policy may be different than those computed for GASB disclosure purposes, and the determination of the NPO at the end of the year should be determined based on the actual amounts received by the fund.

The UAL and the percentage funded by the actuarial value of the assets is shown in the schedule of funding progress, as well as the UAL expressed as a percentage of payroll. The schedule of employer contributions compares the ARC to the contribution amount received by the plan's fund for the plan year. Additional disclosures regarding the actuarial assumptions and methods and other items of significance are also required by Statement no. 25 for the plan's reporting.

Statement no. 27 reports on the employer's required contributions and the funded status of the plan. Notes to the employer's financial statements include the plan description and the funding policy. Except for cost-sharing plans, the disclosures also require a development of the APC and the NPO balance for the year, and a comparison of the actual employer contributions made to the APC for the last three years. Thus the changes in a plan's NPO balance from year to year can be used to measure whether or not a plan's funding status has either improved or declined during the period reported, based on the GASB parameters.

As a result of these accounting standards, two new funding measurements are now available for those reviewing a public plan's funding status. First, the funding ratio (the ratio of the actuarial assets to the UAL) is being used more and more as a funding measurement tool. Second, the NPO balance, while not as common, can also be monitored. Since most statewide pension plans are cost sharing plans, where all benefit costs are pooled among a group of employers, the APC and NPO computations are not required, and do not result in a uniform measurement tool. A plan is not a cost sharing plan if there is a single employer sponsor, or if under a pooled investment arrangement each employer has its share of the assets allocated to and its own pension costs determined separately from the other employers (nonshared).

Measurement of funding status. Regardless of the GASB reporting, consideration should always be given to how well a plan is following its own funding policy. Many state plans have funding requirements or minimum/maximum contribution rates. For example, a plan's funding policy may be to achieve a one-year reduction in the amortization period of the UAL. This is what would be expected to occur if actual experience is close to the actuarially expected experience. Almost always, the actual experience will be different than assumed. The treatment of these differences between actual and expected experiences should be addressed in the funding policy. If the contribution rates are fixed, the only acceptable method is to adjust the amortization period of the UAL. However, the funding policy or state statute may require that while fixed contribution rates are desired, if the amortization period exceeds a certain period, say, thirty years, then the rates must be increased. Likewise, if the contribution rates reflect the experience, the funding policy will usually require the UAL to be measured over a certain period in determining how to adjust the contribution rates to reflect the changes.

Pension obligation bonds. A pension obligation bond is a debt instrument sold by a governmental employer for a special pension related purpose as in the New Jersey case discussed elsewhere in this volume (Bryan, this volume). Usually, the proceeds of the bond are used by the employer to fund all or a portion of the UAL for the pension plan. In return for using the proceeds to fund the UAL, the employer may have some special funding agreements put into place to recognize the large deposit of funds into the plan's assets. Usually, this arrangement will make a modification to the UAL contributions otherwise payable by the employer, and will recognize a portion of the investment return on the plan's funds as an additional means of income to meet future required employer contributions. The gain or loss to the employer or the pension plan benefit depends on the level of future investment returns. These arrangements are favorable to the employer when the rate on the bond debt is less than the discount rate used to determine the pension plan's UAL payments. But these cost savings can only be estimated, because the future investment returns on the plan's assets cannot be fixed. There is also the risk that the UAL may reoccur or increase due to future benefit increases, higher than expected inflation, lower actual investment returns, and other factors. A certain amount of flexibility is also lost since the debt payments are fixed, whereas the pension payments may be adjusted. The cost of issuing the bonds must also be considered. These bonds have been issued by relatively few public sector employers.

Caution is needed to avoid the appearance of arbitrage, which can lead to unfavorable tax treatment by the IRS, when compared to other governmental bonds. Some states may prohibit the issuance of a pension obligation bond. Another consideration is if the actuarial assumptions change over the period of the bond debt, which is likely over a period of time, will the changes adversely impact the decision to issue a pension obligation bond? In recent years, the market returns have caused a number of public plans to become fully funded, meaning the actuarial assets now exceed the accrued liabilities and no UAL remains. Thus, interest in these funding vehicles has decreased in popularity.

Investment Policy

The investment policy of any particular public pension plan generally depends on what the plan's objectives are, what if any statutory restrictions exist, and how much control the board has over the funds' investment decisions (see Peskin, this volume). Typically a public plan board has a fairly broad policy, based on reasonable investments given the fiduciary nature of the plan to its members. Certain states have statutes limiting the amount of the total fund assets that may be invested in equities or nontraditional investments such as venture capital (Munnell and Sunden, this volume). However, some state plans have all investment decisions handled by either a separate investment board, which may invest other state funds as well as the pension funds, or by a single trustee—the state treasurer or similar elected position. The resulting investment policy can vary depending on who actually makes the investment decisions.

Where the retirement board has full exclusive authority on making investments, within any statutory limitations, the political pressure from within government may be somewhat reduced if the same governmental official is also a fiduciary to the pension plan. In times of financial distress, state and local governments have been known to look to the public pension fund as a source of relief. This may come in the form of less than the recommended contributions, thus decreasing the funds to the pension plans and freeing up more governmental funds for what are seen as more important needs. This situation has less immediate impact due to the long term nature of pensions than, say, reducing a public service that is required on a regular basis today. In most cases, the lowering of contributions now would not impact the actual payment of members benefit payments until far into the future. The new GASB reporting rules serve to focus and highlight wherever an employer might be using this approach.

Another sometimes politically motivated approach is to have the pension plan's trust fund invest in government securities. One such example is described by Clark et al. (this volume); another example occurred during the late 1970s when the New York State legislature attempted to have the trustees invest in New York City bonds. This direct approach has not been seen much during the past decade. More recently economically targeted investments have been used, as described by Useem and Hess (this volume) and Munnell and Sunden (this volume).

Conclusion

In this chapter we have described U.S. state and local public pension systems and compared them to private plans with regard to history, structures, and key features. There are many similarities between private and public sector retirement programs, but the significant differences also need to be recognized. On the one hand, the ultimate goal in both cases is to provide a retirement benefit. On the other hand, public plans have unique and unusual characteristics that can make analogies to private plans incomplete. Plan design features that perform essential functions for private sector plans do not always apply to the public sector.

Notes

1. In this chapter we offer certain generalizations with the understanding that there are always many exceptions to the rule. We note important exceptions where relevant.

2. A defined benefit plan is one where the benefit provided by the retirement program is a definitely determinable benefit, usually a lifetime annuity based on a formula using years of service and salary.

3. A tabulation of public service retirement plans indicates most pension formulas were based on an annuity from employee accumulated contributions and a matching pension amount funded by employer contributions, with some type of minimum or maximum benefit (1928 Seattle Public Library, Municipal Reference Division).

4. A recent survey by CalPERS indicated 17 of 66 responding public retirement systems have contribution rates set by state statute.

5. The integration of benefits allows employers to recognize the level of benefit earned under the social security program and provides a greater amount to higher paid employees, such that the combined benefits are level. A significant number of private plans still have integrated formulas but the fraction is declining due to recent changes in IRS compliance rules.

6. The term "public safety members" generally refers to police and fire employees, but may include other employees considered to be employed in hazardous duty types of employment and can sometimes include prison guards or other uniformed officers.

7. In a form rarely used, benefit payments cease once the guaranteed number of payments have been made, even if the member is still living. This is known as a "period certain only" form of payment.

8. Private pension plans are subject to certain ERISA provisions that make DROPs less attractive than in the public sector.

9. A discussion of federal legal and tax limitations on governmental plans appears in Crane (this volume).

10. A tax qualified plan is one that has meet all the applicable requirements of IRS Section 401(a) and is permitted to defer taxation of the accrual of benefits for employees and to exempt the fund's investment income from U.S. tax. One such qualification requirement is that the benefits do not discriminate in favor of the highly compensated employees IRS Code Section 401(a)(4).

11. When an employee is eligible to retire regardless of age, but dependent only on the number of years of service earned, for example, twenty years, the retirement eligibility is sometimes referred to as a "twenty year and out" retirement provision.

12. A method under which the actuarial present value of the projected benefits of each individual included in an actuarial valuation is allocated on a level basis over the earnings or service of the individual between entry age and assumed exit age(s). The portion of this actuarial present value allocated to a valuation year is called the

normal cost. The portion of this actuarial present value not provided for at a valuation date by the actuarial present value of future normal costs is called the actuarial accrued liability. See GASB (1994). The description of this method should state the procedures, including whether the allocation is based on earnings or service; where aggregation is used in the calculation process; how entry age is established; what procedures are used when different benefit formulas apply to various periods of service; and a description of any other method used to value a portion of the pension plan's benefits. Under this method, the actuarial gains (Losses), as they occur, reduce (increase) the unfunded actuarial accrued liability.

References

Bleakney, Thomas P. 1972. *Retirement Systems for Public Employees.* Pension Research Council. Homewood, Ill.: Irwin.

Bryan, Tom. This volume. "The New Jersey Pension System."

Bureau of the Census. 1997. *Report on Employee Retirement Systems of State and Local Governments.* Washington, D.C.: U.S. GPO.

Clark, Robert L., Lee A. Craig, and Jack W. Wilson. This volume. "The Life and Times of a Public Sector Pension Plan Before Social Security: The U.S. Navy Pension Plan in the Nineteenth Century."

Crane, Roderick B. This volume. "Federal Regulation and Taxation of Public Plans: A History of Increasing Federal Influence."

Employee Benefit Research Institute (EBRI). 1997. "Defined Contribution Plan Dominance Grows Across Sectors and Employer Sizes, While Mega Defined Benefit Plans Remain Strong." *EBRI News.* Washington, D.C.: EBRI, October.

Fore, Douglas. This volume. "Going Private in the Public Sector: The Transition from Defined Benefit to Defined Contribution Pension Plans.

Georgia State University (GSU). 1997. "GSU/AON RETIRE Project Report." Center for Risk Management and Insurance Research. Research Report 97-2. Atlanta, October.

Government Accounting Standards Board (GASB). 1994. "Financial Reporting for Defined Benefit Pension Plans and Note Disclosures for Defined Contribution Plans." *Statement No. 25, Governmental Accounting Standards Series*: 116-A (November). Financial Accounting Foundation.

Hustead, Edwin C. This volume. "Determining the Cost of Public Pension Plans."

Milliman and Robertson. 1994. "Contractual Rights to Benefits." *PERiScope.* February.

Mitchell, Olivia S., David McCarthy, Stanley Wisniewski, and Paul Zorn. This volume. "Developments in State and Local Pension Plans."

Munnell, Alicia H., and Annika Sundén. This volume. "Investment Practices of State and Local Pension Funds: Implications for Social Security Reform."

National Council on Teacher Retirement (NCTR). 1998. "The State Regulatory Framework." Public Pension Plans Report. Washington, D.C: NCTR, February.

National Education Association. 1996. Characteristics of 100 Large Public Pension Plans. Washington, D.C.: National Education Association Research Division.

Peskin, Michael. This volume. "Asset/Liability Management in the Public Sector."

Public Pension Coordinating Council (PENDAT). 1997. *Survey of State and Local Government Employee Retirement Systems.* Chicago: Government Finance Officers Association.

Rappaport, Anna M., Michael L. Young, Christopher A. Levell, and Brad A. Blalock. 1997. "Cash Balance Pension Plans." In *Positioning Pensions for the Twenty-First Century*, ed. Michael S. Gordon, Olivia S. Mitchell, and Marc M. Twinney. Pension Research Council. Philadelphia: University of Pennsylvania Press.

Sass, Steven. 1997. *The Promise of Private Pensions: The First Hundred Years*. Pension Research Council. Cambridge, Mass.: Harvard University Press.

State of Wisconsin. 1996. *Comparative Study of Major Public Employee Retirement Systems*. Madison: Retirement Research Committee.

U.S. General Accounting Office (GAO). 1995. "Report on Pension COLAs." GAO Report B-261355, HEHS-95-219K. Washington, D.C.: U.S. GPO.

———. 1996. "Section 457 Plans Pose Greater Risk Than Other Supplemental Plans." GAO Report on Public Pensions. Washington, D.C.: U.S. GPO.

———. 1998. *Social Security: Mandatory Coverage for State and Local Employees.* Washington, D.C.: U.S. GPO.

Useem, Michael and David Hess. This volume. "Governance and Investments of Public Pensions."

Chapter 4
Federal Civilian and Military Retirement Systems

Edwin C. Hustead and Toni Hustead

In this chapter we describe the retirement systems that apply to civilian employees and military personnel of the U.S. federal government. More than one out of every twenty Americans are or will be entitled to benefits under one of the federal retirement systems. These are not only the largest retirement systems in the United States, but they also supply an important part of total retirement income now and will continue to do so in the future.

The most important federally run civilian systems are the Civil Service Retirement System (CSRS) for employees hired before 1984, and the Federal Employees Retirement System (FERS) for employees hired after 1983. Employees in both systems have been eligible to participate in the Federal Thrift Savings Plan (TSP) since 1987. Most military personnel are covered by the military retirement system—an informal name for a complex of evolving plans that have merged over time and cover officer and enlisted members of the uniformed services. Prior to 1980, the military retirement benefit formula provided a benefit of 50 percent of final basic pay, but benefits were reduced in 1980 and again in 1986. As is true for state systems, the new military and civilian benefit rules apply only to personnel entering service after the date of the change.[1]

Some 97 percent of federal participants are included either in the CSRS/FERS program or the Defense Department's military retirement system, though there are still many (thirty-three) small retirement systems that also fall under the federal plan heading. The number of plans and active participants in federal plans is summarized in Table 1. Some systems, such those covering the foreign service and judiciary, were established to fit specific types of employment. Other plans, such as Tennessee Valley Authority and Coast Guard, were outside the authority of the sponsors of the pri-

TABLE 1. Employees in Federal Retirement Systems (1993)

Type (number of plans)	Type of employee covered	Employees covered
Civilian retirement systems		
Primary civilian systems (2)	Postal Service—general	683,000
	Hazardous duty	78,000
	Members of Congress	500
	Congressional staff	21,000
	Military reserve technicians	38,000
	Air traffic controllers	26,000
	Other general	1,996,500
	Total	2,843,000
Foreign service retirement systems (2)		12,000
Judicial retirement systems (7)		2,000
Tennessee Valley Authority (1)		19,000
Federal Reserve and other bank systems (11)		35,000
Nonappropriated fund systems and other (9)		55,000
Subtotal (32)		2,966,000
Military retirement systems		
Department of Defense (1)		2,750,000
Coast Guard (1)		55,600
Public Health Service (1)		6,000
National Oceanic and Atmospheric Agency (1)		400
Subtotal (4)		2,812,000
Total federal (36)		5,778,000

Source: U.S. General Accounting Office (1996), Office of Personnel Management Office of Actuaries.

mary civilian and military retirement systems. Table 1 also shows that, within CSRS/FERS, there are special benefits for certain categories of participants. These include hazardous duty employees (such as Federal Bureau of Investigation agents), air-traffic controllers, and members of Congress. The special treatment of employees of the District of Columbia government in CSRS is described in Hustead (this volume).

Almost all the civilian retirement systems are financed on a sound actuarial basis. The major exception is CSRS, which had an unfunded liability of $504 billion in 1998 and only a portion of the liability is being amortized. The primary military retirement system had an unfunded liability of $498 billion in 1998 but the liability is being fully amortized. The other three military retirement systems are on a pay-as-you-go funding basis.

The Structure of Federal Civilian Employee Retirement Systems

Most U.S. federal civilian employees participate in the CSRS and the FERS. The CSRS was established in 1920, before social security, and it was the natural child of the Civil Service Act of 1883, a law that protected employees from arbitrary dismissal for any reason including age. As a consequence, by 1920, there were many federal employees age 70 or older who could not be separated from service. CSRS offered a legal basis for separating those employees and the income necessary to support them after retirement. The original Social Security Act of 1935 excluded government workers, mainly because most had their own retirement plans. Over time, social security coverage was gradually extended to government workers, and new hires in the federal sector were brought in after 1983 (Crane this volume).

Reasons for two systems and choice. Defined benefit pension plans like CSRS that began in the first half of the twentieth century were designed to provide reasonable retirement income for the long-career employee. Below we provide more detail on the program, here it suffices to note that the CSRS benefit is based on service times the high three-years average salary, with a benefit accrual rate of 1.5 percent of pay for the first five years of service, 1.75 percent of pay for the next five years, and 2 percent of pay for each additional year. Many federal employees at that time would work a full career for the government, so the CSRS approach followed the pattern prevalent in so many defined benefit plans developed at the time, offering long-term workers high benefits, but low benefits to short-career employees. In particular, benefits for short-service younger terminating employees have little value by age 62 because there is no inflation protection before age 62. In fact, most terminated vested employees only receive a return of their own contributions.

Extension of social security to federal employees hired after 1983 necessitated the development of a new federal retirement system. Simply adding social security to CSRS would have resulted in unreasonably high benefits and cost to both the federal government and federal employees.

FERS is a three-part retirement system with benefits flowing from (a) a defined benefit plan, (b) a defined contribution plan, and (c) social security. At the time that FERS was under development, defined contribution plans had become very popular in the private sector. This popularity derived from the rapid growth of 401(k) plans, which in the private sector permitted the deferral of taxes on contributions and investment income. Although some wanted FERS to be only a defined contribution system, others favored only the defined benefit approach. The resulting FERS design incorporated both a defined benefit and a defined contribution approach. One constraint on plan design was that FERS should not cost any more than

CSRS. FERS was launched in 1987, retroactive to 1984 for those covered by social security.

Employment patterns when FERS was being designed differed sharply from those pertinent in the 1920s when CSRS was developed. Increased job mobility, downsizing, and reduced job security in recent years produced a federal workforce with employees who were more likely to work for many employers than to spend a full, or even a majority, of a career with one employer. As a consequence, FERS was intended to provide more portable benefit accumulations than CSRS. Career workers still receive the highest benefits, but young short-service FERS workers can expect to take a much greater share of the retirement benefits with them than CSRS workers with the same age and service. This is particularly evident for workers leaving prior to retirement.

CSRS employees with over five years of service at separation (before retirement) can choose between a vested benefit payable at age 62 and a refund of their contributions, without interest. Most separating employees take the lump-sum refund, thereby losing money to the retirement system. CSRS employees also lack social security coverage. By contrast, the employee covered by FERS has social security credits that are fully portable, and separating employees with ten or more years of service may receive reduced benefits payable at age 55 rather than at age 62. Terminating employees are also offered a choice of a refund of contributions with interest or the deferred vested benefit in the FERS plan. But unlike in CSRS, FERS-covered employees who take the refund do not have an opportunity to redeposit the refund and receive credit for the prior service if they reenter federal service.[2]

Participants in CSRS/FERS and in many of the other civilian retirement systems may also choose to participate in the federal TSP, which is a defined contribution plan (about which more is said below). CSRS employees can contribute up to 5 percent of pay to TSP, with no matching employer contribution. FERS employees can contribute up to 10 percent of pay, with the government contributing up to an additional 5 percent of pay. The TSP began to collect and invest contributions in 1987, and most of the TSP contributions are fully vested.

Historically, salaries paid to federal employees have been lower than for similar positions in the private sector. The higher value of benefits, particularly the retirement benefits, somewhat offsets the low salary level. A Hay Group study found that FERS retirement benefits were worth 15 percent of salary, as compared to 9 percent for other large employers. That study also found that total federal benefits were 52 percent of salary compared to 48 percent for large employers (Hustead 1995).

Transfers from CSRS to FERS. CSRS employees have been provided with two opportunities, or "open seasons," during which they could transfer out of CSRS and into FERS. The first occurred in 1987 when FERS began, and the second was in 1998. Employees who transferred from CSRS to FERS would be covered by social security and the FERS defined benefit system, and they would receive matching contributions to the TSP after the date of transfer. The CSRS benefit formula would continue to apply for service to the date of transfer. The federal Congressional Budget Office (CBO) projected that some 40 percent of CSRS employees eligible to transfer to FERS in 1987 would have been better off by making the switch, but in fact only 5 percent eventually transferred (CBO 1986). We estimated that around 25 percent of those in CSRS would have been better off under FERS, but only 2 percent transferred.

Past experience suggests that employees usually exhibit inertia and favor their current plan when offered a choice between an old and a new retirement system. For this reason it could have been anticipated that the actual transfer rates would have been lower than the 40 and 25 percent predicted by simply comparing the relative economic value of the two systems. Nevertheless, these transfer rates were probably too low to simply reflect inertia. Other explanations that may be offered include employee concerns about trading half of a guaranteed defined benefit for what they saw as risky income from social security and the TSP. Concern about social security was partly attributable to general public skepticism about the future of social security, and also to longstanding federal union opposition to social security coverage. Additionally, many CSRS employees were unsure about whether they would remain in government service until they were eligible for full retirement benefits. This was important since many employees would have been better off under FERS if they planned on leaving government employ prior to age 55, but would have been better off under CSRS had they been able to remain until age 55. Finally, many CSRS employees erroneously saw the open seasons as part of a plan by the government to move the workforce to FERS as quickly as possible. In fact, since most employees who transferred did so for improved benefits, the net result of each of the open seasons was to increase retirement costs for the government.

The distrust of FERS was clearly evidenced in a number of counseling sessions provided by the authors during the two open seasons. In many cases, FERS was clearly the better system for the individual but the distrust of the new system and the perceived motivations of the employer kept the individual from making the favorable economic decision to transfer to FERS. In extreme cases, individuals lost over $100,000 by not transferring to FERS.

Even with the small number of transfers during the two open seasons, FERS has grown into the dominant program as a result of its jumpstart in 1987 (it included all hires since 1983), natural attrition, and subsequent new hires. As of the end of 1998, FERS payroll exceeded half of the total covered payroll, and Board of Actuaries of CSRS/FERS estimates that, by 2015, over 95 percent of employees will be covered by FERS.[3]

The Civil Service Retirement System

We turn next to a discussion of CSRS benefit rules and program financing.

CSRS benefit formulas and rules.[4] The CSRS uses an accrual rate based on service times the employee's high-three years average salary. The accrual rate is 1.5 percent of pay for the first five years of service, 1.75 percent of pay for the next five years, and 2 percent of pay for each additional year. The maximum benefit is 80 percent of the high-three average salary. Benefits are paid in full to employees retiring at age 55 with thirty years of service, at age 60 with twenty years of service, or at age 62 with five years of service. There is no mandatory retirement age. Employees who leave before completing five years of service can receive a refund of their contributions with interest. Those who leave with five or more years of service, but before meeting one of these retirement conditions, can either withdraw their contributions without interest, or receive a benefit beginning at age 62. The lower benefit (i.e., refund without interest) for vested employees compared to non-vested employees is a result of a series of legislative actions. When five-year vesting was introduced vested employees were not permitted to withdraw their contributions at all. The government recognized that the deferred benefit was usually more valuable than the employee contributions so that a withdrawal of contributions in lieu of those benefits would result in a loss of system income.

The surge in federal employment that occurred during the Great Depression and World War II was followed by a reduction in employment after the war ended. Many of the employees then leaving CSRS had more than five years of service and complained about the restriction on withdrawing their own contributions. Congress reacted to this pressure by permitting withdrawal of contributions, but left a disincentive by not including interest on those contributions. In practice, unfortunately, few vested separating employees are deterred by the lack of interest credit. The result is that most vested employees actually receive less than what their own contributions would have earned if they had been invested elsewhere.

CSRS provides retirement credit for military service, unless the employee is already receiving a military retirement benefit. Retirement credit is also provided for unused sick leave at retirement; this is applied after the 80 percent limit and, therefore, can result in a benefit greater than 80 percent. Benefits are paid if the employee is disabled, to the degree that he or she is unable to perform his or her job. The disability benefit is usually the greater of the accrued retirement benefit and 40 percent of salary.[5] The disability benefit is discontinued if (a) the employee is found to have recovered through a medical examination, (b) the employee earns 80 percent of the salary on the former job, or (c) the employee is reemployed by the federal government. Benefits for disability resulting from Federal service are paid through the Office of Workers' Compensation Programs (OWCP). A disabled employee receives the higher of CSRS or OWCP benefits.

Benefits are paid to a surviving spouse and children as well as certain former spouses if the employee dies in service. The surviving spouse benefit is 55 percent of the disability benefit. For instance, the surviving spouse of a young short-service employee receives a benefit of 22 percent (55 percent of 40 percent) of high-three salary. Additional lump sum benefits are paid through the Federal Employees Group Life Insurance (FEGLI) program.

Survivor benefits after retirement are available in exchange for a reduction in the retiree's benefit. The reduction is 2.5 percent of the first \$3,600 in annual benefit and 10 percent of the benefit above \$3,600. The survivor benefit is 55 percent of the retirement benefit before the reduction. This differs from the private sector practice of basing the survivor benefit on the reduced retirement benefit. The retiree can elect to provide a benefit on a lower portion of the annuity, or to provide no survivor benefit, but this election must be agreed to by the spouse. If the spouse predeceases the annuitant, the reduction to pay for the benefit ceases and the annuitant can later provide benefits to a second spouse by accepting a reimposition of the reduction.

All benefits are fully indexed to inflation using the same increase formula as under social security. This formula provides an increase every January based on inflation in the previous year, through the third quarter of the prior year.

CSRS employees are not covered by social security during their federal service. If the employee is entitled to social security benefits through other service, or through a spouse, the social security benefits can be reduced through one of two offset provisions. (HayGroup 1999).

Financing CSRS benefits. CSRS is partially financed through a payroll tax totaling 14 percent, flowing from employee and employee contributions of 7 percent of salary each. These contributions were increased temporarily beginning in 1999, by as much as 0.5 percent, to reduce the federal deficit; the contributions will revert to 14 percent after 2001. Nevertheless, the 14 percent of salary contribution falls far short of the CSRS normal cost,[6] which is 24.2 percent of salary. Each year's shortfall is added to prior shortfalls and interest on past shortfalls, to create a substantial unfunded liability (U.S. Office of Personnel Management [OPM] 1999a).[7]

The annual shortfall in CSRS financing is met through direct government payments, which amortize part of the increased liability attributable to salary increases, benefit liberalizations, and cost-of-living adjustments. It also must be noted that for financing purposes, CSRS liabilities are determined on a "static" basis that does not include projection of future inflation. As a result, current total contribution levels fall short of fully financing the long-term CSRS benefits. The CSRS Board of Actuaries determines and publishes a static unfunded liability as the basis to determine the required government payment; this board also determines and publishes a "dynamic" liability that considers the effect of future inflation, as its best estimate of the actuarial status of CSRS (OPM 1999a).

It is projected that the CSRS account will fall to zero in 2026, triggering transfers of FERS funds to pay CSRS annuities after 2026. Thus CSRS financing problems are slated to be covered through a fund transfer from FERS to CSRS, when the CSRS account is depleted, as shown in Figure 1. This Byzantine approach to financing of CSRS is a product of the legislative history of CSRS. Until 1969, the only financing of CSRS had been through the employee and agency normal cost, then at 6.5 percent of payroll. The employee and agency contributions fell short of even the static cost of CSRS and, of course, fell far short of the full cost of CSRS including inflation.

The financial basis of the CSRS was overhauled in 1969. First, the combined employee and agency contribution was increased to approximately equal the static normal cost of CSRS. Second, additional government payments would be made to finance the remaining static liability, but this level of financing was to be phased in over a period of years. Both the static liability and the gradual phasing in of the new financing were selected as a compromise to limit the impact on the budget. At the time the changes were being debated, federal budget rules showed all increases in federal payments as increases in the federal deficit. Now, government financing of the CSRS unfunded liability costs occurs as an intergovernmental transfer with no impact on the overall measured federal deficit. Ironically, the move to the current budget scorekeeping, which would have removed the controversy from the level of CSRS financing, took place before the first additional government payment under the 1969 CSRS law. If current budget scorekeeping rules had been in effect in the 1960s, the CSRS system would undoubtedly be funded on the same sound actuarial basis as FERS.

Even with inadequate financing, projections of the CSRS fund showed that there would always be sufficient cashflow to pay benefits and live within a small fund balance. In effect, benefits for current annuitants would be paid primarily through income from employees and taxpayers. The reforms in 1969 did add a reserve cushion to CSRS financing, rather than relying solely on pay-as-you-go financing, but even in steady state, the fund would still have been far below the financing level required of private sector retirement plans.

Unfortunately, any prospects for a steady state were dashed with the introduction of FERS, since CSRS then lacked the needed continuous flow of new entrants. The government's solution to this problem was to use FERS income to pay for CSRS shortfalls. The amount borrowed from FERS would

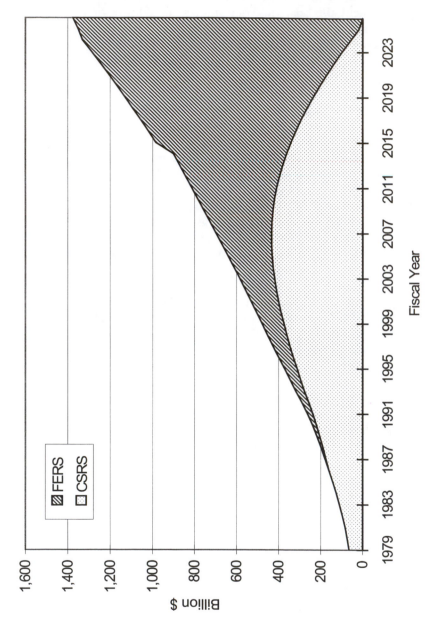

Figure 1. Combined CSRS/FERS fund balances. Sources: OPM (1999a) and data supplied by OPM Office of Actuaries.

be financed through 30-year payments beginning with each year's shortfall. Figure 1 shows the Board of Actuaries' projections that the shortfall will begin in 2026.

As of September 1998, OPM reported that total CSRS liabilities were $962 billion, assets were $361 billion, and the present value of future contributions was $97 billion, for a net unfunded liability of $504 billion. Plan assets were equal to 6.6 times CSRS payroll of ($54.4 billion) and the unfunded liability was 9.3 times payroll. These determinations were made on a dynamic basis that includes the effect of future inflation (OPM 1999a).

In fiscal year 1998, CSRS employer and employee contributions were $33.0 billion and investment income was $25.8 billion for total income of $58.8 billion. Payments to CSRS annuitants totaled $41.9 billion of the total expenditures of $42.3 billion. The annuitant payments were 77 percent of the active participant payroll. The net result was an increase in the CSRS account of $16.5 billion, to $360.6 billion on September 30, 1998. CSRS covered 1,100,000 employees and paid benefits to 2,290,000 retirees and survivors (OPM 1999a).

Figure 2 shows the increase in income and outgo of the CSRS/FERS Fund from 1979 through 2011. While both are growing, income exceeds outgo in all years; this will ensure a growing and viable total fund.

The Federal Employees Retirement System

We turn next to a discussion of FERS benefit rules and program financing.

FERS benefit formulas and rules. The basic FERS benefit is 1 percent of high-three average salary per year of service, with no maximum on the benefit. As with CSRS, the benefit is payable upon achieving one of three eligibility requirements. Two of these, age 60 with twenty years of service and age 62 with five years of service, are the same as under CSRS. However, employees with 30 years of service must have reached a minimum retirement age (MRA). This age is 55 for employees born prior to 1948, age 56 for those born from 1953 to 1964, and age 57 for those born after 1969. The age increases at 0.2 years per calendar year between 1948 and 1953, and between 1964 and 1969.

FERS, unlike CSRS, provides reduced early retirement benefits. Employees who have reached MRA with ten, but fewer than thirty, years of service, can retire and receive a benefit reduced 5 percent a year under age 62. Employees who leave before MRA, with more than ten years of service, can elect the reduced benefit when they reach MRA. Employees can also receive a return of contributions plus interest in lieu of benefits. However, FERS employees who elect a return of contribution cannot receive credit for that service if they later return to federal employment.

Disability benefits are payable under the same conditions as CSRS, but

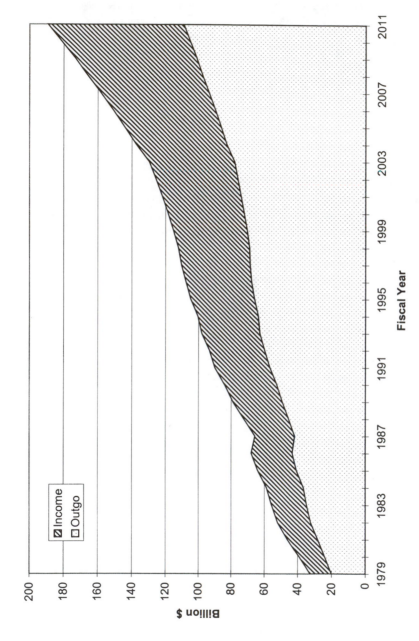

Figure 2. Combined CSRS/FERS funds income and outgo. Sources: OPM (1999a) and data supplied by OPM Office of Actuaries.

with a design that is closer to the long-term disability approach common in the private sector. For the first year of disability, the benefit is 60 percent of high-three salary, less social security. After the first year, the benefit is 40 percent of high-three pay, less 60 percent of social security. After age 62, the annuitant receives the lesser of the pre-age-62 benefit, and a recomputed normal retirement benefit. The normal retirement benefit is computed based on service including the period of disability and a high-three salary projected from the time of disability by inflation. The interaction with OWCP benefits is the same as for CSRS.

There are two benefits payable to survivors of active employees. The first is a lump sum payment, approximately equal to a year's salary, for employees who die after 18 months of service. In addition, a surviving spouse of an employee who dies with more than 10 years of service receives an annuity equal to 50 percent of the accrued FERS retirement benefit at the date of death. FERS employees are also eligible for Federal Employees Group Life Insurance benefits.

Retirees can elect to provide survivor benefits by taking a 10 percent reduction in their benefits. The survivor benefit is 50 percent of the retiree's benefit before the 10 percent reduction. Retirees can also choose a 25 percent benefit or waive the benefit entirely but any choice other than the full 50 percent benefit must be agreed to by the spouse.

Financing FERS benefits. FERS is financed through employee contributions of 0.8 percent of salary with the employer contributing the balance of the normal cost. As with CSRS, these employee and agency contributions were increased temporarily beginning in 1999 by as much as 0.5 percent to reduce the Federal deficit. After 2001, employee contributions will revert to 0.8 percent. The current normal cost is 11.5 percent of salary, so the employing agency contributes 10.7 percent. Unfunded liabilities are amortized over thirty years.

The employee contribution was set at 0.8 percent so that the total contribution rate for social security (currently 6.2 percent of salary) and FERS combined was equivalent to the employee's 7 percent of salary in the CSRS. The total retirement contribution drops to 0.8 percent when social security contributions cease at the maximum taxable wage base ($76,200 in 2000). This lower contribution for higher-paid employees partially offsets two features of the FERS system that favor lower paid employees. One is the tilt in the Social Security benefit design that provides a larger share of replacement income to lower paid employees. The second is the limit on employee contributions to the TSP.

Today there are more FERS than CSRS employee participants, but relatively few retirees are currently receiving benefits; almost all contributions are currently used to build the FERS account. In fiscal year 1998, employer and employee contributions were $7.2 billion and investment income was

$6.8 billion, for total income of $14.0 billion. FERS annuity payments amounted to $0.8 billion, of the $0.9 billion total expenditure. Benefit payments were 2 percent of the total FERS payroll of $55.2 billion. The net result was an increase in the FERS fund of $13.1 billion in fiscal year 1998 to $97 billion in September 1998. FERS covered 1,547,000 employees and paid benefits to 106,000 retirees and survivors (OPM 1999a).

FERS, unlike CSRS, has been fully financed since it began in 1987. The total employer and employee contribution is set equal to the normal cost, which is determined using realistic economic assumptions. Any losses that arise due to adverse experience must be amortized over thirty years. Before 1996, FERS had built up a small unfunded liability because of losses. However, as of September 1996, the plan showed a small surplus, which was preserved by the Board of Actuaries. That group affirmed that a surplus could be held against future losses rather than credited over a thirty-year period, but at the same time that group confirmed that a net surplus would cancel all outstanding amortization payments. As a result, there are currently no FERS payments beyond the normal cost. The transfers from FERS to CSRS to cover the shortfall in financing beginning in 2026 will each be amortized over thirty years. As a result, OPM projects future amortization payments beginning in that year and ending thirty years after the last transfer of funds to CSRS.

As of September 1998, the Office of the Actuary of OPM determined that total FERS liabilities were $191 billion, assets were $97 billion, and the present value of future contributions was $103 billion for a funded surplus of $8 billion. This surplus will be held as a cushion against future losses. Assets were 1.8 times the FERS payroll in 1998 and were projected to be 4.5 times payroll in 2070 (OPM 1999a).

Table 2 summarizes the major features of CSRS and FERS. These include the basis for the formula, retirement conditions and cost-of-living adjustment (COLA) projections. (Other features and details may be obtained through the OPM website <www.opm.gov>.)

CSRS and FERS Governance Issues

CSRS and FERS are administered by OPM with the assistance of the federal agencies. The Federal agencies distribute information on the retirement systems to their employees, channel agency and employee contribution to the CSRS fund, and submit the request for retirement benefits. At retirement, OPM determines the annuity and initiates the benefit payments, and, after retirement, makes any changes to the annuity benefit such as the annual COLA increase.

By law, retirement funds are invested by the Secretary of the Treasury in federal securities. All but a small portion of the investments are in non-

TABLE 2. Key Features of CSRS and FERS

	CSRS	*FERS*
Full retirement benefit	1.5% for the first five years of service, 1.75% for the next five, 2% for the rest; maximum 80%	1% for all service, no maximum 1.1% for all service if retired after age 60 with 20 years of service
Applied to	High-three years salary	High-three years salary
Retirement eligibility		
Full unreduced benefits	Age 55 with 30 years of service Age 60 with 20 years of service	Minimum retirement age (MRA) with 30 years of service
Age 62 with 5 years of service	Age 60 with 20 years of service	Age 62 with 5 years of service
Reduced benefits	None available	MRA and 10 years of service—reduced 5 percent for each year under age 62
Mandatory retirement	None	None
Vested benefit	After 5 years of service, payable at age 62	After 5 years of service, payable at age 62; after 10 years of service a reduced benefit is available at MRA
Cost-of-living increases	Annual increase equal to change in consumer price index (same formula as for social security)	Annual increase in consumer price index (CPI) less 1 percent No increase before age 62 (increase is CPI if that is less than 2 percent and graded if CPI between 2 and 4 percent)
Employee contributions	7.25 percent in 1999, 7.4 percent in 2000, 7.5 percent in 2001, 7 percent after 2001	1.05 percent in 1999, 1.2 percent in 2000, 1.3 percent in 2001, 0.8 percent after 2001

Source: Office of Personnel Management (1998).

marketable bonds issued solely for the purpose of holding the retirement funds. The special issues are created every June 30 for new money with maturities spread over fifteen years and a yield equaling the average of all marketable Treasury securities with four or more years till maturity. Cash balances arising during the year are held in special short-term issues maturing on the following June 30.

Administrative costs charged to CSRS/FERS in 1997 were $102 million or 0.2 percent of total expenditures. These are only the direct costs of OPM and do not include those of the employing agencies nor Treasury investment costs.

Actuarial Assumptions in CSRS and FERS

A three-member Board of Actuaries appointed by OPM is charged with setting the actuarial methods and assumptions used to determine the normal cost and unfunded liabilities of CSRS and FERS. At present the board assumes that inflation will be 4 percent a year and investment return of the CSRS/FERS fund will be 7 percent a year (OPM 1998). Salary scales are projected to grow by 4.25 percent a year with additional individual salary increases averaging 2.15 percent a year. Demographic rates are developed based on plan experience. The current set of rates, adopted in 1994, includes withdrawal, involuntary retirement, voluntary retirement, and disability retirement rates. Separate mortality rates are used for active employees, non-disability annuitants, disability annuitants, and survivors.[8]

The Federal Thrift Savings Plan

The TSP is a defined contribution plan of the 401(k)-type, that permits federal employees to contribute and allocate tax-deferred funds among three investment options. The TSP is administered by the Federal Retirement Thrift Investment Board (FRTIB) established as an independent agency by the Federal Employees' Retirement System Act of 1986 (FERSA).

Employees' choice of funds was restricted when the program began in 1987, but all restrictions were removed in 1991. The three funds are known as the "G fund" or the Government Securities Investment Fund; the "F fund" or the Fixed Income Index Investment Fund; and the "C fund" or the Common Stock Index Investment Fund. Additionally two new funds, a small-capitalization U.S. stock (S) fund and an international stock (I) fund, will be added in 2000.

Employees covered by FERS may contribute up to 10 percent of salary to the TSP. These employees receive an automatic one percent of salary contribution with variable matching on the first 5 percent of salary.[9] FERS participants are fully and immediately vested in their own as well as the government's matching contributions. Participants become fully vested in the one percent automatic contribution after three years of federal service. Employees covered by CSRS can contribute up to 5 percent of salary, but there are no government contributions. Eligible employees are provided two open seasons each year during which they can begin to contribute, change their contribution rate, and/or change how their contributions are invested. Balances on account may separately be transferred among the funds by participants ($10,500 in 2000).

Employee contributions are limited by the elective deferral limit imposed by the Internal Revenue Service. But the TSP is exempt from application of the actual contribution percentage (ACP) test. The ACP test limits contributions of highly compensated employees to a specified amount over the contributions of non-highly-compensated employees. The FRTIB argued that it would be difficult if not impossible to calculate these percentages for the diverse federal workforce. Congress agreed and exempted the TSP from the ACP test, arguing that the TSP was inherently nondiscriminatory.

An employee who separates from service can choose to withdraw the funds, have the TSP purchase an annuity, leave the funds with the TSP, or roll over the balance to an individual retirement account. An employee who leaves funds with the TSP can choose, at any time before age 70½, to withdraw the account balance, select a life annuity, or receive a series of monthly payments.

Active employees over age 59½ are permitted a one-time withdrawal of all or part of their accounts. The TSP does not allow other early withdrawals except for hardship, but loans are permitted for any purpose. As of December 1999, there were 616,000 loans with an outstanding balance of $3.0 billion, or three percent of the total fund.[10] Restrictions and taxes on payments are the same as those that apply to private sector plans established under section 401(k) of the IRS code (McGill 1996).

Governance of the TSP. The FRTIB is composed of five part-time presidential appointees and a full-time executive director selected by those appointees. Each of these officials is required by FERSA to have "substantial experience, training, and expertise in the management of financial investments and pension benefit plans." (5 U.S.C. § 8472(d)). The TSP board members collectively establish the policies under which the TSP operates and furnish general oversight. The executive director carries out the policies established by the board members and otherwise acts as the full-time chief executive of the agency. The board and the executive director convene monthly in meetings open to the public to review policies, practices, and performance. The National Finance Center of the Department of Agriculture has been the TSP recordkeeper, since the fund's creation in 1987 (Mehle 1997).

Costs related to investments are charged against investment return by the fund manager. As with the retirement system, employing agencies disseminate information about the TSP, and funnel agency and employee contributions to the thrift fund. The Thrift Board deals directly with the current or former participant on other matters related to the individual's account. TSP administrative costs are charged to the fund and are offset by account forfeitures. The gross expense ratio (pre-forfeiture offset) has declined steadily as the assets have grown, from an average of 0.67 percent of funds in 1988 to 0.07 percent in 1999. After applying forfeiture credits of 0.02 percent, the net expense ratio was 0.05 percent in 1999. These expenses include the investment management cost of the C and F fund but they do not include the administrative costs of the employing agencies.

As an independent entity, the TSP Board is not subject to the normal review and oversight of federal agencies, but the law did provide for continuing audit and review by outside authorities. The board's annual operations and actions are audited by the Pension and Welfare Benefits Administration (PWBA) of the Department of Labor and an independent auditor. The board is also advised by a 14-member Employee Thrift Advisory Council nominated by employee and retiree groups and appointed by the chairman of the Thrift Board.

TSP investment policy and process.[11] The TSP's investment policy and process was a subject of extensive discussion when the program was under design. Much concern centered around the fact that the fund would rapidly grow to be a major presence in financial markets, and as such, might be used by the federal government to support policy. For example, analysts worried that TSP funds might be used to support social policy such as inner-city investment, or to affect foreign policy, prohibiting investment in corporations doing business in certain countries.

Another concern centered around the perception of investment choices in the C fund. Shifts in investments among firms might be viewed as a sign of insider knowledge about those firms and perceived as manipulation of the market. Even if the investment shift were made based on public information, changes in TSP investment policy could cause much of the market to follow. These concerns moved Congress to consider approaches that would protect the plan's investment policy from any influence by federal policymakers. One possibility would be to permit individuals to freely select investments, while another would be to let workers select any qualified institution to make their investments. The compromise elected for the C fund was to use a passive "indexed" investment approach that was then beginning to be popular among governmental and private sector pension funds. Indexed funds seek to replicate performance of a market index by investing in the same issues in the same proportion as the index. The proportions are based on the market capitalization of all outstanding publicly traded shares.

The board selected the Standard and Poor's 500 stock index as the passive index that would meet the requirements of FERSA; the Lehman Brothers

TABLE 3. Annual Yields of Federal Thrift Savings Plan Funds (1988–97)

Year	C fund (%)	F fund (%)	G fund (%)
1988	11.8	3.6	8.8
1989	31.0	13.9	8.8
1990	−3.2	8.0	8.9
1991	30.8	15.7	8.2
1992	7.7	7.2	7.2
1993	10.1	9.5	6.1
1994	1.3	−3.0	7.2
1995	37.4	18.3	7.0
1996	22.9	3.6	6.7
1997	33.2	9.6	6.8
1998	28.4	8.7	5.7
1999	21.0	−0.9	6.0

Source: U.S. Federal Retirement Thrift Investment Board (web site).

Aggregate Bond index was selected for the F fund. Asset managers of the C and F funds are selected through competitive bidding. The current contractor is Barclays Global Investors (BGI), which invests the C fund assets in the Barclays Equity Index Fund and the F fund in the Barclays U.S. Debt Index Fund. The G fund is invested in nonmarketable U.S. Treasury issues similar to those of the CSRS/FERS fund.

Annual returns on the C, F, and G funds through 1997 appear in Table 3. The C fund has been the most volatile, and had the highest yield with returns varying from a loss of 3.2 percent in 1990 to a gain of 37.4 percent in 1995. The F fund returns have ranged from a loss of 3.0 percent in 1994 to a gain of 18.3 percent in 1995. The G fund returns have been steady ranging from 6.1 percent in 1993 to 8.9 percent in 1990.

Employee participation in the TSP. As of December 1999, there were 1.4 million FERS employees eligible to participate in the TSP, of which 86 percent contributed from their own salaries; the remaining 14 percent received only the mandatory 1 percent federal contribution. There were also 628,000 CSRS employees contributing for a total of 2.1 million contributing participants as of December 1999. Both the number and the percent of participants have steadily increased since the first open season in 1987 when only 29 percent of the 563,000 eligible FERS employees were contributing. (TSP does not track CSRS employees who do not contribute but we estimate that 600,000 eligible CSRS employees do not contribute). Our best estimate is that 1.9 million of the 2.7 million total eligible employees, or 70 percent, are participating in TSP. Figure 3 shows the number of participants since 1987 (information from FRTIB website).

The average contribution rate for FERS participants increased from 3.7 percent in 1987 to 6.8 percent in 1997. One-third of the participants contrib-

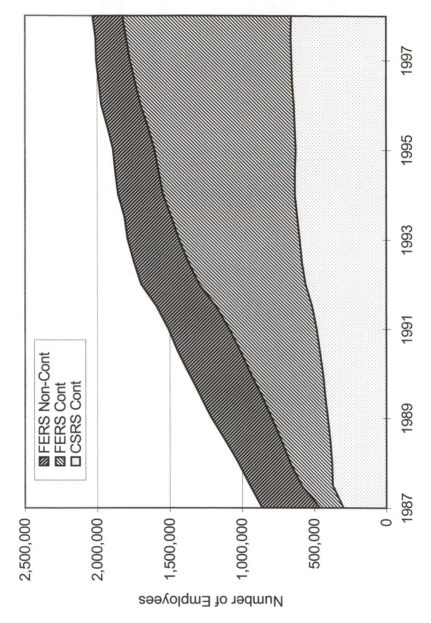

Figure 3. Federal employees contributing to TSP. Source: data supplied by the Federal Retirement Thrift Investment Board.

ute the full 10 percent, and a fifth contribute the 5 percent needed for the maximum employer match. Counting those contributing more than 5 but less than 10 percent, two thirds of FERS participants receive the maximum 5 percent federal contribution. The average contribution rate for CSRS participants increased from 3.2 percent in 1987 to 4.4 percent in 1997, with 76 percent contributing the full 5 percent permitted under the plan (FRTIB 1998).

Growth of TSP funds. Figure 4 shows the growth of the TSP fund and its three accounts since inception. As of December 1999, there was $59.2 billion invested in the C fund (63 percent), $31.5 billion in the G fund (33 percent), and $4.0 billion in the F fund (4 percent) for a combined TSP fund of $94.6 billion.

The Military Retirement System

The military retirement system is part of an integrated pay, benefits, and allowance system used by the Department of Defense (DoD) to recruit, retain, motivate, and ensure a young and vigorous active-duty force. The military's noncontributory defined benefit plan is administered and funded by DoD, and it covers military members of the Army, Navy, Marine Corps, and Air Force. It does not include DoD civilian personnel, inasmuch as they are included in the two federal civilian retirement systems described above. Most of the DoD's system provisions also cover members of other uniformed services including officers of the National Oceanic and Atmospheric Administration (Department of Commerce), officers of the Public Health Service (Department of Health and Human Services), and the Coast Guard (Department of Transportation). This discussion focuses on DoD's military personnel, since this group is by far the largest group covered.

Military retirement must be considered as one of many components of military compensation. Even when the total force size is held constant, 11 percent of the active-duty force is replaced per year. Unlike most employers who hire employees at all ages, new entrants in this system are almost exclusively between the ages of 18 and 22 (with those at the lower ages being enlisted men and women, and those at the older ages being officers). Most of the new entrants (67 percent) serve less than six years, taking advantage of education and other separation benefits designed to recruit and only temporarily employ these members. The turnover patterns result in a force where over half of all members have less than seven years of service at any given time. The average age of the entire active-duty force is 29 (DoD 1998a).

Military benefits. Today's military retirement system for nondisabled retirees provides benefits for active duty personnel retiring after twenty years of service at any age and for reservists (part-time military members) at age 60 with twenty years of service. The system also provides lifetime monthly

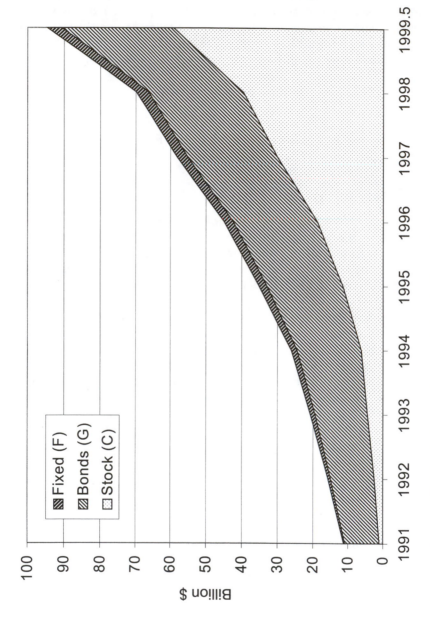

Figure 4. Growth of TSP funds. Source: data supplied by the Federal Retirement Thrift Investment Board.

disability benefits when a member can no longer fulfill the duties of the job; it also pays annuities to survivors of those who die on active duty with over twenty years of service or elect an annuity benefit at retirement.

The military plan is a defined benefit pension, with benefits calculated as a percent of "basic pay." Though basic pay is the main portion of all servicemembers' compensation, it is not directly comparable to private sector earnings. To make such comparisons, one would instead use the concept of "regular military compensation" (RMC), which includes basic pay, cash or in-kind allowances for housing and subsistence, and the tax advantage of these allowances (since they are not federally taxed). Basic pay averages about 72 percent of RMC (DoD 1998b). Consequently, while it is common to hear the twenty-year retirement benefit described as "50 percent pay for life," it is closer to 35 percent (72 percent of 50 percent).

The military retirement system provides an immediate and indexed retirement benefit payable at twenty years of service with no minimum age limitation. These retirement benefits are generally referred to as "retired pay," because most retired members are subject to recall to active duty. (The Uniform Code of Military Justice provides sanctions for the enforcement of the recall.) Unlike other private and government plans, there is no vesting prior to normal retirement in a military pension. In fact, only 18 percent of new entrants complete twenty years of service, but 79 percent of those with ten years of service stay to twenty years, demonstrating the power of this retention tool.[12]

These turnover patterns are the intentional consequence of structured personnel policies in the military. The need for a young and vigorous force, the tremendous investment in training, and the near impossibility of replacing military-specific skills at mid-career or late-career make imperative the careful management of human resources. This explains why numerous reviews of the military pension system reject the notion of allowing vesting prior to twenty years of service, because of its potentially devastating impact on retention and force structure (such as the 5th Quadrennial Review of Military Compensation). Similarly, defined contribution plans are rejected in the military arena, even though private sector employers have curtailed or eliminated defined benefit plans in favor of employer-subsidized defined contribution plans to appeal to an increasingly portable workforce. Indeed, defined contribution plans are seen as a threat to the tremendous retention power of the current "all-or-nothing" military retirement system.

The fact that the system works is signaled by the fact that more than 60 percent of retirees take the benefit at the first chance they get, receiving retired pay beginning at an average age of 42. Promotion, policies, assignments, and dedication—complemented by targeted longevity increases, special pays, and bonuses—allow for the critical retention of selected employees beyond twenty years of service, but even so, most of these leaders

leave by thirty years of service, when the retirement system accruals stop
(DoD 1998b).

A brief history of the military retirement plans. Most societies devote special
care to those hurt defending the country in battle, and the United States is
no exception. In 1636, the Pilgrims at Plymouth declared that wounded soldiers and surviving indigent families would be supported for life. In 1776,
our first national pension law promised 50 percent lifetime pay to the disabled servicemen. Benefits for Navy seamen have been around for many
decades as well (Clark et al. this volume). By 1832, as the numbers of veterans declined and system revenues increased, full pay for life regardless of
need was awarded. All of these disability benefits were administered by bureaus and administrations that were predecessors of today's Department of
Veterans Affairs.

When the Civil War started, there was a need to retire aging military members to replace them with a young and active force, and the first major nondisability retirement act was enacted. This 1861 law separated soldiers after
forty years of service. After the Civil War, Congress enacted legislation to
draw down the force strength by providing retiring officers with benefits
worth 75 percent of pay at thirty years of service (at any age). This fundamental design of 2.5 percent accrual per year of service (2.5 percent times
thirty years equals 75 percent) is still the one in effect today. Each subsequent war and peacetime period since the Civil War brought expansions
and refinements to the system, and the military has also changed its recruitment policy from time to time, sometimes using a volunteer and other times
using a draft induction system. But for more than a century, retiring servicemembers' benefits have been calculated using this same formula.

Between 1920 and 1949, numerous laws shaped the distinction between
disability benefits that continued to be administered by the Department of
Veterans Affairs (VA), and separate *disability and nondisability* benefits transferred to the Department of Defense as part of the military retirement system. No one act clearly defined how these two entitlement systems were to
be separated. The resulting military retirement system includes a lifetime
permanent disability benefit that is awarded when the military member cannot
continue to fulfill job obligations. Disability-specific rating scales developed
by the Department of Veterans Affairs are used by DoD to determine the
percentage of disability. Generally speaking, this percentage is multiplied
by basic pay to determine the benefit at the time of separation. This benefit
is indexed to inflation over time.

The *disability* compensation benefits administered by VA loosely resemble
workers' compensation benefits of the sort designed during the early 1900s.
These are the descendants of the original disability benefits established by
the Pilgrims, and they are not part of the military retirement system. Un-

like DoD disability benefits, these benefits do not depend on a worker's ability to continue service, but rather they are awarded for changes in health status between entry and departure from the military. VA compensation is awarded for combat disabilities, other accidents that take place during a military career, and natural-life diseases acquired in the military (such as high blood pressure and diabetes). Prior to the Civil War, disability benefits were mainly combat-related. Because more soldiers died from disease than any other cause during the Civil War, in 1862 President Lincoln signed an innovative act that extended compensation to cover diseases incurred while in service (VA 1994).

The VA disability rating scales are used to determine initial flat amounts that are then indexed annually to inflation. As veterans age and disabilities worsen, reopened claims can increase monthly benefits. For example, a 30 percent initial disability benefit for high blood pressure could become a 100 percent disability benefit for a heart attack years later. Two out of every three claims adjudicated within the VA compensation system in 1998 were reopened claims. There were approximately 25 million veterans in the United States in 1998, and monthly VA disability compensation benefits were awarded to 2.3 million of them (VA 1994). About one fourth of the VA disability recipients were also entitled to DoD military retirement benefits (DoD 1998a).

DoD military retirement system benefits, including nondisability, disability, and survivor benefits, are offset for any amounts paid by the VA. However, since VA benefits are tax-free and can become greater than the DoD benefit over time, many members apply for both. Approximately 27 percent of DoD *nondisability* retirees and 70 percent of DoD *disability* retirees also receive VA *disability* compensation benefits (DoD 1998b).

Military members were brought under social security as of 1957. At that time, the social security old age, disability, and survivor benefits were simply added to existing military and VA benefits; no attempt was made to integrate the two systems. After the draft ended in the mid-1970s, military pay was increased to ensure that DoD could compete with the private sector for its all-volunteer force. The end of the draft also forced the military retirement system to undergo an evaluation, and in 1980 the system was revised for new entrants. This produced two different retirement benefit structures, one for those already employed prior to 1980, and another for new hires. After continued analysis Congress and the administration adopted in 1986 some of the recommendations of the Fifth Quadrennial Review of Military Compensation,[13] changing the system again for new entrants. This process resulted in the three different retirement benefit structures described above. In 1998, the services expressed concern with recruiting and retention during an unprecedented period of low unemployment. As a result, the National Defense

TABLE 4. Military Nondisability Benefit Formulas (as of February 1999)

Employees entering:	Name of formula	Base pay used in formula	Factor employed in formula	Annual COLA	Other
Before 9/8/80	Final pay	Basic pay at retirement	2.5%/year service capped at 30 yr	CPI	—
9/8/80–7/31/86	HI-3	Average highest 36 months basic pay	2.5%/year service capped at 30 yr	CPI	—
On or after 8/1/86	Redux*	Average highest 36 months basic pay	2.5%/year service capped at 30 yr with 1% penalty for each year retired under 30 yr	CPI minus 1% (even after age 62)	Age 62: one-time benefit adjustment to restore the <30 yr of service penalty and COLA reductions

Source: Authors' compilation of data supplied by the DoD Office of Actuary.
The President's FY 2000 Budget proposed eliminating the penalty for this population.
*At 15 years of service, participant may switch to HI-3 formula or receive a bonus and stay in Redux.

Authorization Act for FY2000 (P.L. 106-65) included language that allows post-1986 members at fifteen years of service a choice between a bonus or moving to the higher 1980 retirement plan.

Nondisability benefits for active duty personnel. As a result of these changes in the system rules over time, different benefit formulas apply to the three distinct populations within the military retirement system. Anyone may retire at twenty years of service (at any age), and his or her benefit is derived by multiplying base pay by a total accrual factor. After the initial pay is calculated, nondisability benefits are then indexed using an annual cost-of-living adjustment.

The specific benefit accrual factors do, however, differ by date of hire. Members entering military service prior to September 8, 1980, have an initial retirement benefit equal to (final basic pay)* (2.5 percent)* (years of service). Beginning with members entering military service on September 8, 1980, the average highest thirty-six months of basic pay was used instead of final basic pay in the initial benefit calculation. Members entering on or after August 1, 1986, were subject to additional changes. There was a one percent penalty for each year of service under thirty years of service at retirement. Consequently, a twenty-year retiree has a 50 percent (2.5 percent for twenty years) total accrual factor reduced by 10 percent, for the ten years of service not served, to equal 40 percent. In addition, the COLA for these members is reduced by one percentage point. At age 62, there is a one-time "catch-up" adjustment in the benefit to reinstate the accrual and the COLA reductions, but the annual COLA is subject to reductions thereafter. At fifteen years of service, a member can accept a $30,000 bonus and remain under this plan, or give up the bonus and move to the higher 1980 benefit levels. This retention bonus is not considered part of the retirement system, and obligates the member to serve five more years. Table 4 summarizes the benefit formulas for the three populations, which are referred to as "Final Pay," "HI-3," and "Redux" respectively.

The FY 1993 defense authorization act (PL 102-484) included temporary early retirement authority (TERA) for the military services, as part of an effort to reduce the size of the active duty force. Unless extended again, this authority expires September 30, 2001, and it allows the military services to offer retirement to members with between fifteen and twenty years of service. These members receive an immediate annuity calculated normally, but with 1 percent penalty for each year under twenty years of service. Part or all of the penalty can be restored at age 62, if the retiree works in a qualified public service job for the period from retirement until twenty years of service would have been completed. As of September 30, 1998, there were 52,000 TERA retirees receiving $615 million annually (DoD 1998b).

Nondisability benefits for members of the reserves. The Reserve Components of the Armed Forces include the Army National Guard of the United States, the Army Reserve, the Naval Reserve, the Marine Corps Reserve, the Air National Guard of the United States, the Air Force Reserve, and the Coast Guard Reserve. The Ready Reserve is comprised of military members of the Reserve and National Guard organized in units or as individuals, liable for recall to active duty to augment the active components in time of war or national emergency as provided by law (Hunter 1998). Members of the reserves are part-time military members, and may be fully employed in a civilian capacity for the federal government or the private sector. These members may retire after twenty creditable years of service (the last eight of which must be in a reserve component), but their retirement benefits are not payable until age 60. The benefit formula is equal to (base pay) * (2.5 percent) * (years of service). A member entering military service before September 8, 1980, has a base pay equal to the active duty basic pay in effect for the reservist's grade and years of service at the time that retired pay begins. A member entering service after this time has a base pay equal to the average basic pay for the reservist's grade in the last three years in service. Since reservists are part-time employees, their years of service are calculated using a point formula that translates effort into years. One point is awarded for each day of service or drill attended, and fifteen points are earned for each year's membership in a component. A creditable year is one in which fifty or more points are earned. While a member must have at least twenty creditable years to retire, points earned in a noncreditable year are counted towards years of service. The sum of the points divided by 360 equals the years of service. For example, a reservist who has 25 years of creditable service and 1,500 points in total would have an initial benefit at age 60 of 10.4 percent of base pay (1,500 divided by 360, times 0.025).

Military disability benefits. As stated earlier, military members are eligible for disability benefits from Social Security, the Department of Veterans Affairs, and the military retirement system. If the disabled member cannot fulfill job duties and has at least a 30 percent disability, then a disability annuity is calculated. If this disability is temporary, then it must be rated at least 50 percent, physical exams must take place every eighteen months, and a final determination must be made within five years in order to terminate the annuity or consider it permanent. The annuity is equal to the larger of the nondisability calculation or the benefit derived by multiplying the percentage of disability by base pay. Base pay is determined exactly like the base pay used in the nondisability formula, depending on when the member entered military service. Federal income taxes do not apply to the part of the annuity equal to the disability percentage times base pay.

Survivor annuities from the military. At retirement, military members have the option to have a portion of retired pay continue to their dependents upon the retiree's death. In return, the member's retired pay is reduced to cover all or a portion of the cost of this benefit. Several design changes have altered survivor benefits over time, following its institution in 1953. Between 1953 and 1972, the Retired Servicemen's Family Protection Plan (RSFPP) was in effect; here members paid the entire cost of this program, as it was not federally subsidized. However RSFPP came to be seen as both inadequate protection and too expensive.

Consequently in 1972, the Survivor Benefit Plan (SBP) was enacted for new retirees, and those already retired were given the option to convert to SBP. The government subsidizes the SBP benefit, directly by paying for benefits in excess of revenues and indirectly by not taxing members' pay directed towards SBP premiums. Overall, the total subsidy averages about 34 percent (information from DoD, 1998b). Benefits to survivors are a percentage of the base amount elected by the retiree; premium reductions are also based on the elected base amount. This base amount cannot be greater than retired pay or less than $300. As a result of a 1998 law, the retiree pays premiums for a maximum of thirty years.

SBP annuities are 55 percent of the base amount if the annuitant is under age 62, and 35 percent of the base amount for older persons. This two-tiered benefit structure was designed around the concept that the reduction at 62 is offset by social security benefits available at that age. Initially, SBP was equal to a flat 55 percent for everyone, with benefits offset by social security at 62; the automatic reduction to 35 percent at age 62 was implemented for administrative ease. Beginning in 1992, retirees electing the maximum base amount can eliminate all or a portion of the reduced second tier by paying the full cost of this added benefit through increased premiums.

Members who die on active duty after twenty years of service are assumed to have retired on their date of death and to have elected survivor benefits. Just as for retired pay, all SBP annuities are offset by survivor benefits awarded by VA, but any past retiree premium payments relating to the reduction are returned to the survivor. Cost-of-living increases and other adjustments are applied as they would have been to the retiree. For example, a survivor of a retiree under the Redux retirement system would get annual increases equal to the consumer price index (CPI) minus one percent, and a one-time catch up to full inflation on the anniversary of the deceased member's sixty-second birthday.

Reservists are eligible to elect SBP at age 60 when they begin to draw retired pay. A reservist who accumulates twenty years of service before age 60 can elect to participate in the Reserve Component Survivor Benefit Program (RCSBP), which provides survivor benefits in the event of death before age 60. The added cost of this benefit is fully borne by the member through future additional reductions in retired pay and survivor annuities.

Cost-of-living adjustments in military pensions. Prior to 1958, military retired pay was generally increased by the same percentage as the increase in basic pay. Since military pay increments exceeded the inflation rate during that period, annuity increases were greater than if they had been based on the CPI. This process was replaced with an automatic mechanism in 1963 that tied increases to the CPI. Two years later, the COLA formula was altered to ensure that annuities were increased, whenever the CPI increased by 3 percent. Between 1969 and 1977, each automatic calculation included an additional one percentage point, designed to make up for a supposed lag between the calculation of and implementation of the COLA. The designers did not recognize that compounding of the one percent increases would soon greatly exceed the effect of a one-time lag. In 1977, the extra percent was eliminated and cost of living increases were then set for March and September of each year.

Increases to annuities in a public system this large are always vulnerable to temporary minor modifications in timing and amount, because of the huge Federal savings that this generates. This occurred in late 1997 to early 1998, at a time when annuitant payments were running close to $30B annually, or $2.5B a month. Increasing the monthly checks by 2.1 percent beginning January 1998, for example, resulted in a monthly increase in spending of $53 million. If legislation had delayed this COLA increase by three months it would have saved over $150 million in fiscal year 1998. Granting a 1.1 percent increase instead of a 2.1 percent increase would have saved over $225 million in 1998 alone, compounding thereafter. Because several such changes occurred over time, a different strategy was adopted in 1984. At this point the military and civilian retirement systems adopted the indexing mechanism used by the social security system. Henceforth, January benefit payments are increased by the percentage increase in the average of the CPIs for July, August, and September over the averaged CPIs for the same three months of the prior year. Using a common mechanism for indexing all federal plans has made temporary changes to only one of these plans nearly impossible.

Military system financing. Prior to 1984, the military retirement system was operated on a pay-as-you-go basis. In other words, there was no trust fund backing military promises, and the amount paid out to retirees in any one year came directly from the DoD budget. To illustrate the impact on DoD budgets, there were 3,000 military retirees with an annual cost of $3.5 million in 1900; by 1984 the number of retirees had risen to 1.35 million with an annual cost of $16.5 billion—a figure that represented approximately half of the military's payroll (DoD 1998a). Projections at the time indicated that retirement outlays would increase to 70 percent of payroll within the ten-year budget window (DoD 1998b).

The movement toward a funded system began in the mid-1980s. Most federal pension plans have had to adhere to standardized reporting requirements under P.L. 95-595 since 1980. Using an aggregate entry-age normal cost funding method to value system liabilities, the system actuaries estimated that the normal cost of the system was approximately equal to the plan disbursements in FY 1984 (50 percent of basic pay). The decision was taken to make the switch to a funded plan in 1984 because after that year, retiree payments would begin to increase rapidly over normal cost payments. Charging DoD with only the accruing liability of the current force would quickly lower the cost of the retirement obligation in the military budget.

The Military Retirement Fund was therefore created under PL 98-94 to move the military retirement system from a pay-as-you-go to a funded system. It charged the military budget with the accruing retirement cost of the current active-duty and reserve force using the aggregate entry-age normal methods. This normal cost is calculated as a percentage of basic payroll and transferred to the trust fund throughout the year when pay is dispersed. The law specified that payments on the initial unfunded liability ($529 billion) would be made to the trust fund at the beginning of each fiscal year from the General Fund of the Treasury. Payments to amortize annual changes in unfunded liabilities (for plan amendments, changes in assumptions, and experience gains and losses) are handled similarly. The legislation passed with little controversy because it ensured that the defense budget would not continue to rise due to past manpower decisions, and current manpower decisions could be made with the full knowledge of the cost of current decisions.

Figure 5 compares the retirement charges to the military budget under the funded and the pay-as-you-go systems since 1984. Specifically, it compares the normal costs for the method used since 1984 to the plan disbursements as a percentage of basic payroll which was the method used prior to 1984.

DoD's retirement contribution in any one year includes a full-time normal cost contribution (for the active-duty force), and a part-time normal cost contribution (for reservists). The annual full-time normal cost percentage (NCP) is derived as the weighted average of the NCPs relating to the three distinct benefit formulas; the weights reflect the percentage of payroll that year relevant to each of the systems. Since the newer systems offer less generous benefits, the weighted NCP drops annually. It should also be noted that half of the basic payroll goes to members with less than eight years of service, so it does not take long for the budget to noticeably change when new benefit rules are implemented for new entrants. The annual part-time NCP is calculated in the same manner as that for full-time personnel.

In FY 1998 the full-time "weighted" normal cost percentage was 30.4 percent and the part-time normal cost percentage was 8.8 percent. These amounts are obtained by multiplying by the basic pay of their respective members to determine the amount transferred from the DoD military budget to the trust fund. As shown in Table 5 (DoD 1998b), the total basic payroll was a little over $37B and the normal cost contributions to the trust fund were $10.4B in FY 1998—a figure that represented 28 percent of basic pay. This percentage is smaller than the 1985 original percent (50.7 percent) be-

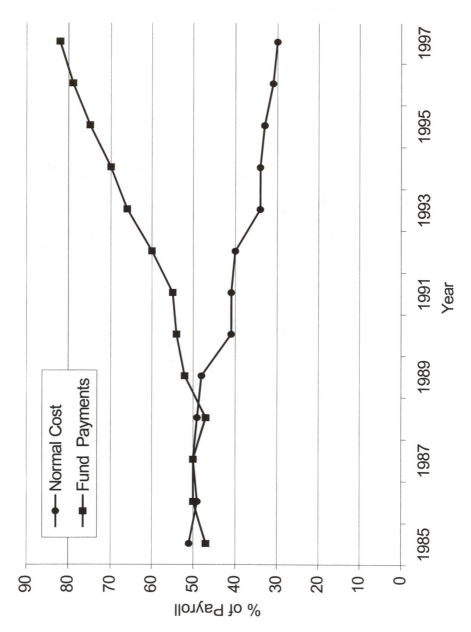

Figure 5. Plan costs as percent of basic payroll. Source: data supplied by the Department of Defense.

TABLE 5. Development of FY 1998 Full-Time and Part-Time Normal Cost
        Percentages

	Final pay (%)	HI 3 (%)	Redux (%)	Weighted (%)
Weighting factors*	17.0	19.3	63.7	
Full-time NCP	36.7	33.0	28.0	30.4
Part-time NCP	9.8	9.3	8.4	8.8

Source: Department of Defense Office of the Actuary (1998b).
*These factors are the percent of basic payroll attributable to members under each benefit
formula.

cause of the introduction of less generous benefits in 1986, and because of
increasing real interest rate assumptions.

The unfunded liability of the system is intended to be paid off in fifty
annual payments, with the last being in year 2033. Changes in unfunded
liability due to benefit formulas, changes in actuarial assumptions, and experience gains and losses are amortized over thirty years by payments that
increase in absolute value at the same rate as the annual long-term pay scale
assumption (currently 4 percent). Total annual payments on the $496 B un-
funded liability (made by Treasury to the retirement fund) were $15 billion
in FY 1998. Unfunded liability and normal cost payments include the cost
of projected inflation so they are adequate to fund the retirement system
(DoD 1998b).

Each year the retirement fund is credited with normal cost contributions
from DoD, payments on the unfunded liability from Treasury, and investment income. It pays all benefits to retirees and survivors. Under law, the
assets of the retirement fund are invested in special issue Treasury securities bearing interest equal to current market yields for federal securities of
comparable maturities. The fund balance increased from zero at the end of
FY 1984 to $150B at the end of FY 1998 (five times payments to annuitants).

Governance of military pension plans. The military retirement system is administered by the DoD, and trust fund assets are invested by an Investment
Fund Manager employed by DoD. P.L. 98-94 (currently chapter 74, title 10,
U.S.C.) established an independent three-member DoD Retirement Board
of Actuaries. The members each serve fifteen-year terms, and one new member comes on every five years (original terms were five, ten, and fifteen in
order to achieve this ultimate arrangement). The DoD chief actuary serves
as the executive secretary of the Board and the Office of the Actuary provides all technical and administrative support to the board. This support is
proactive in nature instead of reactive, and includes recommendations as
to assumptions and methods. The DoD Office of the Actuary produces all
aspects of the actuarial valuations of the system. It has a valuation model
that produces the normal costs, unfunded liabilities, and open group pro-

TABLE 6. Military Retirement System: Key Plan Statistics

Total active-duty members and full-time reservists	1,459,000
Total monthly basic pay ($M)	$2,850 M
Total selected drilling reservists (part-time)	817,000
Total monthly basic pay ($M)	$296 M
Total number of nondisability retirees	1,556,000
Total monthly retired pay ($M)	$2,362 M
Total number of disability retirees	111,000
Total monthly retired pay ($M)	$116 M
Total number of surviving families	234,000
Total monthly survivor annuities ($M)	$144 M

Source: Department of Defense Office of the Actuary (1998b).

jection over the next 100 years. Other models allow the office to project the unfunded liability over time, amortize the payments to the fund, produce a cash-flow analysis for the DoD investment fund manager to use in determining investment criteria, and analyze gains and losses. The office produces military-specific mortality and other decrement rates; analyzes economic indicators and trends that are key to the development of long-term cost-of-living, basic pay, and trust fund investment income assumptions. Experts in the office can analyze the effect of any proposed direct change to the system, or the effect of indirect adjustments that affect the system (such as pay or force size adjustments).

The designers of the 1984 funding law realized the importance of independence in determining assumptions and methods that significantly affect the annual costs of the system. To demonstrate this importance, only one small example need be examined: in fiscal year 1985, we determined that the DoD military budget could have been lowered by $5 billion by merely increasing the actuarial assumption for the annual assumed investment income rate by 1 percentage point. The law requires that the Board of Actuaries determine valuation methods and assumptions, review valuations of the system, determine the method of amortizing unfunded liabilities, report annually to the secretary of defense, and report to the president and the Congress on the status of the fund at least once every four years.

Key plan statistics appear in Table 6. There were almost 1.5 million active duty members, 1.6 million nondisability retirees, 111,000 disabled retirees, and 234,000 survivors as of September 30, 1998.

Future Challenges for Federal Pension Systems

One challenge facing federal pension systems has to do with the way in which the accounting is handled for federal plans that accumulate, and invest, assets in their fund portfolios. By law, any federal retirement assets must currently be invested in U.S. Treasury securities, and these assets are counted in the government's "unified budget." As a result, only payments from "outside" sources (e.g., employee contributions) and payments made to "outside" sources (e.g., annuity benefits) affect the federal deficit. By contrast, government payments to federal pension systems do not affect the federal deficit. One result of this accounting framework is that policy debates tend to focus on contributions from employees and payments to annuitants, rather than structural changes such as an increase in retirement age, since the latter has little or no impact on the measured unified deficit.

To understand how federal pension financing affects the government budget, one first must recognize that an intragovernmental transfer consists of a debit from one government account and a credit to another. An example of an intragovernmental transfer is a payment of interest by the Treasury (debit) to a government pension trust fund (credit). These two transactions cancel each other out and have no overall effect on the federal deficit. Similarly, the accruing cost of retirement in a federal pension system is charged against the employing agency (debit), and some or all of these funds are transferred to the federal pension plan's trust fund (credit). Another federal entity, such as the Department of Treasury, may be responsible for making payments on the unfunded liability (debit) to the trust fund (credit). When the federal pension trust fund receives the income (debit) it invests its assets in special issue Treasury obligations (credit) bearing interest at rates determined by the secretary of the Treasury, taking into consideration current market yields for outstanding marketable U.S. obligations of comparable maturities. Each year the Treasury pays (debits) interest to the trust fund (credit). Each of these is an intragovernmental transfer with no effect on the Federal deficit. Indeed, only payments from the fund to retirees and refunds of contributions are counted as outlays from the federal budget and hence affect the deficit level.

Although budget flows are unaffected by the purchase of securities by a federal pension trust fund, this action does increase the gross federal debt and the debt subject to statutory limit, specifically the portion of the debt held by government accounts. The portion held by the public will not change. But the resultant increase in government debt subject to statutory limit tends to be small, likely having only a negligible effect on the timing of the next debt limit increase and the political issues surrounding that legislation.

Consequently, the decision to accumulate assets in a government-run pension fund has no effect on the annual government deficit, and only a minor effect on the national debt. From an accounting point of view, unless one invests federal pension funds outside the federal government, it is impossible to recognize long term liabilities generated within the system. But investing federal pension assets in capital market assets has been rejected in the past by policymakers for many reasons, including (1) the risk associated with investing pension assets in less secure portfolios, (2) the possibility that the federal government might exert undue influence over private companies by virtue of is large holding of stocks and bonds, and (3) the potential difficulty of convincing the public to buy federal securities when the government invests elsewhere.

Given these complexities, it may be asked why should any federal pension system prefund or hold assets in excess of current pay-as-you-go benefit payout needs? One reason is that adopting a funding policy alerts policymakers to the long-term cost or savings implications of proposed benefit changes and unexpected annual experience (inflation, pay increases, mortality, actual interest income, etc.). These changes are then reflected in the budgets and integrated into policy and management decisions. For example, for many years it was widely believed that the military retirement system needed to be altered, and furthermore, policy required that benefit reductions could only apply to new entrants into the military. As a result of having pay-as-you-go accounting, there was no compelling budgetary reason to implement any changes because it take twenty years before the defense budget would see the result of the policy change. But in 1984 when DoD moved to an entry-age normal cost funding method, it quickly became clear that there was a huge cost impact of changing benefits for new entrants, since the majority of members had less than six years of service. It took Congress and the administration less than two years after this new funding law was enacted to implement a totally new retirement system for new entrants. Another example of the beneficial effect of prefunding is that the long-term consequences of a federal pay raise are better measured. Focusing only on current cashflows reveals how a pay raise affects current year federal outlays, but ignores outyear effects. Of course, most funded plans require agency contributions that are a percentage of payroll, so a current increase in payroll automatically boosts retirement obligations not only in the first year, but in future years as well. Hence funding requires proper measurement of the full cost of federal compensation changes (including in the retirement benefits).

Another reason to fund a federal pension is that funding affords some additional security that annuitants will receive promised benefits when due. One might argue that since funding does not affect the Federal deficit, this security is apparent rather than real. Of course, the current focus on when the Medicare and social security trust funds will run dry indicates that voters and policy experts do perceive some risk associated with the time when outlays come to exceed tax receipts.

Other challenges also await the Federal and military pension systems in the future. Currently a strong economy combined with better financing suggests that these retirement systems are stronger than ever before. But poor economic performance could generate pressures from employees, annuitants and taxpayers for future benefit and tax changes. For instance, automatic indexing of benefits after retirement is always controversial, and immediate budgetary savings can be achieved through cutbacks in the COLA. Indeed, FERS already has a "diet" COLA (reduced by 1 percent) and this may be adopted for CSRS and the military systems in the event of budgetary pressures. The federal systems are also likely to respond to current and future social security reforms. The social security retirement age has already been raised to 67, which will likely lead to pressure for change in the federal systems. The age 55 and thirty years of service under CSRS, and for older FERS employees, is gradually phasing out over time, but there will be pressure to increase the age 57 and thirty FERS provision as well as the age 60 and twenty provision.

Finally, workforce demographics coupled with improvements in medical care will create important challenges for the federal retirement programs in years to come. Both the military and civilian systems have diverse disability programs that should be coordinated more effectively, in order to ensure effective use of disabled employees and efficient design of the disability benefit plans. Postretirement medical costs are a major part of the federal budget and, as yet, have only been estimated approximately but not prefunded.[14] The TSP thrift plan has been quite popular, and it is seen an effective element of FERS compensation. But as economic conditions change, and investment options are expanded, this plan will have to track and incorporate responses to these changes. There may be pressure for including military personnel into the TSP or an equivalent system in the future, though it is unlikely that a defined contribution plan would replace the existing defined benefit model.

Appendix: Postretirement Medical Plans for Civilian Employees and Military Personnel

While the main focus of this chapter is pension benefits, a brief discussion of retiree medical benefits is instructive. As above, a wide range of programs applies to these employees. The federal government does not prefund postretirement medical (PRM) benefits. However, federal agencies are required to report on the PRM liabilities.

Federal civilian employees and their dependents are covered by the Federal Employees Health Benefits Program (FEHBP); here, benefits and the share of contributions after retirement are identical to those that apply to employees before retirement (with the exception that postal employees are covered by FEHBP but pay a lower share of the cost of FEHBP than do nonpostal employees). CSRS/FERS employees entitled to an immediate annuity at retirement and who participated in FEHBP at least five years immediately before retirement can continue to participate in FEHBP after retirement. FEHBP permits retirees to choose among over 300 plans, but the largest one, a national Blue Cross/Blue Shield plan, covers half of the 1.9M participating annuitants. Retirees pay one fourth of the cost of most plans but do bear a higher percentage of the cost of the higher-premium plans. The total PRM liability was $176B as of September 30, 1998, with an annual cost of $23B. The system is not funded so participants and the government cover each year's costs (OPM 1999b).

Health care for military retirees and their dependents may be handled by three health care systems. First, military retirees and dependents can receive treatment at military hospitals. Second, retirees and dependents lacking access to a military hospital can participate in Tricase, which covered 6.8 million people eligible for current or future benefits in 1995 including current and former members of the armed forces and their dependents and survivors. The total unfounded liability was $210B in 1998 with a current cost of 13.7 percent of pay for active duty members (Milliman and Robertson 1998). The third option open to military retirees is that they are also eligible to receive treatment from the health care system administered by the Department of Veterans Affairs.

Notes

1. However, CSRS employees have had two opportunities to elect FERS, and a 1999 change allows military members under the 1986 benefit formulas a choice between the higher 1980 benefits or a bonus.

2. Federal rules that apply to private sector contributory plans require the employer to pay the value of any deferred benefit in excess of the value of the refund. These rules require the former vested employee to be able to redeposit any refund and regain the prior service credit on return to employment. Both CSRS and FERS fall short of these requirements on private sector plans.

3. This and other information on CSRS/FERS was provided by the Federal Office of Personnel Management (OPM 1999a, b). Michael Virga, the Senior Actuary for Pension Programs of OPM, kindly provided the authors with additional unpublished data maintained by the Office of the Actuary of OPM.

4. The information in this section is taken from OPM (1998a) and the OPM website <www.opm.gov>.

5. If the employee is hired after age 38, the minimum benefit is less than 40 percent.

6. The normal cost is the percent of salary that, with interest, will pay the benefits of new entrants to the retirement plan. The Board of Actuaries determines the normal cost for a typical recent group of new entrants. This differs from the traditional approach of determining the cost from entry for all current active participants.

7. The unfunded liability of CSRS is the present value of all benefits for current active and retired participants less (1) the present value of future employee and agency contributions and (2) the fund.

8. See Hustead (this volume) for a detailed discussion of CSRS/FERS actuarial assumptions including illustrative rates.

9. The government matches 100 percent of the first 2 percent in employee contributions, and 50 percent of the next 3 percent. With the 1 percent automatic contribution, the total government contribution is 5 percent if the employee contributes at least 5 percent.

10. Personal communication from the Office of External Affairs, FRTIB, 1999.

11. This section draws from Mehle (1997).

12. New entrant projection provided by the DoD Office of the Actuary (personal communication, 1999).

13. Federal law calls for a Quadrennial Review of Military Compensation (QRMC). As with the Fifth QRMC, many of the reviews have at least partly focussed on retirement benefits. (DoD 1985)

14. See the Appendix for more discussion of postretirement health benefits for military and civilian federal employees.

References

Clark, Robert L., Lee A. Craig, and Jack W. Wilson. This volume. "The Life and Times of a Public Sector Pension Plan Before Social Security: The U.S. Navy Pension Plan in the Nineteenth Century."

Crane, Roderick B. This volume. "Federal Regulation and Taxation of Public Plans: A History of Increasing Federal Influence."

HayGroup. 1999. *1999 Social Security Summary*. Philadelphia: HayGroup.

Hunter, Ronald S. 1998. *Reserve Forces Almanac 1998*. 24th ed. Falls Church, Va.: Uniformed Services Almanac.

Hustead, Edwin C. 1995. Personal communication to Dennis Snook, Research Analyst, Congressional Research Service, Washington, D.C., February 6.

———. This volume. "Determining the Cost of Public Pension Plans."

McGill, Dan M., Kyle N. Brown, John J. Haley, and Sylvester J. Schieber. 1996. *Fundamentals of Private Pensions*. 7th ed. Philadelphia: University of Pennsylvania Press.

Mehle, Roger W. 1997. Statement to the Subcommittee on Securities of the Senate Committee on Banking, Housing, and Urban Affairs. Washington, D.C., April 30.

Milliman and Robertson. 1998. *Analysis of the U.S. Military's Projected Retiree Medical Liabilities for Fiscal Year 1997*. Submitted to Benjamin Gottleib, Chief Actuary, U.S. Department of Defense, Washington D.C., May 29.

Myers, Robert J. 1993. *Social Security*. 4th ed. Pension Research Council. Philadelphia: University of Pennsylvania Press.

U.S. Congressional Budget Office (CBO). 1986. *Analysis of FERS May 22, 1986*. In U.S. House of Representatives Conference Report on HR 2672. Washington, D.C., May 16.

U.S. Department of Defense (DoD). 1985. *Fifth Quadrennial Review of Military Compensation*. Washington, D.C.

———. 1998a. *Statistical Report on the Military Retirement System*. Fiscal Year 1997. Office of the Actuary, Washington, D.C.

———. 1998b. *Valuation of the Military Retirement System*, 1997, Office of the Actuary, Washington, D.C.

U.S. Department of Veterans Affairs (VA). 1994. *The Veterans Benefits Administration: An Organizational History: 1776–1994*. Washington, D.C.: Veterans Benefits Administration.

———. 1999. *FY 2000 Budget Submission*. Washington, D.C., February.

U.S. Federal Retirement Thrift Investment Board. 1998. *Analysis of 1997 Thrift Savings Plan Participant Demographics*. Washington, D.C., December.

————. Website, <www.tsp.gov>

U.S. General Accounting Office (GAO). 1996. *Public Pensions: Summary of Federal Pension Plan Data.* Washington D.C.: Office of the Actuary, Social Security Administration, February.

U.S. Office of Personnel Management (OPM). 1997. *Financial Statements Fiscal Year 1996.* Washington D.C.

————.1998a. *FERS Transfer Handbook.* Washington, D.C.

————. 1998b. Civil Service Retirement and Disability Fund (CSRDF). *An Annual Report to Comply with the Requirements of Public Law 95-595*, September 30, 1997. Washington D.C., May.

————. Website. <www.opm.gov>

Chapter 5
Canadian Public Sector Employee Pension Plans

Silvana Pozzebon

Pension plans covering public sector employees are major players in the Canadian pension market. Public plans account for over half (56 percent) of the pensions ranked by *Benefits Canada* magazine as being among the 100 largest in terms of assets held (Bak 1998a).[1] Eight of the top ten Canadian pension plans were public sector plans, and they held 47 percent of total market value assets of $397.4 billion reported by the 100 largest plans, at the end of 1997 (Bak 1998a).[2] Workers covered by public sector plans include those employed by federal, provincial, or municipal governments and enterprises. While a fair number of federal workers are civil servants, provincial public sector employees generally include teachers, hospital workers, and employees of government enterprises such as hydroelectric power facilities. Finally, municipal public sector employees may encompass such varied groups as police, firefighters, and transit and blue collar workers.

Data on pensions sponsored by employers or unions have been collected by Statistics Canada as far back as the late 1950s, and *Benefits Canada* magazine has surveyed and ranked such plans for some twenty years. Yet there has been little systematic study of pension issues, and even less written about them, by those outside the industry. This is particularly true of pensions covering public sector employees, which motivates the present effort to provide an overview of such plans. We begin by describing the relative importance of public and private sector employee pension plans in Canada and compare key plan characteristics across sectors. The financing of public sector employee plans is then examined, followed by a brief conclusion.

Relative Importance of Public and Private Sector Plans

At the beginning of 1997, 42 percent of paid Canadian workers were members of pension plans sponsored by employers or unions (called "registered"

TABLE 1. Public and Private Sector Plans, Canada 1997

	Public (%)	Private (%)
Active members (total: 5.1 million)	47	53
Male	45	66
Sub-sector		
Municipal	20	—
Provincial	63	—
Federal	16	—
Other	1	—
Plan size		
1–99 members	1	9
100–999	3	28
1000–9999	13	34
10,000–29,999	13	15
30000 +	70	15
Members as % of paid labor force	20	22
Type of plans (total: 15,308)	8	92
Plan assets as % of reserves held in all major retirement programs in Canada[1]	44	22

Source: Author's calculations, Statistics Canada (1998a, Tables 2 and 3); Statistics Canada (1998b, Tables 3 for the public and private sectors); Statistics Canada (1998d, Table A).
[1]Based on author's calculations using available data from 1996 (Statistics Canada 1998d, Table A). The public sector numerator was obtained by adding assets held in two subcategories of registered pension plans—trusteed public sector plans and government consolidated revenue funds; the private sector numerator was based on the remaining assets held in registered pension plans. The denominator is the sum of all monies invested in the Canada and Quebec Pension Plans, registered pension plans and registered retirement savings plans.

pension plans in Canada).[3] Historically, pension coverage rates for the paid workforce have varied in the range of 42 to 45 percent since 1983 (Statistics Canada 1996, 1997, 1998a). Pension plan membership was evenly divided between the public and private sectors as indicated in Table 1, with covered public sector employees representing only a slightly smaller proportion of the paid work force and of active pension plan members at the beginning of 1997. Table 1 also shows that close to two thirds (63 percent) of public sector pension plan members are employed by provincial governments or enterprises. And most public sector plan members are probably covered by a collective agreement. In 1998, 76 percent of Canadian public sector employees were covered by a collective agreement; the comparable figure was 24 percent for private sector workers (Akyeampong 1998).[4]

Male employees represent a minority of plan members in the public sector while the opposite is true of private sector pension plans, according to the figures presented in Table 1. Yet these numbers mask gender differences in changing membership patterns over time (Statistics Canada 1996, 1997, 1998a). The overall number of active members in Canadian employer or union sponsored pensions rose from 1984 to 1992, largely due to the increase in the number of women covered by plans. This is, in turn, a reflection of the growing labor force participation of women and legislation extending pension coverage to part-time employees. Since that time, the increase in female membership has not offset the decline in male membership, so that overall membership fell from 5.3 million in 1992 to 5.1 million in 1997. The decline in male membership occurred primarily in the private sector from 1992 to 1994, but since 1993 the decrease has been more prominent in the public sector as male civil servants and defense employees accepted early retirement packages in the face of large-scale government rationalization programs. As a consequence, public sector plans have experienced a 5 percent fall in membership from 1993 to 1997, while private sector plans have seen little variation in membership levels during this same period.

Despite the relative importance of public sector plans as suggested by the membership figures above, they represent less than one tenth of all Canadian registered pension plans in 1997 (see Table 1). This is better understood if considered concurrently with data on membership distribution by plan size. With the help of Table 1, it can be seen that a majority of public employees are covered by large pension plans, notably those with more than 30,000 members. The pattern is quite different for the private sector, with 71 percent of members in plans with fewer than 10,000 active employees. In 1997, plans with 30,000 members or more numbered 19, and 13 of these covered public sector workers (Statistics Canada 1998a).

Perhaps the most telling statistics testifying to the prominence of public employee pension plans is the relative proportion of assets held by these plans. As indicated in Table 1, public pensions held 44 percent of the aggregate book value of monies held in all major retirement income programs in Canada, which totaled $804 billion at the end of 1996. Although figures are only indicative, this proportion is twice as big as that held by private sector plans. The relative gap is even wider when one compares the market value of assets invested by the 100 largest Canadian public and private pension plans. At the end of 1997, public sector plans ranking in the top 100 held reserves that were approximately three times as large as those of private sector plans in the same group.[5]

Characteristics of Public and Private Sector Pensions

General characteristics. Most workers whose employers offered a pension at the beginning of 1997 were required to participate in the plan. Voluntary participation was an option for only 5 percent of public sector employees and 14 percent of private sector employees covered by a pension plan (see Table 2). On the other hand, a little over half of all public sector employees in Canada are members of plans that impose no eligibility requirements

TABLE 2. General Characteristics of Public and Private Sector Pension Plans, Canada 1997 (percent of members)

	Public (2,419,022 members)	Private (2,696,268 members)
Total members, plans with compulsory participation	50	50
Compulsory participation in sector	95	86
Total members, plans with no eligibility conditions	54	46
No eligibility conditions in sector	54	41
Total members, defined contribution plans	17	83
Defined contribution plans in sector	4	18
Total members, defined benefit plans	52	48
Defined benefit plans in sector	95	80

Source: Author's calculations, Statistics Canada (1998b, Tables 10–12).

and they, in turn, represent a slight majority of members in all pension plans with no eligibility restrictions.

The continued dominance of defined benefit plans in Canada is evident from overall pension membership figures and the relative importance of assets held by these plans. At the beginning of 1997, 87 percent of employer or union sponsored pension plan members belonged to defined benefit plans (Statistics Canada 1998a, Table 7). And according to *Benefits Canada* magazine, 75 of the top 100 pension plans in terms of assets held were classified as defined benefit plans in 1997 (Bak 1998a).[6] These figures appear more telling than the fact that defined benefit plans represented 45 percent of employer or union sponsored pensions. Despite the persistence of defined benefit plans, overall membership in such plans declined five percent from 1993 to 1997, largely due to public sector employee staff cuts (Statistics Canada 1998a). In contrast, membership in defined contribution plans increased 25 percent during the same period.

Defined benefit plans are especially popular in the public sector, accounting for 95 percent of the sector's plan members (see Table 2) but only 3 percent of all employer or union sponsored pension plans in 1997 (Statistics Canada 1998b, Table 12). Yet it is interesting to note that six of the 50 largest defined contribution plans in Canada identified by *Benefits Canada* are public sector plans (listing for the year ending December 31, 1997; Bak 1998b).[7] And four of these six plans rank as the top four defined contribution plans in all of Canada, in terms of assets held. Furthermore, the top three defined contribution plans were large enough to be included in *Benefits Canada*'s listing of the 100 largest pension plans, which includes plans of all types.[8]

Specific characteristics. On the basis of information presented in Table 3, it is difficult to conclude that the overall generosity of plans is higher in one sector relative to the other. On the one hand, public sector pension members

TABLE 3. Specific Plan Characteristics of Public and Private Pensions, Canada
1997 (percent of members)

	Public	*Private*
Vesting		
Immediate	2	4
2 years of service	35	24
5 years of service	14	9
10 years of service	6	—
2 years of participation	35	56
Normal retirement		
Age 60	14	2
Age 65	81	91
Special retirement conditions[1]	87	46
Age 55	24	6
Age 60	11	32
Age 62	—	13
Service 30 or more	27	17
Age + service 80 or 85	9	14
Age + service 90	18	5
Early retirement permitted[1]	99	100
Age 55	80	89
Service < 20	44	38
Age + service 90	21	—
No postponed retirement permitted	24	11
Spousal benefit-death before retirement		
None	0	0.2
Contributions	10	8
60 or 100% of commuted value	26	75
60% or less of accrued pension	34	6
Disability benefit provided	65	41

Source: Author's calculations, Statistics Canada (1998b, Tables 24–31, 36).
[1]More than one condition may apply. Special retirement means no reduction in pension.

appear to be subject to slightly more stringent vesting requirements than
are private plan employees, and the proportion of members belonging to
public sector plans that do not permit postponed retirement is somewhat
greater than twice that of private sector plans. Only a very small fraction of
the private sector workforce are in plans that do not offer spousal benefits
in case of death before retirement, as compared to public sector employees; nevertheless the means of determining benefit amounts differs between
the sectors. The provision of early retirement benefits is universal in both
sectors.

TABLE 4. Design Features of Public and Private Defined Benefit Pensions, Canada
1997 (percent of members)

	Public	Private
Benefit formula		
Flat benefit	0.1	41
Earnings-based	99.9	59
Final average earnings	4	6
3 years	24	24
5 years	74	69
other	2	7
Average best earnings	93	69
3 years	5	24
5 years	74	74
other	21	2
career	3	26
% Earnings per yr of service	98[1]	52[1]
<1.25	1	6
1.25–1.74	1	35
1.75–2.00	98	56
>2.00	—	3
Automatic adjustment of pension to CPI	80	17
Full increase	37	7
Partial increase	56	80
Spousal benefit death after retirement		
60% of initial benefit (with reduction)	30	79
50 or 60% of initial benefit (with no reduction)	53	11
Benefit integrated with C/QPP[2]	96	82

Source: Author's calculations, Statistics Canada (1998b, Tables 13, 20, 21, 32, 38).
[1] Includes defined benefit/defined contribution combination plans
[2] Defined benefit plans based on percentage of earnings. CPP is the Canada Pension Plan, the government sponsored retirement program for Canadians living outside of Quebec. Quebec has an equivalent program called the Quebec Pension Plan or QPP.

On the other hand, a larger share of employees covered by public sector pensions than private sector plans have a lower normal retirement age. Fourteen percent of public plan members have a normal retirement age of 60; the respective figure for the private sector is only 2 percent. Perhaps the most prominent difference between the two sectors is the much higher proportion of plan members that can benefit from special retirement conditions (i.e., no pension reduction) in the public sector (87 percent) as compared to their counterparts working for private firms offering pensions (46 percent).

Defined benefit plan features. More marked differences between public and private sector plan provisions are evident from data presented in Table 4, which focus on defined benefit plan features. The benefit formula used in public sector pensions is virtually always earnings-based, whereas two-fifths of private sector members are covered by plans that offer flat dollar benefits. A higher proportion of public sector membership (93 percent) is covered by pay-based plans that use the average of best earnings to calculate retirement benefits, as compared to private sector plan membership covered by such plans (69 percent). A little more that a quarter of private sector employees are members of pay-based plans that use career earnings to determine retirement benefits, but only approximately 5 percent of pension members in both sectors are covered by pay-based plans that rely on final average earnings to calculate benefit amounts.

Public and private plan benefit formulas also vary in the percentage of earnings recognized per year of service; this percentage is between 1.75 and 2.00 for the overwhelming majority (98 percent) of public employee plan members. Yet only 56 percent of private sector workers are members of plans that use a similar multiplier in their benefit formula, with most of the remaining private sector employees belonging to plans using lower multipliers.

Fully four-fifths of public sector membership is covered by pensions that include an automatic pension adjustment, and in over a third of these cases retired employees receive post-retirement adjustments equal to the consumer price index (CPI). The situation is quite different in the private sector, where only 17 percent of employees are members of plans providing full or partial inflation protection. However, a larger proportion of private sector workers are covered by plans providing spousal benefits in case of the retiree's death. The percentage of employees in both sectors that are members of pensions offering benefit integration with the Canadian government-sponsored retirement program, the Canadian Pension Plan (CPP), or its Quebec equivalent, the Quebec Pension Plan (QPP), is relatively high, though integration is more prevalent in the public than in the private sector.

In sum, information on defined benefit plans summarized in Table 4 suggests that public sector employees covered by such plans have relatively more generous benefits than their private sector counterparts. One possible explanation for this outcome is that most public sector employees are required to contribute to their pension plans as discussed below.

Financing Public and Private Sector Pensions

Contributions. Virtually all public sector employees in Canada are members of contributory pension plans, as is shown in Table 5. The vast majority of these workers is required to pay more than 5 percent of their annual earnings into their pension funds, with some three-quarters of them contributing 7 percent or more. In contrast, only half of all workers employed by private firms offering pensions are required to contribute to their plans and

TABLE 5. Contributions to Public and Private Sector Plans

	Public	Private
Employee contributions required (% of members)	99.6	49
% of earnings		
<5.0	3	27
5.0–6.9	19	47
>6.9	77	1
% of contributions made by employer (total ER		
contributions 1996: $12.4 B)	57	75
Current service	88	77
Actuarial deficiencies and unfunded liabilities	12	23

Source: Author's calculations. Data on employer contributions from Statistics Canada (1998a, Table 6 are for 1996); data on employee contributions from Statistics Canada (1998b, Table 14 are for the reference period January 1, 1997).

approximately three quarters of them pay less than 7 percent of annual earnings in contributions.

The actual dollar value of contributions made by both employers and employees in 1996 totaled $19.6 billion, 63 percent of which was made by employers (Statistics Canada 1998a). Table 5 indicates that public sector employers paid a lower proportion of overall plan contributions relative to their private sector counterparts, a statistic that reflects the fact that all but a few public sector plans require employee contributions.

Employer contributions in both sectors are largely used to fund current service pension obligations, though the proportion of contributions devoted by private sector employers to actuarial deficiencies and unfunded liabilities was almost twice as high as that of private sector employers in 1996. However, data on pension liabilities are not generally available in Canada, so the latter discrepancy is difficult to explain. There have been recent reports of large pension surpluses in some highly visible pension plans in both sectors, but it is not known how general this phenomenon is. As such, one as yet untested explanation for the higher percentage of employer contributions allocated to funding deficiencies in the private sector might be stricter legislative funding requirements for private sector employers.

Investment strategies. Data from pension plans that operate according to the terms of a trust agreement provide a good portrait of investment activity by employer or union sponsored registered pension plans (RPP) in both the public and private sectors. Reserves held by trusteed pension plans accounted for two-thirds of RPP book value assets in Canada in 1996 ($3.5 of the $5.3 billion RPP assets) and 90 percent of RPP monies invested in financial markets (Statistics Canada 1998d, Table A). The share of trusteed pension plan reserves deposited with public sector plans was 61 percent

TABLE 6. Asset Allocation of Trusteed Public and Private Sector Plans, Canada
1986–96 (percent of market value)

	Year					
	1986	*1988*	*1990*	*1992*	*1994*	*1996*
Public sector						
Bonds	53.9	50.1	52.3	49.0	39.5	30.5
Stocks	24.2	25.2	25.0	30.5	34.3	37.2
Mortgages	5.7	5.5	4.2	3.1	2.4	1.7
Pooled vehicles	2.2	2.0	2.0	4.3	11.1	21.0
Other	14.0	17.2	16.5	13.1	12.7	9.5
Private sector						
Bonds	35.0	34.3	36.4	36.9	33.1	31.6
Stocks	38.2	36.6	34.4	39.0	38.1	39.5
Mortgages	4.0	3.5	3.5	3.3	2.3	1.7
Pooled vehicles	9.1	9.4	9.9	10.5	16.0	18.4
Other	13.6	16.1	15.9	10.3	10.4	8.9

Source: Statistics Canada (1998d, Table G).

($2.1 billion, book value) in 1996 (Statistics Canada 1998d, Table A). Almost
all of the remaining public sector fund assets ($1.4 billion), which account
for a large share of RPP monies not covered by trust agreements, are held
under consolidated revenue arrangements. The latter funds, sponsored by
the federal government and some of their provincial counterparts, have no
invested assets as such, so that pension plan contributions are included in
government revenue and used for general expenditures.

The largest portion of trusteed public sector assets is held by provincial
governments and enterprises ($1.5 of $2.1 billion or 72 percent). The respective shares of the municipal and federal government subsectors are 25
percent and 3 percent (Statistics Canada 1998d, Statistical Table 5).

Trusteed public sector pension fund investment strategy has shifted considerably since 1990, so that by 1996 it resembled that of private sector funds
as indicated in Table 6. Until 1990 public sector funds had a stock to bond
investment ratio of about 0.5; this ratio reached a value greater than one
for the first time in 1996, a figure more closely resembling the traditional
stock-to-bond ratio of private sector plans. Data for 1997 (based on book
value of assets) and the second quarter of 1998 (based on market value of assets) indicate that the trend in the stock-to-bond investment ratios of public
and private sector plans has been maintained; plans in both sectors had a
stock-to-bond ratio equal to or greater than one during the period (Statistics
Canada 1998c, Table 10; Statistics Canada 1999, Table 6).

Other notable portfolio investment shifts that occurred from 1986 to 1996
in public sector pension plans are also evident for private sector plans, as is

seen in Table 6. These changes include a rise in the proportion of assets invested in pooled vehicles, and a decline in the proportion held in mortgages and other assets. The general trend for the "other asset" category masks a difference in investment strategies between the public and private sectors, however; the former has historically allocated a greater portion of its portfolio to real estate (Statistics Canada 1998c). The respective shares of total assets at market value invested in real estate in 1996 was 3 percent for public sector plans and 1.6 for the private sector (Statistics Canada 1998d, Statistical Table 6). While rising stock prices explain some of the change in the public sector plan investment mix since the early 1990s, portfolio shifts by a few large public sector funds in the provinces of British Columbia (from 1992 to 1994) and Alberta (1994 to 1996) have probably also influenced asset allocation (Statistics Canada 1998d).

A 20 percent foreign investment cap is imposed on Canadian pension funds by legislation. Against this cap, recent trends indicate that pension plan investors have increased their exposure outside Canada to profit from rising stock prices in external markets. According to Statistics Canada (1999), the share of book value assets invested by trusteed pension plans has risen steadily from below 6 percent before 1990 to just over 16.7 percent by June 1998; the corresponding market value figure was 19 percent. In contrast to the distribution of domestic holdings, stocks and pooled funds (largely equities) accounted for 93 percent of foreign assets but 41 percent of nonforeign pension fund investments at the end of the second quarter of 1998; the corresponding percentages of foreign and domestic portfolios held in bonds were 6 and 44 for the same period.

Based on 1996 figures, it appears that trusteed public and private sector plan investors were behaving similarly with regard to their degree of exposure to foreign markets, with both public and private sector plans holding 16.6 percent of their respective assets (market value) outside Canada (Statistics Canada 1998d, Table G). *Benefits Canada*'s survey suggests the top 100 Canadian funds have an average of 20.9 percent of assets allocated to foreign investments for the year ending December 31, 1997 (Bak 1998a). Apparently, funds use derivative products to gain foreign market exposure making the legislated limit an artificial one.

Conclusion

Canadian public sector plan membership represented a slightly smaller portion of overall pension members and the paid work force than private sector members at the beginning of 1997. Yet public employee plan reserves were twice as large as those held by the private sector, as a percentage of assets held in all major retirement programs in Canada. Public sector plan assets represent a larger share of pension reserves than private sector plans even if monies held by government consolidated revenue funds are ignored; in 1996 public pensions held $2.1 of the $3.5 billion (book value) invested by all trusteed pension plans. The latter hold most of the pension monies invested in financial markets in Canada. As a consequence, public pension plans must be said to be major players in the Canadian pension market.

Defined benefit pension plans are still the dominant plan type in Canada with 95 percent of public employee pension members belonging to such plans at the beginning of 1997. The more generous benefits offered by public sector plans are probably related to the fact that virtually all members are required to contribute to their pension plans. Finally, the investment strategy of public pension plans shifted dramatically in the early 1990s, so that today it generally resembles that of their private sector counterparts.

Notes

1. The number of public sector plans (as of December 31, 1997) is based on the author's estimate and differs from the figure of 63 reported by *Benefits Canada*. The discrepancy is probably due to differences in classifying plans whose employees formerly worked for crown corporations that have been privatized in recent years. Similarly, the author identifies fifty-seven public sector plans among the top 100 pension plans as of December 1998, though *Benefits Canada* (Press 1999) continues to report 63 such plans. Note that 1997 data is reported in the paper to enhance comparability across the various data sources used in the text.

2. This share rose slightly to 48 percent of total market value assets of $432.3 billion, by the end of 1998. Throughout the paper, dollars are reported at the current value for the year indicated and in Canadian dollars.

3. Paid workers exclude the self-employed, unpaid family workers, and the unemployed.

4. Some caution should be exercised in extrapolating unionization levels to public and private sector workers covered by pension plans. An exhaustive comparison of definitions used to identify public and private sector workers by the different Statistics Canada divisions charged with gathering data on pensions and union coverage has not been attempted. Yet, on the surface, it appears that unionization data for the public sector is fairly representative since the universe of public sector workers covered by pensions closely resembles that of public sector employees overall. The same cannot be said of private sector employees.

5. Author's calculations using asset values reported for 1997 in *Benefits Canada* (1998a). Public sector plans held $293,683 million versus $103,773 million for private plans.

6. Figure is based on 91 plans reporting their defined benefit/defined contribution status. Data for 1998 suggest that 69 of the 86 top 100 plans reporting their defined benefit/defined contribution status were defined benefit plans (Press 1999).

7. Based on author's estimate since Bak (1998b) does not identify public sector plans in the listing.

8. Among the top 100 plans, the Co-operative Superannuation Society of Saskatchewan and the Saskatchewan Public Employees Superannuation Funds ranked 47th and 48th, while the University of British Columbia Faculty Plan ranked 93rd in terms of asset size for the year ending December 31, 1997.

References

Akyeampong, Earnest B. 1998. "Selected Union Statistics: Special 1998 Labour Day Release." *Perspectives on Labour and Income.* Ottawa: Minister of Industry, Catalogue no. 75-001-XPE.

Bak, Lori. 1998a. "The 1998 Top 100." *Benefits Canada* (April): 28–43.

———. 1998b. "Top 50 Defined Contribution Plans." *Benefits Canada* (June): 57–64.

Press, Kevin. 1999. "The Top 100 Pension Funds of 1999." *Benefits Canada* (April): 19–32.

Statistics Canada. 1996. *Canada's Retirement Income Programs: A Statistical Overview.* Ottawa: Labour Division, Catalogue no. 74-507-XPB.

———. 1997. *Pension Plans in Canada, January 1, 1996.* Ottawa: Labour Division, Catalogue no. 74-401-XPB.

———. 1998a. *Pension Plans in Canada: Statistical Highlights and Key Tables, January 1, 1997.* Ottawa, Canada: Income Statistics Division, Catalogue no. 74-401-SDB.

———. 1998b. *Pension Plans in Canada, January 1, 1997.* Ottawa, Canada: Income Statistics Division, Catalogue no. 74C0002. (Supplemental statistics to 1998a, which are supplied on request for the public and private sectors separately.)

———. 1998c. *Quarterly Estimates of Trusteed Pension Funds: Fourth Quarter 1997.* Ottawa: Income Statistics Division, Catalogue no. 74-001-XPB.

———. 1998d. *Trusteed Pension Funds: Financial Statistics 1996.* Ottawa: Income Statistics Division, Catalogue no. 74-201-XPB.

———. 1999. *Quarterly Estimates of Trusteed Pension Funds: Second Quarter 1998.* Ottawa, Canada: Income Statistics Division, Catalogue no. 74-001-XPB.

II
Investment Policies, Regulation, and Reporting

Chapter 6
Regulation and Taxation of Public Plans
A History of Increasing Federal Influence

Roderick B. Crane

The origin of pension plans in the United States is often traced to the end of the nineteenth and the early part of the twentieth centuries (Allen et al. 1992). It was during this time that both private and public employers began to examine ways to provide for the economic welfare of employees after the conclusion of their working careers. These pension plans, sponsored by such entities as American Can and B&O Railroad, and the early pension plans for teachers and public safety officers, were generally not established under any mandate or initiative from the federal level. Instead, employers were primarily responding to a combination of concerns about social responsibility and the normal forces of existing economic competition and organized labor.

Although the federal income tax laws in the first half of this century did provide some special tax treatments to pension contributions and benefits, it was the Social Security Act of 1935 that marked the first major entrance of the federal government into the arena of national retirement policy.[1] It took many years, however, before the federal government would begin to exercise its authority into the area of the substantive design and operations of employer-provided retirement benefit plans, and even longer before the federal government involved itself in state and local government pension plans.

The U.S. Congress did not focus on the employer-provided pension system in a substantive way until 1974, with the passage of the Employee Retirement Income Security Act of 1974 (ERISA). ERISA required only private sector retirement plans to satisfy minimum coverage, participation, vesting, funding, and fiduciary requirements as a means of improving retirement

TABLE 1. Recent Federal Laws Affecting Public Pension Plans (1987–97)

Law	Impact
Americans with Disabilities Act (ADA)	Restricts ability to limit retirement and disability benefits for protected disabilities.
Uniformed Services Employment and Reemployment Rights Act (USERRA)	Establishes protections for retirement benefits for qualified military service.
Omnibus Budget Reconciliation Act of 1990	Requires state and local government employee coverage in a retirement plan or Social Security.
Age Discrimination in Employment Act (ADEA)	ADEA: Prohibits pension discrimination on the basis of age.
Older Workers Benefit Protection Act (OWBPA)	OWBPA: Extends ADEA age discrimination protection to disability and other nonpension benefits.
Unemployment Compensation Amendments Act of 1992	Imposes 20 percent withholding on eligible rollover distributions not directly rolled over to an eligible plan.
Small Business Job Protection Act of 1996	Requires trust protections for §457 plans.

Source: Author's tabulations.

income security for plan participants. ERISA also established an insurance program for terminating underfunded defined benefit plans.[2]

Since the passage of ERISA, federal laws and regulations have grown to be a powerful influence on how state and local government retirement plans are designed and operated in the United States. As the remainder of this chapter shall demonstrate, this influence can be found in a combination of places, including federal tax, workplace, and civil rights protection laws. Recent federal legislation illustrating this point is summarized in Table 1.

The States' Rights Doctrine and Public Pension Plans

The fact that federal influence has become so strong over state and local pension plans can be credited, in part, to the erosion of what legal experts call the "states' rights" doctrine. Under the states' rights doctrine, experts see the U.S. Constitution as creating a federal government with specified and limited powers, and all other powers reserved to the states.[3] This theory of constitutional government limits the central government powers and it has guided U.S. legal doctrine for most of this country's history. Its purpose is to protect state and federal governments from significant federal regulation and interference, except in the arena of interstate commerce and national defense.

Evidence of the original force of the states' rights barrier in the public pension arena can be demonstrated clearly by two examples. First, employees of state and local governments were excluded from coverage in the original Social Security Act. Second, state and local governments were specifically excluded from the requirements of the Employees Retirement Income Security Act of 1974.

Erosion of the States' Rights Shield

Nevertheless, over time, state and local governments' ability to assert states' rights as a shield from federal regulatory authority has been steadily eroded since the passage of ERISA. Several decisions of the U.S. Supreme Court — most notably, *National League of Cities v. Usery* (1976) and *Garcia v. San Antonio Metropolitan Transit Authority* (1985) — clearly established the ability of the federal government to indirectly affect the business of state and local governments through the federal income tax and interstate commerce powers. In a more recent case, *State of Michigan v. Davis* (1989), the Court stated the Equal Protection Clause of the federal Constitution also extended its authority to affect public employer retirement systems.

This shift away from states' rights has continued over the last twenty to thirty years, producing an expansion of federal laws, workplace and civil rights laws that has directly influenced almost every aspect of public pension benefits, funding, investment and administration policy.

Recent Supreme Court cases limiting federal power to force state action and upholding principles of constitutional federalism and states' rights concepts have focused on other subject areas (e.g., gun control) and have not yet been used by the states to limit federal intervention in employee benefits issues.[4] On the contrary, a strong example of the willingness of the federal government to impose substantive benefits requirements on public plans can be illustrated by the massive federal legislative efforts in the health benefits arena (e.g., the Health Insurance Portability and Accountability Act of 1996 and related laws). That state and local governments have not challenged this federal intervention gives some indication as to the potential weakness of the states' rights doctrine in the retirement arena. In the remainder of this chapter, we will summarize the major areas of federal laws that have influenced the design and administration of state and local government retirement plans.

The Impact of Past and Prospective
Social Security Legislation

For most public employees, social security has and will continue to be a major source of retirement income (EBRI 1997b); currently about three-fourths of public employees are covered (see Mitchell et al. this volume). Social security provides retirement, disability, and survivor benefits to insured workers and their dependents. Insured workers are eligible for full retirement benefits at ages 65 to 67 (depending on the member's year of birth) and reduced benefits at age 62. Social security retirement benefits are based on the worker's age and career earnings, are fully indexed for inflation after retirement, and replace a relatively higher proportion of the final year's wages for low earners. Social security's primary source of revenue is the 12.40 percent of payroll tax (up to a cap) under the old age, survivors, and disability insurance portion of the payroll tax paid by employers and employees.

When first adopted in 1935, the Social Security Act excluded state and local employees from coverage, largely because public employees very often already had their own retirement systems. Equally important, at that time Congress was concerned about the constitutionality of imposing a federal tax on state governments. Voluntary participation in social security was added to the act in 1950. This permitted state and local employers that did not offer a public retirement system to elect to participate in social security. In what came to be known as the Section 218 Agreements (named after the section of the social security law permitting voluntary participation), state and local governments were thereafter allowed to elect social security coverage for their employees. Section 218 Agreements can cover all public employees in a state, or only specified groups of employees. Section 218 was amended in 1954 to permit coverage of most employees participating in a public retirement system.

Prior to 1983, public employers were permitted to withdraw from social security once they were covered, but that policy was reversed in that year. Currently, most (96 percent) of the nation's workforce, including three-fourths of the state and local government workforce, is now covered by social security. This leaves about five million state and local government employees not covered by social security, with police, firefighters, and teachers most likely to be in noncovered positions.

Under the Omnibus Budget Reconciliation Act of 1991 (OBRA), employees of state and local governments not previously covered by any retirement plan were required to participate in social security. (The social security system also covers individuals in the military and other uniformed services.)

The social security program has had many direct and indirect impacts on the design of state and local government retirement plans. These include the fact that public pension plans for employees without social security coverage have tended to provide greater retirement benefits than other plans for employees with social security coverage (cf. Mitchell, Myers, and Young 1999). Also, some public employees, such as firefighters and police, may not be covered by social security because of their need for earlier retirement and their need for greater death and disability protections. It is also likely that raising the social security normal retirement age will create pressure for greater benefits from state and local governments to fill in the "benefits gaps." For those social security employers with plans with earlier normal retirement ages, many have implemented special "bridge" benefits to help employees afford to retire before social security eligibility (The Segal Company 1997).

Recently, a variety of proposals addressing the financial solvency of the social security system have emerged that would further extend federal influence over state and local retirement plans (Mitchell et al. this volume). Virtually all of these proposals involve mandating social security coverage for new hires in the public sector. If mandatory social security coverage were enacted, public sector employers would have to choose between higher total contributions to fund the existing level of pension benefits, or lower benefits to keep costs level. Other specific benefits design concerns may also arise as a result of the social security reform process. One of these concerns is that social security benefits are intentionally redistributive, paying proportionately more to low than high paid employees; therefore, public employers not covered by social security will need to decide whether to keep benefit levels equal for all employment groups, or have a tiered system with different benefit levels for new hires.

Governmental employers would be trading a secure actuarially-funded system for a system that is not funded in advance (pay-as-you-go funding). Further, social security does not have plans to target specific groups of workers (i.e., fire and police, judges, legislators). These groups do not currently exist in the Social Security benefit structure. Making all of the groups "whole" will certainly be expensive. Financially, state and local government plans are, in the main, fairly well funded (Mitchell et al this volume); a conversion to Social Security would undermine this funding status.

The Impact of the Employee Retirement Income Security Act of 1974

As noted previously, the Employee Retirement Income Security Act of 1974, as amended (P.L. 93-406), is the federal law that regulates private sector employee retirement benefit plans. Its substantive requirements are divided into four titles:

Title I. Requires pension, profit sharing and stock bonus plans to meet specific minimum requirements as to participation, coverage, vesting, funding, fiduciary standards, and reporting and disclosure.

Title II. If the plan meets the conditions of availability of the minimum participation, vesting and funding standards of Title I of ERISA, certain tax benefits for employees and employers can be obtained.

Title III. Contains provisions regarding administration and enforcement of the ERISA requirements.

Title IV. Creates the Pension Benefit Guaranty Corporation (PBGC), a government entity that insures protection for defined benefit plans that terminate without sufficient assets.

State and local government plans enjoy a general exemption from most of the substantive requirements of ERISA. Thus, Title I reporting and disclosure, participation, funding, vesting and fiduciary responsibility standards do not apply to governmental plans (ERISA §4(b)). The Title II amendments to the tax code largely do not apply to government plans through specific exemptions. The Title IV defined benefit plan termination insurance provisions do not apply to government plans (ERISA §4021(b)).

A "government plan" is defined as "a plan established or maintained for its employees by the Government of the United States, by the government of any State or political subdivision thereof, or by any agency or instrumentality of any of the foregoing" (ERISA §3(32)).

While ERISA does not directly govern the retirement plans of state and local governments, its requirements do affect public pensions in an indirect but important way. As the following discussion illustrates, ERISA influences the design and administration of government plans in areas ranging from investment and fiduciary standards to pension rights of surviving spouses.

ERISA's impact on public plan governance and investments. ERISA established that, for purposes of federal law, those persons managing the benefits and assets of qualified retirement plans are fiduciaries and, therefore, must act in that capacity under a "prudent person" standard of conduct. Since the passage of ERISA, the prudent person rule has come to be expected as the necessary high standard of care and responsibility for public pension plan managers as well (Moore 1995).

Public plan trustees recognize that similar prudence standards apply to them through the application of the trust provisions of their plans and that of general state laws governing trusts. Thus, public plan trustees have significantly adapted the diversification and monitoring requirements of the "modern portfolio theory" in the private sector. The importance of having uniform trust and fiduciary standards for state and local plans was underscored by the National Conference of Commissioners of Uniform State Laws (NCCUSL), which has drafted and promoted the Uniform Management of

Public Employees Retirement Systems Act (UMPERSA). UMPERSA, if enacted by a state, would hold public plan fiduciaries to ERISA-style fiduciary standards of care and reporting and disclosure requirements for most state and local government retirement plans.[5]

ERISA's impact on public plan design. ERISA has also had an impact on the way governmental plans design their benefit policies. Consider policies regarding the vesting of pension benefits: the five-year or three- to seven-year graded vesting requirements of ERISA have been adopted by most of the public sector. In many cases, governmental plans have been adopting even more rapid vesting schedules than those required by ERISA (Mitchell et al. this volume).

Governmental plans, however, have had a mixed experience with regard to the so-called "break in service" rules. Many government plans recognize all prior service of returning employees, usually only crediting such service on the repayment of withdrawn distributions. Some plans of old design, particularly the "relief association" plans for firefighters, maintain lengthy vesting requirements (e.g., twenty-year continuous service cliff vesting). In addition, while not allowed for ERISA plans, governmental defined benefit plans still tend to provide for the forfeiture of all employer-funded vested benefits if the employee withdraws his or her own contributions upon termination.

ERISA's impact on public plan survivor benefits. ERISA requires that pension plans provide post-retirement qualified joint and survivor annuities (QJSAs) to married members as the standard form of benefit unless another form is consented to by the spouse. ERISA also requires qualified preretirement survivor annuities (QPSAs). Both of these survivor benefits have found their way into a large number of government plans, although they have not been uniformly adopted within the governmental sector.

ERISA's impact on public plan qualified domestic relations orders. Private sector plans are required under ERISA to honor judicial domestic relations orders dividing retirement benefits between the member and a former spouse and dependent children. These provisions have not always been accepted in the government pension community. Some state and local governments have accepted the standard ERISA rules, or some variation of them, while other have refused to recognize them at all.

ERISA's impact on public plan funding. Although minimum funding standards of ERISA do not apply to governmental plans, they have cast a spotlight on the public plan funding status. Partly as a result of this federal government scrutiny there is increased pressure to adequately fund governmental plans. Along with other forces referred to by Munnell and Sunden, as well as Mitchell et al. (this volume), state and local government pension plans have benefited from greatly improved financing over the last twenty years.

The Influence of Federal Income Tax Laws on Public Sector Pension Plans

The federal government has had an uneven but growing influence on state and local government retirement plans through the federal income tax authority. The original provisions of the Internal Revenue Code (IRC) of 1954, §401 in particular, required only limited regulation, requiring only that "qualified" retirement plans must meet certain trust requirements for the holding of assets, certain vesting requirements on termination of a plan, and that at least some funding of liabilities must occur. These early tax rules applied equally to both private and public sector plans. Until the passage of ERISA in 1974, the retirement plans of state and local governments largely operated without specific regard to these §401 requirements. While many did comply with the trust requirements and significant actuarial funding of benefits did take place, it was not because of the influence of the federal Internal Revenue Code. Although ERISA did mark an increase in federal involvement in private sector retirement plans, it left the public sector mostly untouched as the shield of states' rights continued to protect public plans from direct federal government regulation.

Tax Reform Act of 1986. It was not until the Tax Reform Act of 1986 (TRA '86) that it became clear that the federal government was ready to use its taxing authority to influence state and local government plans and Congress showed its willingness to use tax laws for pension benefits to address both federal budget deficit and national retirement policy concerns. TRA '86 signaled a shift in federal income tax policy for governmental plans by clearly applying the IRC §415 limits on the amount of benefits that could be provided by qualified retirement plans to governmental entities.

Since that time, there has been a running battle between the federal and state and local governments over the extent to which the IRC qualified plan rules will be applied to governmental plans. Both sides have gained and lost ground over the years. The most significant area of debate has been the extent to which the IRC nondiscrimination rules of IRC §401 (limiting special benefits for highly paid employees) and the contribution and benefit limits of IRC §415. Table 2 provides a scorecard showing increases or decreases in federal regulation of governmental plans in recent major legislation in these and other areas.

Federal Workplace and Civil Rights Laws Affect Public Pension Plans

The impact of USERRA. The Uniformed Services Employment and Reemployment Rights Act of 1994 (USERRA) provided for a complete rewrite of the previous law governing reemployment rights of veterans of military service,

TABLE 2. Major Federal Laws Since 1986 Affecting Public Retirement Plans

Name of law	Significant changes	Increase/decrease in federal regulations
Tax Reform Act of 1986	Clearly imposed §415 rules on governmental plans	Increase
	Eliminated §401(k) plans for governmental entities	Increase
	Imposed §401(a)(9) required and minimum distribution rules	Increase
	Imposed §401(a)(17) compensation limits	Increase
	Created elective deferral limits and applied to §403(b) and coordinated with §457 plans	Increase
ADEA Amendments of 1987	Extended ADEA protections to governmental pension benefits	Increase
TAMRA of 1988	Allowed election to grandfather governmental qualified plan benefits above §415 limits, but imposed private sector limits for the future	Mixed, but overall an increase
	Clarified that §457 does not apply to bona fide leave programs	Decrease
OBRA 1990	Required employees not covered by a retirement plan to be covered by social security	Increase
OBRA 1993	Imposed mandatory 20 percent withholding and direct rollover rules	Increase
Small Business Job Protection	Allowed governmental §415 excess benefit plans	Decrease
Act of 1996	Eliminated §415(b) 100 percent of average compensation limit	Decrease
	Established trust requirements for §457 deferred compensation plans	Neutral
Taxpayer Relief Act of 1997	Liberalized service purchase contribution §415 limits for governmental plans	Decrease
	Granted permanent moratorium on application IRC nondiscrimination rules	Decrease

Source: Author's tabulations.

the Veterans Reemployment Rights Act (VRRA). While many of the provisions of USERRA restate the previous requirements of the VRRA, the new law provided clarification of how prior law should be interpreted and, in some areas, significantly expands the reemployment entitlements of veterans of military service.

All public and private employers are covered by the USERRA's requirements. The definition of employer is broadly defined and covers entities like employee benefit pension and health and welfare trusts, which may be independently responsible for meeting benefits reinstatement and benefit rights for the returning military service veteran.

USERRA impacts public retirement plans primarily by requiring that qualified military service cannot result in a break in service for retirement vesting and eligibility purposes, and that such service must count as covered service for vesting.

USERRA also requires that a returning veteran must be credited with all benefit accruals under a defined benefit plan and all employer contributions to a defined contribution plan as if he or she had not left the civilian job. USERRA applies to people who apply for reinstatement after the effective date of the act—December 12, 1994.

The impact of ADEA on public pension plans. The Age Discrimination in Employment Act (ADEA) was amended to apply to pension plans of governmental entities effective in 1988.

The ADEA and related laws generally prohibit covered employers from discriminating against persons who are forty years of age or older. ADEA permits governmental employers to impose a minimum hire age and a mandatory retirement age for firefighters and law enforcement officers if the age requirements are established under a bona fide hiring or retirement plan that is not a subterfuge to avoid the purposes of the ADEA. The public safety exemption does not allow an employer or retirement plan to discriminate as to eligibility or benefits if an employee is otherwise permitted to participate in the plan.

The ADEA does not allow governmental employers to exclude an employee from participating in a defined contribution plan on the basis of age before normal retirement age. For governmental defined benefit plans, the ADEA provides that an employee hired at an age that is more than five years before normal retirement age cannot be excluded from the plan unless it is cost-justified. ADEA provides that a defined benefit plan may not cease or curtail benefit accruals because of an employee's age.

The Older Workers Benefit Protection Act of 1990 (OWBPA) amended the ADEA to clarify that an employee benefit plan may not discriminate against an individual on the basis of age. The OWBPA is generally effective for governmental plans beginning October 1992.

The impact of other workplace laws on public pension plans. Other federal workplace laws affecting public pension plans include the Americans with Disabilities Act (ADA), the Family and Medical Leave Act (FMLA), and various gender discrimination laws. The ADA prohibits disability-based distinctions as to eligibility and benefits under employer-provided service retirement and disability retirement plans. A service retirement plan includes the usual defined benefit and defined contribution plans that are designed to provide lifetime income (an annuitized benefit) to employees after they have reached a specified age or a combination of a specified age and years of service. A disability retirement plan is a plan that is designed to provide lifetime income (an annuitized benefit) for an employee who is unable to work because of an illness or injury, without regard to the age of the employee. These benefits could be provided as an ancillary benefit within a pension or retirement plan or could be provided separately under an insurance arrangement. A qualified individual with a disability may not be denied eligibility or benefits under a service retirement or disability retirement plan. The following are examples of actions that would violate the ADA:

- Participation is denied in a disability retirement plan because of the disability;
- A participant is forced to take a lesser disability retirement benefit even if he or she has met the conditions to be paid a service retirement benefit; and
- The qualified individual has a longer waiting period before coverage under the service or disability retirement plan.

The treatment of FMLA leave for retirement and deferred compensation benefit purposes is unclear in some respects. The FMLA language provides that FMLA leave must be "treated as continued service (i.e., no break in service) for purposes of vesting and eligibility to participate." The FMLA regulatory language is generally interpreted to require at minimum that FMLA leave may not result in a loss of benefits that had been accrued before the FMLA leave began, nor can it cause the employee to lose eligibility to participate in the retirement plan.

Federal law addresses the issue of gender discrimination in the area of employee benefits in several areas, including:

Title VII of the Civil Rights Act of 1964. Generally prohibits sex discrimination with respect to an individual's "compensation, terms, conditions, or privileges of employment."

The Equal Pay Act of 1963. Prohibits gender-based discrimination as to wages for work involving equal skill, effort, responsibility, and working conditions.

The Pregnancy Discrimination Act of 1978. Clarifies the Title VII sex discrimination protections to ensure pregnancy-based discrimination is treated the same as sex-based distinctions.

These three federal laws addressing sex discrimination in employment and wages have been interpreted at various times by the courts and by the EEOC to prohibit discrimination as to fringe benefits, including retirement and deferred compensation benefits. Under these laws and regulations, a retirement or deferred compensation plan may not make sex- or pregnancy-based distinctions as to any feature of the plan, including eligibility, vesting/participation, contributions and benefits, and retirement age as well as benefit eligibility. Of these, the areas of contribution and benefit discrimination have seen the most judicial and regulatory activity. In several key cases, including *Los Angeles Department of Water and Power v. Manhart*, 435 U.S. 702 (1978) and *Arizona Governing Committee v. Norris*, 463 U.S. 1073 (1983), the requirements of Title VII have been interpreted to prohibit the use of sex-based actuarial tables to determine employee contributions to a defined benefit pension plan, and to prohibit the amount of benefits payable from a defined contribution plan to be determined using sex-based actuarial tables.

These cases make it clear that Title VII prohibits the classification of employees on the basis of sex for purposes of contribution and benefits. Public sector retirement plans have generally moved to using gender-neutral actuarial tables for contributions and benefit determination purposes. We note that because of state and local laws or contract rights that prohibit benefit reductions, the remedy for violations of Title VII has usually required "equalizing" benefits by bringing all employees up to the highest sex-based benefit formula.

These laws and cases do not prohibit the use of sex-based actuarial tables for purposes of employer contributions to defined benefit plans. Similarly, these laws do not prohibit retirement plans from requiring equal contributions regardless of sex from employees for either defined benefit or defined contribution plans.

Conclusions

The federal laws governing U.S. public pensions highlighted in this chapter are only some of the ways in which the federal government intervenes in how public sector employers perform their functions. In any event, it should be clear that federal regulation has directly and indirectly significantly influenced the design and operation of public sector pension plans in many ways. While the public sector pension community has seen some recent successes in limiting the impact of federal authority (such as in the area of IRC nondiscrimination rules and the §415 limits), it is likely that the large federal interest in national retirement policy acting through tax and workplace laws will continue to have its impact on public sector retirement plans in the future.

Notes

1. The Revenue Act of 1921, as well as amendments to the Internal Revenue Code in 1928, 1938, 1942, and 1954, established the exemption of interest income on pension plan assets from taxation and the deferral of tax to recipients, the employer deduction for contributions to such plans, and Trust and nondiscrimination requirements (EBRI, 1997a; see also Crane 1999).

2. Title IV of the Employee Retirement Income Security Act of 1974 created the Pension Benefit Guaranty Corporation (PBGC), which provides some employer-funded insurance programs to pay benefits of defined benefit plans terminating with insufficient assets to pay all account benefits. Governmental plans are not covered by this insurance program, leaving the risk of underfunding on the participants or the employer through its taxing authority.

3. See, e.g., *Gregory v. Ashcroft*, 501 U.S. 452 (1991).

4. See, e.g., *Printz v. United States*, 521 U.S. 898 (1997).

5. As of this writing, the UMPERSA had been introduced in whole or import only in two with no states having actually enacting it into law.

References

Allen, Everett T., Joseph J. Melone, Jerry S. Rosenbloom, and Jack L. VanDerhei. 1992. *Pension Planning: Pension, Profit Sharing, and Other Deferred Compensation Plans.* 7th ed. Homewood, Ill.: Irwin.

Crane, Roderick B. 1999. *Federal Workplace Laws Affecting Public-Sector Employee Benefit Programs.* Chicago: Government Finance Officers Association.

Employee Benefit Research Institute (EBRI). 1997a. *Fundamentals of Employee Benefit Programs.* 5th ed. Washington, D.C.: EBRI.

———. 1997b. "Integration of Defined Benefit Plans with Social Security". *EBRI Datebook on Employee Benefits.* 4th ed. Washington, D.C.: EBRI.

Mitchell, Olivia S., David McCarthy, Stanley C. Wisniewski, and Paul Zorn. This volume. "Developments in State and Local Pension Systems."

Mitchell, Olivia S., Robert J. Myers, and Howard Young, eds. 1999. *Prospects for Social Security Reform.* Pension Research Council. Philadelphia: University of Pennsylvania Press.

Moore, Cynthia L. 1995. *Protecting Retirees' Money: Fiduciary Duties and Other Laws Applicable to State Retirement Systems.* 3rd ed. Arlington, Va.: National Council on Teacher Retirement.

Munnell, Alicia H. and Annika Sundén. This volume. "Investment Practices of State and Local Pension Funds: Implications for Social Security Reform."

The Segal Company. 1997. "The Cost Impact of Mandating Social Security for State and Local Governments." New York: The Segal Company.

Chapter 7
Governance and Investments
of Public Pensions

Michael Useem and David Hess

Retirement funds for public employees in the United States are scattered
among more than 2,500 public pension plans. States supervise some, but
local municipalities manage most; a few oversee more than $100 billion in
assets, while most husband less than $1 billion.

Unlike the U.S. Social Security system, state and local retirement systems
do not operate a pay-as-you-go scheme. Rather, they compile contributions
from both governments and participants and then invest the assets until the
capital and its gains are later distributed to those in retirement. Those investment decisions are overseen by a governing board, and in that body the
public has placed its trust. If trustees fulfill their fiduciary responsibilities,
they ensure thousands of public employees a comfortable retirement and
hundreds of public officials a balanced budget. If they do not, they furnish
neither employees nor taxpayers what they are due.

Many state and local systems have modified their governance practices
and investment strategies during the past decade, and many will surely continue to do so. In response to intensifying pressures for greater board accountability, for instance, trustees have become more involved in allocating
their system's assets. And in response to surging stock markets in the United
States and expanding investment opportunities abroad, many have placed
more of those assets in equities and turned abroad. Public pension governance policies and their investment consequences should thus be viewed
dynamically, with the practices of many changing in response to shifting
political realities and market conditions.

In light of a growing debate over whether to allow a part of our national retirement system to be managed in much the same way, the evolving governing practices of public pensions can provide a useful model for what public
officials do when they have authority over retiree monies. From observing
how state and local officials oversee, allocate, and invest their retirement

assets, we might foresee how federal officials and trustees would behave if social security assets were placed in their hands. From past practices we can extract forecasts of future practices, and perhaps even best practices.

This chapter thus provides an analysis of public pension governance practices and investment strategies for the practical lessons they contain not only for policies of state and local systems, but also for anticipating what lies ahead if our social security system were to adopt a policy of placing retirement assets in capital markets.

Drawing on surveys of state and local systems during the 1990s, this chapter is divided into five main sections. In the first, we track the evolving governance practices from 1990 to 1996, and suggest where they are likely to move during the next several years. In the second, we follow their investment strategies over the same period. In the third section, we analyze the impact of the evolving governance practices on investment strategies. In the fourth, we examine how the governing practices have led some pension funds not only to buy stock in companies but also to render advice to them. And in a final section, we consider how the governing practices have affected the social and economic targeting of pension investments.

Sources of Information

We are fortunate to have good surveys of the nation's state and local retirement systems for the years of 1990, 1991, 1992, 1994, and 1996. The Public Pension Coordinating Council conducted the studies, and it sought to reach all of the major state and local systems in the United States. In 1996, for instance, the participating systems covered 81 percent of all plan members and held 81 percent of the $1.6 trillion under management by state and local pension systems. Since public officials know that the council makes the data on each fund available to the public, it is fair to assume that the responding officials perceived an incentive to furnish accurate and complete information (England 1996; General Accounting Office 1996; Mitchell and Carr 1996; Zorn 1998).

The number of state and local retirement systems participating in the several surveys and their asset holdings are displayed in Table 1. Signifying the highly skewed distribution of fund assets, the mean value of the holdings is some 10 times the median value. Signifying the surging economy and exuberant stock market in the latter half of the 1990s, the mean value of the assets under management during this seven-year period soared by two-thirds.

Retirement System Investment Strategies

The trustees of state and local retirement systems serve as fiduciaries for the beneficiaries' funds, but they have interpreted their duties in varying

TABLE 1. Number and Average Assets of State and Local Retirement Systems, 1990–96

	1990	1991	1992	1994	1996
No. of systems	202	325	291	310	261
Assets ($ millions)					
Mean value	$3,048	$2,497	$2,721	$3,115	$5,026
Median value	334	176	202	220	419

Source: Authors' calculations.

TABLE 2. Retirement System Governance Policies and Governing Board, 1990–96

Governance policies (% of systems with policy)	1990	1991	1992	1994	1996
Investment restrictions in state constitution	26.2	26.6	26.9	26.1	19.1
Board sets allocations	n.a.	n.a.	72.7	74.0	84.2
Board directly responsible for investments	60.4	53.6	48.6	48.9	55.6
Independent investment performance evaluation	n.a.	n.a.	70.6	80.3	86.2
Governing board (mean and standard deviation)					
Number of trustees	8.12	7.81	8.60	8.53	8.60
	(3.23)	(3.32)	(3.70)	(3.59)	(3.57)
Plan participants as % of trustees	65.3	62.5	63.1	63.0	64.3
	(24.2)	(25.9)	(25.9)	(25.5)	(25.2)
Elected trustees as % of trustees	34.7	33.6	32.1	33.2	35.1
	(27.5)	(26.9)	(26.5)	(25.4)	(25.1)

Source: Authors' calculations.

fashion, as have the legislative bodies overseeing them. In some instances, legislators have imposed rigid restrictions, while in most cases, none; some boards actively guide investment strategies, others prefer passivity.

We focus on four key areas where legislative bodies and governing boards set policy: (1) constitutional restrictions on investments, (2) independent annual performance evaluations, (3) trustee involvement in setting policy on investment allocations, and (4) direct trustee responsibility for investments. We also examine three main characteristics of the governing board: (1) the number of trustees, (2) the proportion of trustees that are participants in the retirement plan, and (3) the fraction of the board that is elected by plan members.

The trend evidence shown in Table 2 and Figures 1 and 2 reveals widespread policy changes among otherwise persistent board structures. Eight to

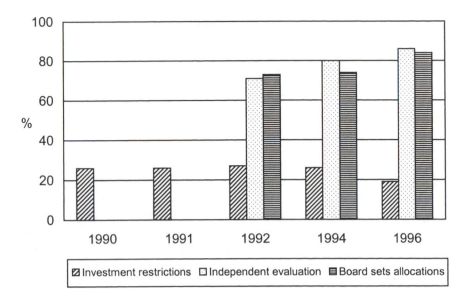

Figure 1. Public pension fund governance policies. Source: Authors' calculations.

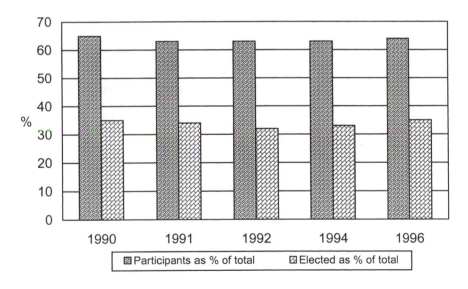

Figure 2. Public pension fund governing board. Source: Authors' calculations.

nine trustees sit on the typical board in both 1990 and 1996, a third of them are elected by plan participants throughout this period, and two-thirds personally participate in the retirement system over which they preside. They have evolved their practices, however, toward greater trustee engagement in investment allocations and more widespread use of independent appraisals of their investment performance. They have also found themselves working within fewer constitutional restrictions.

Consider the evolving policy of trustee involvement in setting investment allocations: Of the 171 systems participating in the surveys in both 1992 and 1996, 128 maintained their practice of having the board set asset allocations, and 24 continued without it doing so. But the adopters far outnumbered the droppers: 14 boards embraced allocation setting, while only 5 abandoned the practice. The weight of opinion among the thousands of investment professionals, pension trustees, and public officials who operate the systems, it seems, is to lodge these critical decisions squarely within the governing board.

Consider as well the diminishing constitutional restrictions. From 1991 to 1994, a quarter of the retirement systems faced such limits, but in 1996 the fraction dropped below a fifth. Indiana voters had rejected measures to abolish the state's total prohibition of equity investing as recently as 1990, but they finally took the equity leap in 1996. The two others states with complete proscriptions on equity investing at that time—South Carolina, and West Virginia—also eliminated their exclusions in 1996. These decisions reflected growing public approval in the mid-1990s of equity markets and their rich returns, or at least less fear about their downside risks.

Other state restrictions have been less limiting: Kansas, for example, maintained a century-old prohibition against ownership of bank stocks. But even these lesser constraints have been lightened. From 1992 to 1994, 20 to 25 percent of the pension funds faced a constitutional or statutory equity cap of 35 percent or less (below generally recommended asset allocations at the time), but by 1996 the fraction of funds facing this cap dropped to 14 percent. Similarly, half of the funds faced equity limits of 50 percent until 1996, but in that year less than a third still reported such a ceiling.

If past trends are predictive of future movements, the recent past suggests that state prohibitions will diminish further, more boards will fix allocations, and outside appraisals will become the standard. Since these directions in the aggregate are the product of thousands of separate decisions by hundreds of retirement systems over seven years, they suggest what emergent best practices are believed to be among those who are most responsible for—and most on the front line of—managing the funds. The rising practices may still not be ideal, but they are certainly road tested.

The most important pension decisions driving investment returns and risks are the allocations of assets among the major classes of investment (investment allocations explain as much as 90 percent of the variance in the returns on assets; Brinson, Hood, and Beebower 1986; Brinson, Singer, and Beebower, 1991). The migration of such decisions into the board signifies its growing prowess in the process, and it also implies that allocation decisions are better vested in system trustees than legislative bodies or executive officials. The trustees are closer to the action and are therefore better positioned to know what actions are required. This principle is consistent with the widespread practice among companies of devolving decisions, responsibility, and accountability whenever feasible to those who are in closest contact with the customer (McKenzie and Lee 1998). Trustees are also shielded from momentary political winds that may be optimal for the state or municipality but suboptimal for the pension beneficiaries, such as economically targeted or social screened investments. This principle is consistent with the equally widespread practice among corporate directors of resisting demands from specific investors for particular changes that may be optimal for them now but not for shareholder value in the long run.

But the trend lines also suggest that allocation decisions are better retained by the overseers than delegated to the front-line investment managers. The publicized bankruptcies of several public and private entities because of excessive leverage during the early 1990s and the near collapse of Long-Term Capital Management in 1998 stand as stark reminders of how insufficient oversight can tempt some money managers too allocate too much money to prospects with too little security. As the trusted agents of the system beneficiaries and public taxpayers, trustees are relatively disinclined, it seems, to delegate further agency on behalf of their principals. Some law markers remain gun-shy as well. "Between Orange County and the Barings failure," offered Richard A. Eckstrom, South Carolina's state treasurer, "legislators are wary of any precipitous change" (Wayne 1995).

The relative constancy of the governing board size—eight trustees give or take three throughout this period—implies a curvilinear optimum somewhere in this range. By way of inference from research on the performance of units ranging from product teams to corporate boards, too few members is to deny the board the diverse experience, expertise, and wisdom that make for good decisions, but too many is also to undermine its communication, consensus, and responsibility that also make for effective actions. A governing body of five members is suboptimal, and so too is a board of twenty-five (Yermack 1996).

The widespread inclusion of elected participants also confirms the desirability of seating representatives from the ranks in the boardroom. In 1990, only 31 percent of the state and local boards included *no* elected members, and by 1996 this had declined to 27 percent. The main concept at work is undoubtedly that the retirement funds ultimately belong to plan members, and their delegates should be present at the creation. Representatives do not dominate the boardroom—only a third of the typical board are so elected—but their presence in the room ensures that their aspirations and fears will be well voiced if not always fully heard. After the Challenger space shuttle disaster on January 28, 1986, the investigating commission recommended that nonflying astronauts be placed in management positions since they bring not only flight experience but also "a keen appreciation of operations and flight safety" (Presidential Commission 1986).

Retirement System Investment Strategies

State and local retirement system investment strategies are intended to optimize assets holdings within the bounds of prudent risk, but system trustees and investment managers have adopted varying ways of doing so. Some have chosen to focus on short-term market trends, others on the longer term; some prefer equities, others bonds; some stay strictly at home, others dabble off shore.

We focus on five retirement system investment strategies: (1) long-term investing, (2) tactical investing based on near-term considerations; (3) management venue—the proportion of funds that are managed in-house or by outside investment companies; (4) equities versus fixed-income—the allocation of funds between stocks and bonds; and (5) international holdings—whether some funds are placed in international stocks and bonds. Long-term and tactical investing are gauged with a survey question that asks if the retirement system asset allocation is "long-term (not often changed with varying economic conditions)" or "tactically set (i.e., changed often with varying economic conditions)." Equities include company stocks, real estate equities, and other forms of equity holding. Fixed-income includes government and corporate bonds, real estate mortgages, and other fixed-income instruments.

Public retirement plans are placing greater responsibility and more accountability in the hands of trustees, and they and their appointed investment mangers in turn are evidently willing to take greater risks in the pursuit of higher returns, as seen in Table 3. They are less tactical and more long term in investment style. Compared with the investment approaches at the start the 1990s, by the latter half of the decade the pension funds were placing more of their assets in equities and moving more of their assets abroad. They were also increasingly relying upon external investment professionals to manage the portfolio. Equity holdings in 1990 typically constituted a third of the total, but by 1996 they had reached half. International holding in 1990 averaged 2.1 percent but by 1996 had risen to 8.6 percent. Half of the systems in 1990 placed all their funds under external management, but by 1996 more than three-quarters were doing so.

TABLE 3. Retirement System Investment Strategies, 1990–96

Investment strategy	1990	1991	1992	1994	1996
Long-term asset allocation	n.a.	n.a.	74.8	82.4	90.0
Tactically set asset allocation	n.a.	n.a	16.3	14.4	11.7
Funds placing *all funds* under *external* management	49.5	66.3	75.0	72.7	78.3
Funds placing *all equities* under *external* management (of those funds with at least some equities)	57.4	73.8	82.9	80.7	85.0
Percentage of funds that manage *all equities internally* (of those funds with at least some equities)	28.7	16.0	10.6	11.5	7.7
Percentage of assets in equities	33.4	36.0	41.7	45.1	50.1
Percentage of assets in fixed income	47.3	46.7	50.0	43.2	41.5
Percentage of assets in international equities	1.56	1.74	2.34	3.70	6.85
Percentage of assets in international fixed income	0.57	0.59	0.82	1.28	1.72

Source: Authors' calculations.

California and South Carolina Retirement Systems

Two pension funds—the California Pubic Employees' Retirement System (Calpers) and the South Carolina Retirement System—usefully illustrate much of the range in governance polices and investment strategies. Examination of them provides tangible examples of what nationwide trends mean when translated into the practices of specific funds. And comparison of them reveals how distinctive governance policies and investment strategies appear to yield distinctive risks and returns on the assets.

As seen in Table 4, the governing board for South Carolina consists of 5 trustees, all plan participants; the governing board for Calpers consists of 13 members, 10 of whom are participants. Consistent with state and local system trends as a whole, the size and structure of the two boards are virtually unchanged over the six-year period. Their respective board sizes and structures are markedly different, however, and so too are their investment styles.

The thirteen members of the Calpers board include six elected representatives, four appointed trustees, and three "ex officio" members. Two of the elected representatives are elected by all Calpers participants, and one each is elected by four other constituencies: (1) employees of California state agencies and public universities, (2) employees of local governments that contract with Calpers for retirement benefits, (3) employees of local school systems that contract with Calpers, and (4) retired employees. The gover-

TABLE 4. South Carolina and California Retirement Systems, 1991 and 1996

South Carolina Retirement System	1991	1996
Governance policies		
Investment restrictions in constitution	yes	yes
Independent performance evaluation	n.a.	yes
Board engagement in investment strategies		
Board sets allocations	n.a.	no
Board directly responsible for investments	no	no
Board composition		
Number of trustees	5	5
Plan participants as trustees	5	5
Elected trustees	0	0
Investment strategies		
Long-term investing of assets	n.a.	yes
Tactical investing of assets	n.a.	no
Equities as % of total assets	0	0
External management of all assets	no	no
International investment of some assets	no	no
Assets under management ($ B)	$9.09	$14.6
California Public Employees' Retirement System (Calpers)	1991	1996
Governance policies		
Investment restrictions in constitution	no	no
Independent performance evaluation	n.a.	yes
Board engagement in investment strategies		
Board sets allocations	n.a.	yes
Board directly responsible for investments	no	no
Board composition		
Number of trustees	13	13
Plan participants as trustees	11	10
Elected trustees	6	6
Investment strategies		
Long-term investing of assets	n.a.	yes
Tactical investing of assets	n.a.	no
Equities as % of total assets	42.7	60.6
External management of all assets	no	no
International investment of some assets	yes	yes
Assets under management ($ B)	$67.9	$100.7

Source: Authors' calculations.

nor appoints two members (one an elected official of a public agency and one an official of a life insurer), and the Speaker of the Assembly and the Senate Rules Committee appoint another. The four ex officio members are the state treasurer, controller, director of personnel administration, and a member of the state personnel board.[1]

TABLE 5. Calpers Internal Investment Allocation Limits, 1991–96

Percentage allowed	1991	1992	1994	1996
Stocks	55	55	50	63
Real estate	10	8	8	7
Corporate bonds	26	37	37	24
Foreign investments	n.a.	16	16	24

Calpers faces no legislative restrictions, but the board does set allocation caps, and the board has changed them in consonance with nationwide public pension trends, as seen in Table 5. Between 1991 and 1996, California increased its permissible equity cap from 55 to 63 percent, and its foreign cap from 16 to 24 percent. Though never quite rubbing against its ceilings, Calpers had come increasingly close: in 1991 it placed 43 percent in stock when it could have allocated 55 percent; in 1996 it put 61 percent in stock at a time the limit had been set at 63 percent.[2]

The South Carolina Retirement System could invest none of its assets in stock due to a 1895 constitutional restriction arising from a scandal in which the governor and other public officials swindled the state out of railroad stock. At the end of 1996, however, South Carolina amended its constitution to permit equity investing, though implementing legislation did not pass until mid-1998 and the system can only increase its equity holdings by 10 percentage points per year until it reaches a cap of 40 percent. Even prior to this legislative uncapping, however, South Carolina investment managers had found ways of enhancing their risks and returns on the fixed-income side, displaying an above average penchant for corporate over government bonds and for single-A over triple-A notes. The ratio of corporate to government bonds, for instance, averaged 0.99 in 1996 for all systems, but for South Carolina the ratio reached 1.23. Yet even then its lower than average returns had left the fund underfunded—by $1.3 billion in 1998, at a time when its assets totaled $17.8 billion—which added an annual burden of $126 million on South Carolina's taxpayers (Rehfeld 1996; Wayne 1995; Sponhour 1998; Parker 1999).[3]

Governance and Investments

When public retirement system trustees set allocation policies, and when their investment managers pick stocks and bonds within those allocations, a plan's trustees and managers are jointly giving shape and content to the fund's investment strategy. That strategy in turn drives and determines their investment's risks and returns. The governance policies of a pension fund can thus be key to its performance: designed well, investment risks will be appropriate and returns will be superior; structured poorly, more tax revenues may be required to make up for the otherwise avoidable and predictable shortfalls. Good governance, then, stands between a fund's success in servicing the public and its failure to do so.

As a case in point, the California Public Employees' Retirement System includes a million participants and more than two thousand participating state and local agencies, and its board convenes on the third Wednesday of every month to ensure that the fund is doing the right thing for them. Board members also guide the fund's investment strategies through four committees:

Strategic Planning Committee. Oversees the strategic planning process, including the selection of consultants

Investment Committee. Reviews investment transactions and investment policy and strategy

Real Estate Subcommittee of the Investment Committee. Develops real estate investment portfolio strategies

Policy Subcommittee of the Investment Committee. Reviews and recommends revisions in investment practices

The time required of trustees for exercising responsible oversight is by no means trivial: Calpers board members typically spend four days per month in meetings. Their compensation, however, is virtually trivial: they receive but $100 per meeting day. The board and its committees oversee the work of 2,500 employees, including a staff of 65 charged with the "successful investment" of Calpers' assets. Decisions on specific equity and fixed-income investments are taken both by the staff and a set of external equity managers under the general guidance of the chief investment officer (formerly Sheryl Pressler, whose prior experience included management of $8 billion in retirement funds for McDonnell Douglas Corporation).

California's investment strategy led to a seven-year average rate of return that exceeded that of South Carolina by 82 basis points (Table 6). On the other hand, it also accepted greater risks in doing so: the standard deviation in the annual rate of return across this period stood at 5.24 for Calpers but only 3.05 for South Carolina. Both systems, however, underperformed the average of all pension funds, though both also assured below average year-by-year variability in their returns. State and local pension funds taken together on average underperformed one of the standard benchmarks for equity investing—the Standard and Poor's index of 500 large companies—but they out-performed three other benchmarks—long-term government bonds, long-term corporate bonds, and U.S. treasury bills.

To examine the extent to which the governance policies shape investment strategies among the retirement systems, we focus on a single year—1992—

TABLE 6. Rates of Return on Investments, South Carolina, California and all State and Local Retirement Systems, 1990–96

Public pensions	1990	1991	1992	1993	1994	1995	1996	Mean	S.D.
South Carolina	10.57	10.15	9.89	9.77	8.83	15.40	5.00	9.94	3.05
California	7.70	6.50	12.50	14.40	2.50	16.40	15.30	10.76	5.24
All systems	6.14	15.46	9.21	11.64	1.94	19.64	13.66	11.10	5.93
Benchmarks									
S&P 500	–3.2	30.6	7.7	10.0	1.3	37.4	23.1	15.3	15.3
Long-term gov. bonds	6.2	19.3	8.1	18.2	–7.8	31.7	–0.9	10.7	13.4
Long-term corp. bonds	6.8	19.9	9.4	13.2	–5.8	27.2	1.4	10.3	11.1
U.S. Treasury Bills	7.8	5.6	3.5	2.9	3.9	5.6	5.2	4.93	1.66

Source: Benchmark data from Ibbotson Associates (1998). Public pension data from authors' calculations; rates of return for 1988 to 1992 are taken from the 1992 survey; rates of return for 1993 and 1994 are from the 1994 survey; and rates of return for 1995 and 1996 are from the 1996 survey (which asked for time-weighted returns).

and we concentrate on six governance policies that are expected to have greatest impact: (1) state investment restrictions, (2) independent performance reviews, (3) board-set asset allocations, (4) board responsible for investments, (5) the size of the board, and (6) the fraction of the board that is plan participants. We draw upon a regression from a companion analysis of five investment strategies—equity investing, long-term investing, tactical investing, reliance on external fund mangers, and international investing—on these governance factors (Useem and Mitchell 1999).

As reported in Table 7, the configuration of a retirement system's governance is seen to have a significant bearing of where it places its assets. Public pensions with state-imposed investment restrictions allocated less to equities and were more long term and less tactical in picking stocks; those with independent performance reviews allocated more to equities and more abroad, and focused more on the long term. Those whose boards set asset allocations are more long term in investment style, and those with larger boards favor stocks, inside managers, and international opportunities. Taken together, these factors explain a substantial share of the diversity observed in the plans' investment strategies. More than a fifth (22.6 percent) of the variation in the proportion placed in the stock market, for example, is explained by how the plans are governed. If a fund added an independent performance appraisal, for instance, by that change in governance alone it was likely to have increased its equity holdings by 14 percentage points. Similar patterns are found in analogous calculations for 1994 and

TABLE 7. Regression of Investment Strategies on Governance Policies, 1992

Governance policy (standard errors in parentheses)	Equities as % of total	Long-term investing	Tactical investing	All external management	Some int'l. investing
Investment restrictions	−7.50 (2.35)**	1.41 (.48)**	−1.10 (.52)*	−0.43 (.40)	−0.24 (.33)
Independent performance evaluation	13.67 (2.50)**	1.58 (.40)**	0.11 (.44)	0.62 (.42)	1.46 (.38)**
Board purview					
Board sets asset allocations	4.65 (2.71)	2.23 (.44)**	−0.35 (.45)	0.58 (.44)	−0.36 (.38)
Board responsible for investments	1.44 (2.15)	0.19 (.40)	−0.61 (.38)	−0.07 (.36)	0.04 (.30)
Board composition/size:					
Number of trustees	0.71 (0.31)*	0.19 (.06)	0.00 (.05)	−0.12 (.05)*	0.10 (.04)*
Plan participants as % of trustees	−3.56 (4.03)	0.04 (.72)	0.22 (.72)	−1.40 (.71)*	0.71 (.58)
Elected trustees as % of trustees	−4.43 (4.06)	−1.02 (.75)	1.47 (.72)*	0.86 (.67)	−0.23 (.57)
R^2 or log-likelihood/concordant pairs	0.226**	188.4/83.4%**	203/83.4%*	217/76.7%*	293/60.4%**

Source: Authors' calculations.
** $p < .01$; * $p < .05$; regression based on 253, 241, 241, 215, and 235 retirement systems respectively; linear regression for equities as % of total; logistic regression for other variables.

TABLE 8. Regression Equity Indexing on Governance Policies, 1996

Governance policy (standard errors in parentheses)	Some equity indexing
Investment restrictions	−0.82 (.43)*
Independent performance evaluation	1.04 (.60)*
Board purview:	
Board sets asset allocations	0.13 (0.49)
Board responsible for investments	0.87 (0.31)**
Board composition/size:	
Number of trustees	−0.00 (0.04)
Plan participants as % of trustees	0.84 (0.65)
Elected trustees as % of trustees	0.08 (0.62)
R^2 or log-likelihood/concordant pairs	253/64.53%**

Source: Authors' calculations.
** $p<.01$; * $p<.05$; regression are based on 203 retirement systems.

1996, signifying the enduring impact of these governance policies on investment strategies.[4]

Another key investment strategy—the placement of at least some equities in an index (further considered in the next section)—was not gauged in the earlier years, but we do have an assessment in 1996. We create a simple measure of whether a system had placed any of its assets in an equity index, and Table 8 reveals that investment restrictions have a predictably negative impact. Pensions that use independent performance appraisals, however, are more likely to invest in an equity index, as are funds whose trustees are directly responsible for investments.

Governance and Activism

Some state and local pension funds concern themselves not only with their own governance but also with that of the companies in which they invest. California, New York, Wisconsin, and other state systems have long led the "shareholder rights"—or perhaps better dubbed—"shareholder power" revolution. They have called for consistently stronger shareholder returns, and they have also sought to ensure robust growth by pressing for annual shareholder elections of all company directors (rather than having directors served staggered terms), company avoidance of takeover defenses such as poison pills, and greater independence of company directors from top management. The retirement systems have pressured companies to make their governance systems more shareholder-friendly through informal dialogue with management, by voting against directors and their proposals, and by publicizing the worst performing companies in their portfolios (Useem 1996, 1998; Tsui 1999).

TABLE 9. Regression of Investor Activism on Governance, 1996 Policies

Governance Policy (standard errors in parentheses)	Investor activism first regression	Investor activism Second regression
Investment restrictions	−0.76 (0.67)	−0.18 (0.75)
Independent performance eval.	1.27 (1.10)	−0.56 (1.38)
Board sets asset allocations	0.16 (0.84)	0.76(1.02)
Board responsible for investments	0.75 (0.43)*	0.84 (0.53)
Number of trustees	0.06 (0.06)	−0.09 (0.08)
Plan participants as % of trustees	−1.23 (0.96)	−1.77 (1.28)
Elected trustees as % of trustees	2.54 (0.93)**	3.03 (1.05)**
Other factors		
Size of fund (ln of assets)		0.70 (0.16)**
% of asset in equities		0.08 (0.03)**
% of assets in equity index		−0.01 (0.02)
Log-likelihood/concordant pairs	161.6/79.9%**	121.2/84.5%**

Source: Authors' calculations.
**$p<.01$; *$p<.05$; logistic regression based 181 retirement systems.

Investor activism should therefore be viewed as yet another investment strategy that pension trustees embrace to ensure that their participants enjoy the risks and returns to which they are entitled. Rather than just picking companies in which to invest, the public pensions pick on companies in which they have already invested.

A significant proportion of many public funds were indexing by the mid-1990s, and this may lead to more activism as well. Close to half—45 percent—of the systems in 1996 had placed at least some assets in an index, and the typical fund had indexed 16 percent of it assets. For these holdings, investment managers are left with no choice once they have picked the index, and activism for them can send a message to management when active buying or selling of a company's stock is no longer feasible.

The 1996 survey of state and local pensions asked, "Has your system actively participated in corporate governance issues by voting against management on annual proxy statements or otherwise encouraging companies you hold stock in to change their management activities?" Almost one in five—40 out of 210—answered in the affirmative. Drawing on nearly the same set of governance factors examined earlier for their impact on investment strategies, we examine the predictors of investor activism as reported in Table 8. The first regression includes only the governance policies, while the second brings in three other factors presumed to foster activism as well: the size of system assets (larger funds have greater resources with which to support activist campaigns), and the proportion of funds in equities and equity indexes. Focusing on the second regression in which the governance effects can be seen apart from the impact of other factors, we see that investment restrictions and independent performance evaluations have no impact, and the same holds for the board's investment responsibilities. Nor is the board size important, but its composition is. The greater the relative presence of elected trustees, the more likely is the fund to be activist. We also note that large funds and those with more of their assets in equities are drawn toward activism, although indexing is seen to have no independent effect.

Governance and Targeting

Voices opposing the formation of a national investment board have contended that such a body could not resist the temptation to favor companies that are of national interest but not beneficiary interest. Such an oversight board might prefer U.S. companies over foreign opportunities, labor-friendly firms over antilabor firms, and tobacco-free corporations over cigarette makers. While such preferencing may make good sense for the country, it may also be a poor choice for participants who want the assets optimized for themselves rather than the nation. Including any political or social criteria in the selection of investment targets would introduce, by this line of argument, untoward bias in participant risks and rewards (Watson 1994; Marr, Nofsinger, and Trimble 1993).

The investing experience of state and local systems in this area is informative, for it suggests that here too governance matters. In 1996, the survey asked the systems whether they have "prohibitions against direct or indirect investments in specific types of companies," such as those doing business with Northern Ireland or manufacturing tobacco. It also inquired whether a fraction of their portfolio is "targeted or directed in-state for economic development purposes." The number of systems engaged in either form of directed investing was modest: in 1996, twenty-eight engaged in social limiting and fourteen in economic targeting (the fraction of assets targeted economically ranged from 0.05 percent to 12 percent, with Calpers anchoring the high end). Paralleling the analysis for investor activism, Table 10 presents a regression of these social and economic measures on the governance factors.

We have already seen that retirement systems with independent performance evaluations and larger boards invest a larger proportion of their assets outside the United States (Table 7). By implication, a national board with these governance characteristics is less likely to favor domestic investments for purely political purposes. On social limiting and economic targeting, however, governance is seen to make no difference. Larger funds are less likely to socially limit and more likely to economically target, but the governance factors have no direct impact once the size of the fund is taken into account.

TABLE 10. Regression of Investment Targeting on Governance, 1996 Policies

Governance policy (standard errors in parentheses)	Social limiting	Economic targeting
Investment restrictions	0.16 (.54)	0.12 (0.23)
Independent performance evaluation	0.74 (.88)	−0.17 (0.31)
Board sets asset allocations	0.28 (.83)	0.06 (0.27)
Board responsible for investments	−0.04 (.47)	−0.17 (0.18)
Number of trustees	−0.02 (.08)	0.03 (0.03)
Plan participants as % of trustees	−1.09 (.95)	0.20 (0.37)
Elected trustees as % of trustees	0.53 (1.01)	0.14 (0.36)
Other factors		
Size of fund (ln of assets)	−0.19 (.11)*	0.12 (.04)
% of asset in equities	0.00 (.02)	0.04 (.01)
% of assets in equity index	−0.01 (.01)	0.00 (.00)
Log-likelihood/concordant pairs	142.6/87.7%	.105**

Source: Authors' calculations.
** $p < .01$; * $p < .05$; regressions based on 203 retirement systems. Social targeting refers to prohibitions on investments in specific types of companies; economic targeting refers to the investment of some funds in-state for economic development.

Governance Matters More

State and local retirement systems have been moving toward greater openness and accountability. They are less constrained by state-imposed restrictions, and their trustees are taking greater responsibility for investment
allocations. More are using professional investment services, and more are
drawing independent performance evaluations. Their boards are little
changing in composition, but their trustees are changing in attitude. So too
are the legislative authorities and public opinions that ultimately shape their
governance policies.

These changes can be seen as part of a nationwide fascination with the
remarkable performance of the U.S. bull market during the 1990s. In the
aftermath of Indiana's vote to end its constitutional prohibition on equities,
an editorial in an Indianapolis newspaper noted the obvious: as the state retirement system began to invest in stocks and, as a result, hopefully raised its
then modest returns from 7.3 percent to even just 8.5 percent, it would lead
to a $70 million to $100 million tax-cut windfall for the people of Indiana
(*Indianapolis Star* 1997).

The way states and municipalities chose to govern their pension funds
has evident bearing on what they do with the funds. Whether they invest
in stocks or bonds, tactically or for the long run, domestically or internationally, is partly a predictable product of how they are governed. So too
are the decisions on whether to manage the investments inside or through
outsourcing, and on whether to take an activist stance or remain passive.
Legislative restrictions, independent evaluations, and trustee compositions

TABLE 11. The Most Important Single Determinants of Key Investment Strategies

Investment strategy	Most important governance determinant
Allocation of funds into equities	Independent performance evaluation
Placement of funds in equity indexes	Board responsible for investments
Long-term investing	Board sets asset allocations
Tactical investing	Trustees elected by plan participants and investment restrictions
External management of portfolio	Number of trustees
At least some international investing	Independent performance evaluation
Investor activism	Trustees elected by plan participants
Social limiting	None
Economic targeting	None

Source: Authors' tabulations.

all affect how and where retiree monies are invested. And, given that legis-latures are loosening their grips and capital markets are opening, pension governance is becoming more important than ever, for those who govern now have more impact than ever before on how their assets are invested.

National Policy Implications

From the recent history of state and local pensions we can suggest that the behavior of a national system that invests in the market will depend on how its governance is configured. The most important single governance deter-minants of key investment strategies by public pensions are identified in Table 11, and although inferring national actions from regional experience is always hazardous, it is better to draw on the public pension experience that we do have than on no data at all.

If a national governing board is established to oversee the investment of social security funds, the state and local retirement system evidence would predict that the body would and should be

- composed of eight to nine trustees, a third of whom are elected by par-ticipants;
- unconstrained by investment restrictions;
- directly responsible for setting investment allocations.

We can anticipate that state and local boards will continue a slow but sure drive toward more equity investing and more international holdings, and if a federal governing body is created to supervise the investment of social security funds, trends in the state and local evidence would predict that the body would and should:

- place most if not all of the funds under active management by outside investment companies;
- eschew tactical, short-term investment styles and favor long-term strategies;
- allocate at least half of the funds to U.S. equities;
- invest close to a tenth of the funds offshore.

Since state and local retirement systems are moving toward less state restriction and more independent appraisal, we anticipate that the systems are likely to move still more assets into equities and more outside the United States during the years ahead. Again, if the Congress were to establish a governing entity to preside over the investment of social security funds, and if it took its cues from trends in public pension governance, we could expect similar trends in its investment strategies. This might be marked above all by a rising favoritism toward equities over fixed-income alternatives, and a declining preference for a purely American portfolio.

The composition of a national board would appear to be a primary consideration in shaping whether it becomes activist of not. Whether it should be activist is a matter for Congress to decide. Most company executives are sure to be opposed, viewing an activist federal investment board as just another thorn in their side. Many investors and plan participants, however, are sure to be supportive, seeing the federal role as one more prod for better corporate performance—and thus larger retirement benefits. But if it is activism that Congress prefers, the evidence from the state and local experience is that electing trustees will take the fund down the activist trail.

As a cautionary note, a governance scheme is ultimately only as good as those board trustees and investment managers who enact it. The quality of leadership counts as much here as anywhere, and the performance of a national system will be critically dependent on the capabilities of those appointed to oversee and operate it.[5]

Notes

1. Board members are profiled at <www.calpers.ca.gov>.
2. By the end of 1998, Calpers had raised its equity fraction to 69 percent of the $151 billion under management, and its international holdings to 24 percent.
3. Indiana and West Virginia joined South Carolina in 1996 in ending their prohibitions on equity investing.
4. For "equities as percentage of total," investment restrictions have a negative effect in both 1994 and 1996, and independent performance evaluation and number of trustees have positive impacts. For "tactical investing," however, the regressions coefficients are not statistically significant for the later years. For "all external management," the number of trustees has negative effects for both years (though is not statistically significant in 1994), while board setting asset allocation has a positive

effect. For "some international investing," independent performance evaluation and number of trustees are positive and statistically significant. These regression results are available upon request to the first author <useem@wharton.upenn.edu>.

5. As a case in point, consider Grinnell College, one of the country's smallest colleges but also one of its richest. Grinnell's endowment in mid-1998 stood at $1.02 billion, not large by comparison with the endowments of some leading universities, but near the top on per capita wealth. Much of its recent affluence—and thus the exceptional benefits received by its participants—can be traced to the investment savvy of its trustees. Joseph F. Rosenfield, a Des Moines businessman, and Warren E. Buffett, an Omaha investment manager, had long served as Grinnell trustees: Rosenfield had joined the board in 1941, and he recruited Buffett in 1968. In 1968, Grinnell College invested in a new firm being built by one of its graduates, Robert Noyce, named Intel. The college also bought $17 shares in Berkshire Hathaway that were later to become valued at $17,000. Rosenfield and Buffett had spearheaded a trustee drive to grow the endowment through such investments, and in doing so they transformed $11 million in college assets at the end of the 1960s into a hundred-times larger endowment three decades later. By the early 1990s, the Grinnell endowment was outperforming the S&P 500 stock index by more than five points (18.7 percent in 1992–93 versus 13.6 percent), and in 1998, Grinnell College achieved an investment return of 38 percent, far exceeding the performance of most mutual fund managers. Regardless of trustees policies and composition, trustee leadership also evidently matters (Siebert 1994, 1998; *Wall Street Journal* 1999).

References

Brinson, Gary P., L. Randolph Hood, and Gilbert L. Beebower. 1986. "Determinants of Portfolio Performance." *Financial Analysts Journal* 42 (July/August): 39–44.

Brinson, Gary P., Brian D. Singer, and Gilbert L. Beebower. 1991. "Determinants of Portfolio Performance II: An Update." *Financial Analysts Journal* 47 (May/June): 40–48.

England, Robert Stowe. 1996."Progress Report for Public Pensions." *Plan Sponsor* (February): 36–45.

General Accounting Office. 1996. *State and Local Pension Funding*. Washington, D.C.: Government Accounting Office.

Ibbotson Associates. 1998. *SBBI 1998 Yearbook: Market Results for 1926–97*. Chicago: Ibbotson Associates.

Indianapolis Star. 1997. "Investing at Last" (editorial). May 10: A14.

Marr, M. Wayne, John R. Nofsinger, and John L. Trimble. 1993. "Economically Targeted Investments: A New Threat to Private Pension Funds." *Journal of Applied Corporate Finance* (Summer): 91–95.

McKenzie, Richard B. and Dwight R. Lee. 1998. *Managing Through Incentives: How to Develop a More Collaborative, Productive, and Profitable Organization*. New York: Oxford University Press.

Mitchell, Olivia S. and Roderick M. Carr. 1996. "State and Local Pension Plans." In *The Handbook of Employee Benefits: Design, Funding, and Administration*, 4th ed., ed. Jerry S. Rosenbloom. Chicago: Irwin. 1207–22.

Parker, Jim. 1999. "Consultant Hired for Pension Fund." *Post and Courier*, February 11: B7.

Presidential Commission on the Space Shuttle Challenger. 1986. *Accident Report of the Presidential Commission on the Space Shuttle Challenger*. Washington, D.C. U.S. GPO.

Rehfeld, Barry. 1996. "Not Just Covering Their Assets." *Institutional Investor* 30 (July): 51.

Siebert, Mark. 1994. "Grinnell's Endowment Performing Brilliantly." *Des Moines Register,* March 14: 1.

———. 1998. "$1 Billion: Quite a Nest Egg, Grinnell College's Endowment in a Class by Itself." *Des Moines Register,* June 14: 1.

Sponhour, Michael. 1998. "South Carolina to Invest $7 Billion of Pension Fund in Stock Market." *The State* (July 31).

Tsui, Rebecca. 1999. "Successful Turnaround Targets for Pension Fund Activism: The Usefulness of Financial Indicators." Philadelphia: Wharton School.

Useem, Michael. 1996. *Investor Capitalism: How Money Managers Are Changing the Face of Corporate America.* New York: Basic Books/HarperCollins.

———. 1998. "Corporate Leadership in a Globalizing Equity Market." *Academy of Management* 12 (1998): 43–59.

Useem, Michael and Olivia S. Mitchell. 1999. "Holders of the Public Pension Strings: Governance and Performance of Public Retirement Systems." Philadelphia: Wharton School.

Wall Street Journal. 1999. "The Old College Try" (editorial). March 4: A14.

Watson, Ronald D. 1994. "Does Targeted Investing Make Sense?" *Financial Management* 23 (Winter): 69–74.

Wayne, Leslie. 1995. "Where Playing the Stock Market Is Really Risky." *New York Times,* May 1: D5.

Yermack, David. 1996. "Higher Market Valuation of Companies with a Small Board of Directors." *Journal of Financial Economics* 40 (February): 185–211.

Zorn, Paul. 1998. "1997 Survey of State and Local Government Employee Retirement Systems." Washington, D.C.: Government Finance Officers Association.

Chapter 8
Investment Practices of State and Local Pension Funds
Implications for Social Security Reform

Alicia H. Munnell and Annika Sundén
with the assistance of Cynthia Perry and Ryan Kling

The investment practices of public pension funds have become a topic of major interest in the wake of President Clinton's 1999 proposal to invest a portion of the Social Security Trust Funds in equities. Both supporters and opponents of the proposal point to the performance of public plans to argue their case. Supporters cite the success of federal plans, particularly the Federal Thrift Savings Plan (TSP), which has avoided picking individual stocks by investing in a stock index and has steered clear of projects with less than market returns. Divestiture of stocks for social or political reasons has also not been a problem, and TSP has avoided government intervention in the private sector since individual portfolio managers vote the proxies. Opponents of Social Security Trust Fund investment in equities point to state and local pension funds. They contend that state and local pensions often undertake investments that sacrifice return to achieve political or social goals, divest stocks to demonstrate that they do not support some perceived immoral or unethical behavior, and intervene in corporate activity. Opponents claim that if social security's investment options were broadened, Congress would use the trust fund money for similar unproductive activities. An important question is the extent to which allegations about state and local plans are true.

This study explores four possible avenues through which social or political considerations could enter the investment decisions of state and local pension funds. The first section focuses on economically targeted investments (ETIs), those investments that are designed to meet some special need within the state. The second section looks at instances of pension fund activism, whereby the fund managers attempt to influence corporate behavior to improve profitability or other aspects of corporate performance. The third section investigates the extent to which state and local pension plans have avoided or divested certain holdings in order to make a political or ethical statement. The fourth section investigates the extent to which states and localities have used pension funds as an escape valve for general budget pressures.

This comprehensive review yields the following conclusions. First, economically targeted investments account for no more than 2.5 percent of total state and local holdings. Although early studies showed plans sacrificing considerable return for targeting their investments to in-state activities, recent survey data reveal no adverse impact on returns as a result of the current small amount of ETI activity. Second, public plans in only three states have seriously engaged in shareholder activism, and this activism appears to have been motivated by a desire to improve the bottom line not to make a political statement. The literature suggests that this activity has had a negligible to positive impact on returns. Third, the only significant divestiture that has occurred was related to companies doing business in South Africa before 1994. This was a unique situation where worldwide consensus among industrial nations led to a global ban on investment in that country. With respect to tobacco, public plans have generally resisted divestiture, and only a few have actually sold their stock. Finally, state and local governments have borrowed occasionally from their pension funds or reduced their contributions in the wake of budget pressures, but this activity has been restrained by the courts and frequently reversed. In short, the story that emerges at the state and local level is that while in the early 1980s some public plans sacrificed returns for social considerations, plan managers have become much more sophisticated. Today, public plans appear to be performing as well as private plans.

Economically Targeted Investments

State and local pension assets grew dramatically during the 1970s, and some observers began to see these funds as a mechanism for achieving socially and politically desirable objectives. Early debate focused on efforts to exclude from pension portfolios companies with "undesirable" characteristics, such as those facing labor problems or holding investments in South Africa. The focus shifted in the 1980s, however, with the publication of two books favoring investments that would foster social goals, such as economic development and home ownership (Rifkin and Barber 1978, Litvak 1981).

At that time, advocates contended that these social goals could be achieved without any loss of return. Early studies, however, suggested that targeting did involve some financial sacrifice. For example, a survey of state-administered pension funds showed that ten states either inadvertently or deliberately sacrificed return in an attempt to foster homeownership (Munnell 1983). Analysis of the risk/return characteristics of the publicly or privately insured mortgage-backed pass-through securities in those states revealed that the sacrificed return sometimes exceeded 200 basis points. Although mortgages accounted for only 5 percent of total state and local assets, it seemed as if state and local pension funds were on a naïve and dangerous path.

During this period, it appeared that public pension managers did not recognize the "Catch-22" nature of the exercise in which they were engaged. The problem is that increasing in-state housing investment is inconsistent with maximizing returns in the United States's highly developed capital markets. This is because any housing investment that offers a competitive return at an appropriate level of risk does not need special consideration by public pension plans. Conversely, pension investments that would increase the supply of housing funds must, by definition, either produce lower returns or involve greater risk. Some sophisticated advocates of ETIs recognized the efficiency of the market for housing finance and argued that pension funds could make a contribution through innovative forms of housing finance (Litvak 1981). But that was not what was going on in 1983; rather the in-state mortgages purchased by public pension funds tended to be conventional fixed-rate thirty-year mortgages. The losses experienced in the early 1980s served as a sharp wake-up call to many public pension fund managers who appeared to believe that they could accomplish social goals without sacrificing returns.

In the last fifteen years, the rhetoric associated with targeted investments has changed markedly. Public pension fund managers now acknowledge the potential for losses and go out of their way to make clear that they are no longer willing to sacrifice returns for social considerations. As discussed below, almost every definition of ETIs includes a requirement that the investment produce a "market rate of return."

Current ETI Activity

Interviews with public pension plan officials in 1993 provide a state-by-state description of past and current experiences with ETI programs and offer a window on current thinking about economically targeted investing (Ferlauto and Claybourn 1993).[1] The study's editors defined successful ETIs as investments that produce risk-adjusted market rates and "provide exceptional corollary or external benefits by meeting specific capital gaps" (p. 4). Since most investments yield some benefit to society, ETIs are expected to produce exceptionally large benefits. The editors recognized that public pensions can do little if markets are perfect, but contended that pension funds can improve the allocation of capital if gaps exist due to redlining, discrimination, or the absence of a secondary market (as was the case for mortgage loans before the advent of Fannie Mae and Freddie Mac in the 1960s).[2]

The Ferlauto and Claybourn study also points out that a successful ETI program requires sensible investment selection procedures as well as a commitment to market returns. They identify three practices as necessary for success. First, state legislatures can authorize ETI activity, but they should not be involved in picking specific investments; the latter decision must rest with the retirement system. Second, ETIs cannot be considered in isolation; they must be incorporated into an overall fund strategy of geographic and asset diversification. Third, the retirement system must institute regular evaluations of ETI investments. They further suggest that those pension funds that have followed these "best practices"—New York City Retirement Systems, Massachusetts MASTERS, the Pennsylvania State System, and California CalPERS—enjoyed solid subsequent performance.

Ferlauto and Claybourn report that some state and local plans that simply targeted investments geographically or violated other guidelines ran into serious trouble. For example, during the 1980s, the Alaska Retirement Systems invested $263 million in nonguaranteed home mortgages, 35 percent of which were located in Alaska. When oil prices dropped dramatically in 1985, the Alaska real estate market crashed and more than one third of the system's in-state loans became nonperforming. Similarly, the Kansas Public Employees Retirement invested in a Kansas Savings & Loan that became insolvent and in an endangered steel mill that closed; the fund also lost tens of millions on its nontargeted direct real estate investments. Kansas failed to diversify its exposure by selecting a number of managers for private placement lending and real estate investment; it also failed to limit its exposure by coinvesting with banks, insurance companies, or other pension funds. Instead, Kansas loaned one-fifth of its private placement portfolio to a single borrower, and it failed to provide oversight of its risky investments.

Although some plans suffered losses during the 1980s, state and local governments learned from their mistakes. Alaska dropped its ETI program, while Kansas expanded and diversified the fund's Board of Trustees, required investments through limited partnerships rather than direct lending, and removed its mandate for in-state investments. Concurrently, other funds designed new programs and improved old programs. Some states created financial intermediaries to identify, underwrite, package, and/or credit-enhance targeted investments. Funds also started to package investments with guarantees and other risk sharing mechanisms in order to meet risk/return benchmarks. They are also now using Fannie Mae and Freddie Mac to securitize affordable home mortgage pools and state or federal government guarantees to back small business loans.

TABLE 1. State and Local Pension Plans' Economically Targeted Investments, 1993

ETI activity	Percent of total
Fixed Income	21.6
Loans to small businesses	4.5
Private placements	17.0
Real estate	69.3
Construction loans	4.5
Residential mortgages	50.6
Commercial mortgages	12.5
Equity	1.7
Venture capital	9.1
Total	100.0

Source: Boice Dunham Group (1993).

Such innovations reduce the risk associated with ETIs, but the necessity to earn market returns and provide large collateral benefits must surely limit the number of possible targeted investment opportunities. How much ETI investing is going on? Three sources of information are available, each with its own purpose and perspective on whether targeted investing is a good or bad idea.

Perhaps the most comprehensive listing of ETI activity is a 1993 Boice Dunham Group study, which was commissioned by Goldman Sachs. This analysis defined an ETI as "an investment by a public pension fund which, in addition to offering financial returns in proportion to financial risk, also offers collateral local economic benefit (e.g., job creation, home ownership)" (p. 1). Using this definition, Boice Dunham concluded that ETIs accounted for $17.5 billion or only 2 percent of the $887.3 billion of public plan assets covered in their survey.[3] ETI activity fell into three categories: fixed income, real estate, and venture capital, with the majority going to residential mortgages (see Table 1).

The second source of information on ETI activity is the General Accounting Office (1995), which reviewed a survey of 139 of the largest public pension plans. Fifty of the 119 respondents indicated that they had invested a total of $19.8 billion in ETIs to promote housing, real estate, or small business development, which amounted to 2.4 percent of total respondents' assets. Since the respondents accounted for 85 percent of the assets of state and local plans, these results are broadly representative.

Another source on ETIs is the set of files known as PENDAT, which were created from the Surveys of State and Local Employee Retirement Systems for Members of the Public Pension Coordinating Council (Zorn 1991, 1993, 1995, 1997). (These data are also the basis for our empirical analysis presented below). The question included in these surveys has varied slightly over time, but generally asks "What percentage of the portfolio is directed in-state for developmental purposes?"[4] The emphasis on "developmental purposes" could easily lead respondents to omit residential mortgages made at market rates and private placements—the two largest categories in the Boice Dunham study. As a result, the percentage of total assets designated for in-state investment averaged between 0.1 percent and 0.3 percent over the four surveys.

Two conclusions emerge from this review of the extent and nature of ETI activity in the 1990s. First, ETIs account for only a small portion of the assets of state and local pension funds.[5] Second, in the wake of early failures pension fund managers have set up procedures to ensure market returns for given levels of risk and to protect themselves from major losses. The question remains, however, whether the new procedures have prevented ETIs from adversely affecting returns. This issue can only be resolved empirically.

The Impact of ETIs on Pension Fund Returns

The most comprehensive data available on state and local plans come from the PENDAT files described above. This periodic survey includes information on system administration, investment behavior, reporting practices, benefits, and actuarial methods and assumptions. Reports regarding public plan attributes in the previous year were published in 1991, 1992, 1993, 1995, and 1997. Sample sizes and response rates vary somewhat by year, but generally include most plan participants and public plan assets. For example, in 1997, 261 retirement systems covering a total of 379 plans responded to the survey, representing about 80 percent of state and local plan active participants and assets (Zorn 1997).

Here we use the PENDAT data to explore whether ETI activity has a significant effect on the economic performance of public pension plans. We measure performance two ways: as the annual rate of return over the preceding year and as the average rate of return over the last five years. The explanatory variables we use fall into four groups. The first concerns investment strategies. This includes whether the fund engages in ETI activity, whether the state constitution imposes investment restrictions, and whether the fund prohibits investments in certain companies (such as tobacco firms). The expected coefficients for these variables are negative, since including criteria other than risk and return diminishes the possibility of an efficient portfolio.

The second group of variables we examine reflects public plan portfolio composition and size. These would be expected to have a positive effect on performance; stocks have higher returns, and large funds tend to be more efficient. The third group of factors concerns management practices, and are expected to have mixed effects: outside evaluation would be expected to increase returns by improving the quality of investment decisions; administrative expenses paid by the fund would be expected to reduce returns; and corporate governance activity (asked only in 1997), generally directed toward underperforming firms, would be expected to enhance the performance of the fund. Finally, we look at the impact of the percentage of the board elected by pension plan membership, and anticipate that the effect could go either way.[6] A summary of the dependent and explanatory variables appears in Table 2.

The results of the multivariate analysis of state and local pension plan performance for the individual years and for the pooled data are presented in Table 3. The ETI variable (INSTATE), which reflects the share of the portfolio directed in-state for developmental purposes, does not have a statistically significant effect on fund performance either in the pooled data or in any of the individual years.[7] Separate estimates using an indicator variable for ETIs also suggest that this activity does not have a significant effect on overall performance (Appendix Table 1). Finally, estimates using the more comprehensive Goldman Sachs information on ETIs yield the same results (Appendix Table 2).

With regard to the other variables in the equation, the only ones that consistently have a statistically significant effect on returns are portfolio composition and size. The share of assets invested in equities has a significant positive effect on fund performance both in the short run and the long run. Large systems are likely to be more efficient in the management and administration of the plan and appear to earn higher returns. Neither the management and reporting practices nor board composition variables have a systematic effect on investment return.

The fact that we fail to find a negative effect of ETIs on returns appears to contradict some prior studies showing a strong and large negative relationship between ETI activity and pension fund earnings.[8] Yet on closer examination, we believe the story is consistent: ETIs are a small part of pension portfolios, managers aim for market returns, and therefore ETI activity does not have a noticeable impact on public plan investment outcomes.

One often-cited study is by Romano (1993), who provides an extensive description of the political pressures on public pension funds' investment practices and an empirical analysis of the relationship between political influence and public pension performance. To explain performance, Romano included the following variables: the proportion of the board elected by fund members, three measures of social investing (preference for in-state investment, active in corporate governance, and restrictions on investments of companies doing business in South Africa), and the proportion of assets in nongovernment securities. Her data were for 50 state pension funds over the five-year period 1985–89. She found that the two variables with statistically significant coefficients are the proportion of assets in nongovernment securities and the South Africa variable.[9] The two other social in-

TABLE 2. Variable Definitions and Means of Characteristics of State and Local
        Pension Plans

Variable	Definition	Mean 1991	1993	1995	1997
Investment strategies					
INSTATE	Percent of pension fund assets invested in state	0.35	0.30	0.37	0.10
RESTRICT	Investment restriction specified in constitution	0.25	0.26	0.24	0.16
SOUTH AFRICA	Prohibitions against invest-ments of specific types	0.45	0.48	0.19	0.13
Portfolio composition					
EQUITY%	Percent of assets invested in equities	35.80	43.26	49.24	53.11
SIZE	Mean assets in the pension fund ($billion)	2.98	3.16	4.88	6.07
Management practices					
OUTEVAL	System obtains independent investment performance evaluation	0.78	0.81	0.87	0.92
ADINVST	Administrative expenses offset by investment income	0.54	0.55	0.60	0.63
PROXY	System has actively participated in corporate governance	—	—	—	0.22
Board composition					
ELCTMEMB	Percentage of board elected by pension membership	34.73	31.60	35.43	32.84
Rate of return					
ROR90	Rate of return on the pension fund received on assets in 1990	7.89	—	—	—
ROR92	Rate of return on the pension fund received on assets in 1992	—	9.33	—	—
ROR94	Rate of return on the pension fund received on assets in 1994	—	—	1.55	—
ROR96	Rate of return on the pension fund received on assets in 1996	—	—	—	13.72
RORAVG	Average rate of return on assets for previous five years	11.53	10.99	8.80	11.29

Source: Authors' calculations using PENDAT (see Zorn 1991, 1993, 1995, 1997).

vesting variables—preference for in-state investments and corporate governance—never had a statistically significant effect on returns at conventional significance levels. Board composition, the variable of greatest interest to the author, was only marginally significant.

Even these modest results should be interpreted cautiously, because the author provided no indication about the extent to which her sample of pension funds represented the broader universe of state and local plans. Also, her dependent variable—earnings on investments "including realized capital gains," divided by book value of total assets—is, in our view, an inadequate measure of performance. The numerator does not include unrealized gains, which were probably important given the increased holdings of equities and the strong stock market performance in the late 1980s, and the denominator can be manipulated—that is, it can be increased or reduced through the purchase or sale of assets.

Mitchell and Hsin (1997) explored the impact of ETIs on investment returns using the 1991 PENDAT data. They related the rate of return on pension assets to the pension board composition, board management practices, reporting requirements, and investment practices—including a variable for the percent of plan assets devoted to in-state investments. The coefficient of the "in-state" variable was not statistically significant when the plan returns were averaged over the previous five years, but it was significant (at the 10 percent level) when the dependent variable was the return for 1991 only. The results suggest that in 1991 every percentage point of plan assets targeted to in-state investments cost public pension funds eight basis points.[10]

Even though we use the same data as Mitchell-Hsin, we do not duplicate their findings. Our 1991 equation shows a statistically significant *positive* coefficient on ETIs when returns were averaged over five years and an insignificant coefficient for the annual return. Because our results are anomalous on theoretical grounds and not consistent with the pattern in later years, we argue that they should be dismissed. The difference in the two studies arises because Mitchell-Hsin imputed missing values and we did not.[11]

The ETI controversy was recently joined by Nofsinger (1998), who claims that ETI activity reduces public pension fund returns by 200 basis points. This claim comes from an empirical model that relates abnormal returns (the dependent variable) to four variables reflecting ETI activity, asset-allocation limitations, social restrictions, and the prudent-person rule. The author estimates this model separately for each of the three years using 1991, 1992, and 1993 PENDAT data, and also a model that pools the three years' data and adds three additional variables: the percentage of board members elected by plan participants, the natural log of assets, and percentage of the portfolio in equities. The results for the ETI variable are mixed. In the year-specific regressions, the ETI variable is negative but not statistically significant from zero. In the pooled data, the ETI variable is negative (at about −200 basis points) and statistically significant at the 1 percent level.

Table 3. Multivariate Analysis of Rate of Return of State and Local Pension Plans

	1991		1993		1995		1997		Pooled	
	ROR90	RORAVG	ROR92	RORAVG	ROR94	RORAVG	ROR96	RORAVG	RORCUR	RORAVG
Management strategies										
INSTATE	-0.31	0.34**	-0.07	0.39	-0.05	0.01	0.35	0.06	-0.12	0.182
	(0.26)	(0.13)	(0.15)	(0.61)	(0.21)	(0.07)	(0.31)	(0.17)	(0.10)	(0.12)
RESTRICT	1.25	1.13**	0.67	0.86**	0.09	0.49	-0.64	-0.19	0.56	0.63**
	(1.00)	(0.52)	(0.50)	(0.40)	(0.79)	(0.27)	(0.62)	(0.35)	(0.37)	(0.23)
SOUTH AFRICA	-0.60	0.07	-0.92	0.16	-0.54	-0.45	1.14	0.35	-0.45	-0.01
	(0.82)	(0.42)	(0.43)	(0.36)	(0.82)	(0.29)	(0.67)	(0.38)	(0.35)	(0.20)
Portfolio composition and size										
EQUITY%	0.02	0.00	-0.01	0.03**	-0.05**	0.01	0.16*	0.07**	0.03**	0.03**
	(0.03)	(0.01)	(0.01)	(0.01)	(0.02)	(0.01)	(0.02)	(0.01)	(0.11)	(0.01)
SIZE	-0.05	0.07	-0.10	-0.04	0.04	0.08	0.21**	0.12**	0.01	0.07**
	(0.18)	(0.09)	(0.09)	(0.07)	(0.13)	(0.05)	(0.10)	(0.05)	(0.06)	(0.03)
Management and reporting practices										
OUTEVAL	-2.35**	-0.11	1.31**	-0.16	-1.23	0.12	-2.75**	-0.94	-0.92	-0.10
	(1.03)	(0.56)	(0.60)	(0.56)	(1.02)	(0.34)	(0.82)	(0.51)	(0.49)	(0.26)
ADINVST	-0.71	-0.85**	0.25	0.23	-0.92	-0.14	-0.01	-0.09	-0.21	-0.19
	(0.81)	(0.43)	(0.43)	(0.35)	(0.65)	(0.22)	(0.45)	(0.25)	(0.29)	(0.16)
PROXY	—	—	—	—	—	—	-0.29	-0.25		
							(0.58)	(0.32)		

	(1)	(2)	(3)	(4)	(5)	(6)	(7)	(8)	(9)	(10)
Board composition										
ELCTMEMB	-0.03*	-0.02**	-0.01	0.00	0.00	0.00	0.01	0.00	0.00	0.00
	(0.01)	(0.00)	(0.01)	(0.01)	(0.01)	(0.00)	(0.01)	(0.00)	(0.01)	(0.00)
Year										
YEAR91									-5.32**	0.54**
									(0.57)	(0.23)
YEAR93									-4.10**	-0.19
									(0.42)	(0.24)
YEAR95									-12.11**	-2.54**
									(0.43)	(0.18)
CONSTANT	11.48**	10.77**	10.87**	10.17**	4.75	6.91**	3.06	5.87**	12.89**	8.68**
	(3.62)	(1.89)	(1.84)	(2.02)	(2.97)	(1.12)	(2.03)	(1.13)	(1.42)	(0.81)
R^2	0.08	0.16	0.07	0.08	0.07	0.08	0.50	0.41	0.55	0.41
Number of Observations	155	132	220	123	144	120	166	156	697	390

Source: Authors' calculations using PENDAT (see Zorn 1991, 1993, 1995, 1997).
"Size" variable is measured as the natural log of assets. Standard errors in parentheses.
** Significant at the 5 percent level.
* Significant at the 10 percent level.

The question is how to interpret these results. One conclusion is that the pooled estimate is implausibly large, given that the average return for funds in the sample is 10 percent and that those plans that do engage in ETI activity hold only 5 percent of their portfolio in such investments. For plans with ETIs to suffer a reduction of 200 basis points in their overall returns, they would have to average a 300 percent loss on their ETI investments. The author acknowledges that the effect is too large to attribute to ETIs and must be picking up the effect of some other unobserved variable that negatively affects returns. A second empirical concern is that the ETI effect is not consistent in the annual versus the pooled data. Our third concern is that the author limits his sample to pension funds that have the necessary data in all three years, which reduces the number of plans in his sample to fifty-six (the original sample of defined benefit plans was 173 in 1991, 280 in 1992, and 260 in 1993). This is troubling because the reduced sample may not be representative, and the results are sensitive to outliers.[12] To test the robustness of Nofsinger's results, we reestimated his model using the entire PENDAT sample for individual years (1991, 1992, and 1993), then with pooled data for those three years, then for 1995 and 1997 individually, and finally with pooled data for all five years available. Our results show that the coefficient of ETI activity does not have a statistically significant coefficient in any of the models.[13]

Our conclusion from this review of ETI activity is that the world has changed since the late 1970s and early 1980s when activists first turned their attention to state and local pension funds. At that time, targeted investing—particularly in the form of in-state mortgages—was associated with lower returns for a given level of risk. Moreover, during the 1980s, a few public plans, such as Kansas, Alaska, and others, suffered large losses, that subjected public plan investments to increased scrutiny. As a consequence, public plan investment practices became more sophisticated; ETIs were redefined as investments that pay market returns and provide opportunities for collateral benefits. The extent to which such opportunities exist today is open to question, but this survey shows that very few state and local pension assets are invested in ETIs—not more than 2.5 percent. Also, the empirical evidence indicates that ETIs do not have a significant impact on pension fund returns.

This conclusion is reinforced by the results of two new studies recently commissioned by CalPERS (California Public Employees Retirement System 1999). Although it is unclear how representative the samples are, both studies suggest that public pension plans are performing about as well as private plans. Wilshire Associates, a California-based pension investment consultant, found no systematic difference in the investment performance of 50 large corporate and 50 large public plans (with total assets of $870 billion combined) (Wilshire Associates 1999). Annualized returns ending September 1998, net of fees and expenses, are shown in Table 4. Private

TABLE 4. Annualized Returns on Public and Private Pension Assets (%)

	Five years	Ten years
1. Median total fund returns		
Corporate pension funds	12.3	12.4
Public pension funds	11.4	11.6
2. Median U.S. equity returns		
Corporate pension funds	16.6	15.4
Public pension funds	16.5	15.6

pension funds had a 1-percentage point higher return over both reporting periods, but this was attributable entirely to their relatively greater holdings of (riskier) stocks. When stock investments were examined separately, the results showed that corporate pension equity portfolios returned 0.1 percentage point per year more than public pension equity portfolios over five years, but 0.2 percentage points less over ten years. Further, using a regression-based methodology to control for risk, Wilshire found that the median public pension plan actually exhibited a higher risk-adjusted return than did the median private pension plan.

The second study by Cost Effectiveness Management Inc. (CEM) (Ambachtsheer, Halim, and Scheibelhut 1999) reported similar results. The firm analyzed four years of data (1994–97) for 51 corporate ($325 billion) and thirty-four public ($632 billion) pension plans. Again, the finding was that corporate plans have a slightly higher average gross return than public funds over the period (14.6 percent versus 13.4 percent), but this reflected greater equity holdings by corporate plans as compared to public plans (63 percent versus 52 percent). A separate analysis of the performance in large-cap U.S. stocks showed nearly identical performance (21.35 percent for corporate plans versus 21.10 percent for public plans). CEM concluded that the type of sponsorship of the fund is not what drove fund performance. The factors that mattered were the size of the plan (economies of scale and a full-time manager), the proportion of plan assets passively managed, and good governance structures with a clear mission. These characteristics appeared to be equally prevalent in the public and private sectors—at least in those plans included in the Wilshire and Cost Effectiveness Management samples.

Shareholder Activism

The most recent avenue through which politics might enter public pension fund investing is shareholder activities—that is, public plans using the ownership rights associated with their equity holdings to influence the behavior of individual firms. Two comments are relevant before describing activity in this area. First, all proposals to invest the Social Security Trust Funds in equities require that voting rights be given to the asset managers, not voted at all, or voted in the same fashion as the other shareholders, which is equivalent to not voting at all. Thus, the voting issue would not arise at the federal level. Second, assuming that improving profitability—not politics—is the motivation for pension fund intervention in corporate activity, the expected effect on returns is positive, not negative.

The Nature of Shareholder Activism

Shareholder proposals are most frequently directed at companies that under-perform their peers (Nesbitt 1994; Karpoff, Malatesta and Walkling 1996).[14] They typically focus on three types of issues: altering the structure of Board governance (eliminating staggered board terms, separating the positions of CEO and chairman of the board, or creating a compensation committee entirely composed of independent Board members); removing takeover defenses provisions (eliminating or weakening a company's poison pill); or changing voting procedures (making shareholder votes confidential or adopting cumulative voting procedures for directors). With one exception, shareholder proposals are only advisory under state law.[15] This means that even if a proposal passes with a majority of votes, management is not required to take the requested action.

In terms of the mechanics, most shareholder activism involves submitting proposals under the Securities and Exchange Commission (SEC) Rule 14 a-8. This rule permits shareholders to include a proposal and a 500-word supporting statement in the proxy distributed by the company for its annual shareholder meeting (Black 1998). This SEC rule allows shareholders to avoid the expense of preparing their own proxy statements and soliciting their own proxies. Keeping costs down is important because even the most activist institutions spend less than half a basis point of assets under management on governance efforts (Del Guercio and Hawkins 1999).[16] While Rule 14 a-8 minimizes costs, it can be used to address only limited subjects. Most importantly, it cannot be used to nominate candidates for the board of directors.

Of the 437 shareholder proposals submitted to companies in 1998, institutional investors accounted for 42 percent; individuals accounted for the rest (IRRC 1998f). Of the institutional investors, labor unions were the biggest players (15 percent of the total), followed by money managers (12 percent), the Interfaith Center on Corporate Responsibility (8 percent), and public pension plans (6 percent). In the case of public plans, three states—California, New York, and Wisconsin—were responsible for most of the activity. The only other participant was the College Retirement Equities Fund (CREF), which is a retirement system used by university and research employees in both the public and the private sector (see Table 5).

TABLE 5. Prevalence of Corporate Governance Shareholder Proposals for Public Pension Plans in 1998

Proposal sponsor	Number of proposals
Individuals	257
Unions	67
Other institutional investors	52
Interfaith Center on Corporate Responsibility	33
Public plans	28
College Retirement Equities Fund	2
California Public Employees Retirement System	5
New York City Employees' Retirement System	7
New York City Fire	3
New York City Police	4
New York City Teachers	4
State of Wisconsin Investment Board	3
Total	437

Source: IRRC Corporate Governance Bulletin (1998f).
Note: Two proposals sponsored by churches are included in the 257 proposals sponsored by "individuals."

In the United States, shareholder activism by institutional investors began in the late 1980s.[17] A key feature of large U.S. corporations is the separation of ownership from control—that is, the shareholders own the firm, but the managers run it. This separation creates an agency problem in that managers may run the firm in their own interests, rather than in the interests of shareholders. In the early 1980s, corporate takeovers provided a measure of discipline by threatening to replace the management of poorly performing firms. With the reemergence of state antitakeover laws and poison pills over the late 1980s, institutional investors concerned about corporate performance turned to alternative means to discipline firms. Shareholder proposals then became a way to address the shareholder-manager agency conflict and to pressure managers to adopt value-enhancing changes (Pozen 1994).

Some critics charge that public pension plans cannot effectively carry out this disciplining task, contending that such plans confront pressure to take politically popular positions that actually hurt firm performance (Romano 1993). Others suggest that public pension plan managers do not face the right incentives to maximize shareholder value. As a result, such managers may use the proposals to generate publicity or enhance their reputations for future employment, rather than to enhance the value of the firm (Murphy and Van Nuys 1994). Thus, the empirical question is whether activism has produced any demonstrable results, and whether these results have been positive or negative.

Impact of Shareholder Activism on Company Performance[18]

Answering this question turns out to be quite difficult. One reason is that the effect of activism may be buried in the noise associated with other factors affecting firm profitability. Our results using the PENDAT data showed that shareholder activism had no significant effect on returns in 1997.[19] Most of the other studies also reveal no correlation, although there are a few exceptions.[20] Nesbitt (1994) documented a rebound in the performance of firms targeted by CalPERS, but it is not clear whether this rebound was a result of the activism or merely a reversion to the mean in stock price returns. Opler and Sokobin (1997) examined the "focus list" of the Council of Institutional Investors and found a significant above-average return in the year after targeting and no mean reversion in their control sample, although other studies did find mean reversion among poorly performing firms.

A different strategy seeks to document abnormal returns around the date when a formal shareholder proposal is announced. Here no obvious pattern emerges, perhaps for several reasons.[21] One is that it is not clear what an "event" means. For example, a formal shareholder proposal could be the result of management's inflexibility, whereas successful informal negotiations could indicate that management responded to shareholder interests. Also, considerable uncertainty surrounds the "event" date, because shareholder proposals are often discussed informally prior to formal announcement (Black 1998).

Yet another strand in the research literature explores the relationship between activism and discrete corporate events, such as CEO turnover, asset sales, or spin-offs. Earlier studies produced mixed results, but Del Guercio and Hawkins (1999) criticized these efforts for failing to account for the heterogeneity in investment strategies among different funds and the impact of these strategies on efforts to affect corporate governance.[22] For example, since the CalPERS, California State Teachers Retirement System (CalSTERS), and the New York City Funds (NYC) rely on indexing and outside managers, they cannot walk away if they do not like the performance of a particular stock. Therefore, these plans are interested in improving the overall performance of the market; as a result they pursue more generic topics, such as confidential voting, and are happy to make their moves very public, since they want spillover effects. In contrast, CREF is 80 percent indexed but actively manages the remainder of the assets, and the State of Wisconsin Investment Board (SWIB) is internally managed and actively engaged in stock picking. These latter plans tend to have narrow firm-specific goals, such as eliminating poison pills, and they generally try to avoid publicity, since they can make money by buying a stock before they target a company and earn a gain from the effort. Taking account of the heterogeneity in strategies, Del Guercio and Hawkins find that targeted companies experience more asset sales, restructuring, spin-offs, and employee layoffs during the next three years than a control sample.

One problem in this type of analysis, however, is that targeted firms are generally poor performers, and poor performers are more likely to experience turnover in top management or a takeover than strong performers. Hence, it is necessary to use a control group of equally poor performers in the same industry. If the researchers use a less sophisticated measure to select the control group than institutions use to target firms, the study could produce a spurious correlation between activism and the governance event (Black 1998).

The conclusion that emerges from the review of the empirical literature is that some studies have found a positive relationship between shareholder activism and firm performance, but the results are still far from robust. Perhaps this should be expected given that funds do not spend very much on this activity, do not act jointly, do not conduct proxy fights, and do not try to elect their own candidates to the board of directors.[23] Alternatively, individual firm data may not be the place to look for success; the impact of shareholder activism may emerge in the form of changing corporate culture. For example, shareholders rarely persuade companies with staggered boards to repeal their provisions, but few companies are making new staggered board proposals because their chances of success are low (Del Guerico and Hawkins 1999).

It is important to reiterate two points before turning to the topic of divestiture. First, the debate with regard to shareholder activism is generally about the magnitude of the positive response from this form of activity, not concern about fund losses. Second, with regard to the social security debate, the issue would not arise at all; all proposals to invest the trust fund in equities require that the proxy voting be undertaken by the individual portfolio managers or not used at all.

Divestiture

It is sometimes argued that public pension plans face pressure to sell assets for political reasons, an issue known as "divestiture." In practice, divestiture has been a one-issue phenomenon, focused on South Africa investments during the apartheid period. Beyond South Africa, politics has not led to divestiture; issues raised in some states by Northern Ireland generally have been resolved by companies promising to adhere to human rights principles not by funds selling stock. Public plans have generally resisted divestiture of tobacco stocks, and to the extent that divestiture has occurred, it has responded to concern about risk-adjusted returns rather than social considerations.

The Issues

Divestiture issues have arisen in three cases: South Africa, Northern Ireland, and tobacco.

South Africa. As opposition against the South African government apartheid policy increased during the 1970s, social activists charged that companies investing in South Africa indirectly supported the government and its discrimination policies. In an initial effort to resolve the conflict, the Reverend Leon Sullivan in 1977 introduced a set of guidelines for companies doing business in South Africa, the so-called "Sullivan principles," that called for nonsegregation of races and equal pay for equal work. However, many felt that the Sullivan principles did not go far enough, and in the wake of the continued controversy, Reverend Sullivan called in 1987 for companies to withdraw completely from South Africa.

During this period, the majority of public pension plans put restrictions on or divested their South Africa holdings (Romano 1993). For example, California banned investment in South Africa in 1986, giving the pension plans four years to unload their investments. By the end of 1990, the plans had sold $11 billion in stocks and bonds, representing about 10 percent of the portfolio (Schnitt 1994). New Jersey banned investments in 1985 and sold $4 billion or 15 percent of its total holdings (Price and Schramm 1991).

In 1993, as the apartheid government started unraveling, African National Congress President Nelson Mandela urged international investors to lift their sanctions. State and local governments and public pension plans quickly responded. New York City's retirement system, one of the country's largest plans managing $48 billion in assets, dropped restrictive legislation the following month (Fortune 1993). California lifted its ban in early 1994, and CalPERS immediately bought $1 billion worth of stock previously barred (Schnitt 1994). Within a few months, a majority of funds had eliminated their policies against investment in South Africa and started to invest in companies previously not available.

Northern Ireland. All references to South Africa have been eliminated from state law; the only country currently cited with any frequency is Northern Ireland.[24] Thirteen states and the District of Columbia have expressed concerns about the discrimination against Catholics in Northern Ireland in their state laws. The state laws and pension board policies regarding Northern Ireland generally do not prohibit investment or call for divestiture. Instead, states have required companies doing business in Northern Ireland to sign onto the "MacBride principles," a set of policies aimed at eliminating religious discrimination (Appendix Table 3).

Tobacco. In the 1990s, attention turned to tobacco companies. In view of pending lawsuits against tobacco companies, investigation of tobacco advertising, and antismoking campaigns, pension funds have faced increased pressure from lawmakers and regulators to sell their tobacco stocks. Some proponents of divestiture base their case on social philosophy; but most argue that pending litigation against tobacco companies and possible legislation have made investing in tobacco stock much riskier.

Among institutional investors, interest in divestiture of tobacco stocks was originally based on health and moral issues. The first wave of divestitures occurred in the mid-1980s when several public health associations, foundations, and religious organizations sold their tobacco holdings citing ethical conflicts. The second wave of tobacco divestitures, which involved university endowments, occurred in the early 1990s. Among private pension plans, CREF created a tobacco-free account in 1990 but has not divested any tobacco stock so far (Investor Responsibility Research Center 1997a).

It was only when the financial risk associated with tobacco holdings was perceived to have increased markedly that states began to advocate divestiture.[25] So far, although several states have proposed banning investments in tobacco stocks, only one state—Massachusetts—has done so.[26] In other states, when state lawmakers have proposed divestiture bills, they have generally been met with strong opposition from the pension plans. For example, in California, CalPERS forcefully opposed divestiture, arguing that any form of divestiture contradicts a passively managed long-term index strategy (*Los Angeles Times* 1998).[27]

Table 6 summarizes the current policy on tobacco investments by public plans. In addition to the Massachusetts state legislation, public plans in eight other states have introduced their own restrictions on tobacco holdings. In some cases, these restrictions have required plans to divest; in other cases, pension funds have kept their current tobacco stock but put restrictions on future investments. Overall public pension plans have sold only between 5 percent and 10 percent of their tobacco holdings (Narayan 1997; Investor Responsibility Research Center 1997a, b, c, d, e, f, 1998). The biggest divestiture occurred in Florida, where the pension system in 1997 sold all its tobacco holdings valued at $835 million, this sale alone accounts for more than two-thirds of public pension plans' total divestiture of tobacco stocks (Investor Responsibility Research Center 1997f).

The Impact of Divestiture on Pension Fund Returns

Investment policies that include selecting assets based on criteria other than risk and return have a negative effect on expected risk-adjusted returns, since restricting the selection of stocks makes it more difficult to eliminate systematic risk through diversification.

South Africa. The experience with divestiture of companies doing business in South Africa turned out to be different in practice than in theory because of some unique circumstances. During the early 1980s, South Africa–free portfolios actually performed better than nondivested portfolios (Grossman and Sharpe 1986; Angelis 1998). Because companies with South Africa

TABLE 6. Investment Policies in Tobacco Stock of State and Local Pension Plans

State	Law	Year
Investment policy by state law		
Massachusetts	Must divest tobacco holdings within three years; local pension boards exempt from divestment requirements but cannot buy additional tobacco stock	1997

Pension plan	Policy	Year
Investment policy by pension board		
Denver Employee Retirement Program	Divest holdings of tobacco	1996
Florida State Retirement Trust Fund	Divest all holdings of tobacco	1997
Maryland State Retirement and Pension Systems	Sold all tobacco stock but retains right to purchase tobacco stock at future date	1996
Minnesota State Board of Investments	Froze tobacco holdings in actively managed accounts; no restrictions on tobacco holdings in index funds	1998
New York State Teachers' Retirement System	Underweight tobacco in index fund by 25 percent	1996
New York State Common Retirement Fund	Froze future investments of tobacco stock in actively managed funds; no restriction on investments in tobacco stocks in the indexed portion of the portfolio	1996
New York City Employees' Retirement System	Froze tobacco investments in index funds; no restrictions on actively managed accounts but money managers have been advised to "use caution" when considering future tobacco investments	1998
Pennsylvania Public School Employees' Retirement System	Froze tobacco investments	1997
Philadelphia Municipal Pension Fund	Divested tobacco stock	1997
San Francisco City and County Employees' Retirement System	Voted to divest tobacco holdings; sold holdings in index fund.	1998
Vermont State Employees' Retirement System and Vermont State Teachers' Retirement System	Divested tobacco stock	1997

Source: Derived from Social Investment Forum (1998) and IRRC Investor's Tobacco Reporter (1997a, b, c, 1998a, b, c, d, e).
Some smaller city plans have also divested their tobacco stock: Boston, Mass., 1997; Burlington, Vt., 1997; Cambridge, Mass., Retirement Systems, 1990, and Fulton County, Ga., 1994.

ties were large companies, the divestiture created a bias toward small capi-talization stocks. During this period, small cap firms returned a premium over their risk-adjusted returns, resulting in overall better returns for the divested portfolios (Grossman and Sharpe 1986).

For the late 1980s, the story is more mixed. For the five-year period 1985–89, the S&P 500 including South Africa stocks performed slightly better than the South Africa–free version of the index (*Pensions and Investments Age* 1989). Using data on a subset of public pension plans, Romano (1993) found that restrictions on South Africa investments had a small but statisti-cally significant negative effect on returns for the same time period. Another study by a consulting firm, the Brian Rom Corporation, shows that portfo-lios without South Africa stock ties performed somewhat better than those portfolios with South Africa stock over the same time period (*Pensions and Investments Age* October 1989). However, the authors attribute the success to the superior management skills of those in charge of the South Africa–free portfolios rather than to restricting investments in South Africa.

Using PENDAT data from the early 1990s, the analysis presented earlier in this paper shows no significant effect on returns of restrictions on investing in South Africa. Thus, taking the pre-1993 period as a whole, while theory would suggest that the South Africa divestiture would reduce returns, spe-cial circumstances produced neutral to positive results.

Tobacco. In contrast to the pervasiveness of businesses involved in South Africa, tobacco companies constituted less than 2 percent of the holdings of state and local plans even before any divestiture. Therefore, any finan-cial effect of divestiture should be quite small. Indeed, over the ten-year period 1986–96, the S&P 500 including tobacco stocks showed a return only 16 basis points higher on an annual basis than the S&P 500 without tobacco stocks. The S&P 500 data also suggests that the risk-return trade-off has worsened in the 1990s. For the five-year period 1991–96, the S&P 500 portfolio including tobacco stock had 15 basis points lower return on an annual basis and a higher coefficient variation than the portfolio exclud-ing tobacco stock (Hemmerick 1997). This trend has continued and recent data show that for the five-year period ending February 1999, every major tobacco stock underperformed the S&P 500 on a risk-adjusted basis (So-cial Investment Forum 1999). This decline in risk-adjusted return provides a justification for selling tobacco stock for financial rather than social con-siderations.[28]

To conclude, divestiture policies do not seem to have affected public pen-sion plans to any great extent.[29] The widespread divestiture of investments with South Africa ties during the 1980s was a unique event. Divestiture of South Africa assets was not limited to public pension plans but reflected a policy supported worldwide to impose economic sanctions against South Africa. Recent experience with tobacco indicate that most public pension plans continue to hold tobacco stocks and argue that investment policies should be based on risk and return considerations, rather than on social arguments.

Pensions as a Safety Valve

The final way in which politics could enter into plan performance arises if states and localities turn to their pension funds in times of fiscal distress. Public pensions are regulated by states, with state law setting investment policies as well as rules for the composition of the pension board. Pension boards usually consist of a combination of members elected by the plans' participants, members appointed by the state, and members named ex officio (for example, the state treasurer or comptroller) (Romano 1993). The role of the state in the regulation of pension plans and the presence of political officials on pension boards can create a conflict of interest between states and plan participants. In particular, states may see pension plans as a source of revenue in times of fiscal stress and be tempted to use pension funds to cover shortfalls in their budgets (Hushbeck 1993).

It has been very uncommon for states directly to transfer money intended for pension contributions to the general budget, so that states would fail to make their legally required pension contributions (Hushbeck 1993). In the cases where states have turned to pension plans, it has been more common to change actuarial assumptions in order to reduce the states' required contributions to the plan. Changing assumptions can free up funds but still allow the state to make its required contribution to the pension fund. However, not every change in assumptions is an attempt to reduce contributions; in many cases, changes are justified by improved economic conditions, increased rate of return, or changes in the funds' asset mix.

Use of Pension Funds in State Budgets

The financial health of public pension plans improved dramatically during the 1980s. They adopted actuarially sound funding methods, benefited from increased contributions to their funds, and were subject to improved oversight. These changes and higher investment returns during the 1980s, helped improve funding. In 1993, the median plan's stock funding ratio had risen to 97 percent and the mean ratio was 95 percent (Mitchell and Carr 1996).[30]

By contrast, many states faced severe budget deficits in the early 1990s. Given the improved financial status of pension funds, a few state governments did in fact turn to their public plans for assistance.[31] One publicized case occurred in California, where the state faced a $14.3 billion budget deficit in 1991. The legislature allowed the state to reduce its required pension contributions to CalPERS by $1.6 billion to help reduce the budget shortfall, an amount representing 2.4 percent of total assets and equal to what the system had earned in excess of projected earnings for the year (Durgin 1991).[32] This was the first time any state government actually used money for general budgetary purposes from funds earmarked for the pension system. CalP-ERS lost its suit in state court and the money was transferred to the general budget. California again failed to make the full required pension contributions in 1992 and 1993 (Vrana 1997). Fund administrators again filed suit in 1994 to stop the practice, and eventually, in 1997, the California Supreme Court ruled that workers had a right to an actuarial sound pension system, and ordered the state to pay back the money to the pension system. The funds were paid back in full during the 1997–98 fiscal year (Hushbeck 1993; Romano 1993; Gunnison 1997; Walsh 1997; Walters 1997).[33]

The direct use of pension funds, as occurred in California, proves to be a rare occurrence in the history of U.S. public pension plans. In times of fiscal stress, it has been more common for states to use indirect methods to free up funds. Instead of reducing already committed contributions to the pension system, states have sometimes changed actuarial methods or assumptions to reduce required contributions. For example, the real discount rate of pension obligations is determined by the difference (the spread) between the assumed rate of return and the rate of assumed wage growth. The higher the discount rate, the lower future pension obligations will be, reducing the state's required contributions to the pension fund.

Many pension systems have changed their interest rate assumptions over time, but the evidence suggests that most of these changes can be justified on economic grounds.[34] For example, Mitchell and Smith (1994) examined the spread for public pension plans over the 1980s, and found a mean spread of 2 percent, a number close to the historic real interest rate. Based on this, they concluded that state governments had not strategically altered the spread to lower required contributions. Dulebohn (1995) reached a similar conclusion in the early 1990s.

In practice, it can be difficult to distinguish between what is actuarially correct, and what is done to help state budgets.[35] Even though the survey evidence does not indicate widespread manipulation of actuarial assumptions, a few states have clearly changed actuarial assumptions or accounting methods to cover budget deficits.[36] As one example, Governor Cuomo of New York argued that public pension assets should be considered one tool among many to deal with the needs of the state. In 1990, the state switched accounting methods creating a surplus for the pension fund and reducing the state's required contribution to zero (Hemmerick and Schwimmer 1992). In response, the pension system filed suit. A state court ruled that the proposed change would divert pension funds to cover current budget deficits and ruled it illegal in 1993. At that point, the state was ordered to pay back $403 million, an amount equal to what would have been contributed under the old accounting scheme (Sorenson 1995).

New Jersey also changed accounting methods in 1992, to increase the value of the public pension fund, which reduced that year's required contributions by $773 million. Since required contributions based on the *old* accounting method had already been deposited into the pension system, and using the *new* accounting method the state had contributed $773 million more than required, the state transferred the "excess" amount from the pension system to the state treasury. A similar bookkeeping change was made in 1994, reducing required contributions by $180 million, with the total adjustment representing approximately 2 percent of assets. The Internal Revenue Service (IRS) launched an inquiry into these transfers arguing that once money was paid into the pension system any removal of money was prohibited. The state counterclaimed that it had the right to recover contributions made in excess of required contributions the same year they were made. Before the case went to court, an agreement was reached in which the state agreed to pay back the money in form of excess contributions over several years (Pulley 1996).

As a final example of politics influencing public pension finance, in a few instances plans have agreed to come to the assistance of a state or local government. When Philadelphia was on the verge of bankruptcy in 1991, the city obtained a short-term loan of $140 million from the state's well-funded public school employees retirement system. The money was paid back quickly and with interest without threatening the financial status of the pension plan (Eithelberg 1991).

To conclude, states have occasionally tried to use pension funds as a source of revenue in times of fiscal pressure. However, in a few instances of obvious misuse of funds, that state courts have protected participants and ordered the payment reinstated. Although states sometimes have changed actuarial assumptions to free up funds, studies prove no evidence of systematic misuse of assumptions. Further, funding ratios have not been reduced; the PENDAT data from 1991–97 indicates that the mean funding ratio has consistently been around 95 percent.

Conclusions

Our exploration of public pension investment policy highlights—despite reports of widespread economic targeting and screening (Franco, Rappaport, and Storey 1999)—the limited extent to which social or political considerations affect the performance of state and local pension funds. Economically targeted investing, which caused such a stir in the 1980s, accounts for no more than 2.5 percent of total state and local portfolios, and does not appear to hurt investment performance. In terms of shareholder activism, very little activity is going on, and the little that is going on is more likely to help than hurt pension fund performance. In terms of divestiture, public plans generally resist selling stocks for political purposes and try to exhaust all avenues of compromise before taking such an action. Finally, the evidence of states trying to use pensions as a safety valve indicates that affected parties will sue, and the courts will protect the rights of participants.

In our view, it is particularly remarkable that so little social investing has taken place at the state and local level given that many of these public plans lack the federal protections afforded corporate pension plans and those envisioned for possible social security equity investment (see Aaron and Reischauer 1998; Advisory Council on Social Security Reform 1996; Ball 1998; and Munnell and Balduzzi 1998). First, little attempt is made to keep politicians away from public plans; in fact, many plans have the state treasurer and other elected officials sitting on the pension board. In the case of Social Security Trust Fund investments, Congress would be expected to establish an expert investment board, similar to the Federal Reserve Board or the Federal Retirement Thrift Investment Board that administers the federal employee Thrift Savings Plan. To insulate such a board from political influence, members would be appointed for long and staggered terms. Second, many state and local plans are still managed in-house where state employees select individual stocks. In contrast, for social security investments, the board would be required to select a broad index fund, such as the Russell 3,000 or the Wilshire 5,000, and it would have to hire private sector money managers on a competitive basis. We believe that such safeguards would prevent even the modest amount of social investing that we found at the state and local level.

One final note, regarding a factor that was not investigated but rather taken for granted throughout this study—namely, the ability of a government entity to contribute to national saving. Some critics argue that it is not possible for the government to accumulate reserves; they claim that any buildup will be dissipated in the form of higher benefits or used to justify a tax cut. But state and local governments have really accumulated reserves to fund their pension obligations; they have not given the funds away in the form of higher benefits; their plans are now roughly 95 percent funded. Nor have they used the large surpluses in their pension accounts to justify deficits in their operating budgets. Their nonretirement budget balance has fluctuated around zero, while annual surpluses in their retirement funds have averaged roughly 1 percent of gross domestic product (GDP). Thus, states appear to be adding to national saving through the accumulation of pension reserves. If it can be done at the state level, it certainly should be possible at the federal level.

The authors would like to thank the editors of this volume, Henry J. Aaron, Pierluigi Balduzzi, Robert M. Ball, Francis Cavanaugh, Peter A. Diamond, James Duggan, Ian Lanoff, Richard Leone, John Nofsinger, and Peter Orszag for helpful comments.

APPENDIX TABLE 1. Multivariate Analysis of Rate of Return of State and Local Pension Plans ETI Activity Measured as an Indicator Variable

	1991		1993		1995		1997		Pooled	
	ROR90	RORAVG	ROR92	RORAVG	ROR94	RORAVG	ROR96	RORAVG	RORCUR	RORAVG
Management strategies										
HINSTATE	-1.94	1.29	-0.56	0.39	-0.59	0.20	0.90	0.02	-0.55	0.60
	(1.61)	(0.83)	(0.82)	(0.61)	(1.17)	(0.42)	(1.18)	(0.64)	(0.56)	(0.46)
RESTRICT	1.21	1.16**	0.68	0.89**	0.10	0.48*	-0.66	-0.19	0.53	0.59*
	(1.00)	(0.54)	(0.50)	(0.40)	(0.79)	(0.27)	(0.62)	(0.35)	(0.37)	(0.23)
SOUTH AFRICA	-0.69	0.21	-0.91**	0.16	-0.53	-0.46	1.09	0.38	-0.45	0.00
	(0.81)	(0.43)	(0.43)	(0.36)	(0.82)	(0.29)	(0.67)	(0.38)	(0.35)	(0.20)
Portfolio composition and size										
EQUITY%	0.02	0.00	-0.01	0.03**	-0.05**	0.01	0.16*	0.07**	0.03**	0.03**
	(0.03)	(0.01)	(0.01)	(0.01)	(0.02)	(0.01)	(0.01)	(0.01)	(0.01)	(0.01)
SIZE	-0.05	0.07	-0.10	-0.04	0.05	0.08	0.22**	0.12**	0.01	0.06*
	(0.18)	(0.10)	(0.09)	(0.07)	(0.13)	(0.05)	(0.10)	(0.05)	(0.07)	(0.03)
Management and reporting practices										
OUTEVAL	-2.33**	-0.10	1.34**	-0.16	-1.20	0.11	-2.75**	-0.94*	-0.87*	-0.04
	(1.03)	(0.58)	(0.60)	(0.56)	(1.02)	(0.34)	(0.83)	(0.51)	(0.48)	(0.26)
ADINVST	-0.66	-0.95**	0.28	0.23	-0.88	-0.15	0.02	-0.11	-0.16	-0.19
	(0.81)	(0.43)	(0.43)	(0.35)	(0.66)	(0.22)	(0.45)	(0.25)	(0.29)	(0.16)
PROXY	—	—	—	—	—	—	-0.31	-0.32		
							(0.58)	(0.32)		

	(1)	(2)	(3)	(4)	(5)	(6)	(7)	(8)	(9)	(10)
Board composition										
ELCTMEMB	−0.03*	−0.02**	−0.01	0.00	0.00	0.00	0.00	0.00	0.00	0.00
	(0.01)	(0.01)	(0.01)	(0.01)	(0.01)	(0.00)	(0.01)	(0.00)	(0.01)	(0.00)
Year										
YEAR91									−5.35**	0.60**
									(0.57)	(0.27)
YEAR93									−4.11**	−0.14
									(0.42)	(0.23)
YEAR95									−12.13**	−2.48**
									(0.43)	(0.17)
CONSTANT	11.46**	10.84**	10.77**	10.17**	4.57	7.01**	2.95	5.83**	12.84**	8.74**
	(3.62)	(1.92)	(1.84)	(2.02)	(3.00)	(1.14)	(2.04)	(1.14)	(1.44)	(0.83)
R^2	0.08	0.13	0.07	0.08	0.07	0.09	0.50	0.40	0.55	0.30
Number of Observations	155	132	220	123	144	120	166	156	698	543

Source: Authors' calculations using PENDAT (see Zorn 1991, 1993, 1995, 1997).
"Size" variable is measured as the natural log of assets. Standard errors in parentheses. HINSTATE is an indicator variable for ETI activity.
** Significant at the 5 percent level. * Significant at the 10 percent level.
For variable definitions see Table 2.

APPENDIX TABLE 2. Multivariate Analysis of Rate of Return of State and Local
Pension Plans ETI Activity Derived from Boice Dunham
Group

	1993	
	ROR92	RORAVG
Management strategies		
GOLDMAN	−1.06	0.15
	(0.83)	(0.59)
RESTRICT	0.71	0.89**
	(0.49)	(0.40)
SOUTH AFRICA	−0.91**	0.15
	(0.43)	(0.36)
Portfolio composition and size		
EQUITY%	−0.01	0.03**
	(0.01)	(0.01)
SIZE	−0.06	0.03
	(0.10)	(0.08)
Management and reporting practices		
OUTEVAL	1.27**	−0.02
	(0.59)	(0.54)
ADINVST	0.36	0.27
	(0.44)	(0.35)
Board composition		
ELCTMEMB	−0.01	0.00
	(0.01)	(0.01)
CONSTANT	10.05**	9.85**
	(1.88)	(1.61)
R^2	0.07	0.09
Number of Observations	223	126

Source: Authors' calculations using Boice Dunham Group (1993) and PENDAT (see Zorn
1993). GOLDMAN is an indicator variable for ETI activity derived from Boice Dunham Group
(1993).
Note: Standard errors are in parentheses.
**Significant at the 5 percent level. *Significant at the 10 percent level.
For variable definitions see Table 2.

APPENDIX TABLE 3. State Investment Prohibition Laws

State	Policy	Source
Alabama	None	Code of Alabama
Alaska	None	Code of Alaska
Arizona	None	Code of Arizona
Arkansas	None	Code of Arkansas
California	General prohibition of investment in firms furthering or complying with *Arab League* boycott of Israel.	California Government Code §16649.81 (1999)
	On or after January 1, 1994, state trust moneys shall not be used to make additional or new investments in business firms that engage in discriminatory business practices in furtherance of or in compliance with the *Arab League's* economic boycott of Israel.	California Government Code§ 16649.81 (1999)
Colorado	None	Code of Colorado
Connecticut	Urge companies to follow MacBride principles. Beginning in 1987, divest all holdings in *Northern Ireland* and invest no new funds unless such corporations have implemented the MacBride principles.	Connecticut General Statute §13–13h (1997)
	No investment in *Iran*.	Connecticut General Statute §3–13g (1997)
District of Columbia	Any assets of the funds invested after March 16, 1993, in stocks, securities, or other obligations of any institution or company doing business in or with *Northern Ireland* shall be invested to reflect advances to eliminate discrimination made by these institutions and companies, pursuant to the MacBride principles.	D.C. Code §1–721 (1998)
Delaware	None	Code of Delaware

APPENDIX TABLE 3. Continued

State	Policy	Source
Florida	Any moneys or assets of the System Trust Fund, which shall remain or be invested on and after October 1, 1988, in the stocks, securities, or other obligations of any institution or company doing business in or with *Northern Ireland*, or with agencies or instrumentalities thereof, shall be invested subject to the provisions of Mac Bride principles.	Florida Statute §121.153 (1998)
	The State Board of Administration shall divest any investment and is prohibited from investment in stocks, securities, or other obligations of any institution or company doing business in or with *Cuba*.	Florida Statute §215.471 (1998)
Georgia	None	Code of Georgia
Hawaii	None	Code of Hawaii
Idaho	None	Code of Idaho
Illinois	None	Code of Illinois
Indiana	None	Code of Indiana
Iowa	None	Code of Iowa
Kansas	None	Code of Kansas
Kentucky	None	Code of Kentucky
Louisiana	None	Code of Louisiana
Maine	The treasurer of state and the Board of Trustees shall review the extent to which U.S. corporations or their subsidiaries doing business in *Northern Ireland*, in which the assets of any state pension or annuity fund are invested, adhere to the MacBride principles.	Maine Revised Statutes §1955 (1997)
Maryland	None	Code of Maryland

State	Provision	Citation
Massachusetts	No funds shall be invested in any bank or financial institution which has outstanding loans to any individual or corporation engaged in the manufacture, distribution or sale of firearms, munitions, including rubber or plastic bullets, tear gas, armored vehicles or military aircraft for use or deployment in any activity in *Northern Ireland*, and no assets shall be invested in the stocks, securities or other obligations of any such company so engaged.	Massachusetts Annotated Laws Ch. 15A, §40 (1999)
	No new investment of funds shall be made in stocks, securities or other obligations of any company that derives more than 15 percent of its revenues from the sale of tobacco products.	Massachusetts Annotated Laws Ch. 32, §23 (1999)
Michigan	None	Code of Michigan
Minnesota	Whenever feasible, the board shall sponsor, cosponsor, or support shareholder resolutions designed to encourage corporations in which the board has invested to pursue a policy of affirmative action in *Northern Ireland.*	Minnesota Statutes §11A.241 (1998)
Mississippi	None	Code of Mississippi
Missouri	Whenever feasible, the state treasurer shall sponsor, co-sponsor or support shareholder resolutions designed to encourage the bank, financial institution or other corporation in which the state treasurer or other state agency has invested state funds to pursue a policy of affirmative action in *Northern Ireland.* Nothing in this section shall be construed to require the state treasurer or any other state agency to dispose of existing investments or to make future investments that violate sound investment policy.	§30.720 Revised Statutes of Missouri (1997)
Montana	None	Code of Montana

APPENDIX TABLE 3. Continued

State	Policy	Source
Nebraska	With respect to corporations doing business in *Northern Ireland*, the state investment officer shall, consistent with the MacBride principles, invest in corporate stocks or obligations in a manner to encourage corporations that in the state investment officer's determination pursue a policy of affirmative action in *Northern Ireland.*	Revised Statutes of Nebraska §72-1246.07 (1998)
Nevada	None	Code of Nevada
New Hampshire	Whenever feasible, the treasurer shall sponsor, cosponsor or support shareholder resolutions designed to encourage corporations doing business in *Northern Ireland* in which the treasurer has invested to adopt and implement the MacBride principles.	Revised Statutes Annotated 6:33 (1999)
New Jersey	Consistent with sound investment policy and prudent fiduciary standards, the treasurer shall, with respect to state funds available for future investment in corporations doing business in *Northern Ireland*, invest such funds in corporations conducting their operations in *Northern Ireland* in accordance with the MacBride principles and fair employment practices.	Revised Statutes Annotated 6:34 (1999)
New Mexico	None	Code of New Mexico
New York	Consistent with sound investment policy, the comptroller shall invest the assets of the common retirement fund in such a manner that the investments in institutions doing business in or with *Northern Ireland* shall reflect the advances made by such institutions in eliminating discrimination as established pursuant to the MacBride principles.	New York Consolidated Law Services Retirement & Social Security S §423-a (1998)

State		
North Carolina	None	Code of North Carolina
North Dakota	None	Code of North Dakota
Ohio	None	Code of Ohio
Oklahoma	None	Code of Oklahoma
Oregon	None	Code of Oregon
Pennsylvania	Consistent with sound investment policy, the board shall invest the assets of the fund in such a manner that the investments in institutions doing business in or with *Northern Ireland* shall reflect the advances made by the institutions in eliminating discrimination as established pursuant to the MacBride principles.	Title 24 Pennsylvania Consolidated Statutes § 8527 (1998)
Rhode Island	The general treasurer, in accordance with sound investment criteria, is encouraged to make future pension fund investments in U.S. firms which conduct business in *Northern Ireland* and which abide by the MacBride Principles of fair employment.	Rhode Island General Laws §35-10n-14 (1998)
South Carolina	None	Code of South Carolina
South Dakota	None	Code of South Dakota
Tennessee	None	Code of Tennessee
Texas	The comptroller may not use state funds to invest in or purchase obligations of a private corporation or other private business entity doing business in *Northern Ireland* unless the corporation or other entity (1) adheres to fair employment practices and (2) does not discriminate on the basis of race, color, religion, sex, national origin, or disability.	Texas Government Code §404.024 (1999)
Utah	None	Code of Utah
Vermont	None	Code of Vermont
Virginia	None	Code of Virginia
Washington	None	Code of Washington
West Virginia	None	Code of West Virginia

APPENDIX TABLE 3. Continued

State	Policy	Source
Wisconsin	None	Code of Wisconsin
Wyoming	None	Code of Wyoming

Source: Derived by authors from state laws.

The MacBride Principles are used to determine the existence of affirmative action taken by institutions or companies doing business in Northern Ireland to eliminate ethnic or religious discrimination based on actions taken for: (1) increasing the representation of individuals from underrepresented religious groups in the work force, including managerial, supervisory, administrative, clerical and technical jobs; (2) providing adequate security for the protection of minority employees, both at the workplace and while traveling to and from work; (3) the banning of provocative religious or political emblems from the workplace; (4) publicly advertising all job openings and making special recruitment efforts to attract applicants from underrepresented religious groups; (5) providing that layoff, recall and termination procedures should not in practice favor particular religious groupings; (6) the abolition of job reservations, apprenticeship restrictions and differential employment criteria which discriminate on the basis of religion or ethnic origin; (7) the development of training programs that will prepare substantial numbers of current minority employees for skilled jobs, including the expansion of existing programs and the creation of new programs to train, upgrade and improve the skills of minority employees; (8) the establishment of procedures to assess, identify and actively recruit minority employees with potential for further advancement; and (9) the appointment of senior management staff members to oversee affirmative action efforts and the setting up of timetables to carry out affirmative action principles.

Notes

1. The compendium, which supports targeted investing, was designed as "the first step in the creation and analysis of a detailed database that pension fund trustees, public officials, pension consultants, and others can use when considering ETI programs and evaluating their appropriateness for funds" (p. 1).

2. A similar view of ETIs is expressed by U.S. Department of Labor (1992) and Watson (1994). Freddie Mac and Fannie Mae were established originally by the federal government to ensure that affordable mortgages are available to low- and middle-income households. To increase the supply of mortgage funds, Freddie Mac and Fannie Mae buy mortgages in the secondary market and sell them as securities to investors thereby freeing up more funds for mortgage lending. Both entities are now owned by private investors.

3. Boice Dunham Group surveyed the 50 state public employee retirement funds (representing $535.7 billion of assets) and the 54 largest other public employee retirement funds (representing $318.9 billion of assets), 6 of which (representing $30.3 billion of assets) refused to participate. The participating funds with $887.3 billion of assets represented about 73 percent of estimated total state and local pension fund financial assets as of June 1993 ($1167.6 billion as of end of 1992 and $1255.9 billion as of end of 1993 suggests about $1211.8 billion as of mid-year).

4. The survey asked in various years: "What percentage of the portfolio is directed in-state for developmental purposes? (1991 and 1993)" "What percent of the portfolio is targeted in-state? (1995)" "Is a portion of the portfolio targeted or directed in-state for economic development purposes? If yes, what percentage of your portfolio is targeted in-state? (1997)"

5. In addition to the comprehensive surveys reported above, partial surveys yield similar results. For example, a 1996 report on the twenty largest public plans showed that ETIs accounted for 2.9 percent of total holdings. Given that large plans are more likely than small ones to engage in ETI activities, this survey is fully consistent with those reported for the nation as a whole (*Spencer's Research Reports* 1997).

6. Nofsinger (1998) and Romano (1993) both included a variable for the percentage of the board elected by fund members, but they did so for opposite reasons and expected coefficients of opposite signs. Romano's hypothesis was that board members who are elected by fund members, as opposed to appointed or ex officio, are not political and therefore would not be pressured or lured into ETI activity. Romano expected and found a positive relationship between elected board members and rate of return. Nofsinger included the identical variable to represent agency costs resulting from organizational inefficiency, in that beneficiaries will not take account of the burden they are imposing on future tax payers if ETIs have a negative impact on returns. He anticipated and found a negative (but generally not statistically significant) coefficient.

7. In 1991, ETI activity appears to have a significant positive effect on rate of return, but this is not consistent with either theory or results for later years. It can only be regarded as an anomaly.

8. GAO (1995) conclusions are consistent with the findings reported in this paper, but they cannot be used as supporting evidence since the agency examined only seven plans that had a history of success in ETI investing and therefore were not representative. GAO found that the returns for the ETIs promoting business development were generally similar to the returns of benchmark investments. The only exception was that the performance of ETI venture capital (3.2 percent of total ETI activity) sometimes appeared to lag the comparison investments.

9. At first glance, Table 3 in the Romano article gives the reader a very different impression about the success of the empirical analysis because the author uses a one-tailed rather than a two-tailed test to evaluate statistical significance.

10. Even though this study provides little support for the contention that state and local pension plans sacrifice large returns for social objectives, critics of government investment have repeatedly mischaracterized the results. For example, the original text read "The results imply that 10% more in-state investments are associated with a 1% drop in return" (p. 109). Based on this statement a 1995 Joint Economic Committee *Economic Update* "The Economics of ETIs: Sacrificing Returns for Political Goals" claimed that "After controlling for differences in size and type of investment, she [Olivia Mitchell] concluded that ETIs were associated with an average 2 percentage point reduction in investment returns." In a September 18, 1995 letter to the Committee, Mitchell clarified that the JEC *Economic Update* had misinterpreted her results. She wrote, "The reported coefficient was quite small: −0.08. To gauge the magnitude of this estimate, suppose we hypothesize that the fraction of in-state holding in state and local pension plans were to grow to 150 percent of their 1990 level, holding all else constant including risk. The predicted effect on returns would be a decline of 0.17 of 1 percentage point −17 basis points, and not the figure of 200 basis points your press release proposes." Similarly, Alan Greenspan (1999) appears to be referring to this article when he says "it has been shown that state pension plans that are required to direct a portion of their investments in-state and those that make 'economically targeted investments' experience lower returns as a result."

11. One problem with the PENDAT data is the large number of missing values on key variables, which means that without imputation many plans must be dropped from the analysis. Diligent researchers try to avoid eliminating a large number of observations by making educated guesses about what the missing information might be. If those are not well documented, however, it is difficult to duplicate the results.

12. Our analysis indicates that the author may have omitted the 7 largest systems, including California, New York, Texas, and Florida; and the reduced sample has a much higher percentage of systems with ETIs than in the original survey.

13. Results are available from the authors upon request.

14. For example, CalPERS and the Council of Institutional Investors, an umbrella organization for large institutional investors, regularly identify a handful of poorly performing firms.

15. The exception is a recent bylaw amendment calling for repealing a poison pill, which, if passed, is binding rather than advisory. The poison pill, created in the early 1980s, is a provision adopted by a number of companies to avoid hostile takeovers. Although the details of the provosions differ by company, one common technique is to issue large numbers of shares to existing shareholders. This tactic increases the price of the company by forcing the buyer to purchase the perferred stock as well as the common stock of the company. Critics have attacked the poison pill bylaw, saying that it improperly interferes with ability of the management and board of directors to run the company. Since the poison pill plays so prominently in the ability of companies to ward off hostile takeovers, the future of the poison pill bylaw is uncertain.

16. One reason why fund managers spend relatively little on shareholder activism may be that they generally do not want to hurt their returns relative to their peers nor allow their peers to free ride on their efforts.

17. The activity was a response to developments in the corporate control market (Pound 1992). In 1982, the U.S. Supreme Court dramatically changed the structure of takeover laws prevailing at the time, by effectively invalidating the restrictive take-

over laws in thirty-seven states. Without any statutory protection against hostile outside takeovers, many managers sought new anti-takeover defenses. In the year following the Court decision, 206 firms adopted antitakeover amendments compared to 22 in the previous year. The adoption of poison pills and state antitakeover legislation accelerated in 1985 after the Delaware Supreme Court and others upheld their use as an antitakeover device. By the late 1980s, poison pills and restrictive state laws posed a formidable obstacle to hostile takeover activity, and hostile takeover activity virtually ceased by 1990. Since the traditional mechanism for replacing management were not functioning effectively, many institutional investors sought to affect firm policies through the use of shareholder initiatives and proxy fights with incumbent managers.

18. Much of the following discussion reflects an excellent survey of the empirical literature by Black (1998).

19. 1997 was the first year that the corporate activism question was included in the survey. The question was framed as follows: "Has your system actively participated in corporate governance issues by voting against management on annual proxy statements or otherwise encouraging companies you hold stock in to change their management activities?"

20. For example, Daily, Johnson, Elstrand, and Dalton (1996) fail to find to find any relationship between shareholder activism and firm performance.

21. Del Guercio and Hawkins (1999) and Smith (1996) find significant negative response to proposals to eliminate a takeover defense. Strickland, Wiles, and Zenner (1996) and Wahal (1996) find significant positive returns to successful "jawboning." Smith finds significant positive returns (1.1 percent) to companies acceding to Calpers proposals, but significant negative returns (1.2 percent) to companies that resist.

22. For example, Karpoff, Malatesta, and Walkling (1996) find no correlation between activism and subsequent CEO turnover.

23. Pension funds do not coordinate their activism; in fact, they try not to target the same company in the same year. When asked why, they often cite a regulatory barrier—shareholders who act together on a voting issue and together own more than 5 percent of a company's shares must file with the SEC and risk a lawsuit by the company and other shareholders (Black 1998). But a SEC filing is not an insurmountable hurdle and companies rarely sue major institutional investors. It may be that most activist investors are trying to change the corporate culture as much as to improve the returns to any one firm, so spreading their interventions gives them maximum leverage.

24. The only other countries cited are the Arab League, Iran, and Cuba. California prohibits investment in firms furthering or complying with the Arab League boycott of Israel, Connecticut bars investment in Iran, and Florida prohibits investments in companies doing business with Cuba.

25. The City of Cambridge, Massachusetts, divested its tobacco stock in 1990, but no other divestment activity occurred until 1996 (Investor Responsibility Research Center 1997a).

26. The ban was signed into law in 1997 giving the public pension system three years to divest its tobacco holdings, which constituted about 1 percent of the overall portfolio. However, the public pension plans sold their tobacco holdings within 3 months (Investor Responsibility Research Center 1998a).

27. The divestment bill in California has not been approved by the legislature.

28. The perceived riskiness of tobacco investment was further evidenced by a recent move by RJR Nabisco, in which the company separated tobacco production from its food production.

29. Aside from tobacco, the only other divestiture activity in recent years occurred in Texas. Texas tried to ban investments in companies that produce music that glamorizes violence and denigrates women, but the ban was ruled unconstitutional. In addition, the Texas Permanent School Fund has decided to sell its holding of Disney stock, citing an ethical stand against Disney's depiction of sex, drugs, and violence in some movie productions (Guy 1998).

30. The funding ratio is measured by the ratio of accrued pension liabilities to the funds assets. However, plans use different actuarial assumptions to calculate their accrued liabilities. In order to compare funding ratios across plans, the Government Accounting Standards Board in 1987 required plans to report their liabilities using a standardized method, the stock funding method. This requirement was withdrawn in 1994, again making it difficult to compare funding ratios (Zorn 1997).

31. An early instance of misuse of pension funds took place in New York in the mid 1970s when the state pension plan bought bonds of four financially distressed agencies to avoid the state diverting contributions intended for the pension plan. The state and city pension plans also bought city bonds worth $125 million when New York City was on the verge of insolvency. A state court originally ruled against the action, but the purchase was made possible through legislation passed by the New York State legislature and Congress (Romano 1993; Eaton and Nofsinger 1999). The city of Detroit also used pension funds to bail itself out in the early 1980s (Franco, Rappaport, and Storey 1999).

32. At the same time, the actuarial function for the pension system was transferred from CalPERS' board to an actuary appointed by the governor. The governor also tried to change the board composition so that political appointees would be in the majority rather than members elected by the plan participants; this move failed. However, in 1992 California approved a state constitutional amendment intended to protect public pension funds from similar incidents and the actuarial function was returned to the pension system (Romano 1993).

33. On a much smaller scale, but similar to California, Illinois transferred $21million (less than 1 percent of total funds) to the general budget in 1991. In response, the pension participants filed suit and the Illinois Supreme Court barred the transfer temporarily but lifted the block (Vosti 1991; Wheeler 1992).

34. Interest assumptions were raised in the early 1990s in Connecticut, New York, Louisiana, Minnesota, Missouri, Rhode Island, and Vermont (Eitelberg 1991).

35. Prudent pension fund management requires regular review of the validity of assumptions, and most plans follow this practice decreasing the risk that changes in actuarial methods are used to divert pension contributions (Hushbeck 1993).

36. Maine changed actuarial assumptions in 1993 but a federal court ruled the changes unconstitutional after participants filed suit (Naese 1996). In 1991,Texas reduced contribution from 7.6 percent of earnings to 6 percent of earnings, decreasing the state's required contribution by $422 million over two years (Hushbeck 1993).

References

Aaron, Henry J. and Robert D. Reischauer. 1998. *Countdown to Reform: The Great Social Security Debate.* New York: Century Foundation Press.

Advisory Council on Social Security Reform. 1996. *Report of the 1994–1996 Advisory Council on Social Security.* Washington, D.C.: Department of Health and Human Services.

Ambachtsheer, Keith, Sandra Halim, and Tom Scheibelhut. 1999. *Do Public Funds Underperform Corporate Pension Funds?* Working Paper. Toronto: Cost Effectiveness Management Inc.

Angelis, Theodore J. 1998. "Trust Fund Investing in Equities." In *Framing the Social Security Debate,* ed. R. Douglas Arnold, Michael J. Graetz, and Alicia H. Munnell. Washington, D.C.: National Academy of Social Insurance. 287–354.

Auerbach, Stuart. 1987. "Sullivan Abandons S. African Code; Activist Minister Urges U.S. Firms to Leave Country." *Washington Post,* June 4: E1.

Ball, Robert M. 1998. *Straight Talk About Social Security: An Analysis of the Issues in the Current Debate.* New York: Century Foundation Press.

Black, Bernard S. 1998. "Shareholder Activism and Corporate Governance in the United States." In *The New Palgrave Dictionary of Economics and Law,* ed. Peter Newman. New York: Grove's Dictionaries.

Boice Dunham Group. 1993. *The Nature and Scale of Economically-Targeted Investments by the Largest U.S. Public Pension Plans.* New York: Prepared for Goldman, Sachs.

California Public Employees Retirement System. 1999. *Public Pension Funds Success Ignored in Social Security Debate, Says CalPERS CEO.* Sacramento: Press release (March 3).

Congressional Research Service. 1999. "State and Local Pensions Plans: Economically Targeted Investments and Social Responsibility Screening." *CRS Report for Congress* (May 25): 1–15.

Daily, Catherine M., Jonathan L. Johnson, Alan E. Ellstrand, and Dan R. Dalton. 1996. "Institutional Investor Activism: Follow the Leaders?" Working Paper. Bloomington: Indiana University.

Del Guercio, Diane and Jennifer Hawkins. 1999. "The Motivation and Impact of Pension Fund Activism." *Journal of Financial Economics* 52, 3.

Duhlebohn, James H. 1995. "A Longitudinal and Comparative Analysis of the Funded Status of State and Local Public Pension Plans." *Public Budgeting and Finance* 15, 2.

Durgin, Hillary. 1991. "Politicians Grabbing Pension Assets." *Pensions and Investments* (July 8): 1.

Eaton, Tim V. and John R. Nofsinger. 1999. "An Examination of ERR and Asset Allocation in Public Plans." Unpublished manuscript, Marquette University, Milwaukee, Wis.

Eitelberg, Cathie. 1991. "Public Pension Funds: A Balancing Act." *Government Finance Review* 7, 6.

Ferlauto, Richard and Jeffrey Clabourn. 1993. *Economically Targeted Investments by State-Wide Public Pension Funds.* Washington, D.C.: Center for Policy Alternatives.

Fortune, Mark. 1993. "U.S. Government Funds Free Their Assets from S. African Investment Restrictions." *Emerging Markets Week* (November 15): 1.

General Accounting Office. 1995. *Public Pension Plans: Evaluation of Economically Targeted Investment Programs.* Washington, D.C.: U.S. GPO. GAO/PEMD-95-13.

Greenspan, Alan. 1999. *On Investing the Social Security Trust Fund in Equities.* Testimony before the Subcommittee on Finance and Hazardous Materials, Committee on Commerce, United States House of Representatives, March 3.

Grossman, Blake R. and William F. Sharpe. 1986. "Financial Implications of South African Divestment." *Financial Analysts Journal* 42, 4: 15.

Gunnison, Robert B. 1997. "Wilson Orders $1.2 Billion Repaid to Retirement System." *San Francisco Chronicle* (July 30): A13.

Guy, John W. 1998. "Disney and Texas Fund's Investment Policy." *Pensions and Investments* (July 27): 12.

Hemmerick, Steve. 1997. "Funds Say Clinton's Actions Snuffing Out Tobacco Stock Allure." *Pensions and Investments* (September 29): 3.

Hemmerick, Steve and Anne Schwimmer. 1992. "State's Pension Grab Fought: CalPERS Appeals; NY System Wins." *Pensions and Investments* (August 17): 2.

Hushbeck, Clare. 1993. "Public Employee Pension Funds: Retirement Security for Plan Participants or Cash Cow for State Governments?" Working Paper 9301. Washington, D.C.: American Association of Retired Persons.

Investor Responsibility Research Center (IRRC). 1997a. *Investor's Tobacco Reporter* 1, 1 (July).

———. 1997b. *Investor's Tobacco Reporter* 1, 2 (September).

———. 1997c. *Investor's Tobacco Reporter* 1, 3 (November/December).

———. 1998a. *Investor's Tobacco Reporter* 2, 1 (January/February).

———. 1998b. *Investor's Tobacco Reporter* 2, 2 (May).

———. 1998c. *Investor's Tobacco Reporter* 2, 3 (July).

———. 1998d. *Investor's Tobacco Reporter* 2, 4 (May).

———. 1998e. *Investor's Tobacco Reporter* 2, 2 (August/September).

———. 1998f. *Corporate Governance Bulletin* (July/October): 1–9, 41–43.

Karpoff, Jonathan M., Paul Malatesta, and Ralph A. Walkling. 1996. "Corporate Governance and Shareholder Initiatives: Empirical Evidence." *Journal of Financial Economics* 42, 3: 365–95.

Litvak, Lawrence. 1981. *Pension Funds and Economic Renewal.* Washington, D.C.: Council of State Planning Agencies.

Los Angeles Times. 1998. "California: News and Insight on Business in the Golden State; The State/Pensions; CalPERS Opposes Tobacco Divestment." February 19: 2.

Mitchell, Olivia S. 1995. Letter to Dan Miller at the Joint Economic Committee. September 18.

Mitchell, Olivia S. and Roderick M. Carr. 1996. "State and Local Pension Plans." In *Handbook of Employee Benefits: Design, Funding, and Administration,* ed. Jerry S. Rosenbloom. Chicago: Irwin. 1207–22.

Mitchell, Olivia S. and Ping-Lung Hsin. 1997. "Public Pension Governance and Performance." In *The Economics of Pensions: Principles, Policies, and International Experience,* ed. Salvador Valdés-Prieto Cambridge: Cambridge University Press. 92–123.

Mitchell, Olivia S. and Robert S. Smith. 1994. "Pension Funding in the Public Sector." *Review of Economics and Statistics* 126, 2: 278–90.

Munnell, Alicia H. 1983. "The Pitfalls of Social Investing: The Case of Public Pensions and Housing." *New England Economic Review* (September/October): 20–40.

Munnell, Alicia H. and Pierluigi Balduzzi. 1998. "Investing the Social Security Trust Funds in Equities." Working Paper 9802. Washington, D.C.: Public Policy Institute, American Association of Retired Persons.

Murphy, Kevin and Karen Van Nuys. 1994. "State Pension Funds and Shareholder Inactivism." Unpublished manuscript, Harvard Business School, Cambridge, Mass.

Naese, Susan. 1996. "Public Pension Funds Fight States." *Pensions and Investments* (September 16): 28.

Narayan, Shoba. 1997. "The Smokeless Portfolio." *Institutional Investor* (September): 187.

Nesbitt, S. L. 1994. "Long-Term Rewards from Shareholder Activism: A Study of the CalPERS Effect." *Journal of Applied Corporate Finance* 6 (Spring): 75–80.

Nofsinger, John R. 1998. "Why Targeted Investing Does Not Make Sense!" *Financial Management* 2, 3: 87–96.

Opler, Tim C. and Jonathan Sokobin. 1997. "Does Coordinated Institutional Activism Work? An Analysis of the Activities of the Council of Institutional Investors." Working Paper. Fisher College of Business, Ohio State University, Columbus.

Pensions and Investment Age. 1989. "South Africa-free Portfolios Don't Suffer; Managers' Abilities Make the Difference as Restricted Funds Outperform Others." October 16: 40.

Pound, John. 1992. "Raiders, Targets, and Politics: The History and Future of American Corporate Governance Reconsidered." *Journal of Applied Corporate Finance* 5, 3: 6–18.

Pozen, Robert C. 1994. "Institutional Investors: The Reluctant Activists." *Harvard Business Review* (January/February): 140–49.

Price, Margaret and Sabine Schramm. 1991. "No Rush Toward South Africa." *Pensions and Investments* (July 22): 3.

Pulley, Brett. 1996. "Trenton and IRS Settle State Pension Fund Issue." *New York Times,* March 23: 27.

Rifkin, Jeremy and Randy Barber. 1978. *The North Will Rise Again: Pensions, Politics and Power in the 1980s.* Boston: Beacon Press.

Romano, Roberta. 1993. "Pension Fund Activism in Corporate Governance Reconsidered." *Columbia Law Review* 93, 4: 795–853.

Schnitt, Paul. 1994. "PERS Jumps into S. Africa Investment." *Sacramento Bee,* May 17: A1.

Smith, Michael P. 1996. "Shareholder Activism by Institutional Investors: Evidence from CalPERS; California Public Employees' Retirement System." *Journal of Finance* 51, 1: 227.

Social Investment Forum. 1999. "Tobacco's Changing Context." *1999 Tobacco Report.* Washington, D.C.: Social Investment Forum.

Sorenson, Jon R. 1995. "Pataki Budget to Tap State Pension Plan." *Buffalo News,* January 27: 1.

Spencer's Research Reports. 1997. "Economically Targeted Investments Are Generally Limited to Government and Nonprofit Pension Plans." Chicago: Charles D. Spencer & Associates, Inc., October 17. 142–51.

Strickland, Deon, Ken Wiles, and Marc Zenner. 1996. "A Requiem for the USE—Is Small Shareholder Monitoring Effective?" *Journal of Financial Economics* 40, 2: 319–38.

U.S. Congress, Joint Economic Committee. 1995. "The Economics of ETIs: Sacrificing Returns for Political Goals." Washington, D.C.: U.S. GPO, September.

U.S. Department of Labor. 1992. *Economically Targeted Investments: An ERISA Policy Review.* Washington, D.C.: Advisory Council on Pension Welfare and Benefit.

Vosti, Curtis. 1991. "Court Stops Illinois from Diverting Assets." *Pensions and Investments* (September): 42.

Vrana, Debora, 1997. "State Loses Battle over Withholding from CalPERS." *Los Angeles Times,* February, 1.

Wahal, Sunil. 1996. "Pension Fund Activism and Firm Performance." *Journal of Financial and Quantitative Analysis* 31, 1: 1–23.

Walsh, Denny. 1997a. "PERS Due Its Cash, State Told." *Sacramento Bee,* February 21: A1.

———. 1997b. "PERS Victory a Pyrrhic One." *Sacramento Bee,* June 26: A3.

Watson, R. D. 1994. "Does Targeted Investing Make Sense?" *Financial Management* 23, 4: 69–74.

Wheeler, Charles N. 1992. "Pension Funds Transferred to Pay Illinois Bills." *Chicago Sun-Times,* May 30: 5.

Wilshire Associates. 1999. "Private Versus Public Pension Fund Investment Performance." Santa Monica, Calif.: Wilshire Associates, February 4.

Zorn, Paul. 1991. *1991 Survey of State and Local Government Retirement Systems: Survey Report for Members of the Public Pension Coordinating Council.* Chicago: Government Finance Officers Association.

———. 1993. *1993 Survey of State and Local Government Retirement Systems: Survey Report for Members of the Public Pension Coordinating Council.* Chicago: Government Finance Officers Association.

———. 1995. *1995 Survey of State and Local Government Retirement Systems: Survey Report for Members of the Public Pension Coordinating Council.* Chicago: Government Finance Officers Association.

———. 1997. *1997 Survey of State and Local Government Retirement Systems: Survey Report for Members of the Public Pension Coordinating Council.* Chicago: Government Finance Officers Association.

Chapter 9
Asset/Liability Management in the Public Sector

Michael Peskin

Public defined benefit pension plan investing is in a transitional phase,
evolving from one that had an asset-only focus, to one that encompasses the
full asset/liability relationship. This chapter argues that this shift may accelerate as politicians, sponsors, participants, trustees and others, realize that
asset/liability management (ALM) within a finance framework is not just a
theoretical nicety. Rather, it reduces cost and risk and thus enhances the
efficiency of the retirement system. Additionally, ALM can help remedy the
significant investment, funding, and benefit policy inefficiencies in the public sector pension system sometimes caused by a lack of integration of the
system and weak accounting. This chapter also discusses the sorts of political imbalances that tend to pass cost and risk onto future generations in a
public pension system, and how such imbalances are also ameliorated by
ALM.

What Should a Public Pension System Maximize?

Public pension systems are complex and dynamic. As in any complex system,
everything impacts everything else. Unfortunately, common practice tends
to compartmentalize and segregate benefit policy from investment policy
from funding policy. This practice, coupled with unscientific accounting,
produces substantial increases in cost and risk. Examples include improper
asset allocation, insufficient bond durations, incorrect measurement of the
price of benefits, especially options, inappropriate issue of pension obligation bonds (POBs) and inefficient funding. I argue that a public pension
plan's proper objective should be to provide intended benefits at the lowest
cost. Savings in cost and risk can be achieved by integrating assets, liabilities,
and funding within a corporate finance framework.

TABLE 1. Comparing the Traditional Approach to the ALM Approach

Policy	Traditional	ALM
Investment objective	Maximizes return per unit of volatility; peer group comparison	Minimizes cost per unit of volatility of cost; overall peer group comparison not relevant
Equity exposure	Subject to risk tolerance of trustees	Virtually dictated by nature of liabilities and funded status
Bond duration	Intermediate duration provides highest return per unit of volatility	Long duration provides lowest cost per unit of volatility of cost
Funding policy	Set through regulations and "negotiated" assumptions	Integrated with investment policy to minimize risk adjusted PV of future contributions
Benefit policy	Maximize benefit per unit of cost on deterministic actuarial basis	Maximize benefits per unit of risk-adjusted cost as measured on fully integrated basis

Source: Author's compilation from data supplied by MSDW Global Pensions Group.

Key differences between an ALM framework and the traditional framework are outlined in Table 1. I recognize that the traditional approach is in a state of flux, with some public plans moving slowly in the direction of ALM. Nonetheless, the table affords an overview of problems and proposed solutions, with a perspective on the overall operation of a public pension plan.

An Overview of the Pension Contract

A pension plan can be viewed as a contractual arrangement between the public employer and public sector employees that sets aside deferred wages in exchange for current service. The foregone earnings take the form of both indirect payments (employer provided benefits) and direct compensation (employee contributions). Deferred wages are usually determined by a formula based on pay and service (at or near retirement), with the policy objective of providing postemployment income that, together with personal savings, social security and medical benefits, will be sufficient to maintain living standards. Public plans generally have multiple benefit formulas (see Steffen this volume; Mitchell et al. this volume) that depend on date of hire and many other factors. Not only do the benefit formulas tend to be complex, but also public plans often provide alternate formulas that apply depending on an employee's circumstances (such as date of hire, circumstance of retirement, etc). Public plan benefits are often also indexed to inflation after retirement, either fully or partly.

These defined benefit promises translate into a pension obligation, one that is typically a "general" obligation of the sponsoring public entity. What this means is that the benefits are seen as very secure, since they have the full backing of the public sponsor's ability to tax to meet obligations. This applies irrespective of how well funded the plan may be at any given moment in time; to the extent that the plan has assets, the deferred wage promise is said to be collateralized with trust assets. From a capital market perspective, then, a defined benefit pension plan should be thought of as a collateralized general obligation bond of the sponsoring public entity. The collateral adds to the security of what, in most instances, is an already very secure bond. It is interesting to note that security is not the prime reason for the funding of public pension plans (although this may be a perceived advantage even if untrue). The key reason for funding public pension plans is to improve intergenerational equity—that is, to reduce the transfer of unfunded costs of currently accruing benefits to later generations of taxpayers.

The "pension contract" is an agreement between employees (plan participants) and the public sector employer. In the public plan case, the employer is a public entity typically represented by elected and appointed officials (administration and regulatory bodies; see Useem and Hess this volume). The group eventually at risk is, of course, the electorate—current and future taxpayers. Employee interests are generally entrusted to the unions (as employee representatives) and public plan trustees who exercise considerable control and usually hire an actuary and investment consultant to help make decisions and analyze alternatives. The primary stakeholders are thus the employees and taxpayers; the other key stakeholders are the elected administrators and regulators, unions, plan trustees, and the plan actuary. There are, of course, many other parties in interest including the professional staff (who are also usually beneficiaries), consultants, money managers and many others.

Cash Flow, Expense, Benefit, and Credit Issues

There are four methods by which year-to-year changes in the financial status of a defined benefit pension plan affect the financial position of key stakeholders. These are as follows:

* Cash flow changes: contribution requirements are paid out of taxes.
* Expense changes: accounting expenses are recognized charges to budgets.
* Changes in benefit security and borrowing costs.
* Changes in participant promises.

Each of these is directly related to pension assets minus pension liabilities, or the funded status of the plan. Plan assets on a stand-alone basis have no economic impact on the key stakeholders. Consequently, proper management of the asset/liability relationship is critical. We delve into each in turn:

Cash flow changes. A defined benefit pension plan should be viewed as part of the capital structure of the sponsor. The plan participants have been promised deferred wages. This promise is met through payments from the pension trust and the trust is funded through required contributions as dictated by regulation and negotiation. The economic cost of the plan consists of the present value of future contributions; in this sense, future contributions are taxpayer liabilities.

Contribution requirements are usually calculated using a deterministic basis; that is, the expected benefit cash flows are discounted at the expected rate of return on the assets to yield a present value. Plan assets are then deducted from the liabilities to determine the unfunded obligation and hence the annual contribution requirements. In practice, plan assets are usually measured using a moving market average value. It is well known that current-period contributions are extremely sensitive to the assumptions, particularly the discount rate (see Hustead this volume), which at times allows the system to be "gamed." For instance, a higher assumed discount rate would permit cuts in current contributions without any other change in policy, although this increases the probability of higher contribution requirements in the future. In addition, investment policy can be changed to increase equity exposure. If a higher expected rate of return is used to calculate contributions but the higher risk is not recognized, then current costs appear to be reduced, but there is a higher chance of needing additional contributions in the future.

Measuring liabilities deterministically ignores the asymmetry that almost always exists in pension systems. For example, benefits are often upwardly indexed to inflation, but benefits cannot generally be cut in a period of deflation; many plans raise benefits when plan funding rises, but cannot cut benefits when funding deteriorates; and finally, some employers have "skimmed" excess returns from one plan to provide benefits in an affiliated plan. The New York City Variable Supplements Funds are an example of such "skim" funds, albeit not particularly egregious ones.[1] These funds provide for supplemental retirement benefits funded entirely from returns in the pension plans in excess of a hypothetical fixed income return. There skim is limited to defined benefit caps on the supplemental benefits provided by these particular plans that limit the transfer of "excess" returns.

Changes in expense. In a public pension plan, the accounting objective is generally to assign a cost to the period in which it is incurred. It is usually the accounting cost that would be treated as the cost for administrative budgeting purposes. Most public systems consider the required contribution amount as the accounting cost. In other words, the contribution require-ment for any year is also the cost of the plan that the administrative budget must meet. This has the virtue of preventing gaming on two fronts—funding cost as well as accounting cost– but it makes plan funding more politically salient and more important for the administration to game. Funding, in its role as the accounting cost, is also the cost recognized for budgetary pur-poses and thus reduces the capacity of the administration to spend on other, more politically desirable, projects. Thus the elected administration would prefer the funding cost to be as low as possible (at least until the next elec-tion) so that more of the budget is available to finance the administration's goals.

Of course, any accounting system that does not mark assets and liabilities to market will be "gameable," and this is often a problem with public pen-sions. Assets tend to be kept at "book" value or some smoothed market value measure (such as a moving five year market average). Furthermore, an arti-ficial discount rate (such as the long-term expected return on the portfolio, without adjustment for either risk or changes in the level of interest rates) is used to measure liabilities. It has been suggested that one way to avoid such gaming is to require that both assets and liabilities be accounted for on a market value basis. The "market value" of liabilities would be the liabilities discounted at market rates of interest. One problem with this approach is that there is no "market value" of ongoing plan liabilities; public pension liabilities are politically influenced and not particularly transparent. A more important issue is that the degree to which the plan is prefunded is also de-termined by the discount rate and cost method used. Thus simply discount-ing the average or expected liability cash flows at market rates of interest is also an artifice and does not lead to optimal or efficient answers.

Changes in benefit security and borrowing costs. As noted above, public pen-sion promises are a general obligation of the public plan sponsor and thus in most instances, deemed very secure. Of course, a pension liability may be at greater risk when there is also a significant general obligation risk. In my view, the key reason for funding public pensions is not to enhance secu-rity or manage borrowing costs, but rather to reduce the intergenerational transfer of wealth implicit in a pay-as-you-go financing framework.

Changes in participant promises. Many public pension systems have at least partial inflation protection through cost-of-living allowances (COLAs; see Mitchell et al. this volume). To some, it seems inappropriate to have one sec-tor of the economy (state and/or local taxpayers) guarantee payment for in-flation caused by macroeconomic policy. In any event, most public plans do provide partial COLAs, and those that do not try to provide ad hoc increases if investment performance allows.[2] This latter practice is encouraged by the widespread view that a defined benefit (DB) public pension surplus belongs to participants. This is contrary to the view expressed in the private pension arena under the Employee Retirement Income Security Act (ERISA), since DB pension participants do not bear investment risk. In fact, the practice of delivering plan surplus to participants provides a costly option, one not typically recognized in pension budgeting.

Public Pension Stakeholders and Their Economic Interests

To understand public pension systems, it is helpful to outline the economic interests of the major stakeholders.

Plan beneficiaries. This set of stakeholders seeks to maximize compensation, which is comprised of both earnings and pension income, subject to risk constraints. The constraints include the possibility of losing employment, the chance of losing current or deferred compensation, and the chance of losses in benefits caused by a loss in pension assets.

Table 2 provides a sketch of the "financial T account" of plan beneficiaries. Here, prospective pension benefits are divided into four different risk types (many other subdivisions are possible):

- Benefits secured by current funding including guaranteed COLAs (i.e., collateralized with plan assets as well as secured by general obligation of the sponsor)
- Accrued benefits (if any) in excess of the current funded level that are dependent on the ability of the sponsor to fund
- Future benefit accruals, dependent on both the sponsor's ability to fund and future employment
- Future benefit improvements and COLAs beyond those guaranteed in the formulas, also dependent on negotiation and in turn dependent on the plan's funded status. In other words, the participants own a partial call on any emerging plan surplus.

Some important observations that flow from this schema include the fact that benefits are very secure except for future negotiated benefit improvements. In addition, COLAs beyond those guaranteed and other benefit improvements may be easier to negotiate when the plan is well funded. This would appear to be the major reason why participants should have an interest in funding the plan.

This format also highlights the important but subtle distinction between the value of increased pension benefits to employees in active service in the public versus the private sector. In the private sector, benefit and wage costs are closely integrated, more so than in the public sector (mainly because total compensation costs appear to be set more competitively in the private sector). For this reason, private sector benefit improvements are likely

TABLE 2. Financial T Account of Beneficiaries with Respect to Pensions

Assets	Liabilities
PV funded accrued benefits (secured by trust assets)	Marginal future work to earn future accruals
PV unfunded accrued benefits (subject to sponsor risk)	PV employee contributions out of future wages
PV future accruals (as per current benefit formulae)(subject to sponsor and/or job risk)	
PV future benefit improvements including COLAs in excess of guarantee (subject to sponsor, job, and negotiation risk)	

Source: Author's compilation from data supplied by MSDW Global Pensions Group.

to be accompanied by offsets in other forms of pay. By contrast, unionization in the public sector constitutes a formidable political force, one that sometimes succeeds in enhancing both pay and benefits. Also, public sector wages are a direct cost against the budget of the public entity, so they tend to be sticky. In the past, public pension benefits have sometimes been used to boost compensation, inasmuch as pension costs are not as directly observable and can be "hidden" or deferred to some extent especially if the plan is well funded.

Significant employee contributions are common in public pension plans, and benefit improvements tend to be accompanied by an increase in employee contributions. It must be noted that such benefit improvements are not necessarily a wash from an economic perspective: older, longer service employees' gain as the value of the benefit increases often exceeds the cost of their additional employee contributions. This subsidy is not necessarily made up by contributions of new hires or younger mobile employees, since labor market competition will require that new hires be paid at market rates. High employee contributions also seem to give more weight to the participants' claim on emerging surpluses, which further reduces their value to taxpayers. In other words, if employees are paying half or more of the total contributions more of the emerging surplus is assumed to belong to them than if they were paying no or a small percentage of the contributions. The economic case for ownership of surplus should, however, be based on who bears the risk of investment returns. A fixed (nonrisky) employee contribution is more properly viewed as part of the defined benefit formula. An example may make this clear. Consider a benefit formula of 1.2 percent of final pay per year of service with employees contributing 0 percent of pay. Suppose an alternative benefit formula providing a larger pension, say, 2 percent of final pay per year of service, but requiring compensating employee

TABLE 3. Financial T-Account of Taxpayers with Respect to Pensions

Assets	Liabilities
PV of future work of participants financed by pensions	PV of future contributions in respect of pensions required to hire and retain staff on basis of efficient asset/liability management
PV of deferrals to future generations of taxpayers	PV of future contributions in respect of inefficient management
	PV of future contributions for benefit improvements based on emerging surplus and weak taxpayer representation
	PV of deferrals by past generations of taxpayers

Source: Author's compilation from data supplied by MSDW Global Pensions Group.

contributions of, say, 6 percent of pay, were proposed. These two formulations may be equally attractive to employees and employer. There would be no economic rationale for the view that the latter plan should share surplus with employees to a greater extent than the former plan, through reduction in employee contributions, if the employees are not equally at risk for an increase in contributions if investment performance is poor.

Taxpayers. It would be reasonable for taxpayers to seek to achieve the public services they require, at the lowest feasible cost. In other words, the goal of state and local governments in this arena should be to hire and retain needed staff, while minimizing the present value of future taxes needed to pay the pension obligations. Since pensions are an important component of the total compensation package, financing the pension sensibly ensures that public employees will ultimately be less of a taxpayer burden after retirement; pension funding also takes advantage of the federal tax-free buildup of pension assets prior to retirement. (Local taxes may also be deductible at the federal level). The financial T account of taxpayers with respect to the pension plan looks something like the matrix in Table 3.

The great challenge to taxpayers in the present context, of course, is how to manage a public pension plan efficiently in the face of enormous agency risk and with very little representation. It is important to design administrative structures that can successfully fend off often ingenious raids made on the large pool of assets built up to meet the pension obligations, and these generally occur in a highly politicized environment (Clark et al. this volume; Munnell et al. this volume). The basic problem arises from a key and very important asymmetry in pension finance: pension liabilities cannot be exactly hedged in the capital markets. For this reason, at any point in time there will be a perceived shortfall or surplus in the fund. Emerging shortfalls have to be made up by taxpayers in higher contributions. Emerging surpluses, however, are only partly used to offset future contributions and partly used to finance enhanced benefits (or reduced employee contributions, which are the same thing).

Elected administrators and regulators. Taxpayers' key "agents" are the elected officials and those who run the public pension systems. But problems arise because public pension plans represent an extremely long bond obligation, poorly understood, not marked to market by anybody, and backed by an enormous pool of assets. In this regard, public pension plans are far less tightly governed by an economic bottom line than are their private sector cousins. For this reason they are more susceptible to political pressures, thus increasing complexity and long-term costs in exchange for short-term accommodation. The short-term accommodation is in the form of both higher benefits and lower current costs. The higher, longer-term cost is usually hidden in an unmeasured risk transfer to the next generation.

In practice, this means that everyone connected to the pension plan may be well intentioned, but the time horizon of elected officials rarely extends much beyond the next election. In hard-fought battles for budget resources, therefore, long-term concerns are least represented and lose out to nearer-term considerations. This political imbalance may manifest itself in numerous ways, including the issue of pension obligation bonds, benefit improvements with an underestimated current cost, and investments focused on specific constituent groups.

The solution to this political imbalance is to adopt a rigorous and disciplined framework within which to calculate liabilities and assets, and to establish policies. Such a framework must make the price of options and transfer of costs or risks to future generations transparent. It thus includes a comprehensive stochastic model of the plan going forward many years with explicit modeling of investment, funding and benefit policies. The core economic cost is the present value of contributions to fund the appropriate level of benefits. It is possible to reduce the present value of contributions with appropriate investment and funding policy and a tightening of benefit policy to avoid the provision of expensive options. The sources of these savings are discussed in the next section.[3]

Sources of Public Pension Saving

A traditionally-managed public plan that changes its polity to minimize the present value of future contributions in a fully stochastic framework will experience several types of savings, listed next.

Better asset/liability matching. Designing the assets to move in tandem with the liabilities saves taxpayers money. The reason for these savings lies in the asymmetric payoff pattern described above. An example illustrates this point. Assume a pension plan is 140 percent funded; that is, assets are 140 percent of the plan's accrued liability. Let us further assume that at this point no further contributions (taxes) are required. Now suppose an asset was available that would perform in tandem with the liabilities so as to maintain the ratio at 140 percent, regardless of what occurs with capital markets; that is, asset returns would be sufficient to pay out benefits for the period, and then assets would rise at exactly the same rate that the liabilities increased. Let us call this hypothetical asset the "liability asset." In point of fact, no such asset exists, but it is sufficient in practice to move in this direction to generate savings.

If the plan were fully invested in this "liability asset," no contributions would be required this year or in any future year. Therefore, the present value of future contributions would be zero. Suppose further that there was an alternative asset class, called the "risky asset," with an expected return of 4 percent per annum above the "liability asset." Unfortunately, this 4 percent premium also has a 15 percent standard deviation (i.e., the return differential between the risky asset and liabilities has a 15 percent standard deviation). If the plan invested in this "risky asset" in lieu of the "liability asset," the expected funded ratio would be well in excess of 200 percent after a period of thirty years or so. However, many scenarios would result in funded ratios substantially below 140 percent. Even on those paths that generate large funded ratios at the end of the period, there may be some years where the funded ratio drops below 140 percent. If these points coincide with the actuarial funding valuation, taxpayers will be called on to make contributions. Thus, the present value of contributions will be substantially higher despite the higher expected returns. This increase in cost can only be recouped if surplus at the end of the period can be recaptured by taxpayers. If surplus is used to increase benefits then the situation is even worse, as high returns will lead to higher benefits and higher future costs.

In practice, it is impossible to find a "liability asset." It is, however, possible to cause the assets and liabilities to move more closely in tandem than a traditional management approach can achieve. The "lowest risk" portfolio, as measured by present value of future contributions, is usually a combination of equities and long duration bonds. The actual mix for this "lowest risk" portfolio can vary substantially among plans and has ranged, in my experience for corporate plans, from a low of 20 percent equities to a high of 90 percent equities. The optimal bond duration is specific to each plan and each level of equity exposure. It usually exceeds ten years and is much higher than any of the commonly used bond indices.

Extending the dollar duration of the fixed income portfolio. One way of synchronizing assets and liabilities is to extend the dollar duration of the fixed income portion of the portfolio, by changing how much plan assets rise or fall per 1 percent fall or rise in interest rates. Liabilities, like long duration bonds, are extremely interest sensitive (Leibowitz 1987). This is true even if the pension is partly inflation indexed. This sensitivity to real interest rates grows as the degree of indexation rises, but there are very few liabilities that are insensitive to nominal interest rates. Increasing the dollar duration of the assets not only reduces the riskiness of the asset/liability gap, but it also provides a higher expected return. This higher expected return results mainly from the move up the yield curve. This is based on the existence of an imbedded liquidity premium (i.e., it assumes that, on average, the yield curve is upwardly sloped).

Figure 1 illustrates the impact of increasing dollar duration through increasing the duration of the bond portfolio using a futures overlay (Gold and Peskin 1988). In the efficient frontier depicted in the figure and below, the vertical axis (the return measure) is the mean present value of future contributions over all 400 simulations. The horizontal axis (the risk measure) is the mean present value of future contributions in the worst 80 simulations. The simulations are obtained through stratified sampling. In the example above, the optimal duration is 18 years. Both the expected cost (the mean present value of contributions over 400 scenarios) and the cost risk (the mean cost in the worst 80 scenarios) rise as the duration is shortened or lengthened from the optimal 18 years.

Amount of equity exposure. The pension plan's equity exposure is critical to its cost. The traditional split (60 percent equities, 40 percent fixed income) is often not optimal and sometimes is not even on the efficient frontier. As indicated previously, the "lowest risk" portfolio has varied from 20 percent to 90 percent equities; however, the "lowest risk" portfolio is usually suboptimal because decision makers have a utility function that leads them to accept the tradeoff in going to higher equity exposures. The optimal amount of equity exposure also varies dramatically from plan to plan; in my experience the optimal equity exposure has varied from no more than 30 to 90 percent.

In Figure 2, the efficient frontier extends from 40 to 90 percent equities. The trade-off between "expected cost" and "cost risk" is such that between 40 percent and 60 percent—the cost reduces substantially per unit of risk—the optimal equity exposure lies between 60 percent and 90 percent equities.

There are three key factors impacting the optimal amount of equity exposure. The first has to do with the "noise" in the liabilities. Fixed income assets are suitable "liability matching assets" if the liabilities are similar to bonds. When the liabilities look a great deal like bonds, a close match can virtually eliminate risk. When the liabilities look less like bonds, a residual risk remains even with the "best" matched portfolio. In this latter case, add-

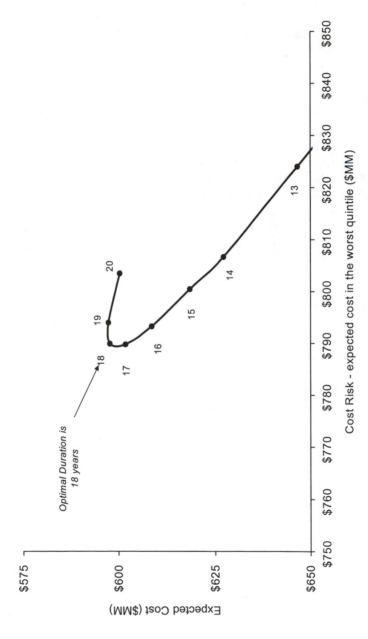

Optimizing Duration
Present Value of Future Contributions
Equity Exposure = 10%

Optimal Duration is 18 years

Expected Cost ($MM)

Cost Risk - expected cost in the worst quintile ($MM)

Figure 1. Optimizing fixed income duration. Source: author's calculations from data supplied by MSDW Pensions Group.

Equity Exposure
Present Value of Future Contributions
Optimal Duration

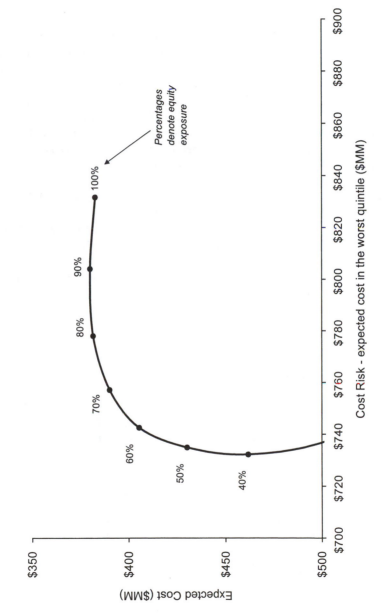

Figure 2. Equity exposure. Source: author's calculations from data supplied by MSDW Global Pensions Group.

ing equity increases returns more sharply than it increases risk. In fact, the equity risk and the liability noise are diversifying and the least risk portfolio will contain some equities.

There are many sources of "noise" including uncertainty in the future demographics in the plan, benefit formulas and design, future pay and future hiring patterns. For example, retiree liabilities are far more accurately represented by bonds than are active liabilities. Salary increases in active liabilities are only partly determined by the level of interest rates and thus create "noise" (volatility in the relationship between bonds and liabilities). The greater the "noise," the greater the optimal equity exposure. This tendency is increased because there is a relationship, albeit small, between the real return on equities over long periods and the real increase in wages that drive active liabilities. Thus the proportion of retirees to actives is an important factor.

Figures 3 and 4 develop the efficient frontiers for plans with identical assets and ABOs but very different "noise" levels. Figure 3 shows the efficient frontier if the liabilities consisted entirely of final pay active liabilities (very high noise). Figure 4 shows the efficient frontier if the liabilities consisted entirely of retirees with no COLAs (very low noise). In the case of the high-noise, efficient frontier, the cost risk increases slowly as equity exposure increases, leading to high optimal equity exposures. In the low-noise case, the efficient frontier ends at 20 percent equities with higher expected cost and much higher cost risk at higher equity exposures.

Also important is the "weight" attached to surplus value. As stated previously, the surplus in a pension plan may have value over and above the reduction in future contributions. It may be recaptured by taxpayers (very rare) or used indirectly to reduce costs elsewhere. The actual value is highly dependent on legislation and the balance of power in the struggle over who owns the pension surplus. Since the appropriate value of surplus is unclear, it is beneficial to examine what the optimal allocation is for a range of possible surplus weights. Generally, the larger the weight, the greater the value of the surplus generated by extraordinary equity returns and the larger the optimal equity exposure.

Figure 5 shows the efficient frontiers in the two extreme cases: that where surplus has no value other than decreasing future contributions (0 percent surplus value) and that where surplus can be recaptured at full value (100 percent surplus value). The efficient frontier in the 100 percent surplus value case is much steeper leading to much higher optimal equity exposures.

Finally, the funded status of the plan matters a great deal. In general, poorly funded plans and well-funded plans lead to higher equity exposures. For poorly funded plans, high equity exposures are necessary because the asymmetry discussed earlier disappears (and may even reverse with little

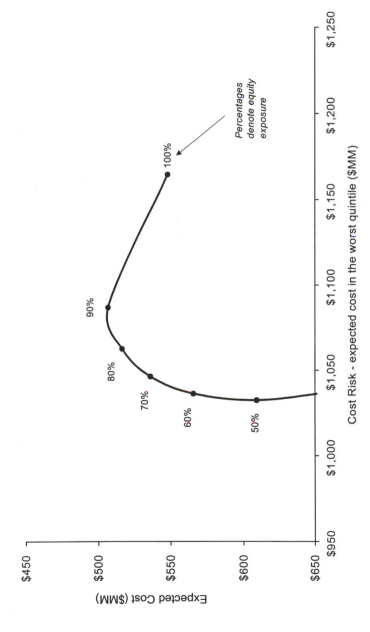

Actives Only
Present Value of Future Contributions
Optimal Duration

Percentages denote equity exposure

Figure 3. High "noise" liabilities. Source: author's calculations from data supplied by MSDW Global Pensions Group.

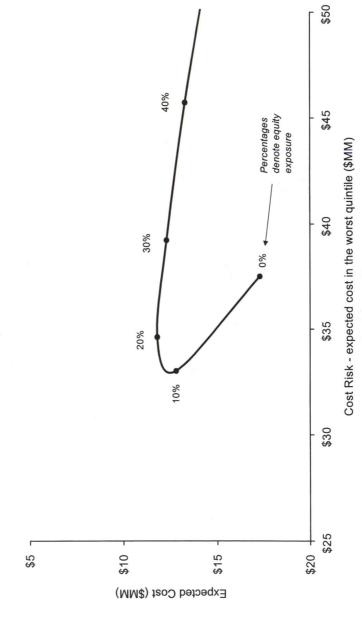

Retirees Only
Present value of Future Contributions
Optimal Duration

Figure 4. Low "noise" liabilities. Source: author's calculations from data supplied by MSDW Global Pensions Group.

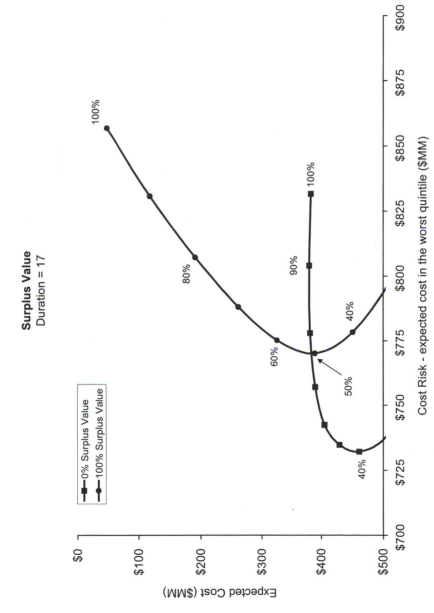

Figure 5. Who owns the surplus? Source: author's calculations from data supplied by MSDW Global Pensions Group.

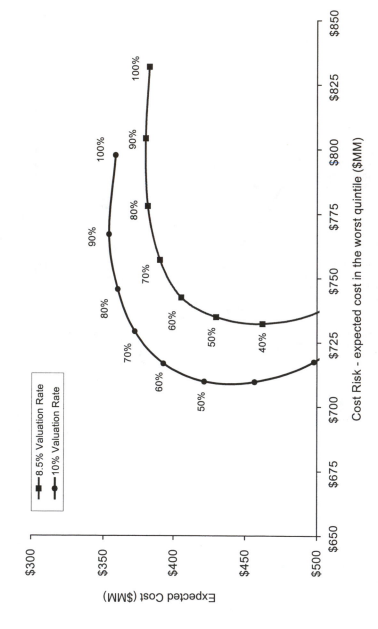

Figure 6. Funding policy. Source: author's calculations from data supplied by MSDW Global Pensions Group.

to lose and much to gain), causing all the upside to be valuable. For well-funded plans, there is a large cushion protecting the plan from future contributions. Thus, even though taxpayers cannot receive full value for the upside, the large cushion limits the downside risk to the extent that it makes the upside of a large equity exposure (a very happy workforce) an attractive trade-off. Plans that are neither poorly nor well funded will usually find that for a given liability noise level, higher equity exposures are economically unattractive.

Rebalancing rules. Another source of savings comes from selecting an appropriate rule for rebalancing the portfolio's optimal asset allocation as the capital markets and other events change the three factors mentioned earlier. It is important to rebalance the portfolio to the mix that is then optimal considering the changes that have occurred.

Funding policy including funding methodology and assumptions. It has long been a tenet of actuaries and financial economists that the pace of pension plan funding is not financially relevant. The cost of the plan is the benefits paid, and funding merely transfers money from one pocket to another. But once it is recognized that the sponsor, or risk bearer, lacks easy access to the surplus in a pension plan, this tenet breaks down. The present value of future contributions can be highly affected by the pace of funding. It is advantageous for taxpayers to make contributions so long as the cost of such additional contributions (the contribution minus the tax deduction) is less than the present value of the future contributions saved if such contributions were made. It is often possible to reduce the present value of future contributions with appropriate changes in funding policy.

Public plans have a tendency to be underfunded for many reasons. One is that surplus assets tend to be used to increase benefits, which in turn leads to increased costs and long run underfunding. Budgets tend to be sticky and once contributions are reduced, it is difficult to get them increased, again leading to long-range underfunding. Administrations tend to defer cost recognition and participants get larger benefit increases if their cost is underestimated. The burden of appropriate funding seems to fall mainly on the shoulders of the plan actuary who is usually a hired consultant and not in a very strong position. It is also usually economically more efficient for taxpayers to aim lower rather than higher given the asymmetries of bearing all the downside risk but not owning all the upside return.

This point is illustrated in Figure 6, where it can be seen that increasing the actuarial discount rate from 8.5 percent to 9.5 percent results in both reduced cost and reduced risk. (There are many situations, however, where it pays instead to decrease the actuarial discount rate and accelerate contributions rather than decelerate them.) Note that the actuarial discount rate is purely a mechanism for determining the pattern of contributions and beyond that has no significance in this framework (i.e., it is one of the outputs from the process of minimizing the present value of future contributions rather than an input).

Many public plan sponsors have issued pension obligation bonds to increase the funding of their plans (Lang 1997). This has been motivated by a budgeting accounting system that allows the sponsor to reduce contributions by more than the cost of borrowing, assuming that the funding earns the expected rate of return on the assets and without adjusting the expected return because of risk. The borrowing cost is the actual borrowing cost. As long as the discount rate (the assumed rate of return) exceeds the borrowing cost, the pension bonds reduce budget outlays. The real financial picture is, of course, quite different and depends on the actual reduction in contributions that occurs over time rather than the assumed reduction using the expected rate of return. It is difficult to envision a situation where the real economics would support the issuance of POBs.

Using a stochastic integrated approach. Measuring costs using a current deterministic basis (expected liability cash flows discounted at expected return on assets) allows considerable gaming of the system through the addition of benefits containing an option feature; it essentially capitalizes the future risk premium on the assets without any cost associated with the risk. The stochastic basis is less "gameable," as it measures risk as well as return and thus assigns a cost to optionality in the benefits. Furthermore, benefits that are more easily matched in the capital markets (i.e., less liability noise) will be assigned an appropriately lower cost as the investment policy can be altered at the same time to reduce overall cost risk.

ALM enforces investment discipline to help avoid political raids on assets. There are advantages to extending the framework from merely minimizing the present value of future contributions to minimizing the present value of contributions as a percentage of tax revenues (i.e., avoid high contribution requirements when the tax basis has eroded). This would make clear that public plans should invest as negatively correlated to the public sponsors tax base as possible. This would help fend off raids such as loans to preferred local businesses. It would also likely lead to more international and other out of state investments.

Defined Benefit Versus Defined Contribution Pensions

A defined benefit plan provides a predetermined level of benefits at retirement; the cost of which is an unknown and largely dependent on investment return. A defined contribution plan provides an unknown benefit at retirement (depending on investment returns) for a predetermined cost. There is a worldwide trend away from defined benefit toward defined contribution plans. A key point, but one frequently missed, is that from a national perspective, any system necessarily translates into a defined benefit system. This is the only system that can ensure that people remain off of welfare.

If a cohort retires under a defined contribution (DC) system with inadequate income (poor investment returns and/or depletion of defined contribution savings prior to retirement owing to economic bad times) then society is going to have to subsidize these retirees. This "insurance," which always becomes payable in particularly trying times (depressed capital markets), turns defined contribution plans into a particularly expensive form of defined benefit plans.

The main problems frequently cited with defined benefit plans are as follows:

- Assets may be insufficient to meet promised benefits (particularly at the national level), causing costs to skyrocket.
- DB systems are complex and can be gamed and manipulated.
- The large pool of assets built up has no direct assigned ownership and thus becomes an easy target for political and other raids.
- When employees change jobs, the vested accrued benefits erode through inflation unless there is inflation protection.

The key perceived advantages of a defined contribution plans are

- There is direct individual correspondence between assets and liabilities.
- There is less opportunity for political and other raids
- DC plans are portable.
- Employees control the investments.
- Employees bear the investment risk.

In fact, many of the perceived disadvantages of DB plans can be cured, or at least ameliorated, by a disciplined structure as outlined here. If these problems can be overcome, DB plans become more efficient for providing retirement income for several reasons. One is that benefit levels can be set to provide desired living standards, with little or no risk of a cohort of retirees needing public assistance. By contrast, in DC plans some fraction of retirees may have inadequate incomes and require public support; this is more likely when capital markets perform poorly and the public sponsor budget is also under extreme pressure. Another issue is that defined benefit plan sponsors generally have much longer time horizons and utility for returns over risk than individuals and are thus willing to take more risk (provide more risk capital). Over long periods, risk capital tends to produce higher returns, which probably lowers the cost of the deferred income (even on a risk-adjusted basis). Also, increased risk capital helps the economy (assuming that equilibrium is not so general as to make everything wash out). Efficiently run defined benefit plans are thus probably more economical. Finally, there is a danger with defined contribution plans that retirees will spend their capital in the belief that they will be subsidized by taxes thereafter.

Conclusions

The economic goal of a public sector defined benefit pension plan should be to provide the promised level of benefits at the lowest present value of future contributions. Traditional management approaches to defined benefit pension plans in the public arena result in a present value of contributions and associated risk that is significantly higher than it need be. As we have shown, benefit, funding and investment policies should be integrated using a comprehensive stochastic model to reduce both cost and risk. Investment policy should more sharply focus on the nature and structure of public pension liabilities, and managers should explore more carefully the extent to which public plan assets can be designed to match public plan liabilities.

Notes

1. I thank Robert North, Chief Actuary of the City of New York, for providing this example, as well as for his many helpful insights and comments that improved this chapter.

2. The advent of government provided inflation-indexed bonds will presumably make it easier to hold assets that back these inflation-linked promises; see Brown et al. (1999).

3. What follows borrows heavily from Peskin (1997) regarding the methods of reducing cost and risk in corporate defined benefit pension plans.

References

Brown, Jeffrey, Olivia S. Mitchell, and James Poterba. 1999. "The Role of Real Annuities and Indexed Bonds in an Individual Accounts Retirement Program." In *Risk Aspects of Investment-Based Social Security Reform*, ed. Martin S. Feldstein. NBER Working Paper 7005, March.

Clark, Robert L., Lee A. Craig, and Jack W. Wilson. This volume. "Life and Times of a Public Sector Pension Plan Before Social Security: The U.S. Navy Pension Plan in the Nineteenth Century."

Gold, Jeremy and Michael Peskin. 1988. "Longing for Duration." *Financial Analysts Journal* (November-December): 68–71.

Hustead, Edwin C. This volume. "Determining the Cost of Public Pension Plans."

Lang, Robert M. 1997. "Using Pension Funding Bonds in Defined Benefit Pension Portfolios." In *Positioning Pensions for the Twenty-First Century*, ed. Michael Gordon, Olivia S. Mitchell, and Marc M. Twinney. Pension Research Council. Philadelphia: University of Pennsylvania Press:

Leibowitz, Martin. 1987. "Liability Returns: A New Look at Asset Allocation." *Journal of Portfolio Management* (Winter).

Mitchell, Olivia S., David McCarthy, Stanley C. Wisniewski, and Paul Zorn. This volume. "Developments in State and Local Pension Plans."

Munnell, Alicia and Annika Sundén. This volume. "Investment Practices of State and Local Pension Funds: Implications for Social Security Reform."

Peskin, Michael. 1997. "Asset Allocation and Funding Policy for Corporate-Sponsored Defined-Benefit Pension Plans." *Journal of Portfolio Management* (Winter).

Steffen, Karen. This volume. "State Employee Pension Plans."

Useem, Michael and David Hess. This volume. "Governance and Investments of Public Pensions."

Chapter 10
Determining the Cost of Public Pension Plans

Edwin C. Hustead

The choice of actuarial assumptions is often an esoteric process commanding little interest beyond the pension plan sponsor. Nevertheless, experience has shown that changes in pension actuarial assumptions can become a political issue because of their impact on pension funding and consequent implications for governmental budgets. In this chapter, I discuss methods of determining and reasons for changing the many key actuarial assumptions used in public (and private) pension plans.[1] Actuarial assumptions are essential in projecting the long-term cost of defined benefit pensions. In addition, actuarial assumptions are frequently used in defined contribution plans to project annuities to individuals, but these assumptions are only of incidental importance in the funding of defined contribution plans. I speak not only to plan actuaries and fiduciaries but also to anyone concerned with understanding how actuarial assumptions can drive financial outcomes in the public sector.

The strong macroeconomy has made the selection of actuarial assumptions relatively easy in the last decade. In fact, the question in setting assumptions has often been how far to go in reducing a pension plan's annual contribution requirements, since reducing contributions could put the plan at risk if conditions worsen. Some plans have set very conservative assumptions to avoid an increase in future contributions except in very unusual conditions. Other plans have been less conservative, so they will have to increase contributions if conditions worsen even moderately. In the latter case, adverse economic conditions could produce required contribution level increases that might result in overall redesign of plan benefits.

Actuarial Assumptions in Pension Plans

Actuarial assumptions are used to predict the amount and timing of contributions to the pension fund and benefits paid from the fund. As used by professional actuaries, these assumptions are classified into two groups: *economic* or *demographic*. The economic assumptions include investment return and inflation and are largely unrelated to any specific pension plan. By contrast the demographic assumptions which include retirement and mortality rates are usually unique to each specific plan's provisions and the demographics of the specific group of plan participants.

Actuarial assumptions are typically changed through a two-step process. First, the actuary studies the validity of the existing actuarial assumptions for the pension plan. This study concludes with a report to the plan's governing body, recommending assumptions that should be used in the future. Second, the governing body acts on the actuarial assumptions. The assumptions adopted by the governing body are then used by the actuary in determining the liabilities of the pension plan.

Table 1 shows a typical set of economic and demographic assumptions for a defined benefit pension plan. Demographic assumptions are those used to project how and when participants will leave active participation in the plan and how long benefits will be paid after retirement. The three main economic assumptions pertain to inflation, investment return, and salary growth.

Many of the assumptions interact with each other. For example, as will be illustrated below, a 1 percent increase in all of the economic assumptions for a fully indexed plan will result in little change in the present value of benefits. In the past, actuaries have often used implicit assumptions that combine one or more of these offsetting factors. For example, an actuary might use a lower-than-expected investment return in lieu of an explicit salary scale. However, modern computers permit and the actuarial profession strongly advises that each economic and demographic assumption be explicit.

The projection of contributions and benefits for a hypothetical plan that pays a benefit equal to 50 percent of final salary at age 65 is presented as an example. No benefits are paid to participants leaving before age 65 and all remaining participants are assumed to retire at age 65. The retirement benefit is indexed to inflation after retirement.

In this example, the employee is enrolled in the pension plan at age 30 with a salary of $10,000. For this hypothetical plan, the actuarial demographic assumptions predict that 90 percent of enrollees leave the system before age 65, so only 10 percent are expected to retire at age 65. Annuity payments will be made as long as the retired worker is alive. The actuary applies a mortality table to determine the probability that the retiree will be alive in any future year. In the present case, the actuary predicts that 60 per-

TABLE 1. Types of Actuarial Assumptions for Typical Governmental Pension Plan

Economic	Demographic
Inflation	Death of
Investment return	Active participant
Salary growth	Disabled participant
General	Retired participant
Individual	Survivor
	Retirement with eligibility for full benefits
	Retirement with eligibility for reduced benefits
	Disability
	Termination with vested benefits
	Termination before vesting

Source: Author's tabulation.

cent of annuitants will survive from age 65 to age 80 and receive a payment at age 80.

The economic assumptions are then used to determine the workers' projected amount and present value of her benefit. Salary growth assumptions predict that the individual's salary will be $30,000 at age 65 so the benefit will be $15,000 (50 percent of final salary). Projections of inflation after retirement predict that the $15,000 at age 65 will have grown to a $20,000 benefit at age 80. Finally the benefits are discounted to the current age, using the expected fund investment return, to determine the present value of the benefit. If, for instance, the discount rate is 8 percent, the fund will need $426 today to pay the benefit at age 80. A full calculation will include benefits paid at other ages and for other terminations.

Economic Assumptions

The three economic assumptions used in the pension valuation—inflation, general salary growth, and investment return—are related and must be considered as a set. Table 2 shows the five-year average of the economic factors from 1951 through 1996. As would be expected, general salary growth and Treasury Bond returns, the least risky investment, followed inflation fairly closely for most of the period. One exception is that the return on Treasury Bonds has been substantially greater than inflation in the 1980s and 1990s. A second is that salary growth was substantially higher than inflation in the 1950s and 1960s.

While equity returns are partially driven by inflation, the relationship of investment returns to inflation is less consistent than with the other factors. With the exception of the 1970s, equity returns were much higher than the other factors throughout the period. A pension actuary must consider the likely relationship between economic assumptions in selecting any given as-

TABLE 2. Economic Factors 1951 to 1996 (%)

Five-year period ending	CPI (W)	Salary growth	Treasury bonds	Stocks
1956	0.9	4.1	2.9	21.5
1961	1.9	3.2	3.9	14.4
1966	1.6	3.7	4.3	6.5
1971	4.6	5.2	6.0	8.9
1976	7.1	6.6	7.6	7.7
1981	9.9	7.8	10.2	8.9
1986	3.8	3.6	11.3	20.0
1991	4.4	3.1	8.7	16.1
1996	2.9	2.8	7.2	15.8

Source: Society of Actuaries (1998).

sumption. It would be unrealistic, for instance, to couple a salary growth assumption of 4 percent with an inflation assumption of 6 percent since that would assume a 2 percent loss in real income each year in the future. While there have been isolated years in which the average person has absorbed a real income loss, the historic trend, as shown in Table 2, has been an increase in real income.

The economic assumptions are also tied closely to each other in their effect on actuarial valuations. Increases of the same percentage in all three assumptions at least partially offset each other. In a system that fully indexes benefits to inflation, a change in all three would result in little change in the liabilities. The degree to which equal changes in the three economic assumptions offset each other in determining the actuarial present values depends on the degree to which benefits are tied to salary growth before retirement and inflation after retirement. Many government plans are fully or partially tied to salary growth before retirement and inflation after retirement.

A 1982 analysis examined the indexing of the Federal Retirement Systems, where prior to 1980 the program had benefits calculated as a percentage of final salary and fully indexed to inflation after retirement (Hustead and Hustead 1982). Table 3 shows that an increase of 1 percent in each economic factor would have had minimal impact on the normal cost of the pre-1980 military retirement system.[2] An increase of 1 percent in all three sets of assumptions would have had minimal impact on the liabilities of the military retirement system. There would be a somewhat greater effect on the federal Civil Service Retirement System (CSRS) normal cost since benefits are tied to the average salary in the three years before retirement rather than final pay. In a system with no indexing after retirement, only about half of the investment return would be offset by an equivalent increase in the salary assumption. Table 3 shows the results for the pre-1980 military retirement

TABLE 3. Effect of Economic Assumptions on Military and Civil Service
Retirement System Normal Cost

	Change in normal cost resulting from a 1 percent increase in annual rate		
Economic factor	Military Retirement System System	Civil service Retirement System	Plan with no COLAs
Inflation	17%	12%	0%
General salary growth	12%	11%	11%
Investment return	(28%)	(25%)	(25%)
Total	1%	(2%)	(13%)

Source: Hustead and Hustead (1982).

system and CSRS. A comparison to a plan without automatic COLA protection was added by the author. The normal cost in the CSRS system falls by 2 percent, and in the unindexed system by 13 percent, when all assumptions are increased by 1 percent.

Inflation assumptions. Since the mid-1980s, the selection of the inflation assumption has been relatively easy because inflation in the United States has been at a fairly consistent level of 3 to 4 percent during that period. During the 1990s actuaries assumed inflation returns of 4 or 5 percent, reflecting their general conservatism. The CSRS Board of Actuaries currently assumes an inflation rate of 4 percent and the average rate among governmental pension plans was 5 percent (Samet et al. 1996).

Experience studies measure inflation using one of the national consumer price indices published by the Bureau of Labor Statistics, which include the CPI for all urban consumers (CPI-U) and the CPI for urban wage earners and clerical workers (CPI-W). The two indices track each other very closely so the difference in using one or the other is very minor. The December 1998 CPI-W was 160.7 compared to 163.9 for the CPI-U, a difference of 3.2 percent in inflation from the base period of 1982–84. The CPI-W is preferred for pension plan purposes since that is the index used to determine COLAs for Social Security benefits.

Investment return. The most critical, and often controversial, assumption is the assumed investment return (see Table 4). In the 1960s and 1970s, governmental pension funds were largely invested in bonds with average returns increasing from around 4 percent in the early 1960s to 8 percent in the mid 1970s. In response to this change in asset mix, actuaries gradually increased investment return assumptions from the 3–4 percent range in the early 1960s to the 6–7 percent range by the early 1980s.

During the 1980s and 1990s, investment returns of governmental funds increased sharply as a result of the high rates of return in the equity mar-

TABLE 4. Investment Mix of Public Pension Plans

	1960	1970	1991–93
Bonds	88.1%	68.1%	41.0%
Equities	2.2	12.0	44.0
Mortgages	6.5	12.6	4.5
Other	3.2	7.3	10.5

Source: Bleakney (1972) and Samet et al. (1996).

kets and the increasing move into that market in response to those high rates of return. Fund investment returns averaged well into the double digits throughout the period. For example the Pennsylvania SERS fund averaged a 13.3 percent investment return from 1981 through 1997 (HayGroup 1998).

Taking the longer perspective, there had been a gradual increase in the investment assumptions over the last thirty years in response to improved investment returns. However, actuaries and the governing boards are conservative and, by the late 1990s, seldom adopted rates greater than 8.5 percent. Ninety percent of the plans studied in SOA (1998) used investment returns of 7 percent to 8.5 percent and the average assumption was 8 percent. Only 13 of the 183 plans used an investment return of 8.75 or 9 percent and none used an assumption greater than 9 percent. The result for most governmental pension funds has been a continual series of large gains from investment return which have, in turn, resulted in both continuing improvement in the percent of liabilities funded by assets and continuing decreases in the employer contributions. For example, from 1980 through 1997, the Pennsylvania SERS contribution declined from 18.0 to 6.7 percent of payroll, and the assets grew from 34 to 107 percent of liabilities (HayGroup 1998).

Most government retirement systems receive an annual report on investment returns from their investment advisors. In that case, the actuary can simply refer to these results in analyzing the historic rate of return. The actuary does need to make sure that the measurement period and method for calculating the rates of return are consistent with the analysis of other assumptions and the use of the rates in the actuarial valuation. This might require, for example, that the actuary convert fiscal year rates of return to calendar year rates of return.

In the absence of an investment advisors report, the actuary needs to adopt a consistent and reasonable rate of measuring investment return. One classic method is to divide the investment return during the year by the average of (1) the value of the fund at the beginning of the year adjusted for new contributions and benefits and (2) the value of the fund at the end of the year less the investment return during the year.

Salary growth. Salary growth is composed of two elements. One is the rate of general increase that applies to all employees and the other is the additional increase associated with any given individual moving through his career with the employer. For example, in a given year, a federal employee might be promoted from a salary of $69,924 at General Schedule 14, Step 4, to a salary of $77,265 at General Schedule 15, Step 2. At the beginning of the next year, the salary for all pay levels might increase 3 percent so the employee is then earning $79,582. The total increase in salary for the individual over the year has been 13.8 percent of which 3 percent is from general increases that apply to all employees and the remaining 10.8 percent is associated with the individual.

These general and individual salary increase elements should be measured separately. The rate of general salary increase can be measured by analysis of the pay practice of the employer. In the case of a public sector employer such as the federal government that pays according to a specific schedule, the general increase is equal to the increase in salary rates in that schedule. If the increase varies by grade and step, then the general increase is determined by weighting the average increase by the number of plan participants at each pay level.

Lacking specific pay schedules, as is generally true in the private sector and increasingly common in the public sector, the actuary can compare the average salary for all employees at the beginning of the year to the average at the end of the year. The result can be taken directly as the general salary increase if there has not been a significant change in the size or composition of the workforce. If there has been, however, the actuary must control for such a change.

Measurement of the individual element of salary growth begins by comparing the end and beginning of year salaries for all employees who participated in the plan throughout the year. The individual salary growth is then the total salary growth less the general salary growth. The calculation of salary growth is usually performed by service and/or age since individual increases are usually substantially greater in the early part of the career as the individuals are promoted to their final position.

A typical individual scale runs from over 4 percent per year early in the career to less than 1 percent later in the career. Combined with a typical general salary increase assumption of 4 percent, the total annual salary increase assumption ranges from 8 percent to 5 percent as age increases.

Economic Factors for Pension Plans

Table 5 compares the economic assumptions used to determine the cost of governmental and private sector pension plans. It can be seen that the public plan economic assumptions reflect a more conservative basis for selecting assumptions: higher inflation and general salary growth assumptions are

TABLE 5. Economic Assumptions Used by Pension Plans

Assumption	State	Federal CSRS	Private	Social security
Inflation (%)	5	4	N/A	3.5
Investment return (%)	8	7	9	6.3
Salary growth (%)	6.5	6.4	5.0	4.4
		(4.25 general, 2.15 average individual)		(general only)

Sources: Samet et al. (1996), OPM (1998), *Pension Forum* (1997), Board of Trustees (1998).

conservative in that they require higher outlays. An assumed lower investment return is conservative in that it increases the present value of future payments.

The 5 percent average inflation rate for governmental plans is much higher than the 3.7 percent average rate in the last fifteen years and, in fact, is higher than the rate in all but one year since 1981. Actuaries for governmental pension plans are gradually lowering the inflation rate but few are below the 4 percent CSRS assumptions or as low as the 3.5 percent social security inflation rate. Private plan actuaries seldom select an explicit inflation assumption because few private plans have automatic retirement cost-of-living adjustments (COLAs). Most large private sector plans do apply ad hoc COLAs every three to five years but, even if these regularly recur, IRS does not permit the actuary to prefund the COLAs before they occur.

The average 8 percent governmental pension plan investment assumption is also conservative in that it is significantly lower than the experience of most plans and of the general market return since 1980. The average private sector investment assumption of 9 percent is closer to actual long-term investment returns but still well below fund returns over the last two decades. The 7 percent investment return rate for CSRS and 6.3 percent for Social Security are relatively low because the only investment available for those funds is Treasury backed securities.

The total state salary scale assumption of 6.5 percent is the same as the federal CSRS assumption. However, if inflation is 5 percent, the average individual salary growth would only be 1.5 percent compared to 2.15 percent for the federal CSRS. This suggests that the total salary growth assumption is less conservative than the other economic assumptions. The private sector salary growth assumption is lower than that of the government plans but it may not include individual salary growth. The social security assumption of 4.4 percent is for general increases only so it is in the neighborhood of the governmental plan assumptions.

Demographic Assumptions

Compilation and analysis of demographic data is a complex process and must be performed very carefully to avoid incorrect selection or application of assumptions. The analysis and interpretation of plan experience must be consistent with demographic rates applied in the pension valuation. For example, if retirement rates in the pension valuation are applied only to those eligible for full retirement at the beginning of the year, then the experience rate should be all retirements divided by those eligible at the beginning of the year. In the past, actuaries set assumptions under the general professional guidelines that require actuarial findings to be based on the actuary's best estimate. The Academy of Actuaries is developing an Actuarial Standard of Practice on Selection of Demographic and Other Noneconomic Assumptions for Measuring Pension Obligations that will offer specific guidance on measuring and setting demographic assumptions for pension plans.

The actuary usually begins the study of demographic assumptions by comparing actual-to-expected ratios for each assumption. For example, the actuary might find that there were 1,200 actual retirements during the experience study period compared to 1,000 expected using the actuarial assumptions. This would be an actual-to-expected ratio of 120 percent (100 percent times 1,200/1,000). This actual-to-expected analysis is a good measure of the overall applicability of the assumptions but can mask differences by age and service. For example, if a plan permits retirement any time after age 60, a simple actuarial assumption might predict that all individuals retire in the year following age 62. An alternative set of assumptions would be that one-fifth of participants retire at each age from 60 to 64. If the actual average retirement age is 62.5 the actual-to-expected ratios would show that either set was reasonable but the two different sets of assumptions could produce significantly different liabilities.

While one aggregate ratio can mask significant differences by age and service, too great a disaggregation can produce results that fail to reveal any overall pattern. Few pension plans are large enough to permit analysis of all demographic rates at every age and service combination but the larger systems usually have enough experience to provide significant results by at least five-year age and service groupings.

Retirement. Retirement rates are measured by dividing the number of participants who retire during the year by the number eligible for that retirement benefit. The rates of retirement are usually unique to the plan provisions and demographics, and most plans can develop credible rates from their own experience. In the absence of sufficient experience the plan actuary can use large plans such as CSRS and statewide plans as a guide to establishing retirement rates.

In general, the retirement rate in the first year of eligibility for unreduced retirement benefits is between a fourth and a half of eligible participants if eligibility is before age 60. The rate then usually drops to 20 percent or less a year with an upturn after age 60 and a spike at age 62 when participants first become eligible for social security.

Different retirement rates should be established for each group of participants with differing retirement conditions. For example, if the general retirement requirement is age 60 but law enforcement officers can retire at age 50, the actuary should establish separate rates for the law enforcement officers. The actuary should select different rates for those eligible for reduced and unreduced benefits.

Retirement rates are much lower among those eligible for reduced than for full benefits, even if the reduction is less than a full actuarial reduction of 4 to 6 percent a year. For example, the number of CSRS retirements doubled after a 1 percent per year reduction was removed in 1966 (U.S. Civil Service Commission 1969).

Determination of the rate of retirement in the first year of eligibility presents a technical problem. The usual practice in determining demographic rates is to divide the number who leave during the year by the number of eligible participants at the beginning of the year. But, if 55 is the first age of retirement eligibility there will be retirements among participants age 54 at the beginning of the year since all of these will become eligible for benefits during the year. One approach is to add a half year of exposure for those who become eligible during the year. The key consideration is that the determination of the rates in the experience study and the application in the valuation have to be consistent.

Disability. Disability rates also vary widely because of differences in plan benefits, eligibility conditions, and demographics. The SOA study found that disability rates for statewide plans are generally based on plan experience. Smaller plans often used published tables with an adjustment to fit the plan's own overall experience. Published tables that are often used are those of the CSRS, social security, and railroad retirement systems. The 1994 CSRS disability rates increase from one per thousand at age 22 to one per hundred at age 61.

Participants who are eligible for either disability or full retirement benefits present another technical problem. If the benefits do not differ, the actuary will often count the disability cases as nondisability retirements in determining the full retirement rates. Disability rates will then stop in the year before full retirement eligibility to simplify both the analysis and the application of disability rates.

Mortality. As with disability, mortality experience for a specific plan, at least before retirement, is usually too sparse to determine tables based totally on the plan's experience. Actuaries often compare actual-to-expected rates on the most widely used mortality tables at the time and select the table that most closely fits each plan's experience.

Most plans use mortality tables produced by the Society of Actuaries (Samet, et al. 1996). These include the tables produced from group annuity mortality experience. The latest tables produced from the group annuity mortality experience are the 1971 and 1983 Group Annuity Mortality (1971 GAM and 1983 GAM) tables and the 1994 Group Annuity Reserving table. An alternative series is the set of tables developed from uninsured pensioner experience. These are the 1984 and 1994 Uninsured Pensioner tables.[3]

The most common table in use for governmental pension plans in the early 1990s, according to the SOA study, was the 1971 Group Annuity Mortality table, usually with projection to years after 1971. One method of implicitly reflecting mortality improvement is to set back the mortality rates by, for instance, assuming a 65-year-old male in the future will have the same mortality as a 60-year-old when the mortality table was developed. The 1983 GAM table was used by a large number of plans in the SOA study and is probably now the most popular table among large state plans.

Recent legislation requires some of the valuations performed by private sector actuaries to be based on a standard table. The standard table is the 1983 GAM table today and will be a table promulgated by the secretary of the treasury after 1999. Many private sector plan actuaries have adopted the 1983 GAM for all purposes rather than to use different mortality tables for different valuations. Public sector plans are not subject to this standard so, while the 1983 GAM plan is popular, it will not become as dominant as in the private sector. For mortality, as for other assumptions, public sector plans only have to conform to the Governmental Accounting Standards Board (GASB) and professional requirements that the mortality tables used in the plan reasonably reflect the mortality of the group.

An important consideration connected with adoption of a new mortality table is the relationship with the mortality table used for determining optional benefits, such as lump sum or joint and survivor benefits, under the plan. If the interest and mortality basis used to determine the optional benefits is different from the valuation assumptions, the selection of an option will increase or decrease the cost of the plan.

The mortality table used to determine optional benefits (the actuarial-equivalence table) often does not automatically change with the adoption of a new table for actuarial valuation purposes. However, even where the tie is not automatic it is good practice to eventually move to the same table for both purposes. Otherwise, there could be significant actuarial gains or losses for both the plan and the participants. If, for example, the retiree were permitted to take a partial or full lump sum benefit, in lieu of the regular retirement benefit, use of an outdated mortality table to determine the lump sum would result in lower lump sum payments than the actuarial equivalent in the plan.

Other terminations. A termination occurs when an active employee leaves the plan. The above decrements dealt with instances in which the terminating employee became entitled to an immediate benefit. Other terminations are those who are not entitled to an immediate annuity. These could be vested, entitled to a later annuity, or not entitled to any annuity. Terminations of participants not eligible for immediate benefits are high in the first year of employment and drop with each year that the participant remains with the employer. As a result, many larger plans vary assumed termination rates by service although others vary the rates by age as a surrogate for service. Some plans, such as CSRS, vary the rates by both age and service. The CSRS termination rates for males vary from 9 percent a year at the earliest age and service to less than 1 percent for the older age and service combinations. The average termination rate is around 7 percent for employees under age 45 in the SOA study. However, the rate varies widely by age, sex, and plan.

As with retirement, the termination rate must be carefully and consistently calculated in the first year after employment since the exposure at the beginning of the year is zero. Termination rates end when the participant becomes eligible for immediate retirement benefits.

Other assumptions. In addition to the primary demographic assumptions there are often other assumptions needed to accurately project all of the benefits of the retirement system. For example, a subsidized survivor benefit would require assumptions about the percentage and characteristics of retirees who elect the subsidized benefits. If joint and survivor options are determined using the actuary's valuation mortality and interest then the actuary does not need to project the number of optional elections. In that case, the present value of a joint and survivor benefit would be the same as for a straight life annuity and the plan would not be adversely or favorably affected by any option selected by the new annuitant.

There should be different sets of demographic assumptions for participants entitled to different benefit levels under the plan. For example, law enforcement officers usually are able to retire at earlier ages than under the general rules so their retirement, disability, and other termination rates are much different than for the general participant population.

Other assumptions include an allowance for administrative expenses to the extent that these are paid by the plan. Administrative expenses for investments are typically netted from the investment return and should be considered in comparing plan investment return with national indices of investment performance.

When and How Are Actuarial Assumptions Changed?

It is important to know who selects the actuarial assumptions. In the public sector actuarial assumptions are typically set at the time of the first valuation of the retirement system based on national data or assumptions for similar plans since the governmental plan in question does not yet have experience to be evaluated. The assumptions are then reviewed periodically with the results, including any recommendation for change in assumptions, reported to the plan sponsor. The review of assumptions is commonly made every three to five years. The actuary reviews the results to determine whether changes in the assumptions should be recommended. The effects of proposed assumption changes in demographic assumptions are then compared to the results without the change to determine the extent to which the validity of the results would be improved by adoption of the recommended changes.

Different plan sponsors will approach the selection of assumptions from different viewpoints depending on the financial circumstances of the plan and budgetary considerations. An actuary will accept assumptions that vary from his or her recommended assumptions as long as the assumptions are within a reasonable range. For example, an actuary might recommend an investment return assumption of 8.5 percent but accept a rate as low as 8 percent or as high as 9 percent if preferred by the plan sponsor.

Actuarial assumptions for private sector pension plans are, at least formally, set by the actuary. The actuary must assure the Internal Revenue Service, through filing of Form 5500, Schedule B, that "in my opinion each assumption, used in combination, represents my best estimate of anticipated experience under the plan" (IRS 1997). In practice, the private sector plan sponsor often exerts a good deal of influence on the assumptions. In the public sector, the formal authority for selection of assumptions varies widely depending on the governance and history of the fund. In many cases (for instance, the Pennsylvania state retirement systems), the assumptions are formally set by the governing board. In other cases (e.g., the federal retirement systems) the assumptions are set by the actuary or a Board of Actuaries.

Whatever the formal arrangement, selection of the actuarial assumptions is usually best achieved as a joint effort of the actuary and the client. If the selection is formally made by the actuary, but the plan sponsor does not agree with the assumptions, the sponsor probably will dismiss the actuary. If the selection is formally made by the sponsor, but the actuary does not agree, the actuary has two choices. The first is to issue a qualified report stating that the actuary does not agree with the assumptions. The second is to resign from the case. Cases of a disagreement that leads to dismissal or resignation are rare.

Underlying Philosophy Regarding Assumptions

There are significant differences in the criteria for selection of actuarial assumptions in the public and private sector. Private sector plans sponsors often attempt to design the amount and timing of pension plan contributions to meet plan sponsor financial goals. For example, a private sector plan sponsor may have an unusually high surplus in a given year and want to maximize contributions in that year. The actuary will usually work with the sponsor to select assumptions within the actuary's range of reasonableness and legal constraints that will best fit the plan sponsor's financial goals.

The often conflicting goals of the private sector plan sponsor, auditors, and the IRS have resulted in a complex and arcane set of funding patterns in the private sector. The actuary for a private sector plan must produce a number of different actuarial valuations to meet all requirements. In addition to the traditional actuarial valuation that presents the actuary's best estimate of the plan funding levels a valuation is required to determine the net periodic pension cost for plan expense purposes, and another valuation to determine the funded status for the Pension Benefit Guaranty Corporation (PBGC). While actuaries for private sector plans attempt to keep assumptions as consistent as possible among the alternative valuations, there are unavoidable differences in assumptions. In particular, the discount rate used for accounting expense purposes, the investment return rate required for PBGC measures, and the actuary's recommended investment rate, usually differ. In 1998, for example, the PBGC rate was below 5 percent, the plan expense discount rate was typically around 7 percent and the long-range actuarial assumption was usually 8 percent or higher.

Government plans are not covered by the PBGC and government accounting rules permit a wide range of assumptions and funding methods. As a result, the actuary for a governmental plan only needs to perform one valuation with one set of assumptions for governmental pension plans. As with the private sector actuary's traditional approach, this is the public sector actuary's best estimate of plan costs and liabilities.

Whatever the formal arrangement, the selection of the assumptions for a public sector plan is usually an interactive process involving the actuary, the pension board, the treasurer and, often, political considerations as described elsewhere in this volume (Bryan this volume; Peskin this volume).

Timing of review of assumptions. The process of adopting new assumptions begins with an actuarial investigation of experience under the plan. The timing of this experience study is often specified in the governing legislation, as it is with the Pennsylvania and federal plans. If the frequency of experience studies is not formally specified in the governing legislation, it is the responsibility of the board and the actuary to determine when a new study

TABLE 6. Hypothetical Results from An Actuarial Review ($B)

Unfunded liability at beginning of year	$20.0 B
(Gains) and losses	
Change predicted by actuary	1.7
Gain due to investment return	(2.0)
Loss due to early retirements	1.1
Loss due to low mortality	0.3
Loss due to high salary increases	0.7
Other gains and losses	0.4
Subtotal gains and losses	0.5
Unfunded liability at end of year	$22.2 B

is needed. Both GASB and the Actuarial Standards Board provide guidance on the timing and content of an experience study (GASB 1994; ASB 1999). Whether formal or informal, experience studies are commonly performed every three to five years as they are with large private sector plans.

It is also considered to be good practice to review the continuing overall validity of the set of assumptions each year, through a gain-and-loss study usually presented as part of the annual actuarial valuation. These studies show the primary reasons for unexpected changes in the liabilities of the pension plan. For example, a gain-and-loss study might show the results in Table 6. An unusually large gain or loss or continuing high gains or losses attributable to a particular assumption, suggests that that assumption should be reviewed before the next scheduled experience study. Confirmation that the assumption was no longer valid could either trigger an early experience study or simply result in a change of the specific assumption without further action on assumptions.

The experience study. The findings of the actuarial study of assumptions are usually presented in an experience study which includes the results of the analysis and the actuary's recommended changes in assumptions, if any. Experience studies usually begin with a presentation of the review of assumptions. The presentation shows the actual-to-expected ratios and other important findings for each of the assumptions with an explanation of significant differences between actual experience and that expected using the current set of actuarial assumptions. The study then presents recommendations for changes in assumptions, if any. Studies should include an estimate of the financial effect of making the recommended change.

The recommendations are usually based on the analysis of experience. For example, the actuary might find that disability rates during the study period proved to be substantially lower than expected and recommend a reduction in those rates. However, the actuary must be careful to consider unusual circumstances that make the experience inappropriate as a basis for setting assumptions about the future. For example, the system might have had an early retirement window open during the experience period that resulted in a high actual-to-expected ratio of retirees. In that case, the actuary should estimate the rates of retirement that would have occurred in the absence of the early retirement window in developing recommendations for long-term assumptions. Conversely, if the plan has adopted a window to begin after the experience study, the actuarial assumptions for retirement should be increased to predict higher retirements while the window is open and reduced to predict lower retirements in the year or two after the window is closed.

The actuary then presents the experience study to the governing body, which tends to focus on the economic assumptions since these are neither as esoteric nor as numerous as the demographic assumptions. Further, since the bulk of the time of the governing body is usually spent on establishing investment policy and selecting investment firms, the governors will be particularly interested in the investment return assumption.

The actuary will make recommendations, and the governing body will consider those recommendations, in light of their overall financing strategy. If, for example, the governing body prefers that changes in cost in future years will likely be reductions rather than increases, the plan sponsor may select a lower investment return rate than a large private sector plan with the same investment history and philosophy. Plan sponsors who are less concerned with potential increases in costs will select assumptions that are closer to the actuary's best estimate. The general approach of governmental plan sponsors is to be somewhat conservative or very conservative in selecting assumptions. For example, in response to double-digit investment returns, the actuary for a plan with a current investment return assumption of 7.5 percent might recommend that the assumption be set at 8.5 percent. A somewhat conservative philosophy might result in an assumption of 8.25 percent but a very conservative plan sponsor might prefer 7.75 or 8 percent. It is likely that the actuary would agree with a very conservative approach, as long as the actuarial report explained that it was the basis for selection of the plan assumptions.

Often the governing body focuses on the projected effect of the change of assumptions as much as on the assumptions themselves. In recent years, with excess investment return driving down employer contributions, governing bodies will be most comfortable adopting a set of assumptions that result in a small reduction in the employer contribution. If the most likely set of assumptions results in a large reduction in contribution, the governing body will often select somewhat more conservative assumptions as a margin against unexpected adverse experience.

This description of the usual process does not, of course, apply to situations where the selection of assumptions becomes a high-profile political issue. The actuary is then sometimes torn between parties who want to re-

TABLE 7. Permitted Funding Methods of Pension Plans

	GASB no. 25	FASAB	FASB no. 87	IRS
Funding methods	Any accepted method (72% of plans in SOA are entry-age normal)	Aggregate entry age normal cost but others permitted if justified	Projected unit credit	Any of the accepted methods
Amortization of unfunded liability	No more than 30 years	None specified	Average working life	5 to 30 years depending on type
Limits on projected benefits	None	None	None	Limits on salaries and benefits
Assumption restrictions	Reasonable	Reasonable	Market interest for discount, others reasonable	Reasonable but investment return and mortality table specified for PBGC purposes

Sources: Samet et al. (1996), FASAB (1995), IRS (1997).

duce the rate as much as possible and others who want little or no reduction in rate. In those cases, any recommendations by the actuary could be viewed by at least one of the parties as political in nature even though such recommendations seldom are, and never should be, influenced by those considerations.

Level and Incidence of Funding

The actuary then applies the new assumptions in the next actuarial valuation to determine the present value of future benefits and to compare these to the value of the assets. This calculation establishes the overall financial status of the plan, but then further direction is needed to determine how the liabilities will be amortized. The amortization method is defined by the actuarial funding method and the length of the funding period.

A public plan sponsor must set and meet a funding policy that is designed to amortize all liabilities over a reasonable period. Until the issuance of GASB Statement Number 25 in 1994 there were no specific national guidelines for setting funding policy for public pension plans. However, over the years, taxpayers and governing bodies had become increasingly aware of the importance of sound financing. In states such as Pennsylvania, this resulted in establishment of an independent retirement commission charged with monitoring and reporting on the financing of all governmental plans under its jurisdiction. Other states, such as Georgia, legislated funding periods and methods for all governmental plans in the state. The guidance of the commissions, assisted by strong fund performance, has greatly improved the financial soundness of many governmental funds.

The FASB expense rules and IRS funding requirements place specific limitations on the range of funding required and permitted in the private sector. GASB No. 25, however, permits a range of funding policy (see Table 7). The typical governmental retirement plan had established specific funding requirements, through legislation or adoption of a requirement by the governing board, before 1996 when GASB No. 25 had to be applied. GASB No. 25 was designed to encompass the large majority of funding patterns among governmental pension plans. While GASB No. 25 only requires a report on the relative funding pattern, governmental plan sponsors hesitate to adopt or continue funding that is lower than the amount required to be reported by GASB No. 25.

As in the private sector, government plans typically smooth out gains and losses in investment income, commonly over five years. This has proved another level of conservatism in recent years as the large market gains in the 1980s and 1990s have been gradually brought into assets, and used to reduce contributions, over five years.

Inflation Protection

Pension plans are usually designed to achieve a benefit that produces a specific replacement ratio at retirement after a full career with the sponsoring employer. For example, a typical state retirement plan design might produce replacement income of 75 percent of salary, including social security, at age 65 with thirty years of service. Benefits for participants who die, become disabled, or retire early are often tied to the full retirement replacement ratio.

The protection against erosion of benefit value from inflation differs before and after retirement. Inflation before retirement for active plan participants is covered by tying the benefit to salary at or near retirement. Governmental plans typically use the high-three (61 percent) or high-five (20 percent) salary average (BLS 1994). Private sector salary related plans are somewhat less liberal with a large majority using the five-year averaging period (HayGroup 1998).

Inflation after retirement is often, but not always, covered by periodic increases in the retirement benefit commonly called cost-of-living allowances. Protection against inflation after retirement is quite different in the public and private sector. About half of governmental plans include automatic COLAs (BLS 1994). Only 12 percent of private sector plans provide automatic COLAs, but many do provide periodic ad hoc increases (HayGroup 1998; Mitchell et al. this volume).

Few plans in the private or public sector protect former participants with vested benefits from inflation between the end of participation in the plan and commencement of retirement benefits. The result can be a substantial loss in the real value of a vested benefit. For example, a $10,000 benefit vested at age 40 would only be worth $4,200 at age 62 if inflation was 4 percent a year.

Most plan sponsors who do not provide full automatic protection are deterred by the high cost of such protection. Sponsors of pension plans that do not provide full inflation protection are somewhat comforted by the fact that social security is fully protected from inflation before and after retirement. Table 8 illustrates the loss to inflation that can occur in a system that is not indexed if inflation is 4 percent a year.

One approach to protection against inflation after retirement has been for the retired participants to share in the investment return. A typical investment-sharing plan would allocate part or all of the earnings on assets earmarked for retirees to provide increases in retirement benefits. This type of allocation would proceed as follows:

Asset allocated for retiree liabilities $1,000 million
Investment return   12%

TABLE 8. Replacement Ratios with No Indexing of Plan Benefits and Inflation at 4 Percent a Year

	Annual benefit in 1999 dollars	*Replacement ratio*
Final salary	$35,096	
Benefit at age 62	21,841	62%
Benefit at age 80	16,557	47%
Benefit at age 95	13,789	39%

Source: Author's calculations.

Actuarial assumption	8%
Allocated to COLA account	$40 million
$(0.12-0.08) \times \$1,000$ million	

Part or all of the earnings in excess of the actuarial assumption would be directed to a reserve account to be used to pay future COLAs.

Postretirement Medical Costs

Actuarial assumptions are also essential in the measurement of postretirement costs of medical plans (referred to as PRM costs). With the rising cost of medical care and the absence of prefunding, the annual cost of postretirement medical can approach or even exceed the cost of the pension plan. Many of the assumptions are the same as those used for the pension plan but some, such as salary growth, are not used in PRM valuations and others, such as medical inflation, are not used in the pension plan.

The economic assumptions used to determine PRM liabilities are the investment return and health care inflation. Investment return is the same as for the pension plan unless there are significant differences in the fund allocation. Health care inflation is used instead of general inflation because medical costs are driven by the health care segment of the economy where costs have increased much more rapidly than in the overall economy. Salary growth is not used because medical benefits are not affected by salary and usually not financed as a percent of salary.

Health care cost changes are measured by looking at both the governmental plans' experience and national changes in health care costs. One source for the national health care costs is the National Health Expenditure analysis produced by the Health Care Financing Administration of the federal government. Trends in health plan costs are determined by reviewing recent cost and premium experience of the plan. It is important to split the trend into experience among retirees under and over age 65 because of the sharp drop in plan costs when Medicare benefits begin at age 65.

Actuaries tend to place the greatest credibility on the last year or two of health cost experience rather than a longer term analysis as is common for the pension economic factors. This much shorter time horizon is necessitated by the much more volatile trend in health care expenditures than in general inflation. For instance, the Federal Employees Health Benefits Plan (FEHBP) experience shows trends that range from –11.4 percent in 1986 to a 25.8 percent increase in 1988 (Hustead 1999).

The PRM valuation uses the demographic assumptions for the pension system since eligibility for PRM benefits is usually tied to pension plan eligibility. In many plans all participants eligible for unreduced retirement benefits are also eligible for PRM benefits. In other plans, the PRM benefit eligibility is more stringent than for the pension benefits. In those cases the retirement rates for both plans must recognize the effect of eligibility for PRM benefits. If, for example, employees can retire on full pension benefits at 55 but will not be eligible for full PRM benefits until age 60, the retirement rates below age 60 will be lower than expected based on pension benefits alone.

The PRM valuation requires additional demographic assumptions if, as is usually the case, dependents are also eligible for PRM benefits. The assumptions include the probability that the annuitant is married, the age of the spouse, and the number of children eligible for benefits.

Actuarial Assumptions: Future Challenges

The bull market of recent years, coupled with increasing investment in equities, has lead to a well-funded situation for many public systems similar to those in the private sector. This has, in turn, greatly reduced employer contributions for many of the public systems. The immediate challenge has been seen to be how to "spend" the unexpected savings. Pressures are to improve benefits for participants, use the money to fund PRM and other benefits, or to simply let the reductions lead to lower taxes. On the other hand, the concern is what might happen when and if the economy turns down. Fiscal conservatism leads many plan sponsors to let large margins build up against the downturn; for these plans, a sharp downturn will simply return contribution rates to their former level. For plans that have used the favorable results to increase benefits and/or reduce contributions, a sharp downturn could lead to the need to boost contributions.

Few governments have faced the potential cost of post-retirement medical benefits and many have not even calculated those costs. With continuing pressure for determination of the cost and at least recognition of the expense on the government financial statements, governments could well face the pressures that impacted on private sector PRM plans in the last decade. Those pressures often lead to curtailment or even termination of PRM benefits to private sector employees. Those changes, in turn, have exacerbated the problem of lack of health insurance for over 40 million Americans.

Notes

1. Similar assumptions are used in funding and costing postretirement medical promises as well.

2. The normal cost of a pay-based retirement plan is the percent of career pay that, with interest, will pay the benefits of the new entrants to the retirement plan.

3. These tables can be obtained from the Society of Actuaries website <www.soa.org>.

References

Actuarial Standards Board (ASB). 1999. Standard No. 35. "Selection of Demographic and Other Noneconomic Assumptions for Measuring Pension Obligations." Academy of Actuaries, Washington, D.C.: December.

Bleakney, Thomas P. 1972. *Retirement Systems for Public Employees.* Pension Research Council. Homewood, Ill.: Irwin.

Board of Trustees of the Federal Old-Age and Survivors Insurance and Disability Insurance Trust Fund. 1998. *1998 Annual Report.* Washington, D.C.: Social Security Administration, April.

Bryan, Tom. This volume. "The New Jersey Pension System."

Bureau of Labor Statistics (BLS), U.S. Department of Labor. 1994. *Employee Benefits in State and Local Governments, 1994.* Washington, D.C.: U.S. GPO.

Government Accounting Standards Board (GASB). 1994. Governmental Accounting Standards Series, Statement No. 25. Norwalk Conn.: GASB.

HayGroup. 1998. *The 1998 Hay Benefits Report,* Philadelphia: Hay Group.

Hustead, Edwin C. 1996. *Fourteenth Investigation of Actuarial Experience of the State Employes' Retirement System of the Commonwealth of Pennsylvania.* Arlington, Va., March 20.

———. 1998. *Commonwealth of Pennsylvania State Employes' Retirement System, 1997 Actuarial Report.* Arlington, Va., May 6.

———. 1999. *Trends in Medical Premiums from the Hay Benefits Report and the Federal Employees Health Benefits Program, 1981 Through 1999.* Arlington, Va.

Hustead, Edwin C. and Toni S. Hustead. 1982. "Indexing of Federal Retirement Systems for Inflation." *Transactions of the Society of Actuaries* 34: 57–77.

McGill, Dan M., Kyle N. Brown, John J. Haley, and Sylvester J. Schieber. 1996. *Fundamentals of Private Pensions.* 7th ed. Philadelphia: University of Pennsylvania Press.

Mitchell, Olivia S., David McCarthy, Stanley C. Wisniewski, and Paul Zorn. This volume. "Developments in State and Local Pension Plans."

Peskin, Michael. This volume. "Asset/Liability Management in the Public Sector."

Samet, Michael J., Timothy P. Peach, and Paul W. Zorn. 1996. *A Study of Public Employees Retirement Systems.* Society of Actuaries Monograph M-RS96-1. Schaumburg, Ill.: Society of Actuaries, September.

Society of Actuaries (SOA). 1998. *Statistics for Employee Benefits Actuaries.* Schaumburg, Ill.: Society of Actuaries, April.

——— website. <www.soa.org>.

Pension Forum. 1997. 10, 1 (March). Pension Section of the Society of Actuaries, Schaumberg, Ill.

U.S. Civil Service Commission. 1969. *Report on Civil Service Retirement System.* Washington, D.C.: U.S. GPO, June 30.

U.S. Federal Accounting Standards Advisory Board (FASAB). 1995. *Statement of Federal Financial Accounting Standards* 5. Washington, D.C.: U.S. GPO, December 20.

U.S. Internal Revenue Service (IRS). 1997. Schedule B, Form 5500, OMB No. 1210-0016. Washington, D.C.: IRS.

U.S. Office of Personnel Management. 1998. *Civil Service Retirement and Disability Fund—An Annual Report to Comply with the Requirements of Public Law 95–595, September 30, 1997.* OPM RI 10-27. Washington, D.C.: Office of Personnel Management, May.

Chapter 11
The Life and Times of a Public Sector Pension Plan Before Social Security
The U.S. Navy Pension Plan In the Nineteenth Century

Robert L. Clark, Lee A. Craig, and Jack W. Wilson

Military pensions have a long history in Western civilization as the practice of rewarding loyal warriors dates from antiquity. Pensions for military personnel have been established prior to the development of pensions for other public sector employees, and military pensions have also predated pensions for workers in the private sector. Standardized systems of military pensions existed as early as the sixteenth century in England. During its 1592–93 session, Parliament established "reliefe for Souldiours . . . [who] adventured their lives and lost their limbs or disabled their bodies" in the service of the Crown (Congressional Research Service, n.d. p. 5). Annual pensions were not to exceed 10 pounds (roughly 50 Spanish gold dollars at subsequent exchange rates) for "private soldiers," or 20 pounds for a "lieutenant." The English were not alone in providing pensions for their soldiers, as Spain also maintained pensions for its Imperial forces. Although a formal pension plan was not established until the eighteenth century, the Spanish Crown had financed military pensions beginning in 1613.[1]

The Continental Congress established pensions for American military personnel shortly after the onset of the American Revolution, creating a naval pension plan in 1775 and an army plan in the following year. In 1800, Congress established the U.S. Navy pension plan to finance the payment of pensions to qualified naval personnel. Over the next century or so, Congress passed dozens of acts covering various aspects of naval pensions including rules pertaining to eligibility, coverage, benefits, and funding. In the absence of (and occasionally even in the presence of) some historical context, many of the characteristics of these acts seem idiosyncratic at best. This study reviews the history of the U.S. Navy pension plan from its inception until World War I, focusing on several economic and policy lessons that emerge from the operation and management of the plan. These historical events provide an interesting background for the development of public and private pensions in the United States. In addition, insight gleaned from the development and management of the navy pension plan in the nineteenth century has considerable relevance for contemporary debates regarding today's social security system.

Creation of U.S. Naval Pensions

Shortly after the onset of the American Revolution, the Continental Congress established a pension plan for naval personnel to be paid out of a fund financed by the sale of prizes captured by the Revolutionary Navy. Unfortunately, neither the pension fund nor its records survived. Legislation passed by the U.S. Congress in 1797 and 1798 revived the navy pension plan, and in 1800, a fund for the payment of benefits was formally established.[2]

Today the term "pension" generally refers to income payments in retirement after the end of a working career. In the nineteenth century, however, a wider range of retiree benefits, survivor's annuities, and disability payments, were also considered as pensions. In the beginning, the navy pension system was primarily a disability pension plan, although the way in which the navy defined disability often included superannuation—that is, incompetence due to infirmities associated with old age. Over time, however, the fund was called on to support dependents of deceased seamen and ultimately to provide old-age benefits. Thus, at one time or another, the fund was responsible for providing the same range of benefits as the modern social security system, although the size and scope of the twentieth-century social security system far exceeds that of the nineteenth-century navy pension plan. Before providing a detailed history of the navy pension system, two interesting characteristics of the fund's creation are worth noting. These are the early date at which the pension system was established, and the motivation for creating a funded plan rather than a pay-as-you-go system.

Broad-based pension systems for military personnel date from sixteenth century England, but America's first formal, nonmilitary, employer-provided plan was established by American Express in 1875. By the turn of the century, only a handful of private companies, mainly railroads, had adopted retirement pension plans (Latimer 1932). For the most part, disabilities incurred on the job were covered by the common law associated with negligence liability (Fishback and Kantor 1998). While a few municipalities provided pensions for police officers, firefighters, and teachers before 1900, the first pension plan for state employees was established by Massachusetts in 1911, and the federal civil service pension plan was not created until 1920 (Craig 1995).[3] So by the standards of other professions and sectors of the economy, pension plans for U.S. military personnel were established very early in our nation's history. There are sound economic, in addition to patriotic, reasons for the early use of pensions by the military.

Pensions are a form of deferred compensation that can be used to bind workers to firms for longer periods than would be the case if spot wages— that is, current compensation for current work—were the only form of compensation.[4] Therefore, one would expect to see pensions in firms and industries in which long-term employment was particularly valuable or conversely in which turnover was costly. These conditions are most likely to be present in firms that provide large amounts of firm-specific human capital and in those in which the tasks of one worker are closely related to those of another. Such characteristics describe the types of large bureaucratic firms that became prevalent in the United States in the late nineteenth century (Chandler 1977, 1990).

Before that time, most Americans worked on family farms (either tenant or owner-operated) or in artisanal shops. In either case, most workers, with the notable exception of slaves, could aspire to one day own the means of production. The ownership of farms, shops, and equipment often provided insurance for disability and old age. Late in the nineteenth century, this economic system was gradually being replaced by the rise of large corporations. Thus, it is not surprising that early pension plans were found among railroad companies, utilities, and communication firms. These were quickly followed by manufacturing firms and public sector employers.

This analysis only explains why pensions did not exist during the first half of the nineteenth century in other sectors of the economy; however, it does not explain why plans were established prior to 1800 for the army and the navy. Military organizations are inherently hierarchical, and the military relies on longevity to fill its upper ranks of noncommissioned and staff officers. As a result, the typical career path involves promotion through the ranks. In the process of moving up the ranks, soldiers and seamen acquire a great deal of firm-specific human capital. This arrangement of long-term employment contracts along with internal promotions makes the military services good candidates for the use of deferred compensation, such as pensions, as a key element in total compensation (Lazear 1979).

It is interesting to note that in the United States much of the legislation providing pensions for the military was designed to provide benefits for soldiers of specific wars or campaigns. The use of war-specific pensions is consistent with the other primary characteristic of jobs that offer deferred compensation. Specifically, soldiering typically includes job assignments that require employees to work relatively closely together; thus the productivity of one worker depends on that of another. Soldiers who left the trenches to go home for spring planting presented officers, not to mention their comrades on the line, with a particularly difficult situation. Although conscription and the Uniform Code of Military Justice were certainly valuable tools against turnover (desertion), deferring a portion of a soldier's compensation also enabled managers to increase the total productivity (fighting ability) of the group. Finally, tying the lifetime wealth of the warrior class to the long-run viability of the political regime promising to pay the deferred compensation made sense from the regime's perspective.

All of the above factors were particularly important during the American Revolution, when American military pensions were created (1775). The plans were later revised. In order to keep the troops in the field during the crucial months leading up to the Battle of Yorktown (1781), the Continental Congress promised to pay any officer remaining in the service for the duration of the Revolution a life annuity equal to one-half his base pay. Unfortunately, it was not long before Congress realized that the present value of its future tax revenues were insufficient to meet that promise. In the Spring of 1783, Congress therefore converted the life annuities to a fixed term payment equal to full pay for five years. Even these obligations were not paid to qualifying veterans, and only the direct intervention of George Washington prevented a coup attempt by disgruntled officers (Ferguson 1961; Middlekauf 1982). Fortunately, the Treaty of Paris was signed in September of 1783, and the Continental Army was furloughed shortly thereafter. It took another eight years before the Constitution and Alexander Hamilton's financial reforms placed the new federal government in a position to honor its pension obligations.

Throughout most of the nineteenth century, navy pensions were paid from a fund financed by the sale of prizes, whereas army pensions were paid from general revenues. This difference in the methods of funding army and navy pensions is consistent with economic theory. Indeed, tying the compensation of naval personnel directly to their performance by granting them a share of the prizes they captured was a time-honored tradition.

Economic exchange can occur either in a pure market system in which all transactions occur between atomistic agents, or through organizations such as firms or government entities.[5] The advantage of the market system is that there are no monitoring costs. In other words, everyone is literally a free agent who self-monitors and every transaction is a new contract. The disadvantage is that such contracting and recontracting is costly. This is one explanation of why organizations such as firms exist. Bringing some transactions inside the organization lowers the number of firm-to-firm transactions and thus reduces contracting costs. One disadvantage of an internal labor market is that self-monitoring inherent in the price system must now be replaced with employee monitoring within the firm. It is the trade-off in costs, transacting on the one hand and monitoring on the other, that determines the optimal scale and scope of an organization (Coase 1937).

Assessing the advantages of the market system versus the firm in the context of military activities, in general, and those of the navy in particular, we see that the objectives of the government would be difficult to achieve using a pure market system. Although naval operations are by definition an activity of the state, naval objectives conceivably could be carried out through a market system by subcontractors rather than by military personnel. Indeed, privateers—that is, holders of letters of marque and reprisal—fulfilled just such a role for many governments until the twentieth century.[6] During these times, privateers served as state-sanctioned pirates or mercenaries on the high seas.[7]

One problem with relying on private contracting for national defense is that the cost of such contracting can be prohibitive. Throughout history, governments that trusted their defense to mercenaries often found themselves renegotiating their contracts at crucial points, frequently when the enemy was at the gates.[8] Furthermore, monitoring the terms of the contract was costly. Mercenary forces in the field or privateers at sea might systematically shirk by avoiding conflict, but they could still demand pay for services rendered. Who was to force them to honor the contract? Such situations with privateers were partly alleviated by awarding compensation based on performance.[9] This was done by creating share contracts, with privateers receiving a portion of all prizes successfully liquidated through prize courts.[10]

The tradition of sharing prizes with officers and sometimes the crews of ships of war survived the creation of modern navies. Although land forces occasionally supplemented their earnings by pillaging, the sack, as a formal means of compensation, was generally abandoned by Western powers with the rise of the nation state and the establishment of professional armies.[11] Why did modern navies adopt a form of compensation associated with privateers, while armies relied exclusively on tax revenues to formally compensate their troops?[12] The answer lies in the different costs of monitoring the performances of the two groups. An army unit typically works in close association with other army units and its effectiveness is relatively easy to monitor. For example, positions on the battlefield are either taken or successfully defended. In the age of sail, however, relatively small naval units typically worked in isolation, often for long periods, having little contact with either other units or the admiralty. As a consequence, directly monitoring their performance could be quite costly, even had it been possible. Indeed, the primary tasks of navies in the age of sail were blockade enforcement and commerce raiding—that is, attacking merchantmen of belligerent states—both of which could be hazardous and either of which could be avoided quite easily. If a ship's company went to sea with none of its compensation tied to performance, it would have been relatively easy to shirk these primary duties; however, once crews were guaranteed some portion of the prizes they captured, the costs of shirking increased. Every blockade runner not overtaken was compensation foregone by the ship's crew.

Given the incentive to defer or backload a certain proportion of a seaman's compensation through pensions, and given the fact that prizes often made up a portion of the crew's current compensation, it was only natural that the two features would be combined and thus that naval pensions would be funded from prize monies. So from its inception the pension plan for naval personnel was designed to be funded from the assets of the plan. In practice, unfortunately, the flow of prize monies did not always match the plan's legislated liabilities. The lack of actuarial assessments linking inflow and outgo of funds, coupled with the political pressures faced by Congress, and its responses to those pressures made for a rather colorful history of the navy pension plan, a history to which we now turn.

Navy Pension Plan Before the Civil War

The Continental Congress created a funded pension system for the Revolutionary Navy in 1775, but this fund did not survive the Revolution.[13] However, a revised pension plan continued to exist, and from 1790 through 1797, benefits were paid to naval (and army) personnel from general appropriations. In July 1797, new legislation was passed that provided disability pensions to officers, marines, and seamen injured in the line of duty. The pension amount, which was not to exceed half pay for officers or $5 a month for marines and seamen, was based on the extent of the disability in both cases (Seybert 1818). Additional legislation was enacted in 1798, 1799, and 1800 to establish a separate pension fund for naval personnel. The 1800 act provided that "every officer, seaman and marine, disabled in the line of his duty, shall be entitled to receive for life, or during his disability, a pension from the United States, according to the nature and degree of his disability, not exceeding one-half of his monthly pay" (*American State Papers* 1834: 487).[14] The fund was to be financed through the sale of prizes including captured ships of war, merchantmen of belligerent states, and neutral merchantmen carrying contraband.

The laws establishing the navy pension fund specified the fund's administrative organization as well as eligibility conditions for receipt of pension benefits.[15] Fund management was placed under the secretaries of the Navy, Treasury, and War Departments. The 1799 legislation directed pension fund commissioners to invest all funds in "six percent or other stock [bonds] of the United States, as a majority of them, from time to time, shall determine to be most advantageous." However, legislation enacted in 1800 authorized the commissioners to invest fund monies "in any manner which a majority of them might deem most advantageous" (Seybert 1818: 692).

In 1809, taking advantage of this investment flexibility, the commissioners purchased a large number of shares in a local bank, the Bank of Columbia. Additional purchases of shares in the Bank of Columbia and new investments in two other local banks, the Union Bank and the Washington Bank, were made during the next decade. Before these purchases, all assets of the fund had been invested in U.S. bonds, which were relatively safe investments compared to equity positions in local banks. The investment in private equities resulted in a loss of income from the nonpayment of dividends, and the eventual loss of capital when the Bank of Columbia failed in 1823–24. This failure occurred at a time when the fund was experiencing increasing obligations to pay benefits.[16]

Historical data on interest and dividend earning assets of the navy pension plan, annual returns on its portfolio, number of beneficiaries, total amount of annual benefits paid, and average benefit per recipient for years between 1800 and 1842 appear in Table 1. Over time the number of beneficiaries increased as did benefits per capita and total annual pension expenditures.[17] In 1801, there were 22 pensioners receiving annual benefits of $1,605 ($72.95 per recipient). By 1842, the number of beneficiaries had increased to 946 and had an annual cost of $220,053 or $232.61 per recipient.[18]

The number of pensioners and the level of benefits in the navy plan generally trended upward over the first half of the nineteenth century. Instead of focusing on the long-run actuarial conditions facing the fund, Congress seemed to react to the absolute size of the fund. When fund assets increased, new legislation was passed expanding coverage and increasing benefits. For example, in 1813, widows of navy personnel who died from wounds incurred in the line of duty were extended benefits equal to half the monthly pay of the deceased. Payments were to be made for a five-year term and could be renewed for additional five-year terms. If there were no surviving widow, children of the deceased who were under 16 years old could receive survivor's benefits. Further, in 1816, commissioners were authorized to issue benefits in excess of half pay in cases of hardship.

Extension of benefits to widows and orphans coupled with the growth in numbers of naval personnel during the War of 1812 dramatically increased amounts paid out by the pension plan. In 1816, pension payments were made to 327 veterans, widows and orphans totaling $27,627. Additional coverage was extended in 1817 to widows and orphans whose husbands or fathers had ultimately died as a *result* of disease or casualties incurred during naval service. To receive benefits, dependents were required to show only that the veteran's death was in some way connected to his previous service. Pension expenditures rose sharply with this extension, and by 1823, a total

TABLE 1. History of the U.S. Navy Pension Plan, 1800–1842

Year	Number of pensioners	Annual[a] outlays	Per capita outlays	Value of[b,c] plan assets	Annual[d] returns
1800	—	—	—	$ 26,552	1.84%
1801	22	$ 1,605	$72.95	56,556	8.40
1802	—	—	—	79,056	6.94
1803	37	3,567	96.40	126,325	6.69
1804	37	3,261	88.13	129,712	7.05
1805	49	4,413	90.06	164,595	6.37
1806	65	5,298	85.51	165,963	8.05
1807	78	6,396	82.00	177,344	8.01
1808	85	6,863	80.74	175,460	8.21
1809	90	6,671	74.12	220,397	5.15
1810	93	7,043	75.73	192,809	7.69
1811	107	8,045	75.19	206,076	7.75
1812	122	9,287	76.12	210,701	8.17
1813	148	11,273	76.17	206,076	5.29
1814	176	13,667	77.65	484,852	6.47
1815	252	20,547	81.54	598,557	6.56
1816	327	27,627	84.49	594,041	5.49
1817	358	32,036	89.49	724,950	7.19
1818	—	34,970	—	877,236	6.52
1819	438	39,340	89.82	874,672	6.60
1820	480	43,863	91.38	870,862	6.01
1821	491	44,488	90.61	891,895	5.98
1822	431	38,772	89.96	906,662	5.81
1823	423	37,248	88.06	910,515	5.38
1824	524	—	—	819,436	5.66
1825	524	—	—	900,166	5.51
1826	533	49,653	93.16	917,902	5.17
1827	534	—	—	911,252	5.21
1828	570	—	—	642,633	6.31
1829	596	—	—	950,675	3.81
1830	536	31,938	59.58	967,081	4.38
1831	536	—	—	1,003,880	3.43
1832	—	—	—	937,047	4.00
1833	—	—	—	947,545	5.53
1834	—	—	—	1,142,462	4.38
1835	442	54,083	122.36	1,160,162	4.31
1836	466	58,009	124.48	1,143,639	4.45
1837	678	200,689	296.00	1,049,232	—
1838	847	216,042	255.06	390,832	—
1839	901	223,045	247.55	253,139	—
1840	914	221,675	242.53	158,739	—
1841	959	226,825	236.52	23,600	—
1842	946	220,053	232.61	—	—

Sources: Authors' calculations based on Clark et al. (1999a, b) and from original sources cited therein.

TABLE 1. Continued

[a]The figures from 1837 through 1842 include two extraordinary treasury remittances resulting from the act of 1837. These remittances appear to have been passed "straight through" a cash position to beneficiaries. [b]The figures in this column exclude cash holdings; therefore annual returns less outlays do not equal the change in the value of the fund's assets. [c]The value of the plans assets varies according to whether the assets are valued at cost or in terms of par. It is not always clear which definition is being used in the original sources. [d]Annual returns are the ratio of asset earnings to the value of plan assets, *excluding cash and bank deposits*; therefore, the figures in this column overstate the actual returns to the plan's assets.

of $37,248 was being paid annually to 423 beneficiaries. This provision was repealed in 1824, but despite this change, the number of beneficiaries continued to rise and reached 596 by 1829. The fund also continued to increase, and its assets reached $950,675 the same year.

By the early 1830s, the pension plan had assets totaling almost $1 million and the number of pensioners had begun to stabilize. Congress once again chose to increase benefits and expand coverage. Given income and expenditure expectations, it seems unlikely that by today's standards the pension plan would have been considered adequately funded at this time. On the revenue side, plan commissioners should have anticipated a decline in new monies flowing into the fund due to the lack of future naval prizes, and they should have anticipated that benefit payments would increase with the aging of the veterans of the War of 1812.

However, in June 1834, Congress restored the widow and orphan benefits that had been in effect between 1817 and 1824. Furthermore, this legislation extended benefits to widows of officers, seamen, and marines who had died *since* 1824. This extension of benefits resulted in "a heavy charge [being] made upon the fund" (*American State Papers* 1836, p. 863). The number of widows receiving pension benefits under all previous acts totaled 56; the 1834 legislation added 80 widows to the rolls, increasing benefits paid by $20,031 annually, an amount equal to nearly 40 percent of total navy pension expenditures (*American State Papers* 1836: 863).

In November 1835, fund assets totaled $1,160,262; income for 1835 was $66,083. Expenses included $23,842 paid to 306 disabled veterans and $30,241 to 136 widows and orphans. In assessing implications of the 1834 legislation, the fund's commissioners deplored Congress's apparent lack of foresight in expanding benefits at that time. By 1837, the fund had increased to $1,049,232 and interest and dividends were more than $50,000. And once again, Congress expanded benefits with the Jarvis Act, which provided that pensions be paid to widows and orphans retroactively from the dates of veterans' deaths. In addition, pensions granted to veterans were now to be paid from the time they became disabled. This meant that the navy pension plan had to make one-time, lump-sum payments covering arrears from the time of death or the onset of the disability to the awarding of beneficiary status.

The pension plan immediately encountered heavy liabilities associated with this expansion of benefits.

Plan commissioners once again opposed this expansion of pension benefits. Payment of back benefits to individual claimants ran as high as $6,000 to $8,000, roughly 5 to 9 percent of the total annual outlay at that time. The number of pensioners increased to 847 and annual expenditures to $216,042 including arrears. "Arrears payments for these pensions soon consumed nearly $600,000. Between March 3, 1837, and October 1, 1838, about $725,000 of the invested capital of the fund was sold, and the proceeds, with the interest and dividend on the capital were applied to payment of pensions and arrears" (Glasson 1918: 104).

Columns 2 and 3 of Table 1 include these extraordinary expenditures for past claims after 1836. Total expenditures, including the extraordinary benefits, are more than double the per capita outlays from that date (Clark et al. 1999b). After the 1837 legislation was passed, fund assets plummeted over two years from $1,049,232 to $253,139, and by 1841, Congress had to appropriate general tax revenues to make up the shortfall to continue paying pensions to beneficiaries then enrolled. This process of appropriating general tax revenues continued until the plan was reconstituted during the Civil War. The history of legislation regulating the navy pension plan demonstrates that Congress, at times when plan assets were growing rapidly, choose to expand coverage, often beyond the plan's actuarial capacity. The ultimate result was a shifting of the plan's liabilities to taxpayers.

Management of the Navy Pension Plan

Prize monies that provided the basic capital for the plan were not consistently identified in the annual reports of the commissioners. Available data indicate large fluctuations in plan revenues. The irregularity of the flow of prize money into the pension plan is evident from the plan "Statement of the Condition of the Navy Pension Fund," issued in 1829 (*American State Papers* 1829: 323).[19] Between 1814 and 1828, the plan received a total of $451,694 from the sale of prizes. Annual revenues from these sales peaked in 1814 at $150,367 and in 1819 at $174,848; however, in six of the fifteen years, no revenues were received.

A sensible portfolio management strategy would have been to convert prize proceeds into a regular income flow to match the somewhat more regular payments to pensioners. With a buy and hold strategy for government securities redeemed at par, capital gains and losses would depend on whether the original assets were bought at a premium, yielding a loss, or at a discount, yielding a gain.

From 1800 through 1808 the fund's portfolio was invested in U.S. government stocks (bonds) in a mix of coupon amounts—Sixes, Eights, and

Threes (the names for the securities refer to their coupon rates). Although the Threes had a lower coupon, the price in Philadelphia in 1805–6 ranged between $59 and $64, indicating a current yield of about 5 percent (Sylla et al. 1997). Sixes issued to upgrade the navy were redeemed by the federal government in 1807, and the proceeds to the fund were invested in Threes and Sixes issued for the purchase of the Louisiana Territory.

Proceeds from the sale of the Eights, redeemed in 1809, were invested in the stock of a private local bank, the Bank of Columbia, the first example of private investment of public pension funds.[20] Additional shares of Columbia Bank, as it was often called, were purchased in 1810 and the stocks of Union Bank and Washington Bank were purchased in 1811 and 1812 in what appear to have been "initial public offerings." Over the period 1809 to 1813, $89,703 was spent on the purchases of these local bank stocks, which meant that 44 percent of the plan's portfolio was invested in private, locally traded securities.

The fund grew rapidly during this period increasing from $26,552 in 1800, to over $200,000 in 1813, as prize receipts, income, and gains annually outstripped payments to pensioners. Between 1809 and 1813, investment opportunities were plentiful for buying nationally and internationally traded securities. U.S. government debt alone was approximately $50 million, and therefore provided ample opportunity for the plan's commissioners to restrict plan investments to government securities. There is some evidence that area commercial banks were paying dividends of approximately 7 to 8 percent indicating a higher market return than could be achieved from holding government securities. For example, the Bank of the United States paid annual dividends from July 1792 through 1810 of over 8 percent of par, but this asset was never held by the fund (Perkins 1994). Columbia Bank paid dividends of $3,730 to the fund in 1810. This represented a 6.2 percent return on monies invested. Similar dividends were realized from the Union Bank and Washington Bank.

The decision to forfeit liquidity in favor of adding risk from holding these three local bank stocks for the potential of an additional 1 or 2 percent return (above that of U.S. debt) appears unconventional. Bank and insurance stocks were the first private equity stocks traded in the United States, but ownership of these stocks came with considerable risk. Of the first eight banks chartered in Washington, D.C., three had failed by 1831, and one had been merged with one of these failed banks (Gallatin 1831; Fenstermaker 1965). The brief financial panic of 1837 brought about a number of other bank failures.[21] This observation is important in light of the fact that the fund managers chose not to invest in the Bank of the United States, a private bank of which 20 percent was owned by the federal government.

The three local bank stocks were acquired in "half" and "whole" shares and the subscription schedule for initial investment in these stocks was an arrangement similar to a time purchase plan in which one could initially purchase, or make a "down payment" on, a whole share by purchasing a half share. It is possible that the market price was paid for an exchange or that these purchases were arranged in some manner consistent with the initial offerings of the capital stock. Because these, as well as subsequent, bank stock transactions were made through the navy's agent, George MacDaniel, who made these and other trades on his own account, this approach to fund privatization has the scent of insider trading—that is, MacDaniel used his access to information and his control over transactions as the fund's agent to make profitable trades on his own account.

By 1829, the fund had grown to almost $1 million.[22] Assets purchased in 1814 and continuing through 1824 were concentrated in the new sixes issued to finance the War of 1812. However, additional purchases of Bank of Columbia stock were made in 1815, 1818, and 1819. These purchases brought total expenditures for Columbia Bank stock to $99,502. According to the authorized amount of capitalization of Columbia Bank ($1 million), the plan owned almost 10 percent of the bank. In 1819, the plan's total holdings of private securities was $129,266 of the enlarged total portfolio of $874,672; therefore, at that time, 15 percent of the plan portfolio was held in private stocks.[23] Columbia Bank, which stopped accepting new business in 1823, ceased all active operations in 1828. The plan's acquisition of private assets inevitably increased the risk associated with its portfolio. Then with the failure of Columbia Bank, the downside of such acquisitions became apparent as the plan lost roughly 10 percent of its value.

In any pension plan, investment decisions and risk-return calculations should include analysis of who benefits from the greater returns and who must bear losses associated with adverse events. In the private sector (prior to the Employee Retirement Income Security Act, ERISA) the owners of the pension fund and/or the plan's participants would absorb such a loss. For the navy pension fund, this was not the case. In July 1834, the pension fund received $167,164, representing the value of lost equity and foregone interest and dividends "From the Treasurer of the United States, for Columbia Bank stock purchased of the navy pension fund by the United States, per act of Congress, approved 30th June 1834."[24] Thus, it was the taxpayers who bailed out the pension fund as Congress assumed the risk of privatization on behalf of the taxpayers ex post facto. Not coincidentally, all of this occurred at the same time that Congress restored the widows and orphans benefits, as discussed previously.

From 1830 to 1836, the plan's total portfolio remained rather constant at approximately $1 million, but it fell sharply by 1838 when securities were sold to meet increased pension obligations associated with the Jarvis Act. Interestingly, as the threes were being redeemed in 1832, the plan, at the direction of the navy, made large purchases of stock of the Second Bank of the United States.[25] Restricting purchases to the Second Bank of the United States was linked to failure of Columbia Bank and also to the practice of paying commissions to agents of the plan while they were being paid to disburse pension payments.[26] The navy directive came after several audits of the pension plan and much correspondence from the commissioners requesting reimbursement because they could not pay widow and orphan benefits. After its federal charter expired in 1836, the Second Bank of the United States was rechartered in Pennsylvania, where it eventually failed; it was liquidated in February 1841 (Hammond 1957; Smith 1953).

To compensate for the loss incurred in the stock of the Second Bank and to help the plan meet its obligations to pensioners, the Treasury, from October 1837 through the end of September 1838, deposited $510,353 in principal and interest to the plan's account.[27] This action represented the second taxpayer bailout of the navy pension plan. The plan, in addition to its bank stock problems, encountered further financial woes when several states defaulted on their debts (Sylla and Wallis 1998; English 1996). These defaults and the accompanying reduction in bond prices occurred while the fund was selling securities to meet pension obligations. The value of the plan's portfolio declined from $253,139 at the end of 1839 to virtually zero by the end of 1841. The only assets remaining in the plan by this time were shares in the Union Bank and Washington Bank, which were almost worthless. So the navy pension plan was dissolved in 1841, and Congress began paying pensions from general tax revenues.

In an audit of the navy pension plan following the failure of Columbia Bank, a number of facts emerged which indicated that the plan had been poorly administered. There was evidence of excess commissions paid to agents for purchasing assets for the portfolios, commingling of agents' funds to pay pensions and manage the portfolio, receipt by agents of dividends and bond coupons that were not remitted to the fund, and failure to make prompt reinvestment of portfolio income flows (Clark et al. 1999a). These problems were further complicated by the decline of investment opportunities in the national financial markets associated with the paying off of the national debt by 1832 (Bayley 1882; Elliott 1845) and the default by various states on their debt.[28] As a result of the audit, the plan was directed to buy only stock in the Second Bank of the United States. Taken together, these problems suggest the plan would have had serious problems in maintaining solvency in the 1840s even if Congress had not increased the navy's liabilities by expanding coverage in the late 1830s.

Navy Pensions After the Civil War

Twenty years after the liquidation of the navy pension plan, the nation was torn by the Civil War and faced the possibility of secession of its southern states. From the outset of the war, a primary component of the Union's strategy required blockading the Confederacy. This situation provided both a new cohort of claimants for benefits from the navy pension plan and a large number of potential prizes to finance a new fund. By the middle of the Civil War, navy pension payments had reached $159,812 and the prizes sent to prize courts since the start of the war were valued at $13 million. Congress reestablished the navy pension fund, directing Secretary of the Navy Gideon Welles to place half the net proceeds from the sale of prizes into the fund.[29]

In his annual report to Congress, Secretary Welles recommended that

The moiety of prize money dedicated as a pension fund, and now accumulating, should be made a permanent investment in registered government securities. Were such the case, it is believed that the annual interest would be sufficient to meet all liabilities for naval pensions. At least two million five hundred thousand dollars can now be invested without interfering with the prompt payment of pensions. I recommend that the fund now on hand be made permanent, and that hereafter, whenever the amount shall reach one hundred thousand dollars, at least one-half shall be invested in registered government securities bearing six per cent interest. (U.S. Navy 1863: xxx)

Congress approved this proposal in July 1864 and Welles purchased $5 million in U.S. government bonds during the rest of 1864. Thus, navy pension liabilities were again—at least nominally—transferred from the Treasury to the navy pension fund. By the end of 1864, gross proceeds from Civil War prizes exceeded $14 million. After expenses and payment to the captors, roughly $6.5 million remained for the navy pension fund. Pension outlays were $189,659 in 1864, which left approximately $1.3 million in cash in the fund. In his 1864 report, Welles proposed to purchase another $2 million in registered securities. One must assume he anticipated either that an additional $700,000 in prize monies would be forwarded to the fund or that the cash position of the fund was substantially larger than $1.3 million because of other prizes not included in the $14 million he had reported up to 1864. In either case, Welles asserted that the $7 million to be invested by early 1865 in six percent government bonds would yield $420,000 a year in interest and would be "sufficient for the payment of the entire pension roll . . . without calling upon the national treasury" (U.S. Navy 1864: xxxviii).

In his final report covering the Civil War years, Welles listed the total value of prizes taken during the war as $21,829,543. After accounting for expenses incurred in adjudicating and processing the prizes and after subtracting the captors' shares, prize monies allocated for the navy pension fund amounted to approximately $10,251,000, with several "important cases still before the courts" (U.S. Navy 1864: xxxviii). The secretary stated that by January 1866 those monies would be fully invested in government bonds; however, at the close of 1865, the fund held only $9 million in bonds. Thus, the plan either maintained a more favorable cash position than it appeared or the difference between monies expected from prize courts and that which had been invested was held up somewhere along the line. In any case, during 1865, expenditures from the fund had reached $250,000; so it appeared the plan was indeed solvent for the foreseeable future.

Welles remained optimistic concerning the financial status of the plan noting that plan income would "if rightly husbanded, be ample to meet the requirements of the government for the payment of naval pensions, without any tax upon the people" (U.S. Navy 1865, p. xxx). Welles's repeated assurances that the navy pension plan would not impose any new burden on the taxpayers leads one to suspect that he was aware of the history of the navy pension plan in the first half of the nineteenth century.

Ultimately the prizes still being adjudicated in 1865 plus the plan's net earnings (interest less expenses) after that date yielded another $5 million; $2.75 million in 1866, $1.25 million in 1867, and $1 million in 1868. These monies were also invested in government bonds. By the end of 1868, the total (par) value of the plan's holdings of U.S. Treasury liabilities was $14 million, all of which paid six percent interest.[30] It appears the plan maintained a small cash position as well. The growth in the plan's portfolio corresponded with an upward trend in annual outlays (roughly $270,000 in 1866, $320,000 in 1867, and $391,00 in 1868).

At this time, the plan seemed solvent under any reasonable set of assumptions. With nearly 100 percent of the plan's portfolio invested in treasury bonds paying a 6 percent coupon, the plan generated sufficient annual income to pay current benefits based on existing coverage, eligibility, and benefit standards. Welles must have thought so because he formally requested both an increase in benefits and an expansion in the number of persons covered by the plan.

In response to the plan's growing balance in 1866 he wrote: "Further legislation is therefore required in order that 'the surplus shall be applied to the making of further provision for the comfort of disabled officers, seamen and marines' "(U.S. Navy 1866: 37), and a year later he added:

I recommend, therefore, that the pension laws applicable to the navy be revised, and such an increase in the rates of pension be authorized as the fund will warrant. The entire principal of the fund was earned by the officers and men of the navy. . . . It may also be well to consider whether the family of a person dying in the navy after a specified time of service should benefit from this surplus fund, even though the death should not have occurred in the strict 'line of duty.' "(U.S. Navy 1867: 25)

In July 1868, Congress granted half of Welles's request. It revised the pension law as it applied to the navy pension plan, but rather than increase pensions or expand coverage, it enacted legislation that altered the character of the assets held by the plan and in so doing lowered returns from these assets. This fundamentally altered the navy pension plan for the rest of its existence.

Specifically, the legislation authorized the treasury to exercise an implicit call option on the $14 million in treasury bonds held by the plan. None of the sixes issued during the Civil War (and probably held by the fund) were redeemable before five years from their date of issue, and all were trading above par; this suggests that the fund experienced a substantial capital loss as a result of this congressional action. In addition, Congress replaced these bonds with a special issue of three percent nonnegotiable treasury liabilities. We have found no evidence that these bonds ever existed except in treasury and navy department accounts.

This legislation generated lengthy and acrimonious debate. Representative F. A. Pike, congressman from Maine, called the pension fund, as it was constituted during the war, a "contract" and labeled the legislation altering it "a breach of faith on the part of the Government" (*Congressional Globe* 1868, p. 1335). This statement was followed by a lengthy recitation on the history of antebellum navy pension fund by Representative Benjamin Butler from Massachusetts.[31] For his part, Secretary Welles made no attempt to conceal his outrage at what he perceived to be a gross breach of faith. In his 1868 report, he reminded Congress that the original legislation had pledged

that the money arising from the sale of prizes shall be and forever remain a fund for the payment of naval pensions and for the investment in registered bonds bearing interest in gold. It is difficult to reconcile the act of July last, which reduces the interest to three per cent in currency, with the pledge faith previously given, . . . had not the income been reduced over fifty per cent by the act of July last, the rate of naval pensions might be increased, and I should have felt it my duty to renew my recommendation for a revision of the naval pension laws for that purpose." (U.S. Navy 1868: xxvi)

Butler, by all accounts a clever politician, ultimately carried the day, and the bill passed. This action ended the U.S. navy's early experiment in both the funding of its pension plan and the use of investment in private equities as part of its financing strategy.

The exact value of the loss imposed on the plan's assets by the action of Congress is difficult to determine. Dollar value or interest yield comparisons between 1862 and 1878 are suspect in terms of whether references are to greenbacks or gold. Specie payments were suspended in February 1862, and the government issued paper currency, which depreciated. Yet a market existed between the paper currency and gold. Wesley Mitchell (1908) recorded the daily high, low, and closing prices of gold in greenbacks, yielding two sets of prices over this period. Confusion concerning the dollar value and yields of securities played a role in the congressional debate in 1868, which led to the loss of autonomy of the navy pension plan in the management of its portfolio. Mr. Butler argued that the navy pension fund's $13 million was balanced on the other side by a debt of the U.S. Treasury, paying out "$319,878.25, while the interest of that fund is $780,000 in gold" (*Congressional Globe* 1878). Although this stretched the truth in terms of the then current greenback-gold exchange rates, the argument was effective in the debate.

Another factor in Butler's argument involved the "sinking fund" of the United States. Alexander Hamilton, in his plan for the origination of the consolidation of the U.S. debt, set up a scheme to repay any indebtedness incurred by the government. That plan had proved to be effective in paying off the debt by 1832. The Civil War increased the debt from about $50 million to $2.4 trillion (Sylla and Wilson 1999). Butler's argument was that the excess of the navy pension plan's receipts over its obligations should revert to the Treasury for debt reduction.

The value of the navy pension plan confiscated by the Treasury in 1868 was $13 to $14 million in terms of greenbacks, but it had a gold value of only about $9.5 million. The 3 percent interest remitted to the plan by the Treasury was certainly less than higher the greenback coupon rate of 6 percent or the higher gold yield at the time. However, nominal interest yields on government bonds following the Civil War until the first World War ranged between 3.5 percent and 4.5 percent (Wilson and Jones 1997).

From 1869 until World War I, with the exception of 1891, the U.S. Treasury annually credited the navy pension plan $420,000 (3 percent of $14 million). Indeed, the essential features of the plan continued until it was abolished by Congress in 1935. When expenditures exceeded that amount, they were paid from other naval accounts; when they were less, the navy shifted the surplus to other items. In essence, the navy pension plan was a pay-as-you-go system.

Implications

The history of the U.S. Navy pension plan shows that Congress expanded benefits in response to existing fund surpluses. These actions changed the navy pension plan from one that was intended to be funded to one that was ultimately insolvent. It is clear that the acquisition of private equities exposed the navy pension plan to substantial risk and management problems. Once the downside variability that characterizes such risk became evident, Congress shifted this risk to taxpayers and bailed out the fund on two separate occasions.

It is our view that the experience of the navy pension plan throughout the nineteenth century offers a valuable lesson for contemporary debates about the possibility of privatization of the social security system. Specifically, the history of the navy pension fund illustrates many of the challenges that could confront social security in the twenty-first century if a portion of the assets of the social security Trust Fund is invested in private equities.

Currently, revenue in excess of current social security outlays is placed, by law, in the trust fund, which is to say that it is invested in special-issue U.S. Treasury bonds. These bonds are similar to those that Congress required the navy pension fund to hold in the late nineteenth century: both bonds are merely accounting entries in the budget of the U.S. government. Many social security reform proposals have favored diversifying social security funds into private equities and corporate bonds.[32] Although the size and scope of today's social security system are considerably larger than the nineteenth-century navy pension plan, historical lessons regarding coverage and funding of navy pension benefits are revealing for today's social security reformers. We suggest that the history of the navy pension fund provides an interesting case study of potential problems resulting from investment of public pension funds in private equities.

Among these concerns is the risk that investment of the trust fund might respond to political rather than to market forces. The history of the navy pension plan provides some useful examples of problems that can arise with such an investment strategy. For example, the fact that the fund invested in riskier local banks, at least one of which was well connected politically, instead of the safer and nationally traded Bank of the United States may have been due to the opposition of President Jefferson, who adamantly opposed the existence of the Bank. This result may be a useful lesson to those favoring private investment of the assets of the social security trust fund. Will fund commissioners be immune to the political positions of the president, congressional leaders, or other public spokespersons? Also, the experience of the agent MacDaniel trading on his own account illustrates another possible concern over the investment of public trust funds in private markets. Will fund managers channel investments through their friends or those of their political allies?

Another issue associated with investment in private equities is the government's inability to shift risks associated with privatization to those persons insured by the fund. If investments in private equities are made, who ultimately bears the risk associated with adverse investment experience? This question applies to investments in private equities by either a general trust fund or through individual accounts. We also found that the bankruptcies of private firms, whose equity composed a substantial proportion of the navy plan's portfolio, ultimately required taxpayer-funded bailouts. Thus, the taxpayers in general and not the pension participants ultimately bore the risk of those investment decisions.

The authors thank Richard Sylla and Olivia Mitchell for comments, Sean Cox and Bob Wright for research assistance, Ms. Jean Porter of the D. H. Hill

Library at North Carolina State University for diligent assistance in locating many of the original sources cited in the paper and Robert Goldich, Congressional Research Service, for documents on the history of military pensions. This research was partially funded by TIAA-CREF.

Notes

1. Initially, funds to support pension payments to the English military were raised from taxes levied on inhabitants of the locale from which the soldier was impressed or in which he was born. Over the course of the seventeenth century, however, pensions increasingly were paid from general revenues of the national government. The Spanish pension system was formalized as an obligation of the state in 1761 during the reign of Carlos III, who had begun a similar project decades earlier when he ruled Naples and Sicily as Charles IV (Chandler 1991).

2. When the fund began paying benefits in 1801, eighteen years after the Treaty of Paris formally ended the Revolutionary War, there were 22 navy pensioners.

3. Before 1920, Congress granted pensions to federal employees on a case-by-case basis. For a discussion of the history of federal pensions, see Craig (1995).

4. In an era in which private disability insurance did not exist, even the disability features of the navy pension plan worked much like a retirement plan (Fishback and Kantor 1998).

5. This discussion is based largely on the analysis of Coase (1937) and Chandler (1977, 1990).

6. Letters of marque and reprisal were warrants issued to private citizens permitting them to arm private vessels for naval service. They were essentially licenses to engage in piracy with one notable exception—the captured treasure had to be shared with the government granting the warrants.

7. Although mercenaries and privateers have a long history, they have largely been displaced by the uniformed forces of modern nation states.

8. Indeed, this situation precipitated one of the most momentous events in Western history, the sack of Rome in A.D. 410 by an army of Gothic mercenaries led by Alaric. The Goths were not invaders from beyond the imperial frontier; rather they were hirelings charged with defending that frontier. Alaric, a devout Christian and formerly a loyal general, marched on Rome because he felt that he and his troops were undercompensated for their efforts (Norwich 1988, pp. 122–38).

9. This practice was essentially the same as that used by pirates since time immemorial.

10. The letter of marque gave privateers the right to arm private vessels and interdict ships of war or merchantmen of belligerent states or neutral merchantmen hauling contraband. A similar, though not quite as formal, contract was structured for mercenaries. Dating from antiquity, it was customary in both Western and Islamic civilizations that any town or city that unsuccessfully resisted a siege was subjected to three days of pillage and rape (Norwich 1988: 137; Norwich 1996: 436). The privilege of sacking a town occasionally was denied regular troops in hopes of maintaining military order among them, but woe to the general who tried to keep his mercenary forces from what they perceived as the just fruits of their labors.

11. The end of the sack as a means of compensation for ground troops was not the result of humanitarian considerations; rather it was linked to the development of the canon. Artillery made folly of hiding behind the town's medieval fortifications and fundamentally altered the course of land warfare (Keegan 1993: 320–34).

12. We say formally because looting and atrocities have remained informal wages of war well into modern times.

13. The demise of the Revolutionary navy pension system resulted after the Continental Congress, in an effort to relieve its own financial crisis, shifted the burden of pension payments to the colonies from which the seamen were recruited (Paullin 1906). Unfortunately, the public finances of many colonies were in only slightly better shape than that of Congress, and it appears the prize revenues simply went into the general accounts of various government entities that were able to claim them.

14. To actually receive a disability pension, a person had to complete an application indicating the circumstances of the injury, when it occurred, the extent of the injury, and the extent of the disability resulting from the injury. The application had to be signed by the company surgeon and commanding officer. Injuries could result in partial or total disability and the amount of pension awarded depended on extent of the disability. Pensions were forfeited if the veteran was convicted of a felony (*American State Papers* 1833: 427). In June 1812, Congress created a similar fund for privateers. The fund, which was supervised by the secretary of the navy, would receive 2 percent of all U.S. prize money. It was depleted in 1837.

15. The 1800 legislation specified that commissioners of the pension fund provide annual reports to Congress concerning the operations of the fund. These reports provide information on activities of the pension fund and are the primary source of data used in this article for the first half of the nineteenth century.

16. As the pension fund grew, the commissioners found the administrative structure of the pension system increasingly difficult to manage through three federal departments. The Commissioners eventually requested Congress to place the pension plan under a single department. In 1832, the secretary of navy was made the sole manager of the pension plan. At that time, Congress mandated that plan assets be held by the treasurer of the United States, and the secretary of the navy was directed to invest all pension funds in stock of the Bank of the United States (Glasson 1900). Reorganization of the plan's management was related to problems associated with investment in the Bank of Columbia (Clark et al. 1999b).

17. Data through 1836 are from various annual reports of the commissioners of the navy pension fund. These reports, submitted by the secretary of the navy, were required by Congress.

18. These figures include extraordinary payments—that is, payment of benefits from the time the death or disability occurred rather than from the time of application for benefits. This payment of deferred benefits was required by subsequent legislation. See below.

19. The submittal dates of the annual reports of the fund vary between September and the following January. The reports also differ from year to year in the detail and quality of the information provided.

20. Ownership and control of the Columbia Bank reads like a Who's Who of the early republic. For details, see Walsh (1940) and Cole (1959).

21. The lack of a national bank following the failure to recharter to the Second Bank of the United States may have contributed to this problem (Thorp 1926).

22. The fund's holdings are reported in detail in Clark et al. (1999a), which is available from the authors on request.

23. Between 1819 and 1829, the sixes and other government securities were being retired along with some of the new sixes. Meanwhile, the fund acquired the new debt being issued by the Treasury in the bonds bearing 4.5 and 5.0 percent coupon rates. At the end of 1829, most of the fund was invested in these securities, with a lesser amount invested in the new sixes and with the original threes.

24. Net loss to the fund from failure of the Columbia Bank was $99,502. The difference of $67,661 must include foregone interest (at 5.32 percent) since 1822 or so.

25. Like its predecessor, the Second Bank of the United States was a federally chartered, private bank in which the federal government owned stock.

26. This stock was purchased from the Treasury at par with no fees involved. These transactions represent subsidies, as the stock was trading at a premium at that time.

27. No stock of the Bank of the United States appears among the fund's assets after 1837 (Clark et al. 1999a). We do not know how those shares were disposed of, though it is possible they were sold by the Treasury.

28. The Second Bank of the United States failed, after it was not rechartered (with the loss by the fund being absorbed by the Treasury). The increased risk resulting from state defaults brought about a dramatic drop in the prices of state bonds, with interest rates rising to around 20 percent on those obligations (Ayres 1939).

29. This discussion pertains to the payment of pensions to Union personnel. Some of the states in the Confederacy paid extremely small pensions to their veterans. These Confederate pensions are not considered in this chapter.

30. There is no evidence in the navy secretary's reports that the securities held by the reconstituted pension fund were ever purchased or valued at anything other than par. Although the reports do not offer a detailed accounting of exactly what securities the fund held, it was probably some combination of the "6's of 1868," "6's of 1881," and the "6% 5–20s of 1865," all of which sold at a premium according to Homer and Sylla (1996) and the bond price quotations from *Financial Review* (1876–1921).

31. Butler was one of the more colorful political figures of the age. After using his political influence to secure an appointment as a general in the Union Army, he outraged southerners by confiscating slaves on the grounds that they were "contraband" and employing them in support of the Union war effort. Later he commanded the ground troops accompanying Flag-officer, later Admiral, David Farragut's famous capture of New Orleans. Butler eventually became the military governor of the city, earning the name "Beast" Butler for his uncompromising rule. After being recalled to Washington, he commanded a series of military disasters, most notably the failure to capture Fort Fisher, North Carolina. Although he spent various parts of his political career in both the Democratic and Republican parties, he was the Populists' candidate for president in 1884.

32. For a summary of these proposals and their connections with the U.S. Navy pension fund, see Clark et al. (1999b).

References

American State Papers, Naval Affairs. Various volumes and reports; see specific citations in the text.

Ayres, Leonard P. 1939. *Turning Points in Business Cycles.* New York: Macmillan.

Bayley, Rayfael. 1882. *History of the National Loans of the United States.* 1880 Census of the United States, vol. 7. Washington, D.C.: U.S. GPO.

Chandler, Alfred D., Jr. 1977. *The Visible Hand: The Managerial Revolution in American Business.* Cambridge, Mass.: Harvard University Press.

———. 1990. *Scale and Scope: The Dynamics of Industrial Capitalism.* Cambridge, Mass.: Harvard University Press.

Chandler, Dewitt S. 1991. *Social Assistance and Bureaucratic Politics: The Monepíos of Colonial Mexico, 1767–1821.* Albuquerque: University of New Mexico Press.

Clark, Robert L., Lee A. Craig, and Jack W. Wilson. 1999a. "Managing Pension Port-
folios in the Nineteenth Century: The U.S. Navy Pension Fund, 1800–1842." Paper
presented at the annual meetings of the Business History Conference, Chapel
Hill, N.C.
———. 1999b. "Privatization of Public-Sector Pensions: The U.S. Navy Pension
Fund, 1800–1842." *Independent Review* 3, 4: 549–64.
Coase, Ronald H. 1937. "The Nature of the Firm." *Economica* 4, 4: 386–405.
Cole, David M. 1959. *The Development of Banking in the District of Columbia.* New York:
William-Frederick Press.
Congressional Globe. Various years; see specific citations in the text.
Congressional Research Service. n.d. "Uniform Services Retirement System." Un-
published manuscript from the files of Robert Goldich, specialist in National De-
fense, Congressional Research Service.
Craig, Lee A. 1995. "The Political Economy of Public-Private Compensation Differ-
entials: The Case of Federal Pensions." *Journal of Economic History* 55, 3: 304–20.
Elliott, Jonathan. 1845. *The Funding System of the United States and of Great Britain.* First
published by Order of the House of Representatives. Executive Document 15, 1st
Sess., 28th Cong. Reprint New York: Augustus M. Kelley, 1968.
English, William B. 1996. "Understanding the Costs of Sovereign Default: American
State Debts in the 1840s." *American Economic Review* 86, 1: 259–75.
Fenstermaker, Joseph Van. 1965. *The Development of American Commercial Banking,
1782–1837,* Kent, Ohio: Bureau of Economics and Business Research.
Ferguson, E. James. 1961. *Power of the Purse: A History of American Public Finance, 1776–
1790.* Chapel Hill: University of North Carolina Press.
Fishback, Price V. and Shawn Everett Kantor. 1998. "The Adoption of Workers' Com-
pensation in the United States, 1900–1930." *Journal of Law and Economics* 41, 4 (Part
1): 305–43.
Gallatin, Albert. 1831. *Considerations on the Currency and Banking System of the United
States.* Reprint New York: Greenwood Press, 1968.
Glasson, William H. 1900. *History of Military Pension Legislation of the United States.* New
York: Columbia University Press.
———. 1918. *Federal Military Pensions in the United States.* New York: Oxford University
Press.
Hammond, Bray. 1957. *Banks and politics in America: From the Revolution to the Civil War.*
Princeton, N.J.: Princeton University Press.
Homer, Sidney and Richard E. Sylla. 1996. *A History of Interest Rates.* 3rd ed. revised.
New Brunswick, N.J.: Rutgers University Press.
Johnson, Ronald N. and Gary D. Libecap. 1994. *The Federal Civil Service System and the
Problem of Bureaucracy.* Chicago: University of Chicago Press.
Keegan, John. 1993. *A History of Warfare.* New York: Knopf.
Latimer, Murray. 1932. *Industrial Pension Systems in the United States and Canada.* New
York: Industrial Relations Counselors.
Lazear, Edward P. 1979. "Why Is There Mandatory Retirement?" *Journal of Political
Economy* 87, 6: 1261–84.
Macaulay, Frederick R. 1938. *Some Theoretical Problems Suggested by the Movements of
Interest Rates, Bond Yields and Stock Prices in the United States Since 1856.* New York:
National Bureau of Economic Research.
Middlekauf, Robert. 1982. *The Glorious Cause: The American Revolution, 1763–1789.*
New York: Oxford University Press.
Mitchell, Wesley C. 1908. *Gold, Prices, and Wages Under the Greenback Standard.* Berke-
ley: University of California Press. Reprinted New York: Augustus M. Kelley, 1966.

Norwich, John Julius. 1988. *Byzantium: The Early Centuries.* New York: Knopf.
———— 1996. *Byzantium: Decline and Fall.* New York: Alfred A. Knopf.
Paullin, Charles Oscar. 1906. *The Navy of the American Revolution: Its Administration, Its Policy, and Its Achievements.* New York: Haskell House.
Perkins, Edwin J. *American Public Finance and Financial Services, 1700–1815.* Columbus: Ohio State University Press, 1994.
Roll, Richard. 1972. "Interest Rates and Price Expectations During the Civil War." *Journal of Economic History* 32, 2: 476–98.
Seybert, Adam. 1818. *Statistical Annals.* Reprint New York: Burt Franklin, 1969.
Smith, Walter. 1953. *Economic Aspects of the Second Bank of the United States.* Cambridge, Mass.: Harvard University Press.
Sylla, Richard E. and John J. Wallis. 1998. "The Anatomy of Sovereign Debt Crises: Lessons from the American State Defaults of the 1840s." *Japan and the World Economy* 10, 3: 267–93.
Sylla, Richard E. and Jack W. Wilson. 1999. "Sinking Funds as Credible Commitments: Two Centuries of U.S. National Debt Experience," *Japan and the World Economy* 11, 2: 199–202.
Sylla, Richard E., Jack W. Wilson, and Robert E. Wright. 1997. "America's First Securities Markets, 1790–1830: Emergence, Development, and Integration." Cliometrics Society Meeting, Toronto, Canada, May 1997, and NBER Summer Institute, Cambridge, Mass.
Financial Review. Various issues. Washington, D.C.: William B. Dana, 1876–1921.
Thorp, Willard Long. 1926. *Business Annals.* New York: National Bureau of Economic Research.
U.S. Bureau of the Census. 1975. *Historical Statistics of the United States, Colonial Times to 1970, Bicentennial Edition.* Washington, D.C.: U.S. GPO.
U.S. Navy. *Report of the Secretary of the Navy.* Various years; see specific citations in the text.
U.S. Senate. 1839. *Annual Report of the Secretary of the Navy.* Senate Document 1, 26th Cong., 1st sess.
Walsh, John J. 1940. *Early Banks in the District of Columbia, 1792–1818.* Washington, D.C.: Catholic University of America Press.
Wilson, Jack W. and Charles P. Jones. 1997. "Long-Term Returns and Risks for Bonds," *Journal of Portfolio Management* 23, 3: 15–23.

III
Challenges to
Public Pensions

Chapter 12
Going Private in the Public Sector
The Transition from Defined Benefit to Defined Contribution Pension Plans

Douglas Fore

The transition from private sector defined benefit to defined contribution pension plans has been underway in the United States for over a quarter-century, since the passage of the Employee Retirement Income Security Act (ERISA) in 1974 and especially since the introduction of 401(k) accounts in 1982. By contrast, in the state and local government sector, pensions have been and continue to be overwhelmingly defined benefit in type, perhaps because ERISA does not apply to these plans. Additional factors contributing to the continuation of public sector defined benefit pensions likely include the relatively high degree of unionization of state and local government employees, and the fact that early retirement features commonly associated with defined benefit plans have meshed well with many public employer personnel goals in the past.

Nevertheless, there is evidence that the public sector pension environment is beginning to evolve. A small but growing number of state and local governments have switched or are contemplating switching from a defined benefit to a defined contribution plan. If these pioneers prove successful, in terms of employee and employer satisfaction, the public sector may follow the transition trend experienced in the private sector over the last quarter-century. If this transition process spreads, it will mark a major shift in the way in which retirement income is provided for a substantial number of American workers and retirees. And if more state and local government pension plans transition to a defined contribution format, this could potentially have a profound impact on capital markets, given the substantial size of public pension assets.

Key Aspects of Public Sector Defined Benefit Pensions

As noted elsewhere in this volume, public pension benefit formulas vary widely within a state, and between states. My goal here is to highlight several issues pertinent to the public sector transition from defined benefit (DB) to defined contribution (DC) pension plans. I focus on benefit formulas, coverage and vesting rules, and funding patterns, derived from data contained in the PENDAT97 survey described above (see Hustead and Mitchell this volume; Zorn 1997, 1998).

Vesting requirements of public DB plans. Vesting refers to how long an employee must work to earn a legal right to an eventual retirement benefit under a plan. In public sector DB plans, a worker is generally vested after either five or ten years of employment; just under half of all plans vest employees after five years, with a similar percentage vesting after ten years. Only a very few plans grant pension rights immediately, and likewise few delay vesting for more than ten years. It should be noted that one plan can have different vesting rules for workers hired at different points in time, as well as different benefit rules. Eligibility for non-duty-related disability and survivors benefits typically requires the same vesting period as for pension benefits; duty-related disability and survivors benefits generally vest immediately, although some plans do require the same vesting period as for pension rights.

DB plan benefit formulas. Public pension benefit formulas vary widely within a state, and also between states (Hustead and Mitchell this volume). But despite this diversity, retirement benefits are calculated as a percentage of final average salary in most defined benefit plans. Final average salary may be defined as the worker's salary in the last year of employment, or an average of the last three or five years of work. Many plans also establish minimum age and service requirements (e.g., fifty years of age and twenty years of employment) in order to qualify for a pension with full credit for accrued benefits; these are commonly associated with police and fire department plan criteria.

Benefit accrual patterns for public employees covered/not covered by social security appear in Figure 1. Corresponding pension benefits received after 30 years of service, as a percentage of final average salary, are given in Figure 2. In the California State Teachers' Retirement System (calsters), employees accrue benefits at a constant 2.0 percent per year, which happens to be the average annual benefit accrual rate for all public sector workers. In 1996, the average DB benefit for state and local government workers covered by social security and with thirty years of service was 57.8 percent of final average salary; for workers not covered by social security, it was 68.5 percent of final average salary.

Constant-rate accrual of benefits appears to be the exception rather than

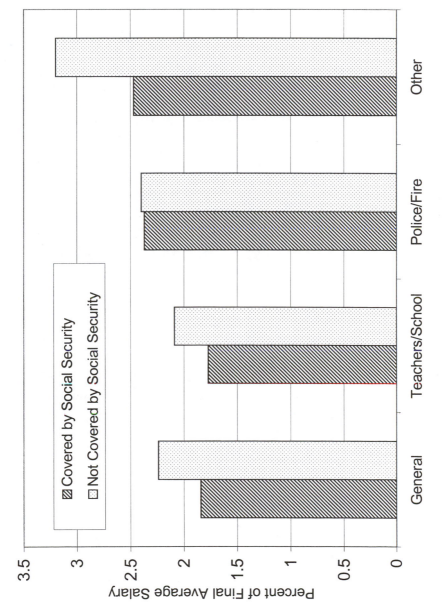

Figure 1. Benefit accrual rates by category of covered employee. Source: author's calculations.

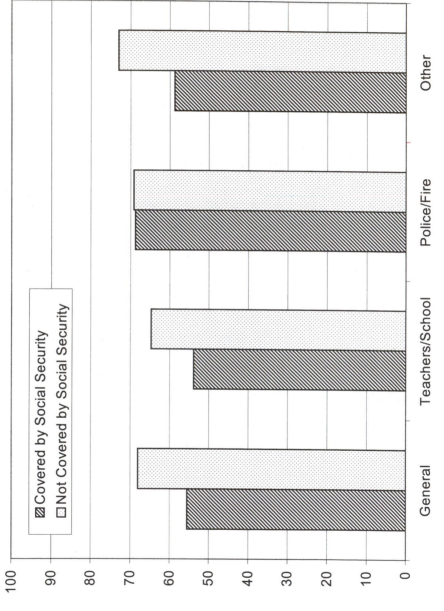

Figure 2. Average benefit after 30 years of service as percent of final average salary. Source: author's calculations.

the norm, however, in the public sector. Most public DB plans have differential accrual rates, usually on either side of twenty years of service. For example, the Alaska Teachers' Retirement System benefit accrual rate is 2.0 percent of final average service for the first 20 years of service, and 2.5 percent per year thereafter. By contrast, the City of Fresno Employees' Retirement System accrual rate is 2.0 percent of final average salary for the first twenty-five years, then falls to 1.0 percent per year thereafter. Some teachers, school employees, and general employees in public DB plans not covered by social security have annual benefit accrual rates rise by 0.30–0.40 percent per year of service on average, but plans for workers not covered by social security do provide lower benefit accrual rates. For example, workers in the California Public Employee Retirement System (Calpers)—who are not in social security—accrue benefits at a constant 1.25 percent per year; their resulting pension equalling only 37.50 percent of final average salary after thirty years of service, the lowest level of benefits offered by any major public plan in the country. This relatively low benefit level provided by Calpers may explain why many counties and municipalities in California have established their own distinct plans with different DB formulas.

Benefit formula design in the public sector appears to be motivated by three factors, the most important of which appears to be whether or not the employee group is covered by social security. Only a minority of plans covering workers covered by social security explicitly integrate their benefit formulas with expected social security benefits by, for example, offering higher benefit accrual rates for salary ranges above the social security earnings threshold. It must also be acknowledged that about a quarter of state and local government employees are not covered by social security; nevertheless as of 1983, state and local governments no longer have the option of opting out of social security.[1] In any event, as noted above, workers outside the social security system have more generous benefit accrual formulas than do workers included in social security. A second apparent factor in benefit formula design has to do with the employee group covered: local government plans are almost always more generous than state plans. For example, the accrual rate in the City of San Jose Federated City Employees' Retirement System is a flat 2.5 percent per year of final average salary, so a worker with thirty years of service would retire with a benefit of 75 percent of final average salary. This is double the benefit of an otherwise similar employee in the state-level Calpers plan. A third factor influencing public plan design is public employee unions, which tend to bargain over pension accrual rates with state and local governments.

DB plan funding status. The U.S. Government Accounting Standards Board has required state and local government pension plans to compute liabilities using a common set of methods to produce a pension benefit obligation (PBO) figure for each plan since 1987. In practice, public pension plan ad-

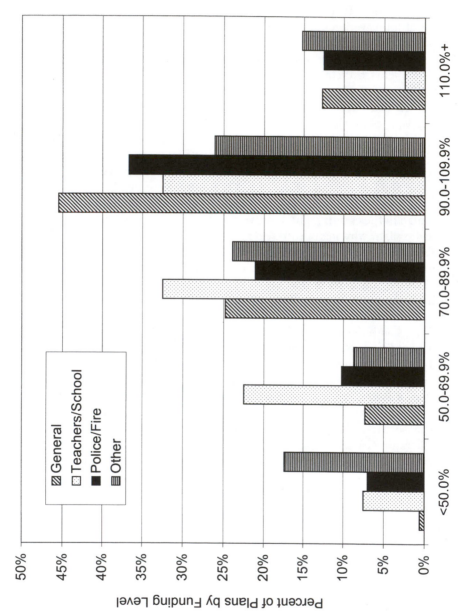

Figure 3. Funding status of plans by category. Source: Zorn (1997).

ministrators have wide latitude in terms of the assumptions used for future real salary increases and turnover rates, as well as future inflation and investment income return rates (Hustead this volume). As Mitchell and Smith (1994) note, the spread between expected investment returns and the expected growth rates of employee compensation is equal to the real discount rate of future pension liabilities, and a larger gap implies a lower present value of future liabilities. Mitchell and Smith found funding status in public DB plans negatively related to the degree of employee unionization and state fiscal pressure, and they also found persistence in past funding patterns.

Public sector defined benefit plans are fairly well funded in the 1990s (Mitchell et al. this volume), but plan funding status varies according to plan type. For example, when we compare teacher/school employee plans, police and fire department plans, and general plans, we find that the general plans have the highest funding ratios and teacher/school employee plans the lowest (in the case of teacher/school employee plans, roughly a third have funding ratios below 70 percent). This is depicted in Figure 3. Where public plans are less than fully funded, the amount is substantial: the mean time to amortization of the unfunded liability is approximately twenty-three years at current funding rates. We find no correlation between a state's per capita income or tax burden and the funding status of its defined benefit plans in the 1996 data.[2] This is perhaps surprising, because different patterns of state income and population growth generate different incentives in terms of funding levels. For example, rapidly growing sun-belt states and municipalities might be expected to underfund their plans relative to slowly growing Northern states. States attracting large numbers of migrants, whether from within or without the United States, might experience more rapid growth in their tax bases than in their actuarially accrued pension liabilities. In this case, DB plan underfunding might be anticipated, since rapid tax base growth could amortize unfunded actuarial liability without changing tax rates. Conversely, states and municipalities with static or declining tax bases have an incentive to fully fund or overfund their plans in order to avoid very large tax increases at some point in the future.

DB plans and mobility within a state. Public pension DB plans diverge concerning how readily they permit employees to transfer their pension rights to other public sector DSB plans *within the same state.* Roughly a third of these pension plans have reciprocal agreements with other plans in the same state for transferring or combining worker benefit rights accrued elsewhere. Where reciprocal agreements do not exist, employees may still have the option of transferring service credits. For example, roughly 40 percent of plans allow veterans to purchase service credits for military service at either full cost or less than full cost. Table 1 shows the matrix of options available to employees. Approximately 60 percent of all public defined benefit plans disallow transfer of any accrued benefit rights across plans; furthermore, fewer

TABLE 1. Defined Benefit Plan Portability Method for Determining Purchase of Service Credits Earned Elsewhere

	Less than			Purchase not allowed
Type of service	Full cost	Full cost	No cost	
State government	22%	15%	4%	59%
Local government	27%	14%	2%	57%
Out-of-state government	15%	6%	1%	78%
Federal government	14%	8%	1%	77%
Military	24%	23%	6%	47%
Other	12%	5%	0%	82%

Source: Author's calculations from PENDAT97 database.

than 20 percent of plans allow workers to purchase service credits earned in either the federal government or other state governments. Plans which do permit employees to purchase service credits are approximately twice as likely to require them to purchase credits at full cost rather than at less than full cost.

DB pension plans' impact on mobility more generally. Lack of portability is one of the well-known drawbacks to defined benefit pension plans. Under a defined benefit pension regime, workers who stay with the same employer retire with larger pensions than similarly compensated workers in similar defined benefit schemes who change employers over the course of their careers. This can be illustrated with a simple numerical example where we assume that pension rights are fully acquired after five years. Consider a worker who begins employment at age 35 with a salary of $25,000, receives annual raises of four percent, and retires at age 65. The worker faces two alternative career path options. On the first path, the worker can remain with the same employer for thirty years, accruing pension benefits at a rate of 2 percent per year that are paid as a percentage of final salary. On the second path, the worker quits his first job after either ten or twenty years. The pension benefits earned under the two paths are shown in Table 2.

Remaining with the first employer until retirement at age 65 would produce an annual pension benefit corresponding to the first year's service of $1,622, two percent of the last year's salary. The annual benefit corresponding to the first ten years of service would be $16,217. However, if the worker quit after ten years, at age 45, the benefit eventually payable at age 65 from the first employer would be only $7,401, corresponding to 2 percent of salary at age 45 for each year of service to the time he quit. Discounted at a rate of 6 percent for twenty years, the present value of the benefit received by staying with the first employer is roughly $2,800 per year larger. This may not seem to be much for a forty-five-year-old worker contemplating a job switch, but at age 65 with expected longevity of twenty more years the future

TABLE 2. Impact of Job Changes on Retirement Benefits in Defined Benefit
Pension Plans

Worker's age	Salary	Benefit based on current salary	Benefit based on final salary
35	$25,000	0	$1,622
45	$37,006	$7,401	$16,217
55	$54,778	$21,911	$32,434
65	$81,085	$48,651	$48,651

Source: Author's calculations.

value of this benefit would be approximately $28,000 larger. A worker who switched at age 55 after twenty years of service loses even more.

Several factors could exacerbate this benefit differential. For instance, high inflation during the latter part of the worker's career could erode the real value of the benefits accrued during prior years, and severely penalize the worker who changes jobs. Additionally, if the benefit formula were back loaded, so that the benefit accrual rate rises at some point (e.g., after twenty years), then changing jobs would also be disproportionately penalized.

DB plan impacts on labor supply. Public DB pension benefit formulas influence older workers' labor supply decisions because of the very nonlinearity of their structure.[3] These plans generally permit early retirement as early as age 55, although required service varies widely: some plans subsidize early retirement by minimizing or even eliminating actuarial reductions for early retirement, while other plans levy "full" or more than full reductions (i.e., over 5 or 6 percent) per year of retirement below age 60 or 65. Not surprisingly, plans covering police and fire department workers tend to have the most liberal early retirement policies. Many of these plans do not specify a minimum retirement age, instead basing the availability of retirement benefits on years of service. These provisions are presumably intended as a means of shedding workers as their physical fitness declines. Hence police and fire department workers may be able to retire with full or (partially) actuarially reduced benefits at age 40, after twenty years of service. Since many of these plans also offer workers the option of purchasing service credits for time spent in the military, many of these workers can earn significant pension rights by their early 40s. This is analogous to the situation in the federal government, where special agents of the Federal Bureau of Investigation can retire with full pensions at age 52 with twenty years of service, and face mandatory retirement at age 55. Similarly, FBI agents receive full credits for military or prior federal government service.

As mentioned above, benefit accrual patterns are rather jagged, with some plans front-loading benefits, others back loading, and still others offering constant benefit accrual rates. Changes in the rate of benefit accrual are typically service related, with changes after twenty years of service, and usually not age related. Additionally, some plans cap benefits at a certain percentage of final average salary. These differing benefit formulas would be expected to impact the labor supply decisions of older workers at several points in time. For example, where the plan does not call for actuarial reductions for early retirement, we would expect to see a spike in retirement at the twenty years of service mark for police and fire department workers, or at age 55 for other state and local government workers. We would expect to see similar spikes at the thirty years of service mark and especially at age 62, the age when three-quarters of state and local government workers become eligible for social security. Researching the empirical links between public plan retirement rates and benefit formulas is a task for future research.

Changes in benefit accrual rates after twenty years of service but before thirty years are also intended to influence the retirement decision. In front-loaded plans, which typically reduce the accrual rate to one percent per year of service after twenty or twenty-five years, employees have an incentive to leave early. Similarly, plans with absolute caps on benefit replacement rates are probably designed to stimulate older workers' withdrawal. This would be expected for the Fire and Police Pension Fund of San Antonio, where plan members are not covered by social security; the benefit accrual rate is 2.0 percent of final average salary for the first twenty years, 4.0 percent for years 21–25, 3.5 percent for years 26–30, and then a modest 1.0 percent of final average salary for each additional year of service past thirty years.[4]

These patterns of benefit accrual rates parallel those of private-sector employers who also tend to want to induce retirement after twenty to thirty years of employment. For instance Gustman, Mitchell, and Steinmeier (1994) show that private DB plans offering subsidized early retirement increased dramatically between 1960 and 1980. The observed heterogeneity in benefit formulas also suggests endogeneity in public plan design. It must also be acknowledged that it is more difficult to fire or lay off a worker with many years of service in the public sector, versus in the private sector. In this light, DB plans offering early retirement incentives provide a substitute method of discharging lower productivity employees. We also recognize that some employers prefer incentive provisions that tie workers to their jobs, especially workers receiving specialized training such as police and fire department personnel and teachers. And for safety workers in particular, early retirement provisions are important to employers where worker productivity may be expected to eventually decline due to physical demands.

The manner in which employee and employer contributions are credited with interest can also impact retirement and mobility decisions. Approximately three-fourths of public DB pension plans currently credit employee contributions with interest.[5] Of those plans that do this, roughly 60 percent use interest rates greater than or equal to 5 percent. Of course, contributions would still compound relatively slowly for most employees at the nominal risk-free interest rate or below. Even where pensions are portable within the public sector of a state, limits on pension accumulations would deter mobility in cases where service credits must be purchased.

There have recently been a variety of legislative proposals introduced, with the aim of increasing portability among different types of pension plans. Most aspects of these proposals refer to DC plans. For example, one proposal would permit rollovers between 401(k) and 403(b) plans which are disallowed under current law. Specifically, this would allow workers with 403(b) and 457 plan assets to use those assets for the purchase of service credits in public sector DB plans. Another proposal allows rollovers from IRAs to defined contribution and defined benefit plans.

The Transition to Defined Contribution Pensions

There are several appealing aspects about DC plans in the public sector. We enumerate these next.

Defined contribution pensions and mobility. When contemplating a job offer, prospective employees must form expectations about job tenure and eventual pension benefits, among other factors. The decision matrix can be expected to vary with the worker's age at time of employment, expected date of retirement, and degree of risk aversion. Younger workers, in particular, may expect to change employers multiple times over the course of their careers, particularly in light of evidence that there has been a trend toward increased employment mobility between the 1980s and the 1990s. For instance, Jaeger and Stevens (1998) report a statistically significant increase in the probability of employees having fewer than ten years of job tenure, over time.

In this environment, defined benefit plans become substantially less attractive, especially those with ten-year vesting periods, and DC plans have increased appeal when long job tenure is not expected due to their enhanced portability. Employee contributions vest immediately, and employer contributions usually vest either immediately or after a wait of one year (a few require vesting periods of up to five years). Employees who change jobs and move from one DC plan to another face only the potential loss of pension rights of nonvested employer contributions. Furthermore, DC pension rights are neutral with respect to job tenure. Thus workers with vested rights in a DB plan who leave the firm after five to ten years see their pension benefits frozen in nominal terms based on their salaries at that time, but similar workers with DC plans continue to accumulate interest income, dividends, and capital gains in their pension portfolios.

Of course, to receive the benefits of tax deferral, employees who change jobs and pension plans must either roll their DC balances into new DC plans, or else leave their original balances untouched to accumulate over time. There is evidence that many workers take partial or full lump-sum distributions from their plans when changing jobs and use the proceeds for investment in housing assets, consumer durables, or immediate consumption (Samwick and Skinner 1996). Restrictions on rollovers between different types of defined contribution plans may well contribute to this phenomenon. Under current law, rollovers are not allowed from 401(k) to 403(b) plans or in the other direction from 403(b) to 401(k) plans. Currently, service credits cannot be purchased with defined contribution plan assets.

Defined contribution pensions and investment risk. In state and local DB plans, taxpayers of each jurisdiction bear two types of investment risk. (Participants do bear default risk, but in the United States, this risk is seen to be low in comparison to the risks borne by taxpayers). First, they bear the risk of underfunding, which could necessitate a higher tax burden. Taxpayers could avoid this risk by moving to another jurisdiction in advance of the future tax increase, but this works only if they move to an area with a better-funded plan. Second, taxpayers face the risk that the DB plan assets will generate inadequte investment performance, again producing a need for higher taxes. Conversely, taxpayers enjoy the upside risk that if investment performance and funding progress are greater than expected, resulting in overfunding of the plan, future contributions may be reduced.[6]

In DC plans, of course, investment risk is borne by plan participants, in exchange for which they receive flexibility in terms of investment choice. This flexibility permits individuals to tailor their portfolios in accordance with their time and risk preferences. While the appeal of a DC approach is obvious, there remains the concern that financially unsophisticated participants may choose portfolios either too conservative or too risky, putting retirement income security in jeopardy. It should also be said that there is no a priori reason to believe that DC plans automatically offer a menu of choices suitable for the varied tastes of plan participants, since investment choices available in defined contribution plans vary widely.

The appeal of DC investment options has been pointed out in a recent study of faculty pension plan choices by Clark, Harper, and Pitts (1997), who examined the choices of new faculty hires at North Carolina State University. These faculty members were given the option of joining either the state government defined benefit plan, or one of three defined contribution plans including TIAA-CREF. Over the subsequent five-year period (1990–94), 75 percent chose TIAA-CREF, 17 percent chose the DB plan, and 8 percent chose one of the other two defined contribution plans.

Defined contribution pensions and labor supply. One key way in which DC plans influence labor supply concerns the interaction between duration of coverage and total accumulations. Older workers continue to receive the same interest accruals on their account balances as do younger workers, subject to portfolio composition. Unlike defined benefit plans, with their reductions in benefit accrual rates after a set number of years of service, or explicit caps on benefits, defined contribution plans have no early retirement incentives. Indeed, as total accumulations continue to accrue with compound interest, employees may have a strong incentive to work longer in order to enjoy higher incomes in retirement. However, once total accumulations are such that retirement income security is assured, employees must then weigh the tradeoffs of continued employment against their desire for leisure.

Trends to DC Pensions at the State Level

As noted above, several states recently introduced DC pensions for particular groups of employees, and more states are studying the idea of making the transition from defined benefit to defined contribution plans. Several factors prompt the increased interest. One is term limits: in states where legislators face limitations on tenure in office, standard DB plans do not provide the legislators with retirement income security. Indeed, this is the main reason why the state of Colorado switched to a defined contribution plan for its state legislators in 1998. A second motivation is the desire to shift risk from the taxpayers to employees; this is related to the goal of cutting total pension contributions and the state's total pension cost burden. Another rationale is the desire of state and local government employees for superior pension portability and investment choice, linked to private employee enthusiasm for investing in 401(k) plans.

Several state and local governments sponsor DC pensions as either their sole plan or as a supplement to their DB plan. In Colorado, in addition to the legislators' defined contribution plan, several municipalities offer defined contribution plans as the only pension plan. In Michigan, newly hired state and local government employees (excluding teachers K-12) may join a defined contribution plan; existing employees were offered the choice of staying in the DB plan or switching to the DC plan. The state of Washington offers a hybrid defined benefit/defined contribution plan. The state of Indiana has a defined contribution supplement to its defined benefit plan for teachers, consisting of 3 percent of salary. Growing interest in making a transition from defined benefit to defined contribution plans is reflected in the number of state legislatures where bills have been introduced to enable the transition. Legislation is currently under consideration in Florida, Georgia, Ohio, South Carolina, Tennessee, and Texas.[7]

The decision to switch from DB to DC is often made in the context of a funding discussion. Ceteris paribus, making the transition is easier when a plan is fully funded or overfunded. The closer a plan becomes to a pay-as-you-go system, and the greater the unfunded actuarial liability, the more expensive the transition and the lower the probability that taxpayers will choose to bear the burden of transition. For example, in Michigan when the new defined contribution plan was introduced, legislation was passed that explicitly stated that K–12 employees could not make the transition until the $3 billion plus unfunded liability of the Michigan Public School Employees Retirement System was erased by December 31, 1997. The liability was not paid off and K–12 employees do not, as yet, have the option of a defined contribution plan. If plan sponsors overestimate the public plan's actuarial liability, perhaps because expectations of future inflation are too high, then the funding status of the plan will be better than it seems at first glance and the transition will seem easier. For instance, some plan administrators are using long-term inflation assumptions in excess of 4 percent, which probably gives an overly pessimistic view of the growth of future liabilities.

When to Stay and When to Go in Defined Benefit Plans

One method of making the transition between a defined benefit to a defined contribution plan is to grandfather existing employees in the old DB system and move new employees into a new DC scheme. This eases the administrative burden, but does not benefit current employees, especially those with limited tenure, who may wish to participate in the defined contribution plan. One way in which costs could be reduced in a transition is if employees assign a high value to the portability, investment choice, immediate vesting, and other features offered by the DC plan. In this case, employees might be willing to accept a lower expected value of future benefits in return for the other advantages of a defined contribution plan. A closer analysis of such trade-offs is facilitated using a simulation model that computes the expected future benefits from either staying in a defined benefit plan or switching to a defined contribution plan after five, ten, fifteen, or twenty years of coverage in a defined benefit plan. First, we assume that the worker begins employment at age 35 with a starting salary of $25,000. The worker receives annual real wage increases of 1.0, 1.5, or 2.0 percent per year. In the DB plan, pension rights are vested after five years of service. Defined benefit pension rights accrue at 1.5, 1.75, 2.0, or 2.25 percent per year. In the DC plan, the overall employee and employer contribution rate is 10.0, 12.5, or 15.0 percent of salary. The investment portfolio in the DC plan is assumed to be 60 percent equities and 40 percent long-term U.S. Treasury bonds, returning 1926–97 historical average real returns of 7.2 and 2.0 percent, respectively (Siegel 1998). The real annual portfolio return is accordingly 5.12 percent. Workers who leave the defined benefit plan with vested rights after five, ten, fifteen, or twenty years of service have their eventual defined benefit pension rights valued based on their nominal salaries at that time. Workers who retire at age 65 in the defined benefit plan have their pension rights valued based on the salary at age 65. Workers who transition to the defined contribution plan eventually receive two pensions. The first is based on their accrued defined benefit rights as of the date they elected to make the transition. The second is based on their final defined contribution accumulations. These accumulations are the basis for a single life annuity based on TIAA annuity rates as of June 1998 that pays a monthly amount of $759 per $100,000 accumulation (Poterba and Warshawsky 1999).

Given these assumptions, we compute the pensions received under the different assumed accrual rates and investment return patterns. The annual pension benefit for a worker who elects to transition to a DC plan after five years of service in a DB plan appear in Table 3. The table shows the importance of high contribution rates in the DC plan. When the contribution rate is 12.5 percent transition is favorable under most combinations of real wage growth and defined benefit accrual rates. However, if the contribution rate is 15.0 percent, then transition is unambiguously favorable under all states except one. Conversely, if the contribution rate is lower, at 10.0 percent, transition generates higher retirement incomes under only a few states.

The simulations also show the interaction of real wage growth with both DB and DC accumulations. For example, in Table 3, when real wage growth is 2.0 percent per year DB pensions after thirty years are higher with accrual rates of 1.75 percent per year than when benefit accrual rates are 2.25 percent per year but real wage growth is only 1.0 percent per year. Similarly, DC accumulations and subsequent annuity payments are an increasing function of real wage growth and contribution rates. Of the two factors contribution rates are more important for parameter values used in these simulations.

Projected DB and DC pension payments if an employee transitions to a DC plan after ten years are shown in Table 4. For mid-range contribution rates of 12.5 percent transition results in unambiguously higher incomes only for low rates of real wage growth and defined benefit accrual. If the contribution rate is 10.0 percent then transition results in lower simulated incomes in all states. However, if the contribution rate is 15.0 percent transition produces higher projected incomes in more than half of the real wage growth/defined benefit accrual states.

Simulation results for transition after fifteen years are shown in Table 5. If the contribution rate is 12.5 percent then transition generates higher retirement income only if real wage growth is 1.0 percent and the benefit accrual rate is 1.5 percent. However, if the contribution rate is 15.0 percent then transition results in higher incomes regardless of real wage growth if the defined benefit accrual rate is 1.50 percent. If the accrual rate is 1.75 percent then transition produces higher income if real wage growth is 1.0 percent, and approximately equal income if real wage growth is 1.50 percent. Transition after twenty years results in lower expected incomes given parameter values simulated here.[8]

Two other significant factors are involved in the determination of pension

TABLE 3. Transition After Five Years in Defined Benefit Plan: Results From Real Simulation

DB plan accrual rate	Real wage gain 1.0% contribution rates of			Real wage gain 1.5% contribution rates of			Real wage gain 2.0% contribution rates of		
	10%	12.50%	15%	10%	12.50%	15%	10%	12.50%	15%
DC pension	14,457	18,071	21,685	15,601	19,501	23,401	16,851	21,064	25,276
DB benefit	1,971	1,971	1,971	2,020	2,020	2,020	2,070	2,070	2,070
Combined	16,427	20,041	23,655	17,621	21,521	25,421	18,921	23,134	27,347
1.50% DB pension		15,163			17,585			20,378	
DC pension	14,457	18,071	21,685	15,601	19,501	23,401	16,851	21,064	25,276
DB benefit	2,299	2,299	2,299	2,357	2,357	2,357	2,415	2,415	2,415
Combined	16,756	20,370	23,984	17,957	21,857	25,757	19,266	23,479	27,692
1.75% DB pension		17,690			20,515			23,774	
DC pension	14,457	18,071	21,685	15,601	19,501	23,401	16,851	21,064	25,276
DB benefit	2,628	2,628	2,628	2,693	2,693	2,693	2,760	2,760	2,760
Combined	17,084	20,698	24,312	18,294	22,194	26,094	19,611	23,824	28,037
2.00% DB pension		20,218			23,446			27,170	
DC pension	14,457	18,071	21,685	15,601	19,501	23,401	16,851	21,064	25,276
DB benefit	2,956	2,956	2,956	3,030	3,030	3,030	3,105	3,105	3,105
Combined	17,413	21,027	24,641	18,630	22,531	26,431	19,956	24,169	28,382
2.25% DB pension		22,745			26,377			30,567	

Source: Author's calculations.

TABLE 4. Transition After Ten Years in Defined Benefit Plan: Results From Real Simulation

DB plan accrual rate	Real wage gain 1.0% contribution rates of			Real wage gain 1.5% contribution rates of			Real wage gain 2.0% contribution rates of		
	10%	12.50%	15%	10%	12.50%	15%	10%	12.50%	15%
DC pension	10,404	13,005	15,606	11,407	14,259	17,111	12,512	15,640	18,768
DB benefit	4,142	4,142	4,142	4,352	4,352	4,352	4,571	4,571	4,571
Combined	14,546	17,147	19,748	15,759	18,611	21,463	17,083	20,211	23,339
1.50% DB pension		15,163			17,585			20,378	
DC pension	10,404	13,005	15,606	11,407	14,259	17,111	12,512	15,640	18,768
DB benefit	4,833	4,833	4,833	5,077	5,077	5,077	5,333	5,333	5,333
Combined	15,237	17,838	20,439	16,484	19,336	22,188	17,845	20,973	24,101
1.75% DB pension		17,690			20,515			23,774	
DC pension	10,404	13,005	15,606	11,407	14,259	17,111	12,512	15,640	18,768
DB benefit	5,523	5,523	5,523	5,803	5,803	5,803	6,095	6,095	6,095
Combined	15,927	18,528	21,129	17,210	20,062	22,913	18,607	21,735	24,863
2.00% DB pension		20,218			23,446			27,170	
DC pension	10,404	13,005	15,606	11,407	14,259	17,111	12,512	15,640	18,768
DB benefit	6,213	6,213	6,213	6,528	6,528	6,528	6,857	6,857	6,857
Combined	16,618	19,219	21,820	17,935	20,787	23,639	19,369	22,497	25,625
2.25% DB pension		22,745			26,377			30,567	

Source: Author's calculations.

TABLE 5. Transition After Fifteen Years In Defined Benefit Plan: Results From Real Simulation

DB plan accrual rate	*Real wage gain 1.0% contribution rates of*			*Real wage gain 1.5% contribution rates of*			*Real wage gain 2.0% contribution rates of*		
	10%	*12.50%*	*15%*	*10%*	*12.50%*	*15%*	*10%*	*12.50%*	*15%*
DC pension	7,086	8,857	10,629	7,888	9,860	11,831	8,780	10,975	13,170
DB benefit	6,530	6,530	6,530	7,033	7,033	7,033	7,571	7,571	7,571
Combined	13,616	15,388	17,159	14,920	16,892	18,864	16,350	18,545	20,740
1.50% DB pension		15,163			17,585			20,378	
DC pension	7,086	8,857	10,629	7,888	9,860	11,831	8,780	10,975	13,170
DB benefit	7,619	7,619	7,619	8,205	8,205	8,205	8,832	8,832	8,832
Combined	14,705	16,476	18,248	16,092	18,064	20,036	17,612	19,807	22,002
1.75% DB pension		17,690			20,515			23,774	
DC pension	7,086	8,857	10,629	7,888	9,860	11,831	8,780	10,975	13,170
DB benefit	8,707	8,707	8,707	9,377	9,377	9,377	10,094	10,094	10,094
Combined	15,793	17,565	19,336	17,264	19,236	21,208	18,874	21,069	23,264
2.00% DB pension		20,218			23,446			27,170	
DC pension	7,086	8,857	10,629	7,888	9,860	11,831	8,780	10,975	13,170
DB benefit	9,796	9,796	9,796	10,549	10,549	10,549	11,356	11,356	11,356
Combined	16,882	18,653	20,424	18,436	20,408	22,380	20,136	22,331	24,526
2.25% DB pension		22,745			26,377			30,567	

Source: Author's calculations.

incomes in these nonstochastic simulations. One is inflation, which erodes the value of the nominal pension benefit earned at the time of transition and may depress nominal investment returns as well. However, where the DB pension formula is computed using final salary, employees are protected until the time of retirement or transition. Income security in retirement is then dependent on the manner in which benefits are indexed, if at all. The second significant factor is the option value of switching to a DC plan. For example, consider the case of an employee in a DB plan, accruing pension rights at the rate of 2.0 percent per year, with real wage growth of 1.50 percent per year, offered the opportunity to switch to a DC plan after five years of coverage under the DB plan. In Table 3 this employee's eventual benefit under the DB plan is $23,446. Assuming a contribution rate of 12.50 percent in the DC plan, and with the small benefit earned under the DB plan, the table gives the eventual pension as $22,194.

Should the employee make the transition or not? That depends on the value the employee assigns to the DC "call option." The value of the option is a positive function of the value to the employee of the advantages such as portability and investment choice offered by the DC plan. Younger workers, in particular, would be expected to prefer DC plans. Additionally, the option value of DC plans would be a positive function of time until retirement. Younger workers can also bear more risk, and may have the ability in DC plans to choose riskier portfolios, with higher expected returns than in the generally conservative simulations shown here. Therefore under reasonable parameters the value of the option would be such that employees would prefer to make the transition to a DC plan even if the simulations show that the transition would result in somewhat smaller incomes in retirement.

The impact of attitudes toward risk on the transition choice is unclear. An extremely risk-averse employee may prefer the status quo and the expected certainty of an eventual DB pension. But at least in the private sector, many employers are converting from conventional DB to cash balance pension plans, a change that may reduce eventual pension benefits of older workers. In the public sector, conventional DB plans may appear more secure, but a jurisdiction which experiences severe fiscal pressure may feel compelled to cut pension contributions and hence future benefits for current workers. Additionally, the DC plan offers control over asset allocation, which often appeals to employees regardless of risk preferences.

Conclusions

Several issues arise when considering the transition from defined benefit to defined contribution pensions in the state and local government sector. While DB plans offer many advantages, a recent trend to DC plans in several public sector contexts suggests that the private sector trend may be spreading to the public sector. We show that the appeal of moving from DB to DC pensions is partly due to the very different retirement wealth accumulations under the two plan types, such that under many transition scenarios, a worker would have greater retirement income security in a DC than in a DB plan. For those who value the option, employers may be able to induce employees to switch pension plans in a way that saves public plan employers — and taxpayers — money in the long run. The cost savings would come from paying only small future DB pensions to employees who switch, as opposed to large DB pensions based on final average salary to those who stay. Hence a transition option in which employees choose whatever plan was in their best interest might actually lower employer costs while improving employee welfare. Calculating the option value of transitioning from a DB to a DC plan is a direction for future research.

Notes

1. Jurisdictions outside social security generally oppose proposals to include them in the system, for fear it would have an adverse impact on plan funding status.

2. This conclusion is based on the author's perusal of PENDAT97 survey results.

3. Data from Europe suggest that early retirement benefit patterns strongly induce early retirement (Gruber and Wise 1999), and in the United States, Costa (1998) shows that eligibility for reduced and full social security benefits produce upward spikes in retirement rates at ages 62 and 65.

4. Front-loaded plans too may be designed to influence the date of retirement. For example, workers in the Illinois Downstate and Suburban Police Fund (who are not included in social security), have an accrual rate of 2.5 percent of final average salary during the first 20 years of service, falling to 2.0 percent per year from years 21–30, and then falling again to 1.0 percent per year after 30 years of service. Conversely, back-loaded plans do not encourage early retirement, unless they have caps on the maximum benefit replacement rate that can be earned. However, back-loaded plans often have fairly ungenerous benefit formulae. For example, workers in the Teachers' Retirement System of Illinois plan have a benefit accrual rate of 1.67 percent of final average salary during the first 10 years of employment, 1.9 percent per year from years 11–20, 2.1 percent per year from years 21–30, and 2.3 percent per year thereafter. Hence a worker retiring after 20 years of service at age 65 would receive a benefit replacement rate of only 35.70 percent of final average salary. A worker retiring at age 65 with 30 years of service would receive a replacement rate of 56.70 percent of final average salary. Plan members are not covered by social security.

5. No data are available on whether and how employer contributions are credited with interest.

6. Alternatively, unions may lobby for benefit increases.

7. Legislation in draft form also exists in Louisiana.

8. Simulations were also calculated with the following assumptions: The worker begins employment at age 35 with a starting salary of $25,000 and a nominal wage growth rate of 4.0 percent per year. In the DB plan, pension rights are vested after 5 years of service. In the DC plan, the overall employee and employer contribution rate is 12.5 percent of salary. DB pension rights accrue at 1.5, 1.75, 2.0, or 2.25 percent per year. Investment returns in the DC plan are alternatively 3.0, 6.0, 7.5, 9.0,

or 12.0 percent per year. Workers who leave the DB plan with vested rights after 5, 10, 15, or 20 years of service have their eventual DB pension rights valued based on their nominal salaries at that time. Workers who retire at age 65 in the DB plan have their pension rights valued based on their nominal salaries at that time. DC accumulations are converted into an annuity as in the simulations described in the text. These simulations generated results quite similar to those in the text. Details are available from the author on request.

References

Clark, Robert L., Loretta Harper, and M. Melinda Pitts. 1997. "Faculty Pension Choices in a Public Institution: Defined Benefit and Defined Contribution Plans." *Research Dialogues* 50 (March).

Costa, Dora L. 1998. *The Evolution of Retirement: An American Economic History, 1880–1990,* Chicago: University of Chicago Press.

Gruber, Jonathan and David Wise, eds. 1999. *Social Security and Retirement Around the World,* Chicago: University of Chicago Press, 1999.

Gustman, Alan L., Olivia S. Mitchell, and Thomas L. Steinmeier. 1994. "The Role of Pensions in the Labor Market: A Survey of the Literature." *Industrial and Labor Relations Review* 47, 3 (April): 417–38.

Hustead, Edwin C. This volume. "Determining Cost of Public Pension Plans."

Hustead, Edwin C. and Olivia S. Mitchell. This volume. "Public Sector Pension Plans: Lessons and Challenges for the Twenty-First Century."

Jaeger, David A. and Ann Huff Stevens. 1998. "Is Job Stability in the United States Falling? Reconciling Trends in the Current Population Survey and Panel Study of Income Dynamics." National Bureau of Economic Research Working Paper 6650, July.

Mitchell, Olivia S. and Roderick M. Carr. 1995. "State and Local Pension Plans." National Bureau of Economic Research Working Paper 5271, September.

Mitchell, Olivia S., David McCarthy, Stanley C. Wisniewski, and Paul Zorn. This volume. "Developments in State and Local Pension Plans."

Mitchell, Olivia S. and Robert S. Smith. 1994. "Pension Funding in the Public Sector." *Review of Economics and Statistics* 76, 2 (May): 278–90.

Poterba, James M. and Mark Warshawsky. 1999. "The Costs of Annuitizing Retirement Payouts from Individual Accounts." National Bureau of Economic Research Working Paper 6918, January.

Samwick, Andrew A. and Jonathan Skinner. 1996. "Abandoning the Nest Egg? 401(k) Plans and Inadequate Pension Saving." National Bureau of Economic Research Working Paper 5568, May.

Siegel, Jeremy J. 1998. *Stocks for the Long Run.* New York: McGraw-Hill.

U.S. House of Representatives. 1999. Bill 739, Retirement Account Portability Act of 1999. 106th Cong., 1st Sess.

Zorn, Paul, 1997. *1997 Survey of State and Local Government Employee Retirement Systems,* Chicago: Public Pension Coordinating Council, c/o Government Finance Officers Association.

———. 1998. *1997 Survey of State and Local Government Employee Retirement Systems: Data Base Users Guide.* Chicago: Public Pension Coordinating Council, c/o Government Finance Officers Association.

Chapter 13
Florida's Public Pension Reform Debate
A Discussion of the Issues and
Estimates of the Option Costs

Kenneth Trager, James Francis, and Kevin SigRist

With assets approaching $100 billion, the Florida Retirement System (FRS) is one of the largest pension plans in the United States. The FRS is comprised of nearly 800 employers and has approximately 600,000 active members and 166,000 annuitants.[1] The Florida Division of Retirement handles the administrative functions of the FRS, while the State Board of Administration's (SBA) responsibilities include the investment of the pension trust fund assets.

Two events transpired over the past year that heightened interest in the costs and benefits associated with the FRS—the elimination of the FRS's unfunded actuarial liability (UAL), and the introduction of optional defined contribution (DC) pension plan legislation. The FRS returned to full funding status mainly due to the bull market in equities, the secular decline in interest rates, and an aggressive asset allocation stance.[2] The defined contribution initiative arose primarily from public sector employer concerns over its ability to compete with the private sector in attracting and retaining workers (Bush 1999; Chiles 1999; Jennings, 1999).

In this chapter we focus on key elements of defined benefit (DB) and DC pension plans that are at the heart of Florida's pension reform debate. We then discuss goals and objectives of Florida's pension reform, including an examination of the DB and DC benefit accrual patterns with a focus on relative benefit portability comparisons. A range of pension reform option costs is then presented. We conclude with an assessment of future public pension reforms in Florida. Although we frame our remarks against the backdrop of FRS data, we believe the discussion is pertinent to all public or private pension plans wrestling with pension reform issues.

Following the 1998 legislative session, Governor Lawton Chiles and the Florida legislature impaneled the Unfunded Actuarial Liability Working Group with a mandate to comprehensively study a number of pension finance issues.[3] The Working Group submitted its pension finance reform proposals to the president of the Senate, the Speaker of the House, and the Board of Trustees of the SBA, and the recommendations were incorporated in the current actuarial valuation (UAL Working Group 1999; Milliman and Robertson, 1998a).[4] The consequent elimination of the UAL (a $3.8 billion surplus was posted on July 1, 1998) and more realistic wage growth assumptions substantially reduced employer contribution costs. For the current fiscal year, the FRS's composite contribution costs fell 611 basis points—from 16.66 percent to 10.55 percent—translating into a systemwide budget savings of approximately $1.1 billion.

Governor Chiles requested that the Working Group also address the various pension reform issues circulating within the Legislature. The Working Group's discussions emphasized the value of a more portable benefit structure, the need to enhance the fairness in the distribution of pension benefits, and the lack of personal control of investment decisions present in all defined benefit pension plans (self-determination). A series of optional DC pension bills was introduced during the 1998 and 1999 Florida Legislative sessions, each with the commonalties of holding FRS employees (existing and future) and beneficiaries harmless while allowing workers to elect the optional DC plan or remain in the DB plan.[5]

Defined Benefit Pension Concerns

Among the many advantages and disadvantages of DB pension plans, two issues are central to the pension reform debate in Florida: the lack of self-determination and portability losses.

DB plan participants currently have no investment options, but they bear little investment risk. The lack of employee participation in DB investment decisions coupled with the fact that employees are insulated from most investment risks appeals to plan members who value guaranteed retirement benefits. But the rigidity of a DB plan's benefit structure and absence of employee choice has become an undesirable pension design element to a segment of FRS employees. Increased interest in self-determination among this segment of members has paralleled the extraordinary investment climate since the end of the 1981–82 recession, a period associated with an elevated rate of increase in stock prices and a secular decline in interest rates. The period from 1994 through 1998 posted the highest five-year return for large company stocks in the 73-year history of the Ibbotson database (measured by the S&P 500 Index; Ibbotson and Associates 1999).[6]

It appears that many self-determination advocates have unrealistically high expectations of future investment returns because they extrapolate returns using one of the strongest bull markets in U.S. history.[7] Since 1988, FRS valuations assume an 8 percent investment return. While this is in step with the majority of public pension plans, according to the Society of Actuaries (Samet, Peach, and Zorn 1996), assumed investment returns proved well below those actually realized over this period. However, FRS member benefits have only marginally participated in these excess returns.[8] Instead, excess returns have mainly been channeled into reducing employer (taxpayer) costs that may have helped to fuel a desire for self-determination among a segment of the FRS membership.

Of course, there are no guarantees that historical financial market returns will be sustained in the future; indeed the last 18-year period stands out because of atypically strong equity and bond market returns.[9] And the desire for self-determination among a segment of the FRS membership probably goes beyond a discussion of financial market returns, since there always remains the possibility that future DB benefits can be changed. There is some risk that the legislature could change the forward looking benefit structure of the FRS, which would negatively impact benefit accumulation; it is also possible that the FRS might not continue its 3 percent cost-of-living adjustment for retired beneficiaries. Some parallel might be drawn by looking at the private sector, where conventional defined benefit plans are being converted to cash balance plans, in some cases adversely impacting the benefits of older, long service workers. In the case of the FRS, however, benefit reductions are highly unlikely. The opening premise of Florida's UAL Working Group formed in 1999 was that the benefits of existing FRS beneficiaries and workers would always be protected.[10]

A second perceived drawback of traditional DB plans pertains to portability losses, which affects workers with discontinuous work histories. This is salient to shorter service employees who might leave FRS covered employment prior to the normal retirement age of 62. Some fraction of short tenure could be voluntary, perhaps arising from opportunities in a dynamic labor market or the desire to remain at home to raise a child. But in many instances, short service is due to reasons that might deemed to be beyond a worker's control, such as a layoff, a forced relocation, or the need to be a caregiver for a parent with deteriorating health.

Workers who leave covered employment prior to meeting the FRS's ten-year vesting requirement (which is double the Employee Retirement Income Security Act's [ERISA's] maximum allowable cliff vesting in the private sector) are the most visible example of FRS portability losses because they leave with no retirement benefits (see Table 1). This group represents a non-

TABLE 1. Employee Termination Counts by Years of Service, Florida Retirement
System

Years of service	Number of employees	Percent of total	Cumulative percent
<1	2,034	3.70	3.70
1	9,927	18.04	21.70
2	6,257	11.37	33.10
3	5,131	9.32	42.40
4	3,884	7.06	49.50
5	2,568	4.67	54.10
6	2,123	3.86	58.00
7	2,056	3.74	61.70
8	1,761	3.20	64.90
9	1,366	2.48	67.40
10–15	6,914	12.60	81.40
15–20	3,607	6.50	87.60
20–25	2,696	4.90	92.50
25–30	2,291	4.20	96.90
30 and over	2,421	4.40	100.00

Source: Authors' calculations from unpublished 1997–98 data kindly provided by the Florida
Retirement System.

trivial number of workers; over two-thirds of the FRS workers who terminated employment over the last actuarial valuation period (July 1997–June
1998) left public service prior to vesting and are entitled to no FRS pension
benefits. Some of these workers may eventually reenter FRS employment
later in their working careers, but the longitudinal data needed to estimate
this proportion is not available.

Another type of portability loss arises from the backloading of benefits
found in most traditional DB plan designs. In Florida, FRS public employee
benefits are based on the average of the highest five years of earnings, which
typically occur at the end of a career, rather than lifetime earnings. Vested
workers who leave FRS employment prior to the normal retirement age of
62 will find that the purchasing power of their retirement benefits is eroded,
since the wage base is frozen in nominal terms. This can cause a substantial
portability loss, nearly double the portability loss of nonvested workers who
leave covered employment (Hay-Huggins and Mathematica Policy Research
1988).

Some skew in the distribution of pension benefits to reward long service may be considered desirable, but DB portability losses also contain two
largely unintentional (and not mutually exclusive) components. First, the
level of inflation affects the portability loss in a DB plan—which, of course, is
beyond the control of employers (Bodie, Marcus and Merton, 1985; Turner
1993). Second, "an age bias" is embedded in portability losses, since shorter-
term younger workers who lose benefits in effect transfer value to shorter-

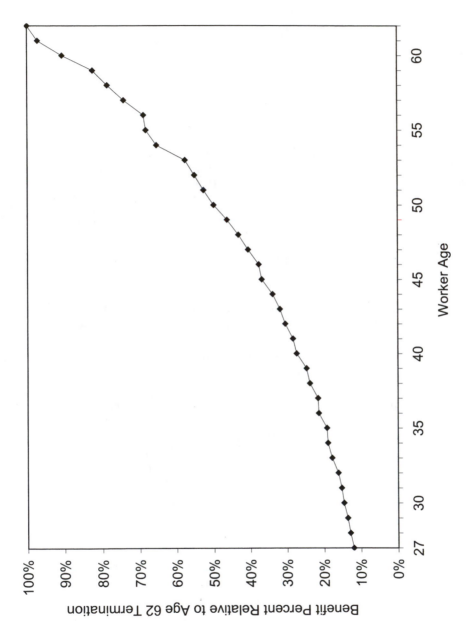

Figure 1. Distribution of FRS benefits for workers terminating employment with ten years of service. Source: authors' compilations of FRS data (7/1997–6/1998).

term older workers. The same can happen in the FRS formula. Figure 1 uses FRS data from the 1998 actuarial valuation to highlight the bias present for workers with ten years of service. Retirement benefits are computed for workers entering covered employment at different ages with equivalent salaries and ten years of service, relative to the benefits of a ten-year service, equal salaried worker terminating employment at the normal retirement age of age 62. The FRS's 6.25 percent salary growth assumption (which was lowered substantially from 7.25 percent in the prior year's valuation) is embedded for workers terminating employment prior to age 62.

The results show that a worker who terminates FRS employment at the age of 32, for example, receives only 16 percent of the pension benefits which an older worker receives, who terminates employment at 62, even though both workers had equivalent nominal salaries and years of service in the system. From another perspective, the pension costs to taxpayers for older workers are over six times that of younger workers hired (since all other variables other than age are identical, both workers are assumed to contribute equal amounts of public services). The age bias imbedded in the FRS penalizes younger mobile workers, while giving disproportional pension benefits to workers with equal years of service hired at older ages. Full-career employees fare relatively well in the current FRS, garnering benefits in excess of what a cost-equivalent DC plan would provide. It has been shown that the pension benefits of young, shorter service FRS workers are nearly 70 percent lower than what they would receive under a cost-equivalent DC plan (UAL Working Group 1999).[11]

Defined Contribution Pension Concerns

Although some groups of public sector employees are attracted by the self-determination and portability of DC plans, other DC plan characteristics are of concern to policymakers and some plan participants. These include the lack of preretirement death and disability insurance, the need to embrace investment risk to increase portability, the ease of preretirement lump-sum distributions and possible increases in labor turnover associated with DC plan portability.

As in most traditional DB plans, FRS benefits include preretirement death and disability insurance. Although these insurance benefits are not typically considered part of a DC pension plan, it is considered desirable to continue them, should optional DC pension plan legislation pass in Florida. The mechanics of assuring the continuation of these benefits are straightforward; the FRS could simply deduct the cost of the death and disability benefits (estimated to be from 50 to 100 basis points) from the DC plan's allocation.

Many workers are attracted to the portability and self-determination aspect of DC plans, but these plans also embody investment risks associated with investment decisions which will fail to appeal to all. DC plan benefits are not guaranteed, and the risk-averse would gravitate toward the guaranteed benefits of DB plans, given the choice. The concern is that public sector workers who take on investment risks in a DC plan might find their retirement security adversely affected given a bad turn in the financial markets near retirement age. Of course DC investment risk during the retirement period could be mitigated if retirees could buy deferred annuities (Bodie, Marcus, and Merton 1985; Turner 1993). On the other hand retirement income security might be less due to the expenses associated with private annuity markets.[12] This in turn implies that plan participants will require extensive, and potentially expensive, financial education which would help workers decide how to invest and how to structure pension payouts. We note that the pension reform bill passed by the Florida Senate during the 1999 legislative session contained an educational program component.

A third type of portability loss occurs when workers cash out their pension as a lump-sum distribution, on leaving covered employment and prior to normal retirement. (It would be more logical to roll over the assets over into a qualified account, from a tax perspective.) The resulting erosion of retirement savings is substantial and it affects younger and lower paid employees, as well as low-dollar accounts (Andrews 1985; Piacentini 1990; U.S. DoD ERISA Advisory Council 1998). We also note that some DB plans permit workers to cash out their accruals at termination; a study by Atkins (1986) found that 40 percent of DB plans permitted this. During the 1999 Florida legislative session, interest was expressed in allowing a transfer of the discounted value of FRS benefits for terminated vested FRS members as part of the pension reform package.

Permitting workers to cash out lump-sum distributions prior to retirement reflects a tradeoff between the dual objectives of self-determination and retirement benefit adequacy, that often imply the need for limitations on preretirement distributions. The ERISA Advisory Council (1998), for example, recommended that preretirement lump-sum distributions in excess of $2,000 be rolled over into a qualified retirement savings vehicle, while also allowing for hardship withdrawals. The President's Commission on Pension Policy (1981) recommended that any cashout of pension benefits over $500 (approximately $900 in 1998 dollars) be prohibited unless it was transferred to an IRA or another qualified plan.

An additional concern to policymakers is the possibility that the increased portability afforded workers in DC plans may increase labor turnover, raise labor costs, and lower productivity. Employers often incur substantial training costs when hiring new employees and the reduced portability provisions of DB plans could increase the likelihood of employers recouping these training costs by offering a financial barrier to terminating employment. While this may be true in some cases, evidence suggests only a modest turnover disincentive of backloaded DB pension plans for short-term, recently trained workers (Gustman and Steinmeier 1987, 1995).

Another side of the pension-portability relationship concerns older workers. DB plans often seek to induce retirement at the so-called "normal" retirement age, when pension accruals are typically maximized and productivity is expected to start declining (e.g., Bodie, Shoven, and Wise 1988; Dorsey, 1995). However, this view has gained little currency in Florida; indeed, the FRS has moved in the opposite direction by providing additional benefits to encourage workers to remain in the workforce beyond the normal retirement age.[13] These targeted benefits impact a small—but costly— segment of FRS members and increase both the transfer of benefits from shorter to longer service workers, and the age bias.

The economics literature offers several theories seeking to explain why employers might want to use DB plans to deter mobility.[14] But to date there is no conclusive evidence of a portability-productivity link that would be useful to Florida policymakers seeking to assess the cost implications of pension reform (e.g., Dorsey 1987; Gustman and Mitchell 1992; Dorsey, Cornwell, and Macpherson 1998).

Goals of Public Pension Reform in Florida

Florida's UAL Working Group recommended that any pension benefit reform changes the Legislature enacted should be paid for (funded) on an actuarially sound basis. It was further recommended that in the course of its pension benefit reform deliberations, the Legislature should thoroughly evaluate the costs and benefits of each alternative and determine the most appropriate goal of pension benefit reform. To this end, a number of pension reform goals were identified in testimony to the Florida Working Group, including bolstering Florida's labor market competitiveness and increasing the fairness in benefits between various groups of employees (UAL Working Group 1999: 2).

A useful perspective for analyzing benefit fairness and portability is to summarize DB and DC benefit accrual patterns graphically by years of service. This approach collapses many variables into a two-dimensional plane, necessitating the selection of a specific worker profile for illustrative purposes. We show benefit accrual patterns for FRS regular service employees who start their careers at age 32 with an entry salary of $32,000. The measure of salary replacement used is the percent of average final compensation, which the FRS defines as the average of a worker's top five years of salary (typically salary at the end of a worker's career). Due to the backloading of FRS benefits and the presence of inflation, salary growth is assumed to grow from termination through age 62 at the current FRS actuarial valuation's 6.25 percent salary growth assumption for vested workers leaving covered

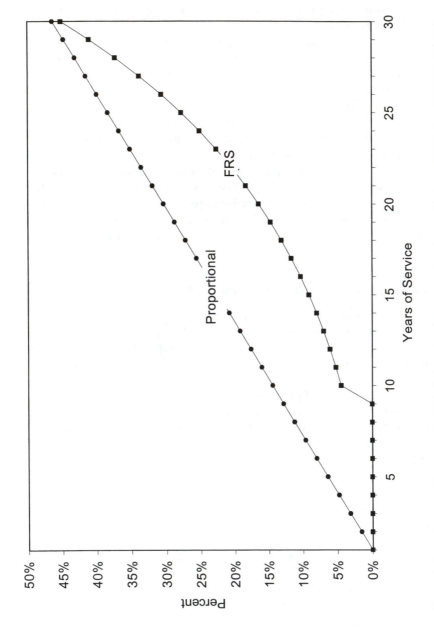

Figure 2. Benefit accrual by years of additional service. Source: authors' compilations of FRS data (7/1997–6/1998).

employment prior to the normal retirement age. For these workers, the vertical axis represents average future compensation.

In Figure 2, the 45-degree (proportional) line depicts the benefit accrual line of a pension plan with full portability, where equal benefit treatment is granted to workers entering and leaving the covered workforce with varying years of service. In this case, a given percentage change in years of service results in an equal percent change in average final (or future) compensation; career interruptions would have no bearing on benefit proportionality. Due to the backloading of benefits, the FRS's current DB benefit accrual line deviates substantially from proportionality. FRS workers accumulate no benefits up to their first ten years of covered employment, after which the benefit accrual line becomes concave from above (over half of the total benefits paid to a career FRS employee are accumulated in the last ten years of service).

When considering moving to a DC plan, it is essential to investigate the employer's position with respect to portability losses. That is, there is no inherent reason for an employer to have different portability provisions between DB and DC plans: rather, portability losses are determined by a plan's accrual pattern (Bodie, Marcus, and Merton 1988). In practice, portability losses can be eliminated or substantially reduced through two DB pension reforms: accelerating the vesting requirements, or indexing the benefits of workers who terminate employment before the normal retirement age of 62. And since high portability and age equivalence can hold in both DB and DC plans, it is reasonable to compare DB and DC plans that are equivalent along these dimensions, when assessing how an optional DC plan might affect funding levels and the contribution rate structure.

DC plans typically have accelerated vesting and do not have backloaded benefits. Providing faster vesting and higher benefits to shorter service employees through an optional DC plan are new benefits relative to the current FRS structure and will add cost unless benefits are reduced for other workers, or workers make the wrong decision in their pension plan election. (Reducing FRS retirement benefits was never a point of discussion in Florida.) Thus a reasonable benchmark for discussing pension reform options is to consider providing those same types of new benefits through reform of the FRS DB system. The two DB reforms suggested above will be sequentially added to the DC/DB accrual analysis.

Simulations were run for a number of vesting schedules. A graded two- to six-year vesting schedule (defined as 20 percent vesting after two years of service, increasing in 20 percent increments per year through the sixth year) was adopted in the Senate pension reform bill. The DC and DB pension plans contained identical vesting provisions (graded two- to six-year) to avoid a two-tiered benefit structure so that FRS members would not be forced into having to embrace a higher degree of investment risk in order to achieve increased pension benefit portability. In addition, a graded two-to six-year vesting schedule permits some skew in the distribution of benefits away from short service workers to career workers, which is considered a desirable goal to many employers and policymakers as long as the transfer enhances productivity. Other attributes of a two- to six-year graded vesting schedule include employers recouping some of the training costs, increased portability when compared to the existing FRS's ten-year cliff vesting requirement and lower relative costs (over immediate vesting).

Determining the optional DC plan's contribution rate, which is a major determinant of the DB/DC election (and drives the ultimate cost of pension reform), is a final methodological issue that needs to be addressed prior to presenting the DC benefit accruals. One avenue is to peg the DC gross contribution rate to the FRS's DB normal cost in order to avoid the perception of a two-tier benefit structure (especially for new FRS members who are expected to gravitate to the DC option). This has a precedent in Florida—the contribution rates of the small optional DC plans for limited classes of FRS employees have historically been set equal to the FRS's normal cost for over a decade.

A number of ancillary issues impact the DC plan's contribution rate. As noted above, the UAL Working Group pointed out the value of having all public workers be covered by preretirement death and disability insurance. Cost estimates ranged from 50 to 100 basis points—and if the upper bound was deducted from the FRS's normal cost for the current fiscal year—the DC contribution rate would have been 8.21 percent for regular class members. Although one of the goals of Florida's UAL Working Group was to stabilize normal costs, year-to-year variability is the norm, and if DC contribution rates were not permanently pegged to the initial DB normal costs, future DB normal costs changes would, of course, change future DC contribution rates. An alternative method of establishing the DC contribution rate would be to establish a target income replacement level for participants.

A final point impacting the DC contribution rate is the treatment of the two offsets, which accompany the election (forfeitures and surplus gain). Forfeitures arise from workers terminating employment prior to vesting. Although the graded two- to six-year vesting schedule increases portability appreciably when compared to the existing FRS vesting schedule, some short-term FRS members will still walk away with either no, or partial, pension benefits. Regular class forfeitures associated with a perfect choice modeling perspective (the modeling assumptions are discussed in the following section) were estimated to be fifty-five basis points as a share of salary, while those associated with the imperfect choice model were estimated to be thirty-three basis points (Table 2). A surplus gain (the difference in the actuarial liability and the accumulated benefit obligation) arises when vested DB members elect the DC option. The DC offsets were not assumed to in-

TABLE 2. Florida Public Pension Reform Option Cost Estimates: Regular Class Members as a Percent of Total Payroll

	Cost Change (%)		Cumulative	Cost Change (%)
	1st year	Long-term*	1st year	Long-term*
Perfect choice model				
Optional DC Plan	0.38	1.55	0.38	1.55
Add two-to-six year graded DB vesting	0.44	0.06	0.82	1.61
Add 3% terminated vested indexation	0.67	0.08	1.49	1.69
Total Option Costs less surplus gain amortized over 30 years (0.23 percent)			1.26	1.46
Imperfect choice model				
Optional DC Plan	−0.76	0.43	−0.76	0.43
Add two-to-six year graded DB vesting	−0.23	0.64	−0.21	0.64
Add 3% terminated vested indexation	1.07	0.57	0.84	1.21
Total Option Costs less surplus gain amortized over 30 years (1.40 percent)			−0.56	−0.19

Source: Authors' compilation of unpublished data for 1997–98 provided by Milliman and Robertson, Inc. and Ennis, Knupp & Associates.
*Long-term is defined in the simulations as over a 30-year period.

crease the DC contribution rate but were used to lower total pension costs. This analysis assumes that a desirable goal of pension reform is cost management and that FRS members and beneficiaries will be held harmless. Given these constraints, the goal of increasing the portability of pension benefits will add to pension costs, and the DC offset was used to help push FRS pension reform toward cost neutrality. Issues surrounding the determination of the DC contribution rate will likely be revisited prior to the next legislative session.

Figure 3 summarizes DC and DB pension accruals under a dual choice structure for Florida plans having the same graded two- to six-year vesting schedules. The DC benefit accruals assume an annuity payout with a 3 percent annual cost-of-living increase to facilitate comparison to the FRS benefit structure and is one of a number of ways to present DB and DC benefit accrual comparisons. The reformed DB pension accruals become more proportional for shorter service workers than under the current FRS's ten-year cliff vesting requirement because the accelerated vesting schedule elimi-

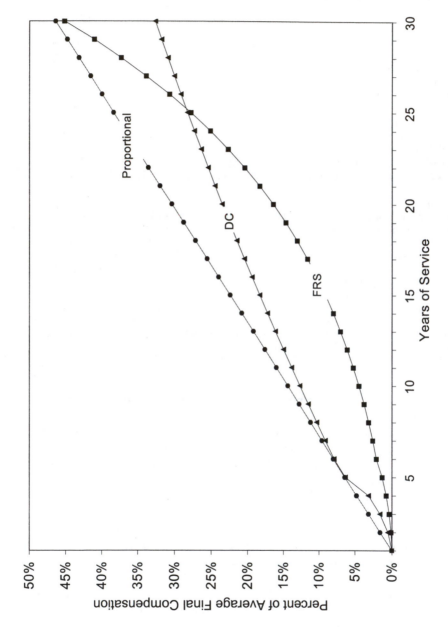

Figure 3. Benefit accrual patterns for FRS and DC plans with graded 2–6-year vesting. Source: authors' compilations of FRS data (7/1997–6/1998).

nates a portion of the forfeiture portability losses. But, as expected, career workers are still better off under a DB plan while the benefit accruals for shorter to intermediate-term workers remain higher under a DC option.

Protecting the purchasing power of FRS retirement benefits of vested workers who left covered employment prior to the normal retirement age of 62 is the last pension reform to be analyzed. DC plans, whose benefits are based on lifetime earnings, are by design fully portable as long as investment returns outpace expected salary growth, but vested FRS workers who terminate employment prior to age 62 suffer substantial portability losses. The portability losses associated with the backloading of DB benefits can be eliminated if the benefits of workers leaving FRS employment prior to the normal retirement age are indexed to the plan's assumed salary increases from the date of termination through age 62.[15] While the Senate bill's 3 percent index provision did not totally eliminate the backloaded portability losses, it took a major step in addressing the needs of the more mobile segment of the FRS workforce. Cost and administrative ease were the primary reasons for settling on a 3 percent benefit index. Secondly, an index below the assumed rate of salary increase permits some transfer of benefits from shorter service to career workers (as did the two-to-six year vesting schedule). Finally, a 3 percent index is considered by some to be equitable (or at least easily understandable) because it is the same annual cost-of-living adjustment FRS beneficiaries receive.

Figure 4 depicts the benefit accrual patterns for an optional FRS DC plan and a reformed DB plan with two- to six-year vesting and a 3 percent index of terminated vested benefits (the same provisions contained in the Senate bill). When compared to a DB plan with no indexation (Figure 3), the benefit accrual line shifts upward toward proportionality. The basic pattern of the DC and DB benefit accruals do not change—longer service workers are better served by a DB plan while shorter service workers receive higher benefit accruals under a DC plan. The crossover point (the years of service where a FRS member is indifferent between selecting the DB plan or DC option) falls by approximately four years of service—from twenty-five to twenty-one years.

Charting the benefits accrual line in this fashion (Figures 2 to 4) offers a useful tool for analyzing pension reform issues, but it is only one of many different perspectives. Focusing on years of service and accounting for entry and termination ages permits us to focus on a measure of portability losses. But by doing so, we are collapsing two key variables into the aggregate analysis: mortality risk, and income (and its associated tax rate). Abstracting from mortality risk misrepresents the benefit accruals by race and gender for individuals. The DB benefit accruals of white females, for example, are expected to greatly exceed those of black males for workers with equivalent average final compensation and equal years of service. Finally, due to the progres-

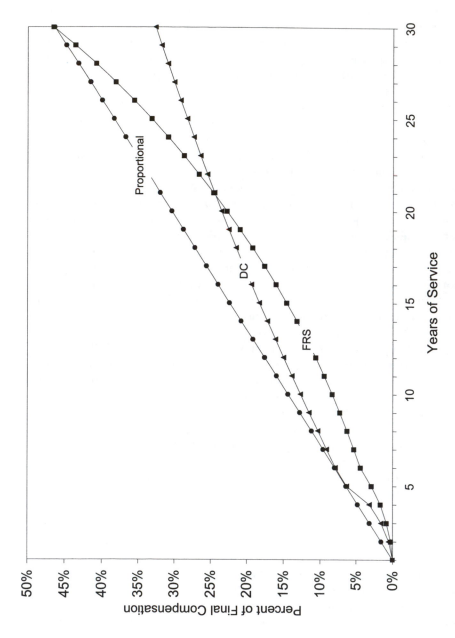

Figure 4. Benefit accrual patterns for FRS and DC plans assuming graded 2–6-year vesting and 3 percent indexation of terminated vested benefits. Source: author's compilations of FRS data (7/1997–6/1998).

sive federal tax structure (and progressive nature of social security benefits), the specific income level needs to be brought into any disposable income analysis of the adequacy of an individual's retirement benefits.

The analysis presented here includes the aggregate effects of mortality risk and income on benefit accruals, but these fields were not available at the individual record level. Although the omission of these two fields does not present much of a barrier to systemwide pension reform analysis, they are key factors influencing individuals' DB/DC election and their retirement decisions. Understanding the effects of these variables can be easily included in the educational material provided workers, including that proposed in Florida.

Option-Cost Estimates of Public Pension Reform in Florida

Since Florida's pension reform plan will permit a voluntary election between two alternative benefit structures, members who elect the DC option will change the resulting demographic profile and long-term cost structure (normal cost) of the DB plan. Logically, employees will select the option that they believe will maximize the future value of their pension benefits. To the extent that employees succeed in making benefit-maximizing choices, the total value provided to all FRS employees will be greater than in the two alternative plans on a stand-alone basis; in general, more benefits translate into higher costs. From the employer's perspective, this additional cost is often referred to as adverse selection (or the option cost) for a dual choice structure.

Currently the FRS relies on cross subsidies to control funding costs, like most traditional DB plans. Nonvested workers and vested workers who leave FRS employment prior to the normal retirement age of 62 subsidize career workers, enabling those long-career workers to receive higher benefits without increasing total plan costs. Under a choice-optional DC structure, younger members who opt out of the DB into the more portable DC plan will drive up the overall FRS retirement system costs. However, attempting to predict how many people would elect which option is a difficult task. Uncertainties surrounding workers' estimates of what their FRS working tenure and wage paths will be at the time of the plan election provides the greatest obstacle to estimating options costs. Other factors that increase the difficulty of costing the option include not knowing individual risk preferences, investment return expectations, what value is placed on self-determination, how much non-FRS savings people have, and mortality risk. Costs can be controlled somewhat by, for instance, equalizing the DB and DC vesting schedules, and offering a one-time, ninety-day irrevocable opt-out election.

But economic fluctuations due to the business cycle provide a dynamic environment in which plans will be selected and costs will be determined.

To make progress on modeling the reform options we differentiate between two modeling perspectives, we seek to quantify recurring costs, which can be objectively measured by assuming persons act in their own economic self-interest and choose to elect the pension option that gives them the greatest expected benefits at retirement. One approach assumes that FRS members have perfect knowledge regarding how many years of FRS service they will eventually attain and behave as income maximizers. This approach, which we dub the "perfect choice" costing model relies on a detailed database of FRS plan members maintained by the state's actuarial consultant, Milliman and Robertson, Inc. Under this scenario FRS members are assumed to choose the pension option that affords them the greatest benefit accruals. This model can also be used to relax certain assumptions, so as to explore the evolution of option costs over time from alternative perspectives.[16]

It is also useful to examine possible costs using an "imperfect choice" approach, which assumes that employee choice across plans will neither be perfect nor random. Specifically, half of the FRS members are assumed to make the wrong choice when they elect a pension option, and this half is assumed to be the 50 percent that will lose the *least* in absolute dollars. Two wrong choices are available: people could elect to remain in the DB plan though they would have been better off electing the DC plan, and vice versa. Assuming that half the members make a wrong election, and that this half has the lowest accumulation of pension assets to lose, provides a conservative pension reform scoring perspective.

Unfortunately there is a dearth of data relating to the election rates associated with dual choice structures, especially for DB and DC plans offering equivalent portability provisions. A few cases suggest that opt-out rates by DB-covered employees prove to be substantially below the DC election rate for new employees. Only 10 percent of the existing FRS DB employees at Daytona Beach Community College (Florida) facing a DC/DB election selected an optional TIAA-CREF DC plan, while approximately 80 percent of new employees elected the DC option (Shunk 1999). The same pattern for new employees was observed at North Carolina State University over a five-year period in the early 1990s when less than 20 percent of the new employees elected the state DB plan (Clark, Harper, and Pitts 1997). These data are not directly applicable to modeling the FRS regular service class election because the great majority of FRS workers do not face the uncertainties of a forced tenure decision. However, model runs using FRS data reveal the same election pattern—DC election rates were much lower for existing FRS members than for new employees. A long-term time horizon (thirty years for the present simulations) offers a more realistic picture of option costs to policymakers because most employees are treated as new, which reduces the possibility of unpleasant cost surprises arising from faulty DC election rate assumptions of existing members.

Table 2 summarizes the option cost estimates associated with the simulated Florida pension reform for regular class service members, which comprise approximately 90 percent of FRS payroll. The estimates include changes in FRS regular class normal costs (9.21 percent) and the cumulative change in costs for regular class FRS members. Estimates are provided for two time horizons: first-year option cost estimates (which are based on the current FRS population), and the long-term impacts.

The evidence indicates that estimated costs for this form of pension reform vary widely, with an upper bound of long-term costs of 146 basis points under a perfect knowledge assumption, to a lower bound of near cost neutrality if enough participants make a poor pension choice. No point estimate can be released with an acceptable degree of certainty, since nonconvexities may be present in the models, making multiple equilibrium points possible. All that can be inferred is that the option costs will likely fall within this range.[17] But it is possible to break out the long-term costs of pension reform. Under the perfect choice model, most of the new costs arise from the introduction of the optional DC plan. If the existing FRS DB plan were not reformed and workers had perfect knowledge, workers with up to twenty-five years of service (the approximate crossover age) would receive greater benefits under the DC plan due to its accelerated vesting and portability provisions; this would increase employer pension costs by 155 basis points. If DB pension reform is layered in by matching the DC plan's accelerated two- to six-year vesting schedule and adding a three percent indexation of the benefits of vested workers leaving covered employment prior to age 62, the DB benefit reform costs add but fourteen basis points. This is largely attributable to new costs associated with accelerated vesting and increased portability, also accounted for in the optional DC plan. If FRS members are modeled as making the wrong choices by not maximizing their pension accruals, the attribution analysis becomes more muddled and the total option costs of Florida pension reform approach cost neutrality.

Conclusions and Implications

The subject of public pension reform has been a lively one in the Florida legislature in recent years. The 1999 analysis of Florida's public pension plan suggested that a lack of portability and self-determination were undesirable for certain segments of the public workforce, mainly mobile workers, younger workers and higher income workers. But other public sector workers prefer to be insulated from most investment risks and do not seem to value employee participation in the FRS's investment decisions. Our examination of a possible reform of the FRS explored the cost implications of permitting employees to select between either a DB or a DC plan.

The specific plan examined would offer a DC option to all FRS regular service class members, pegging the gross DC contribution rate to the FRS's normal cost, and adopting a graded two- to six-year DC vesting schedule. The Senate bill increased the portability of DB benefits by offering the same accelerated vesting schedule, and by indexing the future pension benefits by 3 percent per year of vested FRS members who leave the covered workforce prior to age 62. The Senate's bill would have allowed all regular class members to select the plan that better matches their self-determination/investment risk/portability loss profile without an element of compromise.

Inevitably models of the cost impact of the proposed pension reform legislation produce results subject to wide error. Using a range of behavioral assumptions, offering this option was estimated to have costs ranging from neutral, if enough workers made incorrect pension elections, to 1.46 percent of regular class payroll, if all workers had perfect knowledge concerning their future career paths.

Future legislative sessions will certainly bring up public pension reform again. Several questions are salient:

1. What is the most appropriate DC contribution rate?
2. Should the DC election be open to all FRS workers or just the regular membership class?
3. Should limits be placed on lump-sum distributions?
4. What mechanism should be used for transfers of DB assets (if any) to the optional DC plan?
5. Should vested FRS members who left covered employment prior to the normal retirement age of 62 be included in the pension reforms, and if not, should they be allowed to transfer the discounted value of their FRS benefits into a qualified retirement savings vehicle?
6. Should the choice of moving from the FRS to the optional DC plan be a one-time, ninety-day irrevocable decision, or should there be an annual election window?[18]

The fact that the FRS pension system has eliminated its unfunded liability in recent years offers policymakers a unique opportunity to reform Florida's public pension program. Should optional DC pension legislation be passed that also brings about DB plan reform, it will afford all workers the opportunity to select the pension option best suited to their investment preferences and anticipated tenure. The retirement portion of the overall compensation package offered by FRS employers would then be highly competitive relative to that offered in the private sector.

This paper reflects solely the views of the authors, and it is not necessarily the official position of the Florida State Board of Administration.

Notes

1. The FRS is predominantly a defined benefit pension plan. Limited classes of FRS members (State University System, Community College, and state senior management personnel) are allowed a one-time election into an optional defined contribution retirement plan. The DB accrual rate for regular class service members (which comprises approximately 90 percent of payroll) is 1.6 percent per year (increasing after normal retirement age), and retirees receive an annual 3 percent cost-of-living adjustment. The total compensation package includes pre-retirement death and disability insurance and a retiree health insurance subsidy ($5 a month per year of vested service with a $150 per month cap), and an optional, 100 percent employee contribution, deferred compensation plan. Although the deferred compensation plan is a DC plan, it has the portability constraints associated with Section 457 plans. A deferred retirement option plan (DROP) was established July 1998. The health insurance subsidy is not actuarially funded, and the DROP program is not addressed in the current valuation.

2. The FRS's investment returns for state fiscal years 1995–96 through 1998–99 were 16.6 percent, 20.9 percent, 21.9 percent and 13.8 percent respectively, exceeding the annualized 8 percent investment return assumption over this period. Since 1985, the State Board of Administration outperformed 94 percent of its peers — defined as public plans having assets exceeding one billion dollars (Ennis, Knupp & Associates 1999).

3. The Working Group was comprised of legislators, legislative staff, representatives of FRS employers, staff of the Lieutenant governor and the Division of Retirement, and the executive director of the State Board of Administration.

4. The Working Group's economic recommendations included continuing the investment return/discount rate 8.0 percent assumption and reducing the total salary assumption to 6.25 percent (from 7.25 percent). The salary growth assumption includes a 3.5 percent inflation rate, a real wage (productivity) increase of 1.5 percent, and an age-graded merit scale. Actuarial recommendations included amortizing the impact of future plan benefit changes, assumption changes and funding method changes separately within thirty years; amortizing the impact of future actuarial gains and losses on a rolling 10 percent basis as a level dollar amount (except for gains reserved for contribution rate stabilization); performing an experience study every third year; and utilizing updated mortality tables. In addition, the group expressed clear support for the recognition of contribution rate stability as a public policy goal, and formalized the actuarial assumptions and methods process (UAL Working Group 1999).

5. During the 1998 legislative session, an optional DC retirement bill (HB4333) open to all membership classes of the FRS was passed unanimously by the House but died in the Senate. An optional DC retirement bill, a revision of HB4333 (the portable retirement option or PRO), open only to school board employees (whose payroll accounts for approximately 45 percent of the total FRS payroll), was circu-

lated just prior to the opening of the 1999 legislative session. The Senate enhanced
the bill substantially by broadening it to the entire regular membership and subsequently adopting two DB pension reform amendments: graduated two- to six-year
vesting, and the indexation of the benefits of terminated vested FRS members at a
3 percent rate (CS/CS/SB356). The bill passed unanimously in the Senate, but died
on the final day of the legislative session in the House. Legislation was included
in the bill that set the FRS's contribution rates for fiscal year 1999–2000 (HB1883)
that directs the Appropriation Committees to review the benefit structure of the
FRS prior to the start of next year's legislative session (due February 2000). Pension reform issues will likely reemerge in 2000; see the Florida Legislature's website
.

6. Financial markets had been experiencing atypically high market returns long
before the FRS's existence. Annualized backcasted FRS returns, which reflect what
the historical performance would have been given the FRS's current asset class
weighting, averaged 10.8 percent over the 1952 through 1998 period. A case can
be made to begin a historical analysis as far back as possible, but the 1952 starting
point for the backcast is chosen for policy reasons. Foremost is that even though the
Federal Reserve System was established in 1913, the role of the Federal Reserve was
not clarified until Congress passed the Employment Act of 1946, and the operating
procedures of the Federal Reserve were changed many times over the ensuing decades. Starting the historical analysis in 1946 would bias the fixed income returns,
however, because the Treasury and Federal Reserve artificially kept interest rates low
during World War II and its aftermath to aid in the financing of the war debt. The
independence of the Federal Reserve was not established until March 1951.

7. Last year's surplus also arose, in part, from the low inflationary backdrop which
held back actual salary increases to 4.9 percent, far below the last valuation's 7.25
percent assumed salary increase.

8. No portion of the excess returns (other than increasing the health insurance
subsidy and opening a deferred retirement option plan for a limited subset of the
FRS membership) has been used for benefit enhancements for broad classes of FRS
members. The accrual rate for regular class members remains at 1.6 percent per year
of service through 30 years and the FRS has not accelerated its 10-year vesting requirement, or enhanced benefit portability. The Florida legislature appears to have
operated under the notion as if employers (taxpayers) have the right to all surplus
assets because they bear all of the investment risk. Although this may be a common
stance in traditional DB plans, it is not a universal interpretation. Bulow and Scholes
(1981), for example, present a case for employees and stockholders to share in the
ownership of corporate pension assets. Empirical evidence (cited below) supports
the view that DB employees bear part of the investment risk and should, therefore,
have a claim to share the surplus assets. The FRS's treatment of the independence
of the pension claims from the value of the pension assets has probably prevented
FRS workers from fully benefiting from the atypically high financial market returns
that have accompanied the bulk of their working careers.

9. Studies of financial market returns extending prior to 1952 indicate that recent
experience has been atypical (Bernstein 1997; Bogle 1991; Seigel 1992). Moreover,
long-term analyses of financial markets that attempt to normalize equity market returns for cycles in valuations show that recent stellar performance has been driven by
investors' willingness to pay more for expected earnings. History indicates that this
cycle, too, will eventually ebb and act to depress intermediate-term equity market
returns. Finally, controlling for cycles in inflation over time (inflationary expectations have fallen dramatically since 1981) also leads one to conclude that expected

returns on the FRS portfolio are likely to be well below historical backcasted results. Normalizing equity returns for cyclical valuations is currently a mainstream financial methodology, but its premise rests on a crucial assumption—the independence of the total return residuals over the long-term analysis. Not only are a number of non-contiguous market indices used in this type of analysis, implicit in the independence assumption is that structural changes in the economy over the past two centuries, including the increasing effectiveness of monetary and fiscal policy, do not influence long-term financial market returns. Monetary policy has been refined substantially since the post-World War II era, and has proven to be an effective buffer against external shocks to the domestic economy.

10. The first of the Working Group's guiding principles for redesigning the retirement program structure was: "Do no harm, i.e., current beneficiaries and members cannot be penalized by any changes. Any voluntary election to change to a new plan prospectively must be accompanied by detailed individual statements showing the potential impact on both short-term and long-term benefits." (UAL Working Group 1999, p. 485).

11. Many have recognized these portability losses associated with backloaded DB pension formulas; at the federal government level, the Departments of Treasury, Labor, and the Congressional Budget Office have also examined equity issues associated with the favorable tax treatment afforded private sector DB pension plans (President's Committee on Private Pensions 1965; Subcommittee on Private Pension Plans, 1993; Congressional Budget Office 1987; Hay-Huggins 1988). Recommendations for reducing DB plan portability losses have included accelerating the maximum allowable vesting requirement (President's Committee on Corporate Pension Funds 1965) and setting up a national pension clearinghouse, as is done in a number of industrialized countries (Hay-Huggins 1990; Turner and Watanabe 1995). A national minimum DC pension to be paid entirely by employers, for all workers over twenty-five years old having at least one year of service was recommended by the President's Commission on Pension Policy (1981).

12. We note that investment risk may also influence wage growth and real benefit accruals in DB plans. That is, higher employer DB contribution rates resulting from poor investment returns have been found to negatively impact both wage and benefit increases and ad hoc inflation adjustments (Hyatt and Pesando 1996; Allen, Clark and McDermed 1992).

13. Older FRS members receive increased accruals for service beyond normal retirement age and can elect to participate in a deferred retirement option plan.

14. Implicit long-term wage contract theories point to increased productivity, due to the deferred compensation incentives associated with the backloading of DB benefits that reduce labor turnover, thereby enhancing productive job matches. Short-term auction market theories, however, view the labor market from a totally different perspective. Here, the lack of DB portability reduces productivity because labor market efficiency mandates minimizing the costs and barriers to job change (Ross 1958; Choate and Linger 1986; Allen, Clark, and McDermed, 1993). Many studies analyze the relationship between worker turnover and productivity; see Gustman and Mitchell (1992), Dorsey (1995), Gustman and Steinmeier (1995), and Dorsey, Cornwell, and Macpherson (1998).

15. A national DB pension clearinghouse, previously proposed by Congress and established in a number of industrialized countries, would also facilitate this goal.

16. A two-track approach to estimating reform costs was taken. The state's actuarial consultant prepared estimates with the full valuation system used for regular biennial valuations of the FRS. Estimates were based on considering the actual

and potential economic position of narrow classes of employees, defined by age and sex. A second consulting actuary (Ennis, Knupp & Associates) used an independent model and more aggregated Florida actuarial data to check the first estimates and methods. Finally, both consulting actuaries provided sensitivity analysis of their estimates under varying actuarial assumptions and combinations of potential reforms. This final step provided considerable insight into the impact of certain assumptions and helped to refine the methods for estimating cost impacts.

17. A wide range of option costs associated with Florida pension reform was also recognized by the state's actuary, Milliman and Robertson, Inc., in its November 1998 special study of alternative DC legislation (Milliman and Robertson 1998b) and subsequent analysis focusing more on the likelihood of adverse selection.

18. Due the backloading of DB benefits, an election into a DC plan should be considered irrevocable because of the substantial costs associated with reentering a DB plan late in one's working career.

References

Allen, Steven, Robert Clark, and Ann McDermed. 1988. "The Pension Cost of Changing Jobs." *Research on Aging* 10, 4: 459–71.

———. 1992. "Pensions and Firm Performance." In *Trends in Pensions*, ed. John A. Turner and Daniel J. Beller. Washington D.C: U.S. GPO.

———. 1993. "Pensions, Bonding, and Lifetime Jobs." *Journal of Human Resources* 28, 3: 463–81.

Andrews, Emily. 1985. *The Changing Profile of Pensions in America.* Washington, D.C.: Employee Benefit Research Council.

Atkins, Lawrence. 1986. *Spend It or Save It? Pension Lump-Sum Distributions and Tax Reform.* Washington, D.C.: Employee Benefit Research Institute.

Bernstein, Peter. 1997. "What Rate of Return Can You Reasonably Expect?" *Financial Analysts Journal* 53, 2: 20–28.

Bodie, Zvi, Alan Marcus, and Robert Merton. 1985. "Defined Venefit vs. Defined Contribution Pension Plans: What Are the Real Tradeoffs?" NBER Working Paper 1719, October.

Bodie, Zvi, John B. Shoven, and David Wise. 1988. "Defined Benefit Versus Defined Contribution Pension Plans: What Are the Real Tradeoffs?" In *Pensions in the U.S. Economy*, ed. Zvi Bodie, John B. Shoven, and David Wise. National Bureau of Economic Research, Chicago: University of Chicago Press.

Bogle, John. 1991. "Investing in the 1990s: "Remembrance of Things Past, and Things Yet to Come." *Journal of Portfolio Management* 17, 3: 5–14.

Bulow, Jeremy and Myron Scholes. 1981. "Who Owns the Assets in a Defined-Benefit Pension Plan?" In *Financial Aspects of the United States Pension System*, ed. Zvi Bodie and John B. Shoven. National Bureau of Economic Research. Chicago: University of Chicago Press. 139–60.

Bush, Jeb. 1999. *Fiscal Year 1999–2000 Executive Budget Recommendations.* Tallahassee, Fla.: Office of the Governor.

Chiles, Lawton. 1999. March 12, 1998 letter to the Florida State Board of Administration. In State Board of Administration 1999: 287–88.

Choate, Pat and J. K. Linger. 1986. *The High Flex Society.* New York: Knopf.

Clark, Robert L., Loretta Harper, and Melinda Pitts. 1997. "Faculty Pension Choices in a Public Institution: Defined Benefit and Defined Contribution Plans." *Research Dialogues* 50 (March).

Congressional Budget Office (Larry Ozanne and David Lindemen). 1987. "Tax Policy for Pensions and Other Retirement Savings." Washington, D.C.: U.S. GPO, April.

Dorsey, Stuart. 1987. "The Economic Function of Private Pensions, an Empirical Analysis," *Journal of Labor Economics* 5, 4 Part 2: S171-S189.

Dorsey, Stuart, Christopher Cornwall, and David Macpherson. 1998. *Pensions and Productivity.* Kalamazoo, Mich.: W.E. Upjohn Institute for Employment Research.

———. 1995. "Pension Portability and Labor Market Efficiency: A Survey of the Literature." *Industrial and Labor Relations Review* 48, 2: 276–92.

Ennis, Knupp & Associates. 1999. *Florida State Board of Administration Investment Review First Quarter 1999.* Chicago: Ennis, Knupp & Associates.

Gustman, Alan L. and Olivia S. Mitchell. 1992. "Pensions and Labor Market Activity: Behavior and Data Requirements." In *Pensions and the Economy: Sources, Uses, and Limitations of Data,* ed Zvi Bodie and Alicia H. Munnell. Pension Research Council. Philadelphia: University of Pennsylvania Press.

Gustman, Alan L. and Thomas Steinmeier. 1987. "Pensions, Efficiency, Wages, and Job Mobility." National Bureau of Economic Research Working Paper 2426.

———. 1995. *Pension Incentives and Job Mobility.* Kalamazoo, Mich.: W.E. Upjohn Institute for Employment Research.

Hay-Huggins Company and Mathematica Policy Research. 1988. "The Effect of Job Mobility on Pension Benefit." Report to the United States Department of Labor, July.

———. 1990. "The Transfer of Benefits and Assets in Portable Defined Benefit Plans." Produced for the U.S. Department of Labor, June.

Hyatt, Douglas and James Pesando. 1996. "The Distribution of Investment Risk in Defined Benefit Pension Plans." *Industrial Relations* 51, 1: 136–54.

Ibbotson and Associates. 1999. *1999 Stocks, Bonds, Bills, and Inflation 1998 Yearbook.* Chicago: Ibotson and Associates.

Jennings, Toni. 1999. Opening Address to the Florida Senate, March 2, 1999.

Milliman and Robertson. 1998a. *1998 Florida Retirement System Actuarial Valuation Report.* Washington D.C.: Milliman and Robertson.

——— 1998b. *Florida Retirement System Actuarial Special Study Report 98-1.* Washington D.C.: Milliman and Robertson.

Piacentini, Joseph. 1990. "An Analysis of Pension Participation at Current and Prior Jobs, Receipt and Use of Lump-Sum Distributions, and Tenure at Current Job." Prepared for the United States Department of Labor. Washington, D.C.: Pension and Welfare Benefits Administration.

President's Committee on Pensions. 1965. *Policy and Pensions.* Washington, D.C.: U.S. GPO.

President's Committee on Pension Policy. 1981. *Toward a National Retirement Income Policy.* Washington, D.C.: U.S. GPO/.

Ross, Arthur. 1958. "Do We Have a New Industrial Feudalism?" *American Economic Review* 48, 5: 903–19.

Samet, Michael, Timothy Peach, and Paul Zorn. 1996. *A Study of Public Employees Retirement Systems.* Schaumburg, Ill.: Society of Actuaries.

Shunk, David. 1999. TIAA-CREF presentation to the UAL Working Group, Tallahassee, Florida, January 8.

Siegel, Jeremy. 1992. "The Equity Premium: Stock and Bond Returns Since 1802." *Financial Analysts Journal* 48, 1: 28–38.

State of Florida, Division of Retirement. 1999. *Florida Retirement System July 1, 1997–June 30, 1998 Annual Report.*

Turner, John A. 1992. Comments by John A. Turner to Alan L. Gustman and Olivia S.

Mitchell. In *Pensions and the Economy: Sources, Uses, and Limitations of Data,* ed. Zvi Bodie and Alicia H. Munnell. Pension Research Council, Philadelphia: University of Pennsylvania Press. 109–13.

———. 1993. *Pension Policy for a Mobile Labor Force.* Kalamazoo, Mich.: W.E. Upjohn Institute for Employment Research.

Turner, John A. and Noriyasu Watanabe. 1995. *Private Pension Policies in Industrialized Countries.* Kalamazoo, Mich.: W.E. Upjohn Institute for Employment Research.

UAL Working Group. 1999. *Report of the Unfunded Actuarial Liability Working Group.* Tallahassee, Fla., March.

U.S. Department of Labor, ERISA Advisory Council. 1998. "Report of the Working Group on Retirement Plan Leakage: Are We Cashing Out Our Future?"

U.S. Senate, Subcommittee on Private Pension Plans of the Committee on Finance. 1993. *Private Pension Plan Reform.* 93rd Congress. Washington, D.C.: U.S. GPO.

Chapter 14
Pension Governance in the Pennsylvania State Employees' Retirement System

John Brosius

This chapter describes the governance model utilized by the Commonwealth of Pennsylvania State Employees' Retirement System (SERS). The term "governance model" refers to the way in which the public pension plan is managed and key decisions are made. We begin with an overview of the structure of SERS along with the diverse legal authorities that influence its operation; we then go on to show how both the State Employees' Retirement Board ("board") and SERS are governed.

Characteristics of SERS

The Pennsylvania State Employees' Retirement System was established in 1923 by the General Assembly of the Commonwealth of Pennsylvania; the legislation that created and primarily governed SERS was then recodified in 1959 and again in 1974. Today, SERS is charged with administering two retirement plans: (1) a cost-sharing multiple-employer defined benefit plan and (2) an Internal Revenue Code Section 457 deferred compensation plan, which is a defined contribution plan. These two plans serve the employees of the Commonwealth as well as those of certain independent agencies and educational institutions. The agency today employs approximately 190 people, with headquarters in Harrisburg, and it also has seven regional field offices throughout the Commonwealth of Pennsylvania.

The SERS defined benefit (DB) plan serves approximately 198,000 members and has assets in excess of $24 billion. It was recently ranked 39th in total asset size among all pension funds in the United States (*Pensions & Investments* 1999). Active SERS members (meaning those persons presently making contributions to SERS through their Commonwealth employment) may also elect to participate in the state's deferred compensation plan, a DC plan with around 38,000 participants and investments valued at approximately $725 million. A third-party administrator administers the DC plan under contract with the board, with oversight provided by the board and SERS staff.

SERS is subject to regulatory constraint from both the federal and state level.[1] On the federal level, SERS is subject to the U.S. Constitution and to many federal laws including the Internal Revenue Code of 1986, the Bankruptcy Code, the Americans with Disabilities Act of 1990, Title VII of the Civil Rights Act of 1964, and the Family and Medical Leave Act of 1993 (respectively 26 U.S.C. §1 et seq., 11 U.S.C. §101 et seq., 42 U.S.C. §12101 et seq., 42 U.S.C. §2000e et seq., and 29 U.S.C. §2601 et seq. and 5 U.S.C. §6381 et seq.). On the state level, SERS is subject to the Constitution of the Commonwealth of Pennsylvania and to many state laws. These include the Commonwealth Procurement Code, the Right to Know Law, the Sunshine Act, the Civil Service Act, the Human Relations Act, the Commonwealth Attorneys Act, the Administrative Agency Law, and the Administrative Code of 1929 (respectively 1998 Pa. Laws 57, 65 P.S. §66.1 et seq., 65 P.S. §271 et seq., 71 P.S. §741.1 et seq., 43 P.S. §951 et seq., 71 P.S. §732-101 et seq., 2 Pa.C.S. §501 et seq., and 71 P.S. §51 et seq.). The body of common law governing the public pension environment is also very important, and particularly significant are cases addressing the law of trusts and fiduciary responsibility. In addition, SERS is subject to various executive orders and management directives issued through the governor's office, which controls many administrative issues.

In particular, the most important source of governing authority with respect to the state's defined benefit plan is the State Employees' Retirement Code (the "Retirement Code"; see 71 Pa.C.S. §§5101–5956). The primary sources of authority governing the deferred compensation plan include Section 457 of the Internal Revenue Code of 1986; the state statutory provisions authorizing the establishment of the plan (cf. 72 P.S. §§4521, 4521.2, 4521.3); and the DC plan document, entitled "Deferred Compensation Plan for Officers and Employees of the Commonwealth of Pennsylvania" (originally adopted by the board effective as of January 1, 1989, and known as the "Plan Document"). These sources of authority describe the environment in which the defined benefit and defined contribution plans are managed and governed.

SERS Board Structure and Governance

The Retirement Code establishes the SERS board as an "independent administrative board" (cf. 71 Pa.C.S. §5901(a)). Due to this status, the board operates within the executive branch with a greater degree of independence than many other state agencies. The executive and the legislative branches can influence the actions of the board due to the board's composition, but the board has the authority to make all decisions with respect to the implementation of the Retirement Code and the management of the State Employees' Retirement Fund.

The board's composition is specified in the Retirement Code (71 Pa.C.S. §5901(a)), and must consist of 11 members: the state treasurer ex officio,[2] two state senators or former state senators, two members or former members of the state House of Representatives, and six members appointed by the governor, one of whom must be an annuitant of SERS, subject to confirmation by the state Senate. At least five board members must be active members of SERS, and at least two must have 10 or more years of State service. The Senate members are appointed by the President pro tempore of the Senate, and they must be a majority and minority member or former member. The two members from the House of Representatives are appointed by the speaker of the House of Representatives, and also must be a majority and minority member or former member. The Retirement Code provides that the governor shall appoint the board chairman from among the members of the board. At the present time, the SERS board includes three private citizens (two of whom were formerly members of the House or Senate), two senators, two members of the House of Representatives, the state treasurer, the secretary of the budget, the secretary of Administration, and the executive director of the American Federation of State, County, and Municipal Employees (AFSCME), Council 13. The board is chaired by a private citizen, formerly a member of the House of Representatives.

The board is required by the Retirement Code to meet at least six times a year; in practice, it actually meets eight times per year (71 Pa.C.S. §5902(d)). The board chairman runs the meetings. The board has not adopted written policies, such as bylaws, to govern its meetings.

Unlike some other retirement boards, the SERS board does not rely heavily on the use of committees. Currently, the SERS board has only three standing committees: a personnel committee, a deferred compensation committee, and a corporate governance committee. The personnel committee's primary function is to address the compensation of SERS's senior management and investment office staff. The deferred compensation committee recently reviewed proposals to administer the deferred compensation plan submitted by third-party administrators, and it will address other issues associated with the deferred compensation plan as directed by the board chairman. The corporate governance committee addresses the board's position with respect to shareholder class actions. Other *ad hoc* committees have been formed to review responses to requests for proposals for investment consultants. Generally speaking, however, the board prefers to work as a whole.

With respect to the actions of the board members, the Retirement Code provides that members of the SERS board stand in a fiduciary relationship to the members of SERS regarding the investments and disbursements of the monies of the Retirement Fund, and that they are not to profit either directly or indirectly with respect thereto (71 Pa.C.S. §5931(e)). The Retirement Code also requires that new board members take an oath in which they agree to diligently and honestly administer the affairs of the board, and to not knowingly or willingly permit any applicable provisions of law to be violated (71 Pa.C.S. §5901(c)). In addition to these requirements, board members are also subject to the Public Official and Employee Ethics Act (the "Ethics Act"), which addresses conflicts of interest in Commonwealth employment (65 P.S. §§401–13). Pursuant to the Ethics Act, every year board members, like other public officers and employees, are required to file Statements of Financial Interest with the State Ethics Commission (65 P.S. §404). The form requires certain disclosures with respect to investments, business interests, creditors, sources of income, gifts, and expense reimbursements, as mandated by the Ethics Act (65 P.S. §405). Board members are also required to file a comparable disclosure form under the governor's Code of Conduct (Executive Order 1980-18). The State Adverse Interest Act similarly prohibits board members from having adverse interests in contracts entered into by the board (71 P.S. §776.1 et seq.). Finally, board members are subject to Commonwealth-wide policies regarding travel and expense reimbursement.

SERS Board Responsibilities and Agency Governance

The Retirement Code vests the board with responsibility for managing SERS. There are four areas of responsibility: (1) administration, (2) benefit determination, (3) funding, and (4) investment practices. After describing these, the internal controls in place within the agency to ensure compliance with agency policies and procedures are outlined.

Administration. One of the most important duties of the board with respect to the day-to-day administration of SERS is the appointment of the executive director, who is the chief administrative officer of SERS (71 Pa.C.S. §5902(a.1)). The Retirement Board delegates to the executive director responsibility for almost all administrative functions. The agency is organized into several bureaus and offices, as follows: the Bureau of Benefit Determination; the Bureau of Retirement Counseling; the Bureau of Administration; the Bureau of Management Information Systems; the Office of Financial Management; the Investment Office; the Office of Audit, Reporting, and Compliance; and the Legal Office. The head of each department or office, other than the Legal Office, reports to the executive director. The status of the Legal Office is unique in that SERS does not have the authority to hire its own in-house counsel. The agency's attorneys are instead hired by the governor's Office of General Counsel. Although the chief counsel works closely with the executive director and the board, the chief counsel reports to the General Counsel. The governing law with respect to this area of agency operations is the Commonwealth Attorneys Act (71 P.S. §§732-101–732-506).

Together, the heads of the Bureaus and Offices are referred to as the "executive staff." Each member of the executive staff submits a written report to the executive director on a monthly basis. In addition, meetings between the executive staff and the executive director occur every six weeks, although the executive director will call additional meetings if needed. The purpose of the meetings is to discuss high-level issues, such as the status of strategic planning initiatives, agency performance, and manager and consultant performance. Day-to-day operational issues are generally handled within each Bureau and Office; the executive director becomes involved in operational issues only in exceptional cases.

Many personnel issues, such as the procedures for hiring, promoting and disciplining most employees are governed by the Civil Service Act (71 P.S. §741.1 et seq.). There are employees who are exempted from coverage by the Civil Service Act, the primary examples being the Chief Investment Officer, the Investment Office Directors, and the attorneys in the Legal Office.

Many of the routine administrative issues common to most Commonwealth agencies are addressed through the governor's Directives Management System. The "Management Directives," issued through the governor's office, set forth policies binding on Commonwealth agencies under the governor's jurisdiction. Some of the many topics addressed this way include budget preparation, contract management, accounting processes, payroll, employee training, and supplies. SERS follows the policies established through this state system.

The administration of the deferred compensation plan requires a separate discussion in that, unlike the defined benefit plan, the day-to-day operation of the deferred compensation plan is handled through a third-party administrator under contract with the board (72 P.S. §4521.2(e)(1)). The third-party administrator is supervised by SERS staff within the Office of Financial Management. The head of the Office of Financial Management reports to the executive director regarding deferred compensation issues, with the executive director in turn reporting to the board.

Expenses associated with the administration of SERS are the focus of a yearly budget that is submitted to the General Assembly through the governor's Office, in accordance with the Retirement Code (71 Pa.C.S. §5902(c)). Expenses approved by the General Assembly in an appropriation bill are paid from the investment earnings of the Retirement Fund (71 Pa.C.S. §5902(c)). Expenses associated with both the defined benefit plan and the

deferred compensation plan appear in the same budget. Expenses associated with SERS administration of the deferred compensation plan are initially paid from the investment earnings of the Retirement Fund, and then
they are reimbursed to the Retirement Fund from the accounts of the members participating in the deferred compensation plan (72 P.S. §4521.2(g)).
The state treasurer acts as the custodian of the assets of both the defined
benefit plan and the deferred compensation plan (71 Pa.C.S. §5931(c); 72
P.S. §4521.2(h)).

Benefit determination. The benefit issues associated with the defined benefit plan and the deferred compensation program are very different, and will
therefore be addressed separately.

For the DB plan, the Retirement Code sets forth in great detail how the
benefit structure works (71 Pa.C.S. §§5701–10). There are five types of benefits available: a normal retirement benefit (called a "superannuation annuity"), an early retirement benefit (called a "withdrawal annuity"), a disability annuity, a death benefit, and a return of the member's contributions
and the interest earned thereon. Rather than fully describe all of the benefit
structure, it is useful to highlight key benefit features. For example, the normal retirement age for most members is age 60 or the age at which the member attains 35 years of credited service, whichever occurs first (71 Pa.C.S.
§5102; "superannuation age" defined). All members must have at least ten
years of credited service to qualify for an early retirement benefit, and most
members must have at least 5 years of credited service to qualify for a disability benefit (71 Pa.C.S. §5308). The early retirement benefit is calculated
in the same manner as a normal retirement benefit, but a reduction factor
is applied for the number of years the member is under normal retirement
age (71 Pa.C.S. §5702(a)(1)).

Like many defined benefit plans, the SERS benefit structure focuses on a
member's final average salary and years of credited service. The cornerstone
of SERS's benefit structure is the "standard single life annuity," which is an
annuity equal to 2 percent of the member's final average salary, multiplied
by the total number of years of credited service of the member (71 Pa.C.S.
§§5702(a), 5102; see "standard single life annuity" defined)). The term "final
average salary" is defined by the Retirement Code to mean the highest average compensation received by a member during any three nonoverlapping
periods of four consecutive calendar quarters during which the member was
a state employee (71 Pa.C.S. §5102; see "final average salary" defined).

The Retirement Code establishes five different payment options for members receiving superannuation annuities or withdrawal annuities (71 Pa.C.S.
§5705). Members who leave Commonwealth employment who either are
not eligible for any other benefit, or wish to decline the benefits to which
they are otherwise entitled, may elect to withdraw the contributions they
have made to the Retirement Fund, and the interest which has accrued

thereon, in lieu of any other benefit available under the Retirement Code (71 Pa.C.S. §5701).

Although the Retirement Code sets forth a very detailed benefit structure, some benefit questions require additional interpretation; to this end, the board issued regulations in 1974 that have not changed much over time (4 Pa.Code §§241.1–250.15). Nevertheless these are currently being reviewed, and they may be updated in the near future.

In addition to the Retirement Code and the regulations already described, two other sources of authority also enter into benefit determination decisions including (1) court and board decisions with respect to benefits issues and (2) SERS staff experience as expressed in SERS policy. For greater clarity, SERS recently compiled a manual that attempts to bring together all these sources of authority into a single text.

SERS occasionally is placed in an adversarial position vis-à-vis its members. For example, many different benefit decisions have to be made by SERS's staff prior to the time a benefit is calculated for any given member. These include decisions with respect to membership eligibility, the ability of members to purchase additional service credit, and whether members qualify for a disability benefit. In some cases, members or their families seek to change the benefit option selected by the member at retirement, a practice allowed by the Retirement Code only under very narrow circumstances. When SERS staff makes a benefit determination that is adverse to a member, the member has the right to appeal that determination. The appeal is first considered by the Appeals Committee, which consists of senior level staff not involved in the original staff determination. If the Appeals Committee determination is still adverse to the member, the member has right to request an administrative hearing before an independent hearing examiner. Upon hearing the case, the hearing examiner makes a recommendation to the board. The board will ultimately issue a decision in the case. If the board does not decide the case in the member's favor, the member may appeal first to the Commonwealth court, and then, if necessary, to the Pennsylvania Supreme Court. The source of authority for much of this procedure is the Administrative Agency Law (2 Pa.C.S. §§501–704). More detailed procedures governing the appeals process are found in the General Rules of Administrative Practice and Procedure (1 Pa.Code §31.1 et seq.), which were made applicable to board proceedings by board regulation (4 Pa.Code §250).

Actual benefit calculations rarely give rise to administrative appeals. The computational procedures used in calculating SERS benefit payments have been approved by the SERS actuary, as required by the Retirement Code (71 Pa.C.S. §5902(h)). To ensure the accuracy of benefit calculations, all calculations are done independently by two different employees. Further, a subsample of these calculations is audited by Treasury auditors employed by the state treasurer but housed at SERS. A subsample of benefit calculations is also audited by the board's independent accountants, in conjunction with the annual agency audit.

In the case of the DC plan, the benefit determination process is fundamentally different. Participants here may elect to defer some of their current compensation into the plan. The deferred funds are then invested at the direction of the participant; several investment vehicles are available under the plan. Amounts paid out from the plan to the participant or the participant's beneficiaries are a function of amounts contributed by the participant and investment income earned with respect to those contributions. The DC plan offers great flexibility in the timing and form of withdrawals as compared to the DB plan; the primary requirements are that DC distributions must comply with Sections 457 and 401 of the Internal Revenue Code of 1986.

The Plan Document gives the board, acting as plan "administrator," the authority to decide all matters under the plan, and it states that the board's determinations are final, binding, and conclusive on all interested persons for all purposes. The Plan Document further provides that any determination shall be uniformly and consistently made according to reasonable procedures established by the Administrator. As of this writing, there have been no challenges by plan participants to determinations made under the plan.

Funding. The SERS deferred compensation plan is financed solely through employee contributions, at levels selected by the employees, and investment earnings on those contributions. As with other DC plans, assets are equal to liabilities at all times so by definition, the DC plan is fully funded.

The SERS DB plan is financed through three sources: (1) employee contributions, (2) employer contributions, and (3) investment earnings. Pursuant to the Retirement Code, most Commonwealth employees contribute to the Retirement Fund at the rate of 5 percent of their gross compensation (71 Pa.C.S. §§5501, 5102; see "regular member contributions" and "basic contribution rate" definitions). These contributions are deducted from each employee's biweekly paycheck. The amounts paid annually to the Retirement Fund as employer contributions are determined each year by the board with the assistance of the SERS actuary, pursuant to the requirements of the Retirement Code (71 Pa.C.S. §5902(k)). The amount of employer contributions is expressed as a percentage of payroll (71 Pa.C.S. §5902(k)). For reasons set forth in the Retirement Code, not all employers contribute to the Retirement Fund at the same rate. The average of all employer contribution rates will be referred to herein as the "composite employer contribution rate."

Every five years the board issues a request for proposals (RFP) for actuarial services. The selected actuary performs several services for the defined benefit plan during the contract period, including conducting an actuarial experience study once during the five year period; conducting annual actuarial valuations; recommending appropriate employer contribution rates to the board every year; and determining the funded status of the defined benefit plan every year. For the actuarial experience study, the actuary reviews SERS economic and demographic experience over the previous five-year period. That experience is used as a basis for forming actuarial assumptions, which are essentially highly educated predictions about what will occur in the future with respect to salary growth, investment returns, and other demographic factors. The last actuarial experience study covered the period of 1991 to 1995, and concluded that investment earnings could be projected at 8.5 percent per annum, average career salary growth would be 3.5 percent per year, and that salary schedules would rise by 3.3 percent per year. These assumptions were recommended to the board by the actuary and adopted by the board in accordance with the Retirement Code (71 Pa.C.S. §5902(j)).

Armed with these assumptions, the actuary conducts an actuarial valuation of the Retirement Fund each year, as required by the Retirement Code (71 Pa.C.S. §5902(j)), comparing the prior year's actual experience with the actuarial assumptions. Based on this valuation, the actuary develops recommended employer contribution rates, which are presented to the board. The Retirement Code vests the board with the authority to establish the employer contribution rates. The determination of the board is final, and not subject to modification by the Commonwealth's budget secretary (71 Pa.C.S. §5902(k)).

In recent years, required employer contribution rates have declined, mainly because the fund's investment earnings exceeded the actuarially assumed 8.5 percent return. For instance, the composite employer contribution rate for fiscal year 1998–1999 was 6.70 percent of payroll, whereas for fiscal year 1988–1989 it was 13.09 percent of payroll.

The SERS defined benefit plan is currently fully funded, by which we mean that the actuaries have determined that the Retirement Fund has sufficient assets to cover the fund's net liabilities for the accumulated benefits of all active and retired members. SERS first achieved this status in 1992.

Investment practices. The board's investment responsibilities differ for the DB and the DC plan. Turning first to the DB plan, the Retirement Code provides that the members of the board have exclusive control and management of the Retirement Fund, with full power to invest the same:

subject . . . to the exercise of that degree of judgment, skill and care under the circumstances then prevailing which persons of prudence, discretion, and intelligence, who are familiar with such matters, exercise in the management of their own affairs not in regard to speculation, but in regard to the permanent disposition of the funds, considering the probable income to be derived therefrom as well as the probable safety of their capital. (71 Pa.C.S. §5931(a))

This is commonly known as the "prudent person rule."

Other than the prudent person rule, the Retirement Code contains only a few specific principles with respect to the board's investment authority. First, the board may (when possible and consistent with its fiduciary duties, including the obligation to invest and manage the Retirement Fund for the exclusive benefit of the members of SERS) consider whether an investment promotes the general welfare of the Commonwealth and its citizens, including but not limited to investments that increase and enhance the employment of Commonwealth residents, encourage the construction of adequate housing, and stimulate further investment and economic activity in the Commonwealth (71 Pa.C.S. §5931(e)). The board reports annually to the General Assembly regarding investments made pursuant to this authority (71 Pa.C.S. §5931(e)).

Second, not more than 2 percent of the book value of the total assets of the Retirement Fund can be invested in venture capital investments (71 Pa.C.S. §5931(h)). The Retirement Code further provides that a venture capital investment may only be made if, in the judgment of the board, the investment is reasonably likely to enhance the general welfare of the Commonwealth and its citizens and the investment meets the prudent person standard set forth in the Retirement Code (71 Pa.C.S. §5931(h)). Third, the Retirement Code contains restrictions on investments in Northern Ireland. More particularly, the board is directed to invest the assets of the Retirement Fund in such a manner that the investments in institutions doing business in or with Northern Ireland reflect the advances made by such institutions in eliminating ethnic or religious discrimination (71 Pa.C.S. §5940).

As is apparent, the board's investment authority is quite broad. To help define the exercise of that authority, the board has adopted a Statement of Investment Policy and an Annual Five-Year Investment Plan. This was initially adopted in 1979 but was amended over time, mostly in response to legislative changes. The statement sets forth the board's investment objectives, policies and procedures; defines the duties and responsibilities of the various entities involved in the investment process; and establishes guidelines for the investment of the assets of the Retirement Fund in various investment vehicles. Each year the board also adopts a Five-Year Investment Plan. This plan establishes SERS's asset allocation, and sets specific goals for each asset class in which SERS is investing.

To implement the statement and its five-year investment plan, and to provide advice regarding future policies and plans, the board employs in-house investment professionals and outside consultants, pursuant to authority granted by the Retirement Code (71 Pa. C.S. §5902(b)). The in-house staff consists of a chief investment officer, a director of private equity, a director of real estate, a director of public markets, a director of equities, and a director of fixed income. The directors of private equity, real estate, and public markets report to the chief investment officer. The directors of private equity and fixed income report to the director of public markets. The chief investment officer reports to the executive director.

The board also employs three consultants: one, a general investment consultant, which provides advice regarding the total Retirement Fund portfolio; the second, a private equity consultant, which provides advice regarding the composition of the private equity portfolio and suitable private equity investments for the Retirement Fund; and the third, a real estate consultant, which provides advice regarding the composition of the real estate portfolio and suitable real estate advisors for the Retirement Fund. Working together, the consultants and in-house staff search for managers to fulfill the board's investment policies. Suitable candidates are then interviewed by the board. The board makes all decisions regarding the hiring and termination of managers and consultants.

The managers hired by the board invest the monies of the Retirement Fund. At year-end 1998, the board had 99 external investment managers. The staff and consultants keep the board informed of the performance of the managers through performance reviews. The board is provided with quarterly performance reports for the public market managers and semi-annual performance reports for the private equity and real estate managers. The board is also provided with an annual performance review of all managers upon the conclusion of each calendar year.

The goal of the investment program, of course, is to earn as high a rate of return on the Retirement Fund as possible, with appropriate levels of risk. Attainment of this goal helps to keep the employer contribution rate lower and helps to ease the burden on the Commonwealth's taxpayers. To ensure accountability for its performance, as required by the Retirement Code, each year the board produces a report describing the financial condition of the Retirement Fund during the previous year (71 Pa. C.S. §5902(m), (n)). The financial statements included in the report are audited by an independent accounting firm selected by the board (71 Pa. C.S. §5902(n)). The report is required by the Retirement Code to be submitted to the governor and the head of every department within the Commonwealth for the use of members of the system and the public (71 Pa. C.S. §5902(m)). In actual practice, the report is also forwarded to every member of the state House of Representatives and the state Senate, as well as certain other entities and people who have expressed an interest in receiving the report. The report generally is available to members of the public on request.

Turning next to the DC plan, the board is authorized by statute to contract with investment managers to invest the assets of the deferred compensation plan (72 P.S. §4521.2(e)(1)). In recent years the board has contracted with external managers to provide seven investment products for plan participants to choose from (1) an S&P 500 index fund, (2) an international index fund, (3) a tactical asset allocation fund, (4) an extended market fund, (5) an aggregate bond fund, (6) a stable value fund, and (7) a money market fund. Only the stable value and the money market funds are actively managed. These seven products were chosen by the board to offer the participants different levels of risk, as well as market diversification and low fees. If the board should seek to offer additional investment products to plan participants, the Office of Financial Management, the Investment Office, and the general investment consultant to the Retirement Fund will work together to find appropriate investment products and managers.

The Office of Financial Management reports the returns earned by each deferred compensation manager to the board every quarter. The financial statements of the deferred compensation plan are audited every year by the board's independent accountants at the same time the financial statements of the Retirement Fund are audited. The audited financial statements are provided to the board, and are generally available to the public upon request.

Internal Controls for SERS

The SERS governance model also includes a series of internal controls. This is because governance largely consists of making policy determinations, but any given policy determination is useful only if it is consistently applied by those responsible for implementing it. The goal of internal controls is therefore to ensure that consistent application.

Historically, SERS has taken a rather decentralized approach toward internal controls, and most believe it has worked well. The head of each bureau and office is responsible for seeing that the staff of that Bureau or Office complies with all agency policies and procedures. The SERS Office of Audit, Reporting and Control provides an oversight function through audits. That is, each year the internal auditors select a certain number of agency processes for audit. Those processes are then tested for accuracy, efficiency, and compliance with policies. The head of the Office of Audit, Reporting and Compliance reports to the executive director but direct access to the board is permitted if deemed necessary.

Recently, SERS has moved toward a more standardized approach toward internal controls through the adoption of an internal control methodology developed by the Committee of Sponsoring Organizations of the Treadway Commission (commonly referred to as COSO; Coopers and Lybrand 1992). This was not in response to any particular problems that had arisen within the agency, but instead was a reflection of SERS's commitment to proactively find ways to improve its operations. The COSO methodology provides a standard framework for evaluating internal controls over operations. The result is that while each bureau and office within the agency still has primary responsibility for implementing controls, with oversight provided by the Office of Audit, Reporting and Compliance, all the bureaus and offices are now using one methodology to evaluate the internal controls in place. To date, the Office of Audit, Reporting and Compliance has assisted the Office of Management Information Systems and the Investment Office in completing a COSO review of their internal controls. Soon each office and bureau within the agency will undertake similar reviews and this process is anticipated to improve operational efficiency as a result.

Conclusions

As described above, the governance model used by the Commonwealth of Pennsylvania's State Employees' Retirement board and the State Employees' Retirement System is complex. The model addresses responsibility over the four areas of agency operations: plan administration, benefit determination, funding, and investment practices. It also addresses the agency's internal control system. It must be emphasized, however, that what has been presented is but a snapshot of SERS's operations at a particular point in time. An important component of the corporate culture at SERS is openness to change. SERS constantly strives to find new and better ways to do things. As those ways are found, SERS will continue to evolve.

The author thanks the Honorable Nicholas J. Maiale, Chairman of the State Employees' Retirement board, for helpful comments, and he acknowledges the research assistance of Kathleen B. Bertolette. He also thanks Olivia Mitchell and Edwin Hustead for their guidance and support.

Notes

1. An overview of sources of authority governing public pension plans appears in Martin (1990).
2. The state treasurer is elected by the citizens of the Commonwealth.

References

Texts

Coopers and Lybrand. 1992. *Internal Control-Integrated Framework*. Committee of Sponsoring Organizations of the Treadway Commission.
Commonwealth of Pennsylvania State Employees' Retirement Board. 1989. "De-

ferred Compensation Plan for Officers and Employees of the Commonwealth of
Pennsylvania." Adopted effective January 1.

Martin, Lawrence A. 1990. "The Legal Obligations of Public Pension Plan Governing
Boards and Administrators." In *Public Employee Retirement Systems; Guides for Trustees
and Administrators*, ed. Gary W. Findlay. Chicago: Government Finance Officers
Association of the United States and Canada.

———. 1999. "Top 200 Pension Funds/Sponsors." *Pensions and Investments* (January 25): 30.

Federal Statutes

Americans with Disabilities Act of 1990, 42 U.S.C. §12101 et seq.
Bankruptcy Code, 11 U.S.C. §101 et seq.
Civil Rights Act of 1964, Title VII, 42 U.S.C. §2000e et seq.
Executive Order 1980-18, issued May 16, 1984, revised September 28, 1987.
Family and Medical Leave Act of 1993, 29 U.S.C. §2601 et seq. and 5 U.S.C. §6381
et seq.
Internal Revenue Code of 1986, 26 U.S.C. §1 et seq.

State Statutes

Administrative Agency Law, 2 Pa.C.S. §501 et seq.
Administrative Code of 1929, 71 P.S. §51 et seq.
Civil Service Act, 71 P.S. §741.1 et seq.
Commonwealth Attorneys Act, 71 P.S. §732–101 et seq.
Commonwealth Procurement Code, 1998 Pa. Laws 57
Human Relations Act, 43 P.S. §951 et seq.
Public Official and Employee Ethics Act, 65 P.S. §401 et seq.
Right to Know Law, 65 P.S. §66.1 et seq.
State Adverse Interest Act, 71 P.S. §776.1 et seq.
State Employees' Retirement Code, 71 Pa.C.S. §5101 et seq.
Sunshine Act, 65 P.S. §271 et seq.

State Regulations

General Rules of Administrative Practice and Procedure, 1 Pa.Code §31.1 et seq.
Regulations of the Commonwealth of Pennsylvania State Employees' Retirement
Board, 4 Pa.Code §241.1 et seq.

Chapter 15
The New Jersey Pension System

Tom Bryan

Retirement benefits are big business in the public sector: the Public Pension Coordinating Council found that the number of active participants in the plans was over 11 million and employer contributions to the plans were $31.2 billion for the 261 large public plans responding to its 1996 survey (Zorn 1988). The New Jersey public employee pension system is one of the largest of these funds, ranking ninth among the top 1,000 pension funds in terms of assets (*Pensions and Investments* 1999). For the 1997 actuarial valuation period, the New Jersey retirement systems had valuation assets of $53 billion and an actuarial accrued liability of $52 billion. They paid out $2.9 billion in benefits, and held excess valuation assets of $1 billion with a combined funded ratio of 102 percent. As of 1998, the combined New Jersey retirement systems had over 418,000 active members and 166,000 retirees and beneficiaries. Indeed, one out of every 14 residents of the state participates in a public pension system.

The current healthy state of the New Jersey retirement systems is the result of the state's long history of public retirement systems and also two public policies, which shaped that history. The first was an early recognition of the need to establish public retirement systems on a "scientific" (i.e., actuarial) basis. The second policy was consolidation of retirement benefits for public employees in state-administered retirement systems, an early development and one extended to centralized asset investment and administration of the systems during the 1950s. Because of national and state economic cycles, a dramatic increase in public employment in the 1970s and 1980s, and benefit enhancements provided in recent decades, funding of retirement benefits in New Jersey has presented frequent budgetary challenges as well as opportunities for creative funding of public employee retirement benefits.

Historical Developments in the New Jersey State Retirement Systems

New Jersey has been in the retirement benefits business for a long time. Pensions for various categories of police and fire personnel were authorized under state law beginning in the 1880s (New Jersey State Legislature 1976). A statewide contributory annuity plan for teachers financed by member contributions was established by the Teacher's Retirement Fund Law in 1896 (L. 1896, c. 32). In 1906, pensions payable from public funds were authorized for teachers with 40 years of service. But because no provision was made for funding the liability for these pensions, the Teachers' Retirement Fund experienced financial difficulties almost immediately and collapsed in 1919. In addition, there was a substantial unfunded liability relative to the teachers' service pension law by that time. To address both problems, the Teachers' Pension and Annuity Fund (TPAF) was established in 1919 and continues today as the statewide retirement system for teachers in New Jersey (L 1919, c. 80).

A significant aspect of the law which created TPAF was its recognition as public policies that public funds should be used to fund public employee pensions, and that public retirement systems should be "established on a scientific basis" (actuarial basis) to "protect the future well-being" of their members (L. 1919, c.80, Preamble, p. 157). These policies were also reflected in a 1921 law which established a system similar to TPAF for state employers, the State Employees' Retirement System (SERS). This system was made available to county and municipal employees at the option of local employers.

Uniform provisions for benefits and administration of police and fire pension funds of counties and municipalities were provided under state law in 1920 (L. 1920, c. 160). These provisions were intended to provide financially sound and efficiently administered pension plans for policemen and firemen, but the hope was not realized. In fact, in 1944, the local funds were closed to new members and new employees were required to enroll in a new state-administered plan, the Police and Firemen's Retirement System (PFRS; L. 1944, c. 255). In 1952, some two hundred closed local police and fire pension funds were consolidated into a state-administered fund, the Consolidated Police and Firemen's Pension Fund (CPFPF), to provide for centralized administration of the benefits and funding on an actuarial reserve basis. Provision was made for liquidation of the unfunded accrued liability of the local funds with a substantial State contribution to the liquidation (L. 1952, c. 266).

Investment of pension assets and administration of the retirement systems were initially the responsibility of the boards of trustees of the several state retirement systems. The investment and administration responsibilities were centralized in new state agencies, the Division of Investment and the

Division of Pensions, respectively, in the 1950s (1950, c. 270; L. 1955, c. 70). The two major state systems for public employees other than policemen and firemen, TPAF and SERS, were integrated with social security in 1955. SERS was terminated and the Public Employees' Retirement System (PERS) was established with essentially the same membership and benefits, but it was integrated with social security (L. 1954, c. 84). PERS is currently the retirement system for state employees and local government employees not eligible for other state or local retirement systems. TPAF was reorganized and integrated with Social Security (L. 1955, c. 70). Under the integration, pension benefits under the two systems were reduced by the initial amount of the social security benefits received by retirees.

In 1959, the Prison Officers Pension Fund, which was created in 1941 for officers at the state prisons, was effectively closed to new members. New employees were required to join PERS (L. 1959, c. 170). Prison officers were made eligible to participate in PFRS in 1973 (L. 1973, c. 156). In 1965, the State Police Retirement System (SPRS) was established as the successor of the State Police Retirement and Benevolent Fund, which was created in 1924. The purposes for the new system were to provide for actuarial reserve funding of the system and systematic amortization of its unfunded accrued liability (L. 1965, c. 89).

In 1969, an alternative retirement plan (to PERS and TPAF), the alternate benefit program (ABP), was provided for the faculty at the state colleges and universities and the county colleges (L. 1969, c. 242). It constituted a significant departure from the long-standing public policy for retirement benefits for public employees, that is, defined benefit retirement systems administered by the state, in that it was a defined contribution plan administered by a third party (initially the Teachers' Insurance and Annuity Association and the College Retirement Equity Fund, TIAA-CREF, but now includes six additional vendors). In 1973, the judicial retirement system (JRS) was established for justices and judges of the state and county courts. Numerous prior laws which provided for pension and survivorship benefits for judges were repealed (L. 1973, c. 140).

Today the process of consolidation of public retirement benefits in state retirement systems is virtually complete. Only one municipal system and a few special funds for lifeguards in a few beachfront cities are open to new members.

A Period of Enhancements

The integration of PERS and TPAF with social security was the beginning of a period of enhancement of retirement benefits for public employees that continued for the next three and a half decades. Some of the more significant enhancements are listed in Table 1.

TABLE 1. Retirement Benefit Enhancements in New Jersey's Public Pension
System, 1958–92

- 1958 all systems—Ad hoc percentage increases in retirement allowances provided for persons who retired from state-administered retirement systems through 1951 starting in 1959 (L. 1958, 143).
- 1965 CPFPF—Service retirement benefit formula changed from 1.67 percent of final average compensation for each year of service to 2 percent a year of service up to 25 years and 1 percent thereafter (L. 1964, c. 242).
- 1965 PFRS—Service retirement benefit formula changed from 1.67 percent of final average compensation for each year of service to 2 percent a year of service up to 25 years and 1 percent thereafter; ordinary disability pension (non-service connected) increased from 25 percent to 40 percent of final average compensation (L. 1964, c. 241).
- 1966 PERS—Relationship to social security changed from integration to co-ordination of benefits (offset of PERS retirement benefits for initial social security benefit eliminated, but employee contribution offset related to social security retained); minimum ordinary disability benefit increased to 40 percent from 28$\frac{1}{3}$ percent (L. 1966 c. 67); vesting period reduced from 20 to 15 years; participation in PERS made mandatory for all public employees not required to enroll in another contributory plan under state law (L. 1966, c. 217).
- 1966 TPAF—Relationship to social security changed from integration to co-ordination of benefits (offset of TPAF retirement benefits for initial social security benefit eliminated, but employee contribution offset related to social security retained); minimum ordinary disability benefit increased to 40 percent from 28$\frac{1}{3}$ percent; vesting period reduced from 20 to 15 years (L. 1966, c. 66 and c. 218).
- 1967 PFRS—Member contributions for group life insurance program eliminated and pensions provided for dependent widows/widowers and children (L. 1967, c. 250).
- 1969 all systems—Annual cost-of-living adjustments (COLA) provided for retirees from state-administered retirement systems effective January 1, 1970 (L. 1969, c. 169 and c. 230).
- 1969 PFRS—Special early retirement benefit provided, under which a member could retire at age 51 with 25 years of service on an unreduced benefit (L. 1969, c. 90).
- 1971 PERS, TPAF, PFRS, CPFPF, and POPF—Major benefit liberalizations provided which included the following: reduction in period for final average salary from five years to three years; change in the annual percentage reduction for early retirement with 25 years of service before age 60 from 6 percent to 3 percent; and, payment of noncontributory and contributory (if applicable) group life insurance benefit in addition to an annual pension in cases of accidental death (L. 1971, c. 121, c. 175, c. 179, c. 181 and c. 213).
- 1971 all systems—Annual cost-of-living adjustments extended to eligible survivors effective January 1, 1972 (L. 1971, c. 139).
- 1972 state employees—State payment for retiree health benefits coverage under the State Health Benefits Program for qualified retirees (25 years of service or disability retirement) and their eligible dependents, but not survivors, and reimbursement for Part B Medicare premiums (1972, c. 75).
- 1973 PERS and TPAF—Age for early retirement with unreduced benefit reduced from 60 to 55 (L. 1973, c. 129).

Table 1. Continued

- 1973 PFRS and CPFPF—"25 and out" benefit provided under which a member could retire on a benefit of 50 percent of average final compensation after 25 years of service regardless of age (L. 1973, c. 109 and c. 110).
- 1979 PFRS—Special retirement benefit increased from 50 percent to 60 percent of average final compensation with 25 years of service (L. 1979, c. 109).
- 1981 CPFPF—Special retirement benefit increased from 50 percent to 60 percent of average final compensation with 25 years of service (L. 1981, c. 241).
- 1982 PFRS—Basis for special retirement benefit changed from average final compensation (three years) to final compensation (final year) (L. 1982, c. 198).
- 1984 CPFPF—Basis for special retirement benefit changed from average final compensation (three years) to final compensation (final year) (L. 1984, c. 127).
- 1985 PFRS—Widow/widowers pension increased from 25 percent to 35 percent of average final compensation (L. 1985, c. 393.).
- 1987 TPAF—Postretirement medical benefits (PRM) for qualified retirees (25 years of service or disability retirement) paid by the retirement system; actuarial reserve funding on a phased-in basis provided for COLA and PRM benefits (L. 1987, c. 385).
- 1987 CPFPF—Surviving widow or dependent widowers pension changed to surviving spouse pension and percentage increased from 25 percent to 50 percent of member's final average salary (L. 1987, c. 128).
- 1989 PFRS—Special retirement benefit increased from 60 percent to 65 percent of average final compensation with 25 years of service; actuarial reserve funding for COLA benefits provided; State to pay annual contributions to the system in the amount of 1.8 percent of covered compensation to fund the increase in the special retirement benefit granted in 1979 (L. 1989, c. 204).
- 1990 PERS—Actuarial reserve funding provided for COLA benefits on a phased-in basis (L. 1990, c. 6.).
- 1991 PFRS—Widow/widowers pension increased from 35 percent to 50 percent of average final compensation with the state to pay increased costs to the retirement system for the benefit enhancement (L. 1991, c. 511).
- 1992 PERS and ABP—Payment by the State for PRM benefits provided for qualified retirees of school boards (school district support staff, e.g., secretaries, custodians, cafeteria workers) and county colleges who are not members of TPAF (L. 1992, c. 126).

Source: Author's compilations.

The rising tide of benefit enhancements did not go unnoticed. With the dramatic growth in the number of public employees from 1960 through the 1980s and the high inflation rates in the 1970s, the cost of public retirement benefits began to present significant challenges to state budgets beginning in the late 1970s. Only a few voices sounded the alarm in the wilderness of budgets and benefits.

Storm Warnings of Problems Ahead

The first significant call for attention to public employee pensions and their growth was a program analysis by a nonpartisan staff agency to the Legislature. As part of its responsibility to "ascertain compliance with legislative intent by the conduct of performance audits and efficiency studies," the Office of Fiscal Affairs of the New Jersey Legislature was authorized by its governing body, the Law Revision and Legislative Services Commission, to undertake a program analysis of the contributory public employee pension programs in the mid-1970s. The result was a comprehensive, three-volume report that included expert pension policy and actuarial analysis by pension and actuarial consultants. The second volume, entitled *Program Analysis of the Public Employees' Retirement System,* highlighted the need for the study as follows:

> In terms of growth in coverage and assets, and critical importance in providing for the economic independence of an ever larger proportion of our population, public employee pensions have achieved a role and significance unparalleled in years past. (New Jersey State Legislature 1976: 1)

It documented this statement by highlighting the fact that membership in the four active retirement systems grew by 134 percent from 1961 to 1973, and assets increased by 313 percent over the same time period. The primary purpose of the study was to provide the legislature with the data and analytic tools necessary to undertake policy development in the area of public pension and retirement policy. Legislative involvement in such policy development was necessary due to the "magnitude of the resources contributed by the State, county and local governments in New Jersey to these pension plans and the ever increasing burden of Social Security wage taxes" (New Jersey State Legislature 1976: 7).

The primary recommendations of the study related to the funding of the retirement systems and included the conclusion that the actuarial assumptions used to determine the liabilities and funding requirements for the retirement systems, especially the salary increase and interest assumptions, be closer to the actual experience of the systems to provide a more accurate measure of the liabilities and current funding requirements. In addition, the report examined the relationship of the two major systems, the Public Employees' Retirement System and the Teachers' Pension and Annuity Fund, to social security and recommended that the sizable and increasing state and other employer contributions to social security be considered as part of the overall costs of public employee retirement benefits. It argued that measures to control the overall costs be considered if the trend of increasing cost for social security continued. The report recommended that changing the actuarial funding method from a projected benefit to an accrued benefit method be considered to target the funding of the systems more closely to their ongoing liabilities and to potentially lower employer contributions. Finally, it argued that pension adjustment benefits (cost-of-living adjustments in pension benefits or COLA) be funded on an actuarial reserve basis unless the annual rate of increase in the cost-of-living, the growth in the number of covered employees, and the rate for the increase in the pension benefit (50 percent of the change in the consumer price index, CPI) remained at their current levels. The report may have been too scholarly and "objective" for the political environment to which it was addressed, and in any event it generated little or no action.

The next voice of concern, from State Treasurer Clifford A. Goldman, sounded a clarion call for immediate attention to the potential budgetary catastrophe from "explosive growth" in pension costs. In 1981 he posed the problem starkly:

The independent actuary for PERS and TPAF has just completed a study of the costs and benefit levels for the two major systems. The study confirms our fear that the explosive growth in pension costs will continue and present the next administration with some unavoidable questions about the future of our public retirement systems. I believe that the preservation of these systems is going to require some fundamental change in the benefit structures and that the earlier the need for change is recognized, the less severe it will have to be. (New Jersey State Pension Study Commission 1984a)

Treasurer Goldman identified the critical factors driving up the costs as the actuarial factors of life expectancy and salary levels, and the cost impact of double-digit inflation on COLAs. An aggravating factor was continued pay-as-you-go funding of the cost of living adjustment. Treasurer Goldman recommended that the plan fund cost-of-living adjustments on an actuarial reserve basis; establish a new noncontributory system for new employees with a retirement benefit at age 65 of 1 percent of final compensation per year of service; set a maximum percentage for the cost-of-living adjustment of 4 percent; and, permit current employees to transfer to the new system, trading in future larger benefits for a return of paid-in contributions and ending their contribution requirement. It was too late in the Byrne administration for any action on the recommendations, but they clearly came to the attention of the new administration of Governor Kean in 1982.

The increasing cost of public employee pensions and benefits was a major focus of the Kean administration. In 1982, Governor Kean issued Executive Order No. 7, creating an 11-member pension review commission consisting of: the state treasurer or his designee; a member of the State Investment Council, two elected member's of the boards of trustees of the state retirement systems, and three public members, all appointed by the governor; and, two members of the Senate and General Assembly appointed by the leaders of the respective houses on a bipartisan basis. The preamble clauses to the order described the need for the study as follows:

Whereas, Substantial portions of the annual budgets of the State and its political subdivisions consist of appropriations to fund various retirement systems established by law for the benefit of public employees and their beneficiaries; and Whereas, The State bears an especially large burden with respect to the funding of public employee pension liabilities, being responsible for employee pension contributions on behalf of approximately 87,000 State workers, 137,000 schoolteachers, 300 judges and many other active and retired public employees; and Whereas, The State Treasurer has estimated that for the fiscal year 1983 State contributions to the Teachers' Pension and Annuity Fund and the Public Employees' Retirement System alone, exclusive of payments to fund cost-of-living adjustments to retirees and beneficiaries under those retirement systems, will increase from fiscal year 1982 by approximately 21 percent, with combined cost of $294 million; and Whereas, Forecasts for expenditures suggest regular increases of the same magnitude; and Whereas, It is incumbent upon the State and local governments to maintain the integrity of their pension funds. (Kean 1982: Preamble)

The Pension Study Commission provided its own statement of the problem facing the State relative to retirement and health care costs for public employees:

The problem facing the State of New Jersey is that both retirement and health care costs have escalated over the past 10–15 years more rapidly than any other State expenditure. There are many reasons for this escalation, but if such trends continue, both the State and its local governments will find it difficult, if not impossible, to meet their employee benefit obligations without cutting other services. . . . the cost of mandated retirement and health benefits to State employees has increased from approximately 12.9 percent of the general fund in 1976 to 18.2 percent in 1983. (New Jersey State Pension Study Commission 1984b: 4)

The commission recommended several changes in the benefits under PERS and TPAF. These included an increase in the age for unreduced benefits for early retirement (with twenty-five years of service) from 55 to 60 or 62; an increase in the normal retirement age (regardless of service) from 60 to 65 or 62; a reduction in the retirement benefit formula from 1.67 percent of final average salary (three years) for each year of service to 0.75 percent of final average salary for each year of service; the elimination of employee contributions to the systems; a limit on the percentage of cost-of-living adjustments (60 percent of the CPI change) to 3 percent or 5 percent; the establishment of an incentive savings plan with employee contributions to a maximum of 10 percent of pay with matching employer contributions equal to 50 percent of employee contributions to a maximum of 1.5 percent of pay; the new plan would be mandatory for new employees and employees under 40 years of age with less than ten years of service; other employees would have the option to transfer to the new plan; and, cost-of-living adjustments would be funded on an actuarial reserve basis with the unfunded liability for prior service funded over a forty-year period by level percentage of payroll contributions. The Commission noted in its executive summary that its solutions were consistent with the recommendations of Treasurer Goldman to Governor Byrne (New Jersey State Pension Study Commission 1984c).

A minority report was filed by three members of the commission, a senator, and assemblyman, and a trustee of the Teachers' Pension and Annuity Fund, requesting that the governor not endorse the recommendations of the majority of the commission. The minority report criticized the lack of meetings of the whole commission and the fact that the work of the commission seemed to be conducted by the staff director and the consultants without much guidance, direction or input from the commission members. It stated that

> The impression of several commission members was that the commission was being used to ratify and legitimize a series of predetermined conclusions of the current administration regarding the need to save State monies at the expense of employee and health benefits. (New Jersey State Pension Study Commission 1984d: 3)

It also contained a point-by-point rebuttal of a number of the recommendation in the majority report. The minority members got their wish, as the majority report was quickly abandoned.

Despite the failure of the Pension Study Commission Report to generate any momentum for change relative to the state retirement systems, Governor Kean continued to highlight pension and benefits as mandated major growth areas in the budget, a practice that was begun under the Byrne administration. In his budget message for FY 1989, he addressed the problem of pension and health benefits increases:

> Still, I believe there are a number of areas where legally-required, formula driven state spending is growing at an unsupportable rate. Even in an overheated economy, some areas are growing much faster than revenues. . . . Spending on pensions and employee health care has increased by 140 percent, three times the rate of inflation, since I took office. (Kean 1989: 5A)

His budget message for FY 1990 (the last year of his administration) dramatized the problem with more colorful language:

> The problem is simple: we suffer from mandate-mania. Each year, legally mandated, formula-driven, spending increases at rates far in excess of the rate of inflation. The three problem areas are education funding, pension and employer-sponsored health care and Medicaid. Each year these legally required programs devour an increasingly large share of the budget. . . . State spending on pension and health benefits increased this year by more than $137 million and has grown by 183 percent since 1983. (Kean 1988: 23A)

The message also graphically illustrated the point over fiscal years 1984 through 1990. Other forces were at work that would bring the potential retirement benefit funding crisis to a head.

The Crisis Comes to a Head

The economic recession of the early 1990s precipitated severe budget crises in the new administration of Governor Florio. For fiscal year 1990 income and sales tax revenue increased by only 1.5 percent and 1.9 percent, respectively, and the corporation tax revenue declined by 11.1 percent. The Florio administration was faced with two major budget challenges in its first year in office. The General Fund was awash in red ink and a new court mandate requiring substantial additional state school aid was expected shortly. The budget deficit was estimated to be over a billion dollars. The state budget picture did not improve much in the second year of the Florio administration. Faced with a still bleak budget picture in 1992, Governor Florio proposed a major budget initiative relative to retirement benefit funding. The stated purpose for the initiative was to enable the State to provide more property tax relief. Governor Florio described the initiative in his budget message for fiscal year 1992–93:

I am proposing that we adopt a sound, conservative accounting practice, that will allow us to continue more property tax relief. In this budget, we are taking the prudent and long overdue step of revaluing State pensions by assessing them at market rather than book value. Making this accounting adjustment is required by law in the private sector. . . . For years, the best accounting and auditing firms, as well as the Kean administration and our Senate and Assembly leaders, have suggested that the State adopt this sensible practice. In making this move, New Jersey is joining the majority of other States, which use this more accurate and equitable system. The soundest accounting principles dictate we take this step. Let me say it in no uncertain terms: every penny that has been paid into our State pension system is secure and will remain that way. (Florio 1992: iii)

This budget initiative was commonly known as pension revaluation.

Pension Revaluation

As its name suggests, the primary innovation of pension revaluation was a change in the valuation method for pension assets. Until that time, public pension assets were valued at book value. During the 1980s, the Division of Investment increased the percentage of pension assets invested in equities, and by 1991, there was a $5 billion difference between the book value and market value of pension assets. Although the reasons for making the valuation change were obvious, adoption of the proposal was not straightforward. A struggle developed in the legislature over how the pension asset windfall would be used. The state teachers' association, NJEA, and the state employee unions wanted some of the money for improved funding for COLA and PRM benefits. There was also an effort to enhance the autonomy of the boards of trustees of the systems to give them greater control over the governance of the retirement systems. The two primary governance proposals were to give the boards of trustees the right to choose the actuaries and legal advisors to the retirement systems. The state treasurer had the authority to choose the actuary and the attorney general was the legal advisor to all the state retirement systems. This effort was spearheaded by the NJEA and elected member representatives on the TPAF Board of Trustees.

A compromise was reached over use of the additional assets, under which 60 percent would be used to reduce employer contributions and 40 percent would be used to improve funding for COLA and PRM benefits. The liability for these benefits had been added to TPAF and PERS only a short time previously (1987 for TPAF and 1988 for PERS). Annual COLA benefits had been provided to retirees and beneficiaries beginning in 1969 on a pay-as-you-go basis. The state had been paying the full cost of health benefits coverage and Part B Medicare premiums for its qualified retirees (twenty-five years of service or disability retirement) and their eligible dependents since 1972. The NJEA and other teacher representatives had succeeded in having legislation enacted in 1987 to provide for payment for health benefits coverage by TPAF for qualified retirees under the system. The qualification requirements were the same as for state employees. The rationale offered for providing the benefit to teachers was that they were "state employees" for retirement benefit purposes because the State paid the employer contributions for their pension benefits under TPAF. Because the past service liability and annual normal costs for these benefits would have caused extraordinary increases in employer contributions if they were funded in a more traditional way, recognition of the liability was being phased slowly—over thirty years for TPAF from 1987 and over twenty-five years for PERS from 1988. Both the normal contribution and the unfunded accrued liability contributions were being phased in at the phase-in rate for recognition of the liability. Once the liability was fully recognized, it would still take a substantial additional period of time before the unfunded accrued liability would be fully funded.

Under the compromise, 40 percent of the additional assets were used to accelerate the phase-in percentages for recognition of the liability for COLA and PRM. The additional assets fully funded the accrued liability for basic benefits and for COLA for retirees and thus eliminated the unfunded accrued liability for these items. This permitted acceleration of the phase-in percentages and higher contributions for COLA and PRM.

The legislation which enacted pension revaluation also did several other things (L. 1992, c. 41). It changed a number of actuarial assumptions under PERS and TPAF: increased regular interest (rate of return on investments) from 7 percent to 8.75 percent; increased the average salary increase assumption from 4.75 per cent and 5 percent to 6.25 percent; increased the COLA inflation assumption from 2.25 percent and 2.5 percent to 3 percent;

and, increased the medical inflation assumption (first ten years) from 10 percent to 12 percent. It reduced the percentage rate of total covered compensation for state contributions to PFRS from 1.8 percent to 1.4 percent. It required that local employer contributions for fiscal year 1992 be refunded to the state. This latter provision was in lieu of a reduction in state aid to municipalities which would have been required without the savings. It provided for actuarial reserve funding for COLA and PRM benefits under SPRS and JRS and for use of the additional assets from revaluation for the funding in those systems. The legislation also sought to allay fears of members of the retirement systems that the changes might somehow affect their retirement benefits by stating that "[n]o present or future retirees of the [listing of the affected retirement systems] shall receive any reduction in benefits or incur any additional costs" as a result of the revaluation provisions.

The governance effort led to the passage and presentation to the governor of two bills, one with all the funding changes and some governance changes, and the other with the same funding changes and additional governance enhancements for the boards of trustees. The governor conditionally vetoed the first bill whereupon it was quickly amended to incorporate the governor's recommendations and passed, and signed on the last day of fiscal 1992. The governance changes in this bill included the following:

- Gubernatorial appointments on the several pension boards were made subject to advice and consent of the Senate.
- Public pension boards were given the authority to select and employ legal counsel for any matter for which the attorney general determined that a conflict of interest would affect the ability of the attorney general to represent the board.
- An eleventh member was added to the State Investment Council who would be appointed by the governor from a list of three persons nominated jointly by the senate president and the speaker of the General Assembly.
- The terms of current gubernatorial appointees to the pension boards were terminated at the end of the sixth calendar month following the effective date of the act.

The governor also conditionally vetoed this second bill, but it was amended later in the year to incorporate the governor's recommendation and was enacted (1992, c. 125). The final version of the bill made three additional governance changes:

- It changed the authority to appoint pension actuaries from the state treasurer to a Retirement Systems Actuary Selection Committee consisting of four state officers, including the state treasurer, or their designees, and representatives of the three major pension boards, PERS, TPAF, and PERS.

- It preserved the authority to set the regular interest rate for the state treasurer, but restricted this assumed rate to no more than 3 percent higher than the average percentage of the salary increase assumption, and the pension boards were prohibited from setting the average percentage of the salary increase assumption below 6 percent.
- The Director of the Division of Pensions and Benefits was required to communicate annually to the pension boards the relevant factors used in calculating the state's contributions to the accrued liabilities of the retirement systems, and the pension boards were to have access to all the relevant actuarial information relating to any actuarial matter under consideration by the boards.

On the same day that this bill was signed, another bill, which provided for state payment for retiree health benefits coverage for qualified support staff of school districts and county college employees not in TPAF, was signed.

The budget impact of pension revaluation was immediate and dramatic. State contributions to the public retirement systems were reduced by $733 million in 1992 and $552 million for fiscal 1993; local employer contributions fell by $233 for fiscal year 1993. Table 2 provides a detailed list of the savings for the two fiscal years.

Despite the savings from pension revaluation and improving economic conditions, the state budget was again in trouble during Governor Florio's fourth year. Legislation was enacted to remove the sharp increases in the phase-in percentages for COLA and PRM benefits under TPAF and PERS (L. 1993, c. 6 and c. 182).

One of the first budget initiatives of Governor Whitman's administration involved a major pension funding revision, described in her first budget message:

We are changing the way we fund pensions and health benefits for retirees in a way that will save you more than $600 million this year and more than 3½ billion dollars over the next four years without affecting benefits for a single retiree. We are not taking a penny out of the pension system. We will continue to pay for health benefits on an annual basis. (Whitman 1994: iii)

This budget initiative was commonly known as the Pension Reform proposal.

Pension Reform

Six changes under pension reform were in the plan proposed initially by the governor:

TABLE 2. Effects of Pension Revaluation in New Jersey

	Contributions before reval.	Contributions after reval.	Difference	% change	Contribution rate before reval. (%)	Contribution rate after reval. (%)	Difference
1992 Employer contributions and rates							
PERS-state	$217,810,428	$105,450,960	($112,359,468)	(52)	10.1	4.9	(5.2)
PERS-local	$254,602,473	$66,069,547	($188,532,926)	(74)	7.6	2.0	(5.6)
TPAF	$619,156,837	$272,442,807	($346,714,030)	(56)	15.8	6.9	(8.9)
PFRS-state	$48,408,556	$21,814,788	($26,593,768)	(55)	32.5	41.5	9.0
PFRS-local	$187,604,239	$157,352,074	($30,252,165)	(16)	17.9	15.3	(2.6)
SPRS	$26,192,429	$0	($26,192,429)	(100)	25.9	0.0	(25.9)
JRS	$9,158,741	$7,191,769	($1,966,972)	(21)	29.4	23.5	(5.9)
CPFPF	$6,283,451	$5,461,992	($821,459)	(13)	N/A	N/A	N/A
Total	$1,369,217,154	$635,783,937	($733,433,217)	(54)			
1993 Employer contributions and rates							
PERS-state	$261,424,459	$136,225,509	($125,198,950)	(48)	11.5	5.9	(5.6)
PERS-local	$296,615,200	$101,866,244	($194,748,956)	(66)	8.2	2.8	(5.4)
TPAF	$726,271,036	$350,125,886	($376,145,150)	(52)	17.1	8.2	(8.9)
PFRS-state	$57,325,482	$26,559,078	($30,766,404)	(54)	32.9	15.8	(17.1)
PFRS-local	$217,630,772	$178,898,681	($38,732,091)	(18)	18.9	15.7	(3.2)
SPRS	$18,034,210	$0	($18,034,210)	(100)	18.3	0.0	(18.3)
JRS	$10,689,377	$9,518,759	($1,170,618)	(11)	29.6	26.4	(3.2)
CPFPF	$6,634,211	$5,717,967	($916,244)	(14)	N/A	N/A	N/A
Total	$1,594,624,747	$808,912,124	($785,712,623)	(49)			

Source: New Jersey Division of Pensions and Benefits (1992).

- Eliminate actuarial reserve funding for PRM benefits under TPAF and for state employees under PERS, SPRS, and JRS. Fund the benefits on a pay-as-you-go basis.
- Change the funding method under the state retirement systems from entry age normal to projected unit credit.
- Increase the amortization period for funding the unfunded liabilities of the systems from thirty to forty years.
- Eliminate the 2 percent reduction on employee pension contributions on compensation below the social security compensation limit.
- Extend the phase-in of the impact of revised actuarial assumptions under TPAF from two years to five years.
- Decelerate the phase-in schedule for recognition and funding of COLA benefits to the schedule prior to pension revaluation.

Rationales were provided for each of the proposed changes. Because of the uncertainty over what the health care system in the country would be due to the activity the federal level at the time, it was not prudent to contribute hundreds of millions of taxpayer dollars to prefund PRM benefits. The change to the projected unit credit method for funding the retirement systems would more accurately reflect and fund the liability for retirement benefits on a current basis as the benefits accrue each year. (The study by the Office of Fiscal Affairs in 1976 suggested consideration of such a change in the funding method.) A forty-year amortization schedule for the unfunded accrued liability was a common practice and was authorized under a proposed new rule of the Government Accounting Standards Board. The elimination of the 2 percent offset was long overdue and equitable because it continued long after the basis for it, the offset in retirement benefits for initial social security benefits, had been eliminated (in 1966). The extension of the phase-in for the revised TPAF actuarial assumptions was justified because the primary revision related to improved mortality and the impact of the improved mortality would not be experienced for several years. The deceleration of the phase-in schedule for recognition and funding of COLA benefits was justified because the acceleration under pension revaluation was an unwarranted and costly alteration of the original schedule which was reasonable for funding the benefit.

The proposal generated a bitter battle in the legislature. Led by the NJEA and the state employee unions, the opposition lobbied hard to defeat the proposal. Despite the opposition of these normally powerful interest groups, the proposal passed with all the main elements of the initial proposal included and with a few additional elements some of which enhanced the savings under it.

As enacted by Chapter 62, Laws of 1994, pension reform made several key changes. It eliminated actuarial reserve funding for PRM benefits under TPAF and PERS (state only), SPRS and JRS, and provided for pay-as-you-go funding with additional annual state contributions to the PRM funds under TPAF and PERS to provide a "cushion of reserves" designed to grow at the rate of 0.5 percent of the covered payrolls of the systems. In addition, it changed the actuarial funding method from entry age normal to the projected unit credit method, and reset the amortization period for the unfunded accrued liability from thirty to forty years with required funding progress for ten years until the schedule was reduced to thirty and a flexible schedule which could not exceed thirty years thereafter to accommodate gains and losses. Also, pension reform changed the employee contribution rates under PERS and TPAF from variable rates based on entry age to a flat 5 percent and eliminated the 2 percent offset in the rates on compensation subject to FICA, with a postponement of the change for one year for current members and a transitional one-year flat rate of 4 percent for current members who had effective contribution rates (full rate less the 2 percent offset) of less than 4 percent. It also extended the phase-in of the impact of revised actuarial assumptions under TPAF from two to five years (the TPAF Board of Trustees delayed revision of the assumptions for one year and phased-in the impact over two years). It reverted to the percentage level recognition and funding of COLA benefits under the schedule originally established under the laws which provided for funding the benefit under the retirement systems, and extended the schedule to forty years from the beginning date of the original schedule. In addition the law change reduced the CPI inflation assumption for COLA benefits to 4 percent (the COLA increase assumption is 60 percent of the CPI inflation assumption or 2.4 percent), and gave the pension boards the right to review and change the CPI inflation assumption if the CPI exceeded 4 percent for two consecutive years. In tandem, it reduced the average salary increase assumption to 2.8 percent less than the regular interest rate (8.75 percent) making it 5.95 percent for four years with the pension boards having the right to review and change the rate to a reasonable level if necessary thereafter. It also reduced from 1.4 percent to 1.1 percent the percentage rate of total covered compensation for State contributions to PFRS to fund the increase in the special retirement benefit granted in 1979.

Table 3 shows the estimated savings for five years for each of the elements of the final agreement on pension reform, and Table 4 illustrates the effect of pension reform on employer contributions and contribution rates for fiscal years 1994 through 1996 for each New Jersey retirement system.

The opposition did not give up the fight, but instead moved to another venue. The NJEA and the largest state employee union, CWA, instituted suit in federal court to overturn the pension reform legislation.

Despite the continuing savings from pension reform, the state budget

TABLE 3. Analysis of New Jersey Public Pension Reform: Savings ($ millions)

	FY'94	FY'95	FY'96	FY'97	FY'98	Totals
(A) Change in pre-funding of PRM						
State total	239.0	328.0	228.6	261.3	279.4	1,336.3
Local total	0.0	0.0	0.0	0.0	0.0	0.0
(B) Change to projected unit credit method and 40-year amortization						
State total	58.5	151.8	226.1	278.3	318.3	1,033.0
Local total	80.0	108.8	122.1	148.2	168.6	627.7
(C) Delay assumption change in TPAF from 2 to 5 years						
State total	0.0	60.0	56.0	40.0	23.0	179.0
(D) Revise member contribution to flat 5% rate						
State total	0.0	0.0	30.0	65.0	70.0	165.0
Local total	0.0	0.0	9.0	20.0	22.0	51.0
(E) Return to original COLA phase-in schedule						
State total	33.0	88.0	53.0	64.0	75.0	313.0
Local total	57.0	62.0	67.0	72.0	77.0	335.0
(F) Revise COLA assumption from 3% to 2.4% per year						
State total	23.3	58.5	85.7	108.1	124.8	400.4
Local total	24.8	27.0	48.5	52.9	54.8	208.0
(G) Reduce average salary scale to 2.8% below regular interest						
State total	11.5	21.6	34.3	40.7	39.3	147.3
Local total	18.4	27.2	17.4	4.9	5.6	73.5
(H) Waiver of life insurance over $50,000						
No savings estimated						
(I) SHBP one-year withdrawal moratorium						
No direct savings anticipated						
State savings	365.3	707.9	713.7	857.4	929.8	3,574.0
State aid offset*	180.2	73.7	86.5	97.6	107.4	545.4
Total state savings	545.5	781.5	800.2	955.0	1,037.2	4,119.4
Local savings	180.2	225.0	264.0	298.0	328.0	1,295.2
State aid offset*	180.2	73.7	86.5	97.6	107.4	545.4
Total local savings	0.0	151.3	177.5	200.4	220.6	749.8

Source: New Jersey Division of Pensions and Benefits.
*Estimates 100% of local savings will accrue to the state in FY'94 and 32.75% beginning with FY'95.

continued to face problems. Table 5 shows the actual amounts and annual increases in the three major taxes and total revenues for fiscal years 1993 through 1998 and the estimated amounts for fiscal years 1999 and 2000. Because of pension revaluation and pension reform, it seemed unlikely that there could be another pension funding initiative. However, history shows that one should never underestimate the talents of creative budgeters.

TABLE 4. New Jersey Pension Reform Anaysis: Contributions ($ millions)

System	Contributions			Employer contribution rate		
	FY 1994	FY 1995	FY 1996	FY 1994	FY 1995	FY 1996
PERS-state						
Before reform	$148.4	$198.5	$233.0	6.31%	7.96%	9.54%
After reform	$57.8	$64.8	$91.7	1.26%	0.97%	1.48%
Difference	($90.6)	($133.7)	($141.3)	–5.05%	–6.99%	–8.06%
TPAF						
Before reform	$380.5	$585.0	$725.0	8.32%	11.68%	13.99%
After reform	$119.1	$61.2	$189.4	2.61%	0.96%	1.00%
Difference	($261.4)	($523.8)	($535.6)	–5.71%	–10.72%	–12.99%
PERS-local						
Before reform	$138.6	$191.3	$225.0	3.58%	4.56%	5.28%
After reform	$33.6	$29.5	$38.4	0.84%	0.60%	0.76%
Difference	($105.0)	($161.8)	($186.6)	–2.74%	–3.96%	–4.52%
PFRS-state						
Before reform	$53.2	$111.5	$103.0	33.69%	52.80%	45.98%
After reform	$36.4	$69.8	$78.7	19.53%	33.08%	34.93%
Difference	($16.8)	($41.7)	($24.3)	–14.16%	–19.72%	–11.05%
SPRS						
Before reform	$10.8	$44.8	$47.5	10.70%	39.40%	40.56%
After reform	$13.7	$27.9	$29.8	13.70%	24.50%	25.80%
Difference	$2.9	($16.9)	($17.7)	3.00%	–14.90%	–14.76%
JRS						
Before reform	$9.6	$12.3	$13.1	24.90%	29.90%	31.95%
After reform	$9.1	$11.2	$15.5	23.40%	27.30%	38.40%
Difference	($0.5)	($1.1)	$2.4	–1.50%	–2.60%	6.45%
PFRS-local						
Before reform	$195.1	$195.6	$222.3	19.85%	15.10%	16.01%
After reform	$119.1	$127.8	$178.1	9.65%	9.86%	12.95%
Difference	($76.0)	($67.8)	($44.2)	–10.19%	–5.23%	–3.06%
	1994	1995	1996			
Total state savings	$366.4	$717.2	$716.5			
Total local savings	$181.0	$229.6	$230.8			

Source: Author's compilations from data supplied by the New Jersey Divison of Pensions and Benefits.

Governor Whitman's budget message for fiscal year 1998 unveiled another pension funding initiative:

I am also excited about our pension bond proposal. Here are the facts. Like three dozen other states, our pension fund has an unfunded liability. With this proposal, pensioners can rest easy knowing that their pensions are fully funded and that the money will be there when they retire. We are saving today's taxpayers millions of dollars by taking advantage of favorable market conditions and low interest rates to lock into tomorrow's pension payments at today's prices. And we are protecting future

TABLE 5. Annual Growth of Three Major Taxes and Total Revenues, FY 1993–2000

Year	Sales tax revenue	% change	Income tax revenue	% change	Corporate tax revenue	% change	Total tax revenue	% change
1993	3,651,122		4,325,305		960,754		14,833,258	
1994	3,725,645	2.04	4,493,660	3.89	1,091,142	13.57	14,967,778	0.91
1995	4,132,657	10.92	4,540,400	1.04	1,085,492	(0.52)	15,298,868	2.21
1996	4,318,373	4.49	4,733,786	4.26	1,171,509	7.92	15,873,379	3.76
1997	4,415,429	2.25	4,825,411	1.94	1,286,447	9.81	16,466,605	3.74
1998	4,766,195	7.94	5,590,579	15.86	1,231,629	(4.26)	17,444,555	5.94
1999*	5,015,000	5.22	6,065,000	8.49	1,478,000	20.00	17,961,746	2.96
2000*	5,258,000	4.85	6,477,000	6.79	1,555,600	5.25	18,859,136	5.00

Source: Whitman (1999).
*Estimated.

generations by refinancing this obligation over a shorter period of time. Clearly, this proposal is good for us today and good for our grandchildren tomorrow. (Whitman 1997: ii)

This last pension initiative of the 1990s has become known as the pension security proposal (PSP).

The Pension Security Reform

This proposal was rather more complicated than the two previous initiatives. According to actuarial valuations, the state had an unfunded accrued liability under the retirement systems of $3.2 billion. There was also a projected future unfunded liability from the phased-in recognition and funding of COLA benefits with a present value of $1 billion. Under PERS and TPAF, the basic benefits and retiree COLA were fully funded and had an asset surplus of $543 million. The assets and liabilities for the COLA benefits for active employees were tracked separately from basic benefits and retiree COLA because of the phased-in recognition and funding of the active COLA. This surplus was being amortized over the amortization period for the unfunded accrued liability and was providing an annual credit against the employer normal and unfunded accrued liability contributions. And finally, the last piece of the puzzle was a surplus in the market value of pension assets (the difference between the market value and the actuarial value of the assets) of $1.9 billion.

Governor Whitman's original proposal was to issue pension obligation bonds to fund the state's unfunded accrued liability to the state retirement systems. These bonds would not be general obligation bonds, but rather would be *appropriation bonds* which means that payment would depend on the availability of legislative appropriations and there could be no guaran-

TABLE 6. The New Jersey Pension Security Proposal ($ millions)

	Original proposal	Plan adopted
TPAF/PERS surplus assets (basic benefits)	$543	$543
Surplus market assets	1,919	1,919
Subtotal surplus assets	2,462	2,462
Pension obligation bonds	3,213	2,750
Subtotal pension obligation bonds and surplus assets	5,675	5,212
Unfunded accrued liability	3,213	3,213
Projected COLA unfunded liability	1,042	1,042
Subtotal accrued and projected unfunded liability	4,256	4,256
Pension obligation bonds and surplus assets	5,675	5,212
Interest discount on bond proceeds	357	305
Accrued and projected unfunded liability	4,256	4,256
1997 state pension contributions due	334	334
1997 state pension contributions paid	82	82
1998 state pension contributions due	415	415
1999 state pension contributions paid	67	67
1998 employee contribution reduction	0	47
Net surplus assets	670	3
FY'97 and FY'98 budget savings	$601	$601

Source: Author's compilations from data supplied by the New Jersey Division of Pensions and Benefits.

tee of such appropriations. The valuation assets of the retirement systems would be reset to full market value for the actuarial valuations on which the fiscal year 1998 pension contributions were based. The surplus assets from resetting the pension assets to market value and the surplus assets for basic benefits in PERS and TPAF would be used to fund the projected COLA unfunded liability and the state pension contributions for fiscal years 1997 and 1998 to the extent of availability of surplus assets in the several funds. Table 6 shows the pertinent numbers for the original proposal and the plan actually adopted.

The rationale for bonding the unfunded accrued liability was that due to favorable conditions in the financial market, it could be funded at a lower rate and over a substantially shorter time period than it could through the retirement systems. Most of the unfunded liability was attributable to COLA benefits under PERS and TPAF. Due to the phased-in recognition and funding of this liability under these systems, the liability would not be fully recognized until fiscal year 2029. The liability would not be fully funded until fiscal year 2056. The total contribution to the retirement systems to fund the liability over 59 years would have been $57 billion. The regular interest rate (assumed rate of return on investment of pension assets) under the systems was 8.75 percent. Under PSP, the liability could be funded over 32 years at

TABLE 7. New Jersey State Retirement Systems: Five-Year Projection of Assets, Liabilities, and Employer Contributions ($ Millions)

	PERS State	TPAF	PFRS State	SPRS	JRS	CPFPF	POPF
Fiscal year 2000							
Market assets	8,860	28,703	1,350	1,345	358	56	20
Valuation assets	7,830	24,936	1,233	1,459	333	62	20
Actuarial liability	6,986	23,941	1,208	1,372	312	59	16
Unfunded liability/ (Surpluss)	(844)	(995)	(25)	(86)	(21)	(3)	(4)
Excess assets	(559)	(131)	(25)	(86)	(21)	(3)	(4)
Employer contributions							
Normal contributions	97	339	91	32	13	0	0
Excess asset offset	97	144	30	32	13	0	0
UL contribution	0	0	2	0	0	0	0
PRM contribution	54	131	0	0	0	0	0
Total contribution	54	326	62	0	0	0	0
Net excess assets	(656)	0	0	(55)	(9)	(3)	(4)
Fiscal year 2001							
Market assets	9,391	30,654	1,619	1,800	369	49	19
Valuation assets	8,496	27,374	1,419	1,535	348	54	19
Actuarial liability	7,474	25,741	1,351	1,481	333	52	15
Unfunded liability/ (Surpluss)	(1,022)	(1,633)	(68)	(54)	(15)	(2)	(4)
Excess assets	(737)	(781)	(68)	(54)	(15)	(2)	(4)
Employer contributions							
Normal contributions	107	356	96	35	13	0	0
Excess asset offset	107	356	49	35	13	0	0
UL contribution	0	0	2	35	0	0	0
PRM contribution	58	144	0	0	0	0	0
Total contribution	58	144	48	0	0	0	0
Net excess assets	(844)	(425)	(19)	(19)	(2)	(2)	(4)
Fiscal year 2002							
Market assets	9,939	32,412	1,760	1,968	382	42	18
Valuation assets	9,160	29,558	1,587	1,630	364	47	18
Actuarial liability	8,010	27,553	1,510	1,608	356	46	14
Unfunded liability/ (Surpluss)	(1,150)	(2,005)	(77)	(22)	(8)	(1)	(4)
Excess assets	(867)	(1,173)	(77)	(22)	(8)	(1)	(4)
Employer contributions							
Normal contributions	118	375	101	37	14	0	0
Excess asset offset	118	375	53	22	8	0	0
UL contribution	0	0	1	0	0	0	0
PRM contribution	62	159	0	0	0	0	0
Total contribution	62	159	49	15	6	0	0
Net excess assets	(985)	(798)	(24)	0	0	(1)	(4)

TABLE 7. Continued

	PERS State	TPAF	PFRS State	SPRS	JRS	CPFPF	POPF
Fiscal year 2003							
Market assets	10,501	34,225	1,914	2,151	396	36	17
Valuation assets	9,823	31,742	1,763	1,743	380	41	17
Actuarial liability	8,595	29,447	1,683	1,744	381	40	13
Unfunded liability/							
(Surpluss)	(1,228)	(2,295)	(80)	1	1	(1)	(4)
Excess assets	(945)	(1,485)	(80)	0	0	(1)	(4)
Employer contributions							
Normal contributions	129	394	106	40	14	0	0
Excess asset offset	129	394	56	0	0	0	0
UL contribution	0	0	1	0	0	0	0
PRM contribution	66	175	0	0	0	0	0
Total contribution	66	175	50	40	14	0	0
Net excess assets	(1,074)	(1,091)	(24)	0	0	(1)	(4)

Source: Author's compilations of data for PERS, SPRS, JRS, CPFPF, and POPF supplied by Buck Consultants, and for TPAF supplied by Milliman & Robertson.
Assumed asset investment return 8.75%; assumed market investment return FY2001 8.75%.

a lower interest rate at a cost of $10 billion. This would yield a saving of $47 billion in future pension contributions.

Opposition to this initiative was different from that expressed regarding the pension reform plan. Now employee representatives were divided. The state was proposing to pay off its unfunded liability to the state retirement systems with bond proceeds. It would put several billion dollars into the pensions funds and fully fund the state obligations under all the systems. The NJEA recognized very early in the process the benefits to the retirement systems from the proposal. It wanted some changes in the proposal, such as a limit on the state's ability to continue to use excess assets to offset pension contributions and a benefit for the members of the retirement systems. In exchange, state officials wanted the lawsuit over pension reform to be settled. Concessions to the NJEA led that group to become an early and strong supporter of the proposal. State employees unions were divided on the proposals. They had weak relations with the Whitman administration, leading them to be reluctant to support the proposal. Eventually, the proposal was supported by the national leadership of CWA, but some locals opposed it; the AFL-CIO decided not to oppose it.

A few additional items were added to the proposal while it was under consideration in the legislature. A limit was placed upon the ability of the state to use the full amount of excess assets to offset normal contributions. It could use the full amount through fiscal year 2003. It could use 84 percent and 68 percent over the next two fiscal years, respectively, and 50 percent in

TABLE 8. New Jersey State Retirement Systems: Five-Year Projection of Assets, Liabilities, and Employer Contributions (in Millions)

	PERS State	TPAF	PFRS State	SPRS	JRS	CPFPF	POPF
Fiscal year 2000							
Market assets	8,860	28,703	1,350	1,345	358	56	20
Valuation assets	7,830	24,936	1,233	1,459	333	62	20
Actuarial liability	6,986	23,941	1,208	1,372	312	59	16
Unfunded liability/ (Surpluss)	(844)	(995)	(25)	(86)	(21)	(3)	(4)
Excess assets	(559)	(131)	(25)	(86)	(21)	(3)	(4)
Employer contributions							
Normal contributions	97	339	91	32	13	0	0
Excess asset offset	97	144	30	32	13	0	0
UL contribution	0	0	2	0	0	0	0
PRM contribution	54	131	0	0	0	0	0
Total contribution	54	326	62	0	0	0	0
Net excess assets	(656)	0	0	(55)	(9)	(3)	(4)
Fiscal year 2001							
Market assets	8,626	28,180	1,619	1,656	339	45	17
Valuation assets	8,343	26,879	1,419	1,506	342	54	17
Actuarial liability	7,474	25,741	1,351	1,481	333	52	15
Unfunded liability/ (Surpluss)	(869)	(1,138)	(68)	(25)	(9)	(1)	(2)
Excess assets	(584)	(286)	(68)	(25)	(9)	(1)	(2)
Employer contributions							
Normal contributions	107	356	96	35	13	0	0
Excess asset offset	107	318	49	25	9	0	0
UL contribution	0	0	2	35	0	0	0
PRM contribution	58	144	0	0	0	0	0
Total contribution	58	182	48	10	4	0	0
Net excess assets	(691)	32	(19)	0	0	(1)	(2)
Fiscal year 2002							
Market assets	9,107	29,760	1,619	1,811	349	38	16
Valuation assets	8,860	28,627	1,558	1,576	352	45	16
Actuarial liability	8,010	27,553	1,510	1,608	356	46	14
Unfunded liability/ (Surpluss)	(850)	(1,074)	(48)	33	4	0	(2)
Excess assets	(567)	(241)	(48)	0	0	0	(2)
Employer contributions							
Normal contributions	118	375	101	37	14	0	0
Excess asset offset	118	268	53	0	0	0	0
UL contribution	0	0	1	1	0	0	0
PRM contribution	62	159	0	0	0	0	0
Total contribution	62	266	49	38	14	0	0
Net excess assets	(685)	0	0	0	0	0	(2)

TABLE 8. Continued

	PERS State	TPAF	PFRS State	SPRS	JRS	CPFPF	POPF
Fiscal year 2003							
Market assets	9,596	31,447	1,761	1,991	365	32	15
Valuation assets	9,381	30,462	1,708	1,675	367	38	15
Actuarial liability	8,595	29,447	1,683	1,744	381	40	13
Unfunded liability/							
(Surpluss)	(786)	(1,015)	(25)	69	14	2	(3)
Excess assets	(503)	(205)	(25)	0	0	0	(3)
Employer contributions							
Normal contributions	129	394	106	40	14	0	0
Excess asset offset	129	228	30	0	0	0	0
UL contribution	0	0	1	2	1	2	0
PRM contribution	66	175	0	0	0	0	0
Total contribution	66	341	77	42	15	2	0
Net excess assets	(632)	0	0	0	0	0	(3)

Source: See Table 7.
Assumed asset investment return 8.75%; assumed market investment return FY2001 0.00%.

fiscal years thereafter. In order for there to be excess assets, the valuation assets have to be sufficient to cover the full accrued actuarial liability and the projected liability for COLA benefits under PERS and TPAF. Members of PERS and TPAF were guaranteed a 0.5 percent reduction in their contribution rates (from 5 percent to 4.5 percent) from excess assets 1998 and 1999, and continued contribution reductions of up to 0.5 percent if there were excess assets and the state used them to offset normal contributions. The state employee unions succeeded in obtaining a statutory guarantee against a change in benefits once a member attained five years of service. This was not a change in the vesting period which remained at 10 years and PRM benefits were not included in the guarantee. Ultimately, PSP was passed by a close vote in the Senate and a larger majority in the General Assembly; the Governor signed it immediately in June of 1997, whereupon NJEA and CWA dropped their law suit over pension reform.

Interest from investors was enormous. When the pension bonds were first offered to the market, demand was eight times the value of bonds supplied. Interest in the offering helped to reduce the interest rate, which came in at average rate of 7.64 percent. This pension funding initiative like its two predecessors had a dramatic positive impact on the state budget. Reduced contribution amounts totaled $600 million for FY 1997 and 1998; over $200 million in contribution savings were budgeted for fiscal year 1999, and over $400 million in FY 2000. There were also positive impacts on the public pension funds. One was due to the immediate addition of $2.75 billion to the funds and the second was due to the enhanced investment return on not

TABLE 9. Annual Investment Return on Pension Assets and CPI Change: 1985–1998.

Year ending	Average annual return (%)	5-yr average annual return (%)	Consumer price index (%)	5-yr average annual increase price index (%)
6/30/1985	31.2		3.70	
6/30/1986	30.90		1.70	
6/30/1987	14.90		3.70	
6/30/1988	70.00		3.90	
6/30/1989	14.50	17.50	5.30	3.65
6/30/1990	13.30	14.10	4.30	3.77
6/30/1991	9.30	10.40	4.70	4.38
6/30/1992	13.80	10.10	3.00	4.24
6/30/1993	12.50	12.70	3.00	4.06
6/30/1994	0.70	9.40	2.50	3.50
6/30/1995	19.70	10.70	3.00	3.24
6/30/1996	16.10	12.10	2.80	2.86
6/30/1997	22.10	13.70	2.30	2.72
6/30/1998	22.70	15.60	1.70	2.46
10-year average annual return	14.14%			
10-year average annual CPI change	3.25%			
14-year average annual return	15.43%			
14-year average annual CPI change	3.25%			

Source: Author's compilation of data supplied by the New Jersey Department of the Treasury, and Whitman (2000).

only on the pension bond proceeds, but also the entire fund. For FY 1998, the first full year after the addition of bond proceeds, the Division of Investment had an average rate of return on the pension assets of 22.7 percent. Since the pension funds earned $624 million on the bond proceeds but debt service was $91 million, net earnings totaled $533 million. They were $414 million more than the amount to cover the average interest rate (7.64 percent) on the bonds, and $384 million more than the amount to cover the interest assumption for the systems (8.75 percent). Partly as a result of this plan, and double-digit investment returns on pension assets, fund balances entering the *new* millennium are projected at $647 million.

Outlook for the Future

New Jersey pension funds are expected to do well in the next several years. Estimates of pension assets, liabilities, and employer contribution requirements appear in Tables 7 and 8, under two scenarios. One assumes that the rate of return will be the regular interest assumption, 8.75 percent while the second scenario assumes one flat year of zero return on investment, and three years at the regular interest assumption. Under either scenario, the State is projected to not have to make a normal contribution to PERS in each of the four years. In TPAF, there would be a complete normal cost offset for three of the four years with an 8.75 percent return, and substantial offsets in each year even with one flat investment year.

The ability to undertake the funding initiatives of the 1990s is attributable to the recent favorable investment climate. The State Investment Council and Division of Investments has generated remarkable returns on pension asset investment, since it began to invest more of the pension assets in equities. Table 9 shows the average annual pension returns and CPI changes since 1984, and shows that the fund averaged returns of more than 14 percent in the last decade and over 15 percent in the last five years (inflation averaged 3.25 percent over the same periods). We conclude that the public funds will continue to be in good shape even if there were an economic slowdown in the near future. In fact, with current assets, the pension plans could pay out current annual benefits for over 20 years without another contribution or another dollar in investment earnings.

References

Florio, James. 1992. *State of New Jersey Budget—Fiscal Year 1992–1993.* Trenton, January 28.

Kean, Thomas H. 1982. *Executive Order No. 7.* Trenton, May 4.

———. 1989. *Budget Message for Fiscal Year 1989—The Budget Message and Taxpayers' Guide; New Jersey Budget—Fiscal Year 1988–1989.* Trenton, January 26.

———. 1990. *Budget Message for Fiscal Year 1990—The Budget Message and Taxpayers' Guide; New Jersey Budget—Fiscal Year 1989–1990.* Trenton, February 2.

KPMG PeatMarwick. 1998. *Audited Financial Statements, Combined Statements for the State Retirement Systems (Except the Alternate Benefit Program) as of June 30, 1998.* Trenton: KPGM PeatMarwick.

New Jersey Division of Pensions and Benefits. 1998. *43rd Comprehensive Annual Report for the Fiscal Year Ending June 30, 1998.* Trenton.

New Jersey State Legislature. 1976. *New Jersey's Contributory Public Employee Pension Programs: Program Analysis of the Public Employees' Retirement System.* Trenton: Office of Fiscal Affairs, March.

New Jersey State Pension Study Commission. 1984a. *Report to the Governor.* Trenton, March 15.

———. 1984b. *Appendix of Report to the Governor.* Section V, "Memorandum to the Honorable Brendan T. Byrne, Governor of the State of New Jersey, From State Treasurer Clifford A. Goldman, April 9, 1981." Trenton, March 15.

———. 1984c. *Executive Summary of the Report to the Governor.* Trenton, March 15.

———. 1984d. *Minority Statement Submitted to the Governor.* Trenton, April 4.

Pensions and Investments. 1999. "Special Report: Top 1,000 Funds." January 25.

Whitman, Christine Todd. 1994. *State of New Jersey Budget—Fiscal Year 1994–1995.* Trenton, March 15.

——. 1997. *State of New Jersey Budget—Fiscal Year 1997–1998.* Trenton, January 29.

——. 2000. *State of New Jersey Budget—Fiscal Year 1997–1998.* Trenton, January 29.

Zorn, Paul. 1998. *1997 Survey of State and Local Government Employee Retirement Systems.* Chicago: Public Pension Coordinating Council, c/o Government Finance Officers Association.

Chapter 16
Public Pensions in Washington, D.C.

Edwin C. Hustead

When Congress granted the District of Columbia limited "home rule" in 1974, the fledgling District municipal government inherited numerous responsibilities that usually fall within the ambit of state or city government.[1] To cite but a few examples, the District government found itself both managing and financing a prison system, a land-grant university, a complete trial and appellate court system, and a Medicaid program. Although these functions were expensive—and experience would demonstrate that they would become far more costly than anyone foresaw in 1974—they could be justified as normal attributes of a government vested with home rule powers. Equally important, their costs were defrayed (at least in part) by a "federal payment"—an annual lump sum grant that the U.S. federal government made to the District as part of its annual appropriations process.

This was not the case with District pension liabilities. In addition to buildings and programs, the District inherited employees and retirees, and they came with built-in retirement costs. Congress first began to pass legislation granting pensions to District employees in the last quarter of the nineteenth century, well before the establishment of the Civil Service Retirement System in 1920 for civilian employees of the federal government, and the system expanded over time. By 1974, District employees participated in three major District-only retirement programs:

Police and firefighters. This program was established in 1916, replacing several earlier programs that covered municipal police, as well as members of the secret service and other uniformed federal police forces operating within the District. By 1974, this was the largest retirement program limited to District employees, providing pension and disability benefits to over 13,000 active and retired police and firefighters, as well as limited numbers of secret service personnel. The program had achieved notoriety for its generous treatment of disability pension applications: as of 1969, over 98 percent of the retirees had "gone out on disability."

Teachers. Established in 1920, the program covered about 12,000 active and retired teachers in the municipal elementary and secondary schools.

Judges. The newest and numerically smallest of the systems, the judges' program was created in 1974, when Congress established a new system of local trial and appellate courts.

The majority of the remaining District employees (clerks, sanitation workers, etc.) participated in the Civil Service Retirement System (CSRS), the umbrella retirement program for federal employees, which is described in detail in Hustead and Hustead in this volume.

While the three District systems had different benefit levels, eligibility requirements and administrative structures, they shared several important characteristics with CSRS. They are all defined benefit plans that allow workers to retire earlier than their private sector counterparts, and often provide subsidies for early retirements. Police and firefighters can retire at any age with 20 years' service; teachers at age 50 with 25 years' service; and judges at age 60 with 10 years' service. The District's cost-of-living allowance (COLA) scheme was more generous than even the CSRS. Retired District police and firefighters received COLAs that matched any salary increase paid to active employees, and teachers were entitled to twice-a-year COLAs. (Judges had to manage on a once-a-year COLA).

The District of Columbia 1979 Retirement Reform Act

It would have been relatively simple to draft legislative language in 1974 transferring administrative responsibilities for the retirement programs from the federal government to the District. The deficiencies inherent in the pre-1974 retirement systems were sufficiently apparent, however, that Congress delayed the transfer while efforts were made to craft remedial legislation addressing the most glaring problems. It ultimately proved impossible to pass effective legislation that satisfied the necessary stakeholders, and the resulting "District of Columbia Retirement Reform Act of 1979" (PL 96–122) had the dubious distinction of making a bad situation worse.

The process began with the assumption that the retirement programs would be transferred en bloc to the District. It was also eventually decided that the District would not be allowed to make any significant changes to the existing plan rules regarding defined benefit levels, retirement ages and accrual patterns. Thus the District would be responsible for the benefits of workers who retired before home rule, the benefits earned by current employees after the passage of home rule, and the cost of any future accruals. The only open issue was the extent to which the federal government would contribute to assist the District in discharging these retirement costs. The answer was, not much.

Inherited liabilities. Congress retained Arthur Andersen & Co. to calculate the unfunded liabilities of the District programs as of 1974, and the accountants duly reported that the figure was $2 billion. In 1978, Congress passed legislation that would have provided the District with a series of $65 million payments for twenty-five years, a formula that was reckoned to cover the benefit costs of workers who had retired before home rule (and left the costs of subsequent retirees up to the District). However, the Carter administration vetoed the measure on the grounds that it was excessively generous. By 1979, when the unfunded liabilities had grown to $2.7 billion, Congress and the administration agreed on a single $38 million payment coupled with twenty-five annual payments of $52 million. The payments had a present value of $687 million, which was supposed to cover 80 percent of the retirement benefits (and 33 percent of disability benefits) of pre-home rule retirees. The cost of post-1974 retirees would fall entirely upon the District.

Prospective contributions from the district. The most striking feature of the 1979 Reform Act was the statutory formula that set the District's posttransfer annual contribution to the programs. As long as the federal payment was in effect, the formula directed the District to pay the *lesser* of (1) the programs' "pay as you go" costs and (2) the programs' normal cost plus projected interest. What this meant, of course, was that the original $2 billion in underfunding would steadily grow. After 2004 (when the federal payment was to cease) the District's payment would rise to the sum of the programs' normal cost *plus* interest on the programs' unfunded liability.

Benefit structure. Even tentative suggestions that the DC plans' generous benefit structure warranted modification triggered objections from unions and employee groups, all of whom had excellent relations with the relevant congressional committees. As a result, only minor changes were made to the old benefit system, and even those changes were made prospective, thereby "grandfathering" most of the workforce. Teachers who retired after 1980 would receive "only" one annual COLA rather than two, and police and firefighters hired after 1980 had the salary-related COLA replaced with a twice-a-year consumer price index (CPI)-based formula. No changes were made to the judges' benefits.

Plan administration. The Reform Act created a nine-member District of Columbia Retirement Board composed of mayoral appointees and representatives from the participant groups. Contrary to what one might expect from the nomenclature, the new board did not administer the programs. Instead, tasks such as record keeping, benefit administration, and benefit payments, were all performed by the Office of Pay and Retirement within the Office of the Mayor. The board was charged with investing assets, or more accurately, selecting competing private sector asset managers to invest the assets.

TABLE 1. District of Columbia's Public Pension Plan Costs: 1979–1995 ($ million)

Fiscal year ending September 30	District's contributions	Partici-pants' contributions	Total contributions to plans[a]	Actu-arially deter-mined normal cost	Excess of all contributions over normal costs	Pension plan unfunded liability
1980	$107.6	$21.1	$128.7	$84.6	$44.1	$N/A[b]
1981	107.7	20.2	127.9	81.1	46.8	N/A[b]
1982	135.8	60.9	196.7	85.5	111.2	2,679.7
1983	142.9	22.6	165.5	94.6	70.9	2,677.7
1984	174.1	24.4	198.5	108.4	90.1	3,090.2
1985	165.1	24.6	189.7	113.9	75.8	3,190.7
1986	176.5	26.4	202.9	113.7	89.2	N/A
1987	173.4	28.5	201.9	122.1	79.8	4,213.4
1988	180.3	30.7	211.0	137.3	73.7	4,440.0
1989	194.3	34.8	229.1	121.6	107.5	4,447.0
1990	222.6	34.7	257.3	135.8	121.5	4,941.0
1991	225.3	37.3	262.6	151.0	111.6	4,505.2
1992	255.0	35.2	290.2	148.1	142.1	4,558.6
1993	292.3	36.0	328.3	140.6	187.7	4,418.2
1994	308.1	39.6	347.7	146.4	201.1	4,729.7
1995	297.8	37.7	335.5	136.1	199.4	
Totals	$3,158.8	$514.7	$3,673.5	$1,921.0	$1,752.5	

Source: Appleseed Foundation, 1996.
[a] The $52 million federal contributions required under the Retirement Reform Act of 1979, P.L. 96-122, were *not* included in these data because they did not impact the actuarially deter-mined normal cost.
[b] These unfunded prior service costs were not readily available.

The Appleseed Foundation Report and Counterreformation

Following passage of the 1979 Reform Act, the DC pension programs de-veloped as one could have anticipated, given the parameters established by Congress. Between 1980 and 1995, the District's required contributions nearly tripled, and the programs' inherited liabilities increased. The dismal picture is illustrated in Table 1.

The spiraling rise in annual pension costs took place against a backdrop of general financial difficulty for the District. In a nutshell, the post-home rule District faced a combination of a declining population, a shrinking tax base, and expanding costs for education, welfare, the prison system, and myriad other functions. During the administration of Mayor Kelly (1990–94), the District suspended payments to the pension programs. The D.C.

Retirement Board responded with a lawsuit that resulted in the issuance of an injunction requiring the city to make its annual payments within the time prescribed by the Reform Act.

These developments triggered an unusual response from the private sector. In 1995, a local nonprofit public interest organization composed of lawyers and other professionals operating under the intriguing sobriquet of the "DC Appleseed Center for Law and Justice" took up the study and analysis of the District Retirement Programs. The lawyers and pension professionals funded by the Center issued a report and policy recommendations in June 1996 (Appleseed Foundation 1996).

This Appleseed Report began by affirming that the District government had no responsibility for the massive underfunding of the programs. It showed that the federal government had created the benefit structure and had elected to maintain the Programs on an unfunded basis prior to downloading to the District in 1979. Since that time, the District's contributions (coupled with those of the employees) more than covered the normal costs associated with post-1979 accruals. The report further established that the investment practices of the Retirement Board were prudent and played no part in the underfunding of the programs. Finally, the Appleseed Report warned that an already-dismal situation would get even worse when the federal payments ceased in 2004. The trigger mechanism built into the 1979 Act would then require an annual contribution equal to normal cost plus interest on the programs' unfunded liability (which at that time would equal $7 billion) or $490 million. As the report dryly noted, by that time the District's pension costs would exceed its payroll. Moreover, this heroic expenditure would not reduce the principal of the inherited unfunded liabilities: *that* would require an additional $300+ million a year.

Once it had established that the existing system was doomed, the Appleseed report recommended several proposed changes. It argued that the simplest and fairest method of dealing with the District pension problem was for the federal government to reclaim the District's pension plans. Under this scenario, the federal government would accept financial responsibility for all of the pension programs' benefit costs associated with retirees, active employees and former employees with benefits vested as of the transfer date. The federal government would also receive all the assets held by the pension programs.

The District would then be free to establish new benefit plans covering new hires. The District would have full control over selecting the structure and benefit levels of the new plans—the report went so far as to suggest that the District adopt a defined contribution structure—and the District would be solely responsible for funding them. The District would also provide the federal system with an annual payment equal to the normal cost of the post-transfer benefit accruals earned by the transferred participants.

All too often, public policy analyses and recommendations lie unread, but the Appleseed Report proved to be an exception to the rule. During the summer and fall of 1996, the Foundation's board and staff conducted a remarkably effective education campaign before the Congress, the D.C. Council, and the Clinton administration's Office of Management and Budget. The foundation also obtained solid support from the local news media, as stories and editorials in the *Washington Post* began to stress the urgent need for solutions to the District's pension problem.

In the last week of 1996, President Clinton approved the basic elements of a legislative proposal to address the fiscal and management woes of the District. The first element of the package contained a modified version of the approach to the pension problem presented in the Appleseed Report. Other aspects of the proposal called for a federal takeover of the District's prison, court and criminal justice system, the federalization of the District's tax system, and other elements too numerous to mention here.

In February 1997, the Office of Management and Budget (OMB) summoned representatives from numerous Federal agencies and departments to a meeting in the Treaty Room of the Old Executive Building, to outline the proposal and assign drafting responsibilities. Responsibility for drafting the pension proposal was entrusted to staff of the National Economic Council, the Treasury, OMB, the Department of Labor, and the Pension Benefit Guaranty Corporation (PBGC). Drafters were told to take all the time they needed, so long as the legislative language and proposed descriptive material was finished within three weeks. While most aspects of the bill (prisons, taxes, courts, etc.) ended up requiring several months to draft, the pension team actually completed a passable draft before the three week deadline.

The District of Columbia Retirement Protection Act of 1997

The resulting bill outlining the Administration's proposal to assume the District's unfunded pension liability was introduced as part of the "National Capital Revitalization and Self-Government Improvement Act of 1997." A version of the Administration's proposal passed Congress relatively quickly, and "the District of Columbia Retirement Protection Act of 1997" became effective in October of 1997. (It appeared in Title XI, Subtitle A, of the Balanced Budget Act of 1997, PL 105-32).

In drafting this pension law, the Administration faced two major constraints. The first was that the federal government's assumption of the District's unfunded pension liability could not impact on the recent agreement to balance the budget by the year 2002. For that reason, the federal government could incur no costs before fiscal year 2003. The second constraint was the lack of any department or agency within the federal government with experience or knowledge in administering a public pension plan remotely similar to traditional state and local government pension plans.

Following roughly the model set out in the Appleseed Report, the Act divided the $3.9 billion in pension program assets between the federal government and the District. The Act specified that the District would keep $1.3 billion, which would be used to help fund the replacement programs that the District would establish. The remaining $2.6 billion would migrate to a new Federal Trust Fund with no restrictions on the investments. Permitting investments to continue in the private sector avoided converting the assets to an internal fund. Conversion to federal funds would have reduced the deficit in the year of the conversion but, by drawing on federal funds within the budget for benefits, would have increased the deficit in each succeeding year. This provision satisfied the first constraint mentioned above — assets in the trust fund would be sufficient to ensure that no new net costs resulted in any year prior to 2003. The new fund would be sufficient to pay all federal obligations assumed in the Act until well after the year 2002. A second federal fund invested entirely in federal securities was also established to pay benefits after the assets of the federal trust fund were depleted. The act provides that the new fund will receive annual federal payments (drawn from annual appropriations) in an amount determined by accepted actuarial methods to amortize the original unfunded liability.

The act transferred all liabilities and administrative responsibilities for the smaller judges' plan to the federal government. With respect to the Teachers Plan and the Police and Fire Plan, the act transferred responsibility for paying the retirement benefits of plan participants who retired before June 30, 1997, to the federal government. The responsibility for paying pension benefits to new District employees remained with the District, in the form of whatever replacement plans the District decided to adopt.

Diverging from the Appleseed proposal, the act split both financial and administrative responsibility for current District employees between the Federal government and the District. In rough terms, benefit accruals for the federal portion of the employees' benefits were frozen on June 30, 1997, with the federal government responsible for the prefreeze portion. While the federal government will not be responsible for benefits earned by current employees in future service years (other than judges), their federal benefit will reflect pay increases on the frozen benefit. Frozen benefits will also continue to be subject to cost of living adjustments. All future disabled retirees' benefits were the responsibility of the District. The act also pledged the full faith and credit of the United States to meet its responsibilities to pay benefits for the Police and Teachers Programs.[2]

Any benefit subsequent to the freeze for current workers would be determined by the terms of the District's replacement plans. The drafters had no way of knowing what type of replacement plan the District might choose, and they sought to draft provisions that would not limit the District's choices for a replacement plan. As in the past, however, political realities overcame actuarial theory, and the District Council dutifully enacted a replacement plan for Teachers and for Police and Fire that was substantially the same as the existing plans. Curiously, this did not have an adverse effect on the District's cash flow because the $1.3 billion left behind by the act covered plan costs for the foreseeable future. The District plans have also been placed on a sound actuarial basis to avoid future financing shortfalls.

The act placed responsibility for administration of the trust fund and benefits with the Department of Treasury. (It is a matter of record that no other federal agencies were eager to accept this job.) To deal with the lack of experience at Treasury in administering public pension plans, the act allowed the secretary to delegate much of the responsibility to third-party trustees. The secretary was also given broad regulatory powers under the act. The trustee or trustees were empowered to invest funds, manage the existing plans, and make payments on behalf of participants and beneficiaries. The act called for cooperation and an exchange of information between the District, the District's Retirement Board, and the Treasury Department. These parties have entered into Memorandums of Understanding to coordinate both the transfer of assets to the federal trust fund, and benefit administration.

The Omnibus Consolidated Act of 1998: Pension Protection Protected

By this point, it may be evident that governmental pension reform has proven to be a never-ending process, and this conclusion was reiterated with the Omnibus Consolidated Appropriations Act of 1998 (OCAA 1998). Among other things, section 801 of the law permitted the secretary to allow the pension trustee contractor to hire subcontractors. One should not infer that this was a gesture of confidence in favor of contracting, because another change in the same section clarified that the secretary could have work performed by Treasury employees instead of contractors. The act also allowed the secretary new authority in determining exactly *which* assets should be left behind with the District, a point that had apparently caused controversy.

October of 1998 saw the passage, *twice*, of a myriad of corrections to the judges 1997 legislation. The District of Columbia Courts and Justice Technical Corrections Act of 1998 (Public Law 105–274), managed to secure full faith and credit for the judges' pensions, along with several other changes stretching the meaning of "technical corrections." Apparently concerned that simply getting these corrections passed once was not enough, hours later the exact same set of provisions was enacted into law as section 804 of OCAA 98.

Section 130 of the 1998 amendments merits careful attention. The 1997 legislation had given the Secretary broad authority to invest the old DC pension program assets including permitting investment in private securities. The ability to continue to hold and invest the pension program assets outside the federal budget was necessary to avoid increasing the Federal deficit. The 1998 amendments eliminated investment discretion altogether in favor of "public debt securities" of the United States. By 1998, annual projected surpluses were large and there was no deficit to increase. Instead, the then current need was for spending increases to allow Congress to pass unrelated legislation with offsetting costs. In other words, the arcane rules of deficit reduction, applied in times of surplus, had led the D.C. pension retirement financing back to investment in federal debt issues.

Conclusion

We have at last, therefore, come full circle. Today, a portion of the pensions of D.C. employees accrued before 1997 are again backed by the federal government's own securities and promise to pay. Employees with pension accruals after 1997 are the responsibility of the District. Continued federal government intervention in the District of Columbia's pension system is a near certainty, judging from events over the last thirty years.

Notes

1. The District of Columbia is the capital of the United States, and as such the District is treated differently from states or municipalities in many ways. The legal structure outlining how the nation's capital is governed is spelled out in The District of Columbia Self-Government and Governmental Reorganization Act, P.L. 93-198.
2. The legislative provisions dealing with the judges (drafted by the judges themselves) neglected to obtain a similar commitment.

Reference

Appleseed Foundation. 1996. *The District of Columbia Pension Dilemma: An Immediate and Lasting Solution.* Washington, D.C: Appleseed Foundation.

Chapter 17
Public Pension Design and Responses to a Changing Workforce

Cathie Eitelberg

Workers of the nineteenth century would marvel at the current face of the American workforce. Most obviously, women have entered the workforce in record numbers, the nation's general education level has increased, public unions have grown, and new industries and services have developed. But what would truly amaze those bygone workers would be the benefits enjoyed by many of today's employees. This boom in employer sponsored benefits is the product of demands from a changing, diverse and organized workforce, and wide range of economic conditions favoring benefit growth over increases in salary, such as the wage freezes of the second world war and during the 1970s. Yet the growth in employee benefits is far from a static development. Rather benefits specialists have come to recognized that it takes a dynamic and constant rebalancing of salary and benefits, if employers are to effectively integrate their human resource objectives with those of their workforces.

This chapter traces key workplace trends in the society at large, and then discuss how they have been mirrored in the public sector. In addition, we outline how these trends will influence designers of public employee benefit plans for the twenty-first century. In particular, we argue that retirement systems and expanded employee choice will be essential in attracting and retaining the ideal mix of workers for public employers in years to come. This is because public employers are now recognizing that they confront new and diverse compensation as well as benefit challenges. Competition with the private sector for employees has intensified just as public employers are reevaluating the relationship among personnel, compensation and benefit policies. These will strongly influence the future evolutionary path of public-sector pension benefits design and policy.

Workforce Developments

Key workforce trends that will shape compensation strategies in the next hundred years including population aging, technological change, and new work patterns. Demographers have recognized that the United States will experience a large increase in the fraction of elderly: in 1970, persons 65+ accounted for 9.8 percent of the population, and this figure will rise to 13.3 percent by 2010, and over 20 percent by 2040 (Bureau of the Census, 1975; SSA 1997). One result of this pattern is that employers will seek to retain older workers, as there will be too few younger workers to fill available jobs.

To appeal to older workers, it is likely that there will be pressure to constantly revisit and revise compensation structures. One response, already starting to be seen in practice, is that companies will implement programs with financial incentives embedded in them to induce more worker productivity. Examples include pay for performance, bonus plans, and gainsharing, as well as flexible benefit arrangements permitting employees to choose benefits that best suit their individual needs from a specified list or menu given a specified budget of benefit dollars. For example, an older worker could purchase long-term care insurance, while a younger worker might opt for childcare benefits.

A related workplace shift that has already begun and will greatly influence future benefit design is the movement away from a permanent, full-time workforce to more temporary, part-time, and contract employees. Employers seeking to remain competitive while meeting the needs of their customers on a project-by-project basis will increasingly find that a flexible staff allows more customization of the workforce to the product. Employee teams will be molded to meet clients needs, probably with some permanent employees and supplemented with temporary or specialty employees. Chat groups and e-mail is being used to create a team of workers without using physical office space. Video conferencing allows employees to interact visually, without leaving their individual locations. A specific area where this is occurring is in the information/technology field, where employers are already experiencing difficulty in locating, hiring, and retaining these specialists (Virginia Polytechnic Institute 1998; Violino 1999). With team development and shifting skill needs, employers must design an entire work environment—including benefits—that will both attract employees for short-term assignments, while also providing meaningful benefits to permanent employees.

A more flexible workplace is also facilitated by technological change which will allow employees to be increasingly flexible about where and when they work. The development of the "virtual workplace" concept, and telecommuting, are hallmarks of this movement (Crandall and Wallace 1997).

Many firms still use paper communications media, but increasingly they must expand electronic communications with their constituents. This applies to public as well as private sector entities: for instance, governments are increasingly using the Internet for tax filing or providing information and forms. In our view, the greater value accorded technologic skills will likely drive two trends in employment benefits. First, younger workers will become relatively more attractive, inasmuch as they often have more of these skills than do older workers. As a result, benefits will be designed to attract and keep these younger workers. But second, because of the anticipated shortage of young workers, employers will be faced with the necessity of offering technology training and educational benefits to attract and keep employees of all ages.

Changing Retirement Patterns

In addition to workforce changes, the nature of retirement is evolving as well. Americans' life expectancy is expected to continue to rise in the foreseeable future, a trend that will inevitably drive demands for more retirement income. Thus in 1940, a 65-year old man could expect to live another 12 years; by 1997 this had risen to 15.5 and it is soon expected to be 20 years. His 65-year old female counterpart could expect 13.5 more years in 1940; by 1997, it was 19 years, and her life expectancy too is expected to keep rising over the next quarter-century (The Concord Coalition 1998; Employee Benefit Research Institute 1999).

The lengthening of the retirement period also comes at a time when the nation has recognized that important reforms are needed in our social security system to maintain program solvency. Although the choice of specific policies has not yet been resolved, likely changes will probably include changes in the benefit eligibility age(s) or levels, increases in the tax rate or base, adjustments to inflation indexation, or perhaps the establishment of individual investment accounts (Mitchell et al. 1999). As the social security normal retirement age rises from 65 to 67, and perhaps later, some people may delay retirement, while others may switch careers, working on a new or "bridge" job until they reach social security eligibility age. Such a reform could induce many workers to remain in the labor force longer. A similar effect might follow from a change in the amount of money that a retiree can earn before social security benefits are partially or fully reduced. If this limit were increased in the future so that retirees would not lose social security benefits with each dollar earned, elderly individuals would have a greater incentive to work after beginning to receive benefits.

The possible impacts on work patterns of more far-reaching changes in the social security system are more difficult to predict, although some might induce extended worklives particularly among women workers. For instance, the General Accounting Office (GAO 1997) recently concluded that women's short labor market attachment period translated into lower benefit amounts, despite the fact that the rules are gender-neutral on their face. The agency also found that individual account plans might lower women's benefits relative to men's, depending on the way the reform was structured.

Issues Specific to the Public Sector Workforce

These trends just described influence employers and employees as a whole, but in addition there are several factors likely to be particularly salient in the public sector. It is worth noting that state and local government employment is projected to grow at an overall rate of only 1 percent annually over the next decade, below the 1.3 percent employment growth rate expected for the overall economy. As a result, the fraction of workers in state and local government is projected to fall just slightly, from 12.4 percent in 1986, to 12.2 percent in 2006 (Franklin 1997). Inasmuch as the public sector workforce is not growing in relative terms, it will also be expected to age somewhat.

As this process continues, the government sector as an employer will become more competitive with private sector firms, particularly for employees with high-tech skills. The public sector workforce today is heavily dominated by service, teaching, and public safety workers. It is reasonable to expect that governments will continue to employ relatively more women because of the high concentration of teachers in this workforce. But some changes are likely to be felt. For example, the public sector has had a specific mandate to provide public safety, particularly through the police and firefighting forces. In the past, employees tended to join the uniformed services in their early 20s, and could retire at 50 or 55 years of age from these physically demanding positions. A shortfall of younger workers will no doubt mean that state and local governments will face increasing pressure to keep staffing levels up. In the future, we also anticipate that technological services such as Internet expertise will be in more demand, driving public employers to compete in this increasingly sophisticated labor market.

Implications for Benefits in the Public Sector

What will be the consequences of these changes for public sector compensation and employee benefits? One is that governments may need to increase salaries for particular jobs and occupations. As an example, some states and municipalities are already exploring multiple pay structures, which permits the rebalancing of compensation away from tenure, and toward specific skills for which there is stiff market competition. Related to this is the fact that as competition for employees drives up salaries, state and local governments will need to take a total compensation perspective that combines salary and benefits into a single budget item. Managing these costs in a wholistic way will be needed to balance salary and benefit program costs. It is also likely that benefits packages in the public sector will need to become more flexible. It has been observed that employees who are parents may value benefits differently from their single counterparts, placing high importance on childcare. Others who have aging parents will tend to value eldercare and long-term care insurance benefits more highly. All employees have tended to place high value of flexible work schedules, as well. In the future, public employers will need to develop benefit packages that are flexible enough to attract and retain the needed workforce for these positions. Careful restructuring of health insurance benefits may also be another method of retaining and attracting older workers, though cost considerations require careful attention to these offerings.

As this process unfolds, public employers will evolve from being benefits *providers* to being benefits *facilitators*. That is, instead of the employer offering a single plan that covers all employees, the new model will have the employer assisting employees to find the right benefits combination for their situations. Part of this new role will include employer education, instructing employees how to meet their long-term financial goals. This facilitator role must engender a new view of benefits from both the employer's and employee's perspective. The employer challenge will be to offer benefits that are valued by employees at various career stages. From the employee perspective, more options will be available, but in turn this will require the worker to take more responsibility in planning for his or her financial needs.

Drivers of Public Pension Redesign

In the particular case of public pensions, many state and local governments will find that the changing workforce requires a number of design changes. For instance, some will seek to update their pension system to retain older workers who will carry forward the institutional memory of processes, procedures, and history as technological changes are implemented. In other cases, a pension might be adapted so as to encourage retirees to return to work, which is feasible if governments permit the accumulation of additional retirement benefits for "unretirees."

One factor deserving note is that state and local employers often have rules restricting how much a former worker who has retired can earn if he or she returns to work for the same employer. In some cases, these rules also limit reemployment at *any* participating government in a combined retirement system. In such a case, should the older individual return to the public sector employer or work "too much," the pension benefit paid may be reduced or suspended. Naturally, such limits can be a barrier to work at older ages. Earnings limits do not apply if the retiree is receiving benefits from a private employer and is now working for the government, nor when a retiree from a government works in the private sector.

As public plans recognize a need to retain older workers, and retirees seek to earn some additional income, public pensions will need to review their return-to-work limits. A recent examination of 105 statewide pensions found that there are two primary types of earnings limits: loss of retirement benefits for *any* work, or reduction in retirement benefits when a retiree has worked over a *set limit* (PRI, 1999). Such limits include working over a particular number of hours each week, earning more than a specified amount, and working more than a given number of weeks per year. The survey found that all but two of the 55 respondents imposed some type of earnings limit on retirees who returned to work for their prior employer; the earnings limit centered at around $13,500 per year (or 730 hours). It also found that 89 percent of the plans also imposed a limit if the retiree worked for any employer who participated in the retirement system. The most commonly used limit involved benefit suspension while the retiree is reemployed (58 percent); many also require that no additional benefit may be earned while reemployed (36 percent). Numerous systems (30 percent) impose limits on the number of hours that can be worked or the level of earnings allowed (32 percent) permitted before retirement benefits are reduced. In addition, thirty-six of the fifty-three plans with restrictions had two or more restrictions. For example, a plan might allow participants to choose between several options of how to alter their retirement benefit when they became reemployed.

Another factor that may drive public pension redesign is a controversial proposal that would require all state and local employees to participate in social security. For the approximately 5 million state and local government employees, or a quarter of current public employees, currently outside of social security and their employers, a requirement of universal participation would require plan redesign, increased cost and/or reductions in benefits from the employer plan. This transition would be very costly, on the order of $26 billion over five years (The Segal Company 1999). Further, the General Accounting Office (1998) has concluded that this reform would extend the systems' solvency by only two years. If it were enacted, many jurisdictions would need to completely reassess their total compensation packages. For example, social security earned income limits differ from state and local government earning limits just described. Social security retirement ages also differ from those in the public pension sector, and many governmental plans pay supplemental retirement benefits until a retiree grows old enough to receive social security. Evidently, changes in social security ages would in turn affect public plan costs. Finally, it must be recalled that the public sector tends to hire relatively more women and it employs public safety personnel who tend to retire at earlier ages as compared to the private sector. Therefore social security system changes will have distinct and potentially far-reaching impacts in the public sector.

Encouraging Employee Saving

It appears that public employers in the future must seek to encourage additional employee saving, if they are to achieve target income replacement ratios of 75–80 percent (Salisbury 1997). One way to help state and local employees achieve this goal is to conduct a strategic plan review. Such a review would ask the following questions:

- What personnel objectives is the plan sponsor trying to accomplish through the plan's design? Is the plan meeting these objectives? Are the benefits competitive?
- What income replacement is provided to retirees? Is this rate achieved for most or only a few retirees? Can the plan sponsor afford to provide a higher income replacement goal? Are there retirees or others terminating employment with little retirement income or savings and are there options to assist those individuals? Should the replacement rate be preserved in real terms with inflation adjustments?
- Are employees doing any saving privately, and what vehicles are they using (e.g., IRA, 457 plans, etc)? Should the employer provide more retirement saving opportunities?
- Are employees covered by social security, and what can that system be expected to provide in the future?

As a result of a plan review, the state of Missouri recently instituted a match of employee contributions to its section 457, and in so doing has leveraged employee saving quite successfully. When an employee contributes to this plan, the employer matches up to $25 monthly in a separate account: as a result, participation in the section 457 plan grew from 30 to 70 percent in just two years. Due to the program's popularity and its manageable cost the state has authorized but not yet implemented a new, higher monthly match of up to $75. Similar state programs have been instituted in Oklahoma, Tennessee, and Maryland.

Developments in Portability

In addition to efforts to enhance saving incentives, public sector pension plans are also moving to facilitate portability. This refers to the ability to carry one's retirement accumulation or credits as the employee moves between employers. In an era when the employee remained with a single employer during the entire career, portability was not a concern. However, today portability can mean the difference between a comfortable retirement and needing, rather than wanting, to work through retirement (see Fore, this volume). Two methods are available for making pensions portable: dollar portability or service portability. In a defined contribution plan, the size of the retirement benefit depends on the funds accumulated in the individual's account. Portability may be achieved by transferring funds from a former employer's defined contribution plan account to an individual retirement account (IRA), or to the new employer's plan. In a defined benefit plan, the retirement benefit depends on the retiree's years of service and salary as specified according to a formula. In the public sector, pension portability may be accomplished by permitting the mobile employee to transfer service from one employer to the next. This occurs when a monetary amount is transferred between plans, equal to the value of the worker's accrued benefit. Portability is often thought to be more difficult in defined benefit plans as compared to defined contribution plans, because of the role of assumptions in the valuation of employee accruals.

As public sector employers find they must compete for employees at all age levels and with different benefit preferences, some have already added portability options to their plans. Some portability provisions are attached to defined benefit plans, though some governments have established defined contribution arrangements for all new workers or for a specific subset of employees. For example, the state of Michigan established a defined contribution plan for all new state workers in 1997. In the same year the state of Vermont instituted a defined contribution plan for elected and appointed officials who, through the power of the ballot box may experience higher job mobility. This focus on portability is also influencing the growth of section 457 or 403(b) plans, which are public sector deferred compensation plans similar in concept to section 401(k) plans (Bureau of Labor Statistics 1996). Section 457 and section 401(k) plans are types of defined contribution plans. A section 457 plan account balance from a previous public employer can be transferred to a new public employer's 457 plan without any tax implications. The same is true between section 401(k) plans. Further options may emerge if the federal government passes tax law changes that would permit almost complete portability between and among retirement arrangements. The ability to carry assets from one employer to the next is one type of portability that can preserve the benefits as well.

Three factors unique to public sector defined benefit plans provide some portability under current rules: employee contributions, purchases of service credit, and reciprocity agreements. As noted above, most public sector employees are required to make some contribution to their pension plan (Mitchell et al. this volume). Generally, when employees leave their public sector employment before retirement and they have been required to make contributions, these contributions are returned to them, often with interest. These contributions can then be placed in a subsequent employer defined contribution plan or, in some cases, a defined benefit plan. Purchase of service credit arrangements allow mobile employees to "purchase" years of employment with their new public sector employer. This is common for those serving in the military: for instance, a two-year veteran of the armed forces who then works for a state government for 35 years could, if allowed by the state government, add the two years of military service to his benefit formula by "purchasing" or contributing the cost of the additional service to the plan. The retirement benefit under the state government plan rules would then be calculated using 37 years of service. Most state plans permit this (92 percent) and half of local plans do as well (PRI 1998), generally up to a capped number of years. A third portability approach entails reciprocity agreements between state and local government plans (usually within the same state). Such an agreement would permit two employers to transfer service, funds, or both for people changing jobs if they had worked for two or more employers covered by the agreement. Some 40 percent of statewide plans participate in this type of reciprocity agreement (PRI 1998). It is to be anticipated that similar provisions will proliferate in the future, to accommodate employees seeking portability.

Two additional portability provisions have recently been added to the set of public plan options, distinguished according to whether they offer "front-end" or "back-end" portability. Front-end portability pertains to decisions made around the time someone is initially hired. For example, it is common for public universities to offer new teaching staff a choice between a statewide defined benefit plan and an individual-account model defined contribution plan. Back-end portability provisions specify how employees may receive their benefits at or near retirement. One variant on this theme is the so-called "deferred retirement option plan," known as a DROP plan. This refers to a plan permitting employees to contract to retire at a specified future date (generally as much as five years ahead). The retirement benefit is then frozen as of the current date, and any future retirement accruals earned are paid as a lump sum at retirement. At retirement the individual receives a pension benefit from the general plan and a lump sum from the DROP. This lump sum can then be rolled into an IRA to accumulate additional retirement assets. Giving employees distribution options of this type in the context of a defined benefit plan increases flexibility in response to employee demands.

To illustrate some of the more innovative provisions related to portability we turn next to some salient examples. For example, the Ohio State Teachers Retirement System allows employees to compute benefits two ways, as a defined benefit plan, or as a money purchase plan (which is a type of defined contribution plan). Under the money purchase alternative, the employee may take part of the employer's contributions and interest when they leave employment; thus someone with under three years of service receives the employee contributions plus four percent interest, while someone with more than three but less than five years service receives contributions plus six percent interest. A participant with five or more years in the plan would receive 50 percent of the employer matching contributions. Another public pension pioneer in this arena is the Texas Municipal Retirement System (TMRS), which has a cash balance plan. In this structure, workers accumulate an account balance that is credited with interest; the TMRS cash balance plan guarantees a minimum rate of return, but not the benefit amount (assets are invested by TMRS and are not self-directed.) If the participant separates from service before vesting, then he or she can take the account as a lump sum benefit. A participant's annuity is the actuarial equivalent of the sum of the participant's own monthly contributions plus interest during working years and an equal or greater multiple sum out of the employer's accumulation account plus interest. TMRS also provides a partial lump sum distribution based on a participant's last three years of contributions at retirement.

As a final example, the Colorado Public Employees Association (COPERA) instituted its current plan in 1995, at which time it added a money purchase retirement plan to its set of pension options. Similar to the Ohio State plan, plan assets are invested by COPERA and are not self-directed. Retiring employees may choose between the higher of a defined benefit or a defined contribution amount. The money purchase benefit is calculated using the value of the participant's contributions and interest on these funds since the date of membership. The total amount then is converted to a lifetime benefit using the retiree's life expectancy or that of their co-beneficiary. A participant who terminates prior to retirement eligibility receives his/her contributions, a 25 percent employer match and interest on the total amount. Individuals who are eligible to retire can take a lump sum distribution or an annuity. The lump sum distribution is equivalent to the participant's total contribution, a 50 percent employer match and interest. Interest is credited at 80 percent of the assumed actuarial rate.

Conclusion

A major challenge facing public-sector employers in the next several decades is their ability to respond creatively to workforce and retirement trends. Compensation and benefits structures must support career, core, and contingency workers and the increased competitiveness of the workplace will require a rebalancing of pay and benefits policy. This process will not be static; rather, continued redesign will be needed to encourage evolving employee behaviors. Benefit plans, and pensions in particular, will have to be increasingly flexible, accommodating new work and retirement patterns. Employee choice will be essential in attracting and retaining the ideal mix of workers for each employer. Governments will continue to move away from the role as the sole provider of benefits to one of a partner or "facilitator" of benefits. Increasingly, individuals will take more responsibility for managing their benefits. Augmenting education about benefit choices, investment approaches and financial planning will intensify for all employers. Portability in pension will be needed to attract and retain younger and more mobile employees, as well as to appeal to older people seeking reemployment. These features will place more responsibility on employees to manage and preserve their retirement assets, and will lead employers to better educate those who must manage their own financial matters.

References

Bureau of the Census. 1975. *Historical Statistics of the United States, Colonial Times to 1970*. Washington, D.C.: U.S. GPO.

Bureau of Labor Statistics. 1994. *Employee Benefits in Medium and Large Private Establishments, 1993.* Washington, D.C.: U.S. GPO.

———. 1994. *Employee Benefits in State and Local Governments, 1994.* Washington, D.C.: U.S. GPO.

Commerce Clearing House (CCH). 1997. *1998 Social Security Benefits Including Medicare.* Chicago: CCH Inc. 27–28.

Concord Coalition. 1998. *Financing Retirement Security for an Aging America: Background Information About Population Change, Social Security, and Medicare.* Washington, D.C.: Committee for a Responsible Federal Budget.

Crandall, N. Fredric and Marc J. Wallace, Jr. 1997. "Inside the Virtual Workplace: Forging a New Deal for Work and Rewards." *Compensation and Benefits Review* 29, 1: 27–36.

Employee Benefit Research Institute. 1999. "Retirement Patterns and Bridge Jobs in the 1990s." EBRI Issue Brief 206.

Fore, Douglas. This volume. "Going Private in the Public Sector: The Transition from Defined Benefit to Defined Contribution Pension Plans."

Franklin, James C. 1997. "Industry Output and Employment Projections to 2006." *Monthly Labor Review* (November): 39–45.

General Accounting Office (GAO). 1997. *Social Security Reform: Implications for Women's Retirement Income.* HEHS-98–42. Washington, D.C.: U.S. GPO.

———. 1998. *Social Security: Restoring Long-Term Solvency Will Require Difficult Choices.* T-HEHS-98–95. Washington, D.C.: U.S. GPO.

Mitchell, Olivia S., David McCarthy, Stanley C. Wisniewski, and Paul Zorn. This volume. "Developments in State and Local Pension Plans."

Mitchell, Olivia S., Robert J. Myers, and Howard Young, eds. 1999. *Prospects for Social Security Reform.* Pension Research Council. Philadelphia: University of Pennsylvania Press.

Public Pension Coordinating Council. 1998. *PENDAT 97.* Chicago: Public Pension Coordinating Council.

Public Retirement Institute (PRI). 1998. *Purchases of Service Credit: Portability for Public-Sector Employees.* Alexandria, Va.: Public Retirement Institute.

————. 1999. *The Structure of Earnings Limits in Public Pensions.* Alexandria, Va.: Public Retirement Institute.

Salisbury, Dallas L. 1997. "Benefit Planning and Management in a Changing, Dynamic Labor Market." *Compensation and Benefits Review* 29 (January): 74–80.

Segal Company. 1999. *The Impact of Mandatory Social Security for State and Local Governments.* Washington, D.C.: American Federation of State, County, and Municipal Employees.

Social Security Administration (SSA). 1998. *1997 Annual Report of the Board of Trustees of the Federal Old-Age and Survivors Insurance and Disability Insurance Trust Funds.* Washington, D.C.: U.S. GPO.

Violino, Bob. 1999 "Outside Help Wanted." *Information Week Online,* January 4: 1–7.

Virginia Polytechnic Institute and State University and Information Technology Association of American. 1998. *Help Wanted 1998: A Call for Collaborative Action for the New Millennium.* Richmond: Virginia Polytechnic Institute and State University.

Contributors

John Brosius is the Executive Director of the Pennsylvania State Employees' Retirement System (SERS), with the responsibility of managing the operations of a $23 billion retirement fund serving 85,000 retirees and 109,000 active members employed by 110 different employer agencies. Previously Mr. Brosius was Director of the SERS Office of Financial Management; he also taught college level accounting courses and worked at Main LaFrentz & Co. He received a bachelor's degree from Bloomsburg University of Pennsylvania, and an MBA from Bucknell University. He is a Certified Public Accountant.

Tom Bryan is Deputy Director, New Jersey Division of Pensions and Benefits. He advises on legal, legislative, policy, and actuarial matters for the New Jersey state retirement systems and health benefits program. He also manages the Legislative and Legal Affairs section of the director's office, and serves as liaison with the treasurer's office, the governor's office, the legislature, and other state agencies. Previously he served in the New Jersey Office of Legislative Services. Mr. Bryan earned a JD from Seton Hall University and BA and MA degrees in political science from Rutgers University.

Robert L. Clark is Professor of Economics and Business Management at North Carolina State University. He has published widely on retirement and pension policy, employee benefit policy, the economic well-being of the elderly, and international pensions. Professor Clark serves as Senior Fellow at the Center for the Study of Aging and Human Development at Duke University and as Senior Research Fellow at the Center for Demographic Studies at Duke University. Previous academic positions include a faculty appointment at the Fuqua School of Business, Duke University, and service as Interim Dean of the College of Management at North Carolina State. Dr. Clark earned a bachelor's degree from Millsaps College and a PhD in economics from Duke University.

Lee A. Craig is Associate Professor of Economics at North Carolina State

University, where he teaches economic and business history. His research focuses on the history of pensions, productivity growth, and international economic integration. Dr. Craig is a research economist at the National Bureau of Economic Research, and he has previously held appointments at Duke University and Universitat Munchen. He received bachelor's and master's degrees from Ball State University and MA and PhD degrees from Indiana University.

Roderick B. Crane is a Director of the National Government Compliance practice of The Segal Company, and a company Vice President. His interests include the design and administration of public sector retirement and saving plans, including 401(k) and 403(b) plans. Previously he was counsel to the North Dakota Legislative Council's Committee on Public Employee Retirement Programs. Mr. Crane received a bachelor's degree in economics from the University of North Dakota, and a JD from the University of North Dakota School of Law.

Cathie Eitelberg is the Director of Government Practice for The Segal Company where she coordinates and participates in the firm's consulting, compliance, and actuarial services provided to the public sector. Her special interests include public employee benefits, industry trends, and federal policy as it affects benefits. Concurrently Ms. Eitelberg serves as an adviser to the Government Finance Officers Association Committee on Retirement Benefits Administration. Previously she worked at the National Conference of State Legislatures and the Government Finance Officers Association. She earned a bachelor's degree in business management from the University of Maryland.

Douglas Fore is Manager of Pension and Economic Research at TIAA-CREF. His research interests include the determinants of pension type. Dr. Fore earned a PhD from the University of Colorado.

James Francis is Chief Economist for the Florida State Board of Administration. He is responsible for the FRS and Chiles Endowment investment plans, asset allocation, risk management, performance measurement, and total fund investment research, as well as for the SBA Information Center, an internal library and research services unit. He has been vice-president and consulting economist for the consulting firm CFF Associates, Inc., Director of Research and Analysis for the Florida Department of Revenue, and House Economist for the Florida House of Representatives. He holds a PhD in economics from the Florida State University.

David Hess is a doctoral candidate in the Management Department at the Wharton School of the University of Pennsylvania. His research focuses on corporate governance and corporate social responsibility. He earned a bachelor's degree in economics from Grinnell College and a JD from the University of Iowa College of Law.

Edwin C. Hustead is Senior Vice President in charge of the Hay/Huggins

Washington, D.C., office and governmental actuarial and benefits consulting. He is also the practice leader of the Hay Group for governmental consulting. His interests focus on health insurance, social insurance, pension reform, and policy analysis. Previously he served as Chief Actuary of the Federal Office of Personnel Management, charged with responsibility for the actuarial analysis of the Civil Service Retirement System and the Federal Employees Health Benefits System. Mr. Hustead is a Member of the American Academy of Actuaries, a Fellow of the Society of Actuaries, and an Enrolled Actuary.

Toni Hustead is Chief of the Veterans Affairs Branch of the U.S. Office of Management and Budget, Executive Office of the President. She oversees the development of veterans' programs and policies, and their integration with other Presidential priorities. Previously she was an international benefits consultant for the Hay Group, serving as the European Director of Benefits Consulting, and served as Chief Actuary for the Department of Defense. She is a Member of the American Academy of Actuaries, and an Associate of the Society of Actuaries.

David McCarthy is a doctoral candidate in the Insurance and Risk Management Department at the Wharton School of the University of Pennsylvania. His research focuses on the economics, econometrics, and finance of pensions. Previously he worked in a South African life insurance firm where he initiated the examination process for the Faculty of Actuaries, Edinburgh, and expects to qualify this year. He earned a BS in economic science and also in mathematical statistics from the University of the Witwatersrand, Johannesburg.

Olivia S. Mitchell is the International Foundation of Employee Benefit Plans Professor of Insurance and Risk Management, and Executive Director of the Pension Research Council, of the Wharton School at the University of Pennsylvania. Her research focuses on the economics of retirement and benefits, social security and pensions, and public as well as private insurance. Dr. Mitchell currently serves on the Board of the National Academy of Social Insurance, the Steering Committee for the University of Michigan's HRS/AHEAD projects, and she is a Research Associate at the National Bureau of Economic Research. Previously Dr. Mitchell served on the Board of Directors for Alexander and Alexander Services Inc., and she has held academic appointments at Cornell University and Harvard University. Dr. Mitchell earned a BS in economics from Harvard University, and MS and PhD degrees in economics from the University of Wisconsin.

Alicia H. Munnell is the Peter F. Drucker Professor of Management Sciences at Boston College's Carroll School of Management and Director of the Boston College Center for Retirement Research. Her research interests include pension and social security policy, and the determinants of productivity; in addition she has analyzed bank mergers and tax policy. Previously Dr. Munnell was a Member of the President's Council of Economic Advisers and Assistant Secretary of the Treasury for Economic Policy. She also was Director of Research and Senior Vice President at the Boston Federal Reserve Bank. Among other affiliations, Dr. Munnell is on the Board of the Pension Research Council, and she cofounded the National Academy of Social Insurance. She earned a bachelor's degree from Wellesley College, an MA from Boston University, and a PhD from Harvard University.

Michael Peskin is a Principal in Morgan Stanley's Global Pension Group where he heads the unit responsible for helping insurers, corporate plan sponsors, and others, with investment strategy and asset/liability studies in a corporate financial framework. His published research includes strategic asset allocation and benefit financial theory and he has published widely on pension finance. He is an Associate of the Society of Actuaries and the Institute of Actuaries, a Fellow of the Conference on Consulting Actuaries, and a Member of the American Academy of Actuaries. Previously he worked at Buck Consultants and was President of Michael Peskin Associates, Inc.

Silvana Pozzebon is Associate Professor of Industrial Relations at the Ecole des Hautes Etudes Commerciales, the business school at the University of Montreal. Her areas of interest include union-management relations, as well as private and public benefits including workers' compensation, health and safety management, and pensions. She earned a bachelor's degree in economics from Concordia University in Montreal, and MS and PhD degrees from Cornell University.

Kevin SigRist is the Assistant Chief Economist at the Florida State Board of Administration. His principal research responsibilities are in investment policy and performance measurement. Previously, he was responsible for assessing foreign country risk and preparing economic forecasts at Wells Fargo Company. He has worked as an econometrician and tax analyst at the Missouri State Budget Office and a research assistant at the Center for the Study of American Business at Washington University in St. Louis. He holds a BS in economics from the University of Wisconsin-Oshkosh and an MA in economics from Washington University in St. Louis.

Karen Steffen is a Principal with the Seattle office of Milliman & Robertson, Inc. Her primary practice is in the area of public employee benefit systems, with a focus on retirement and employee benefit plans, actuarial valuation and funding strategies, and postretirement benefits. She also consults on pension calculations in marital dissolution cases. She is a Fellow of the Society of Actuaries, a Member of the Conference of Consulting Actuaries, a Member of the American Academy of Actuaries, and an

Enrolled Actuary. Ms. Steffen earned a bachelor's degree in mathematics from the University of Michigan.

Annika Sundén is the Associate Director for Research at Boston College's Center for Retirement Research. Her research interests include the economics of retirement, pensions, and social security, and the determinants of savings behavior. She previously worked at the Federal Reserve Board on the Survey of Consumer Finance. Dr. Sunden received a PhD in labor economics from Cornell University.

Kenneth Trager is the Total Fund Research Manager at the Florida State Board of Administration. His research interests include applied business cycle theory, regional economic development, tax incidence, and political economy. Previously Dr. Trager served as a Senior Economist in the Florida Legislature's Joint Legislative Management Committee and as the Florida Statistical Analysis Center Director. He earned a PhD in economics from the New School for Social Research.

Michael Useem is the William and Jacalyn Egan Professor of Management and Director of the Center for Leadership and Change Management at the Wharton School, University of Pennsylvania. His research interests focus on corporate organization, corporate ownership, and governance, as well as leadership in both the private and public sectors. He has consulted with numerous private institutions as well as government agencies, and he offers programs for managers throughout Latin America and Asia as well as Europe. Among other affiliations Dr. Useem serves on the Board for the Pension Research Council. He earned a bachelor's degree from the University of Michigan, and MA and PhD degrees from Harvard University.

Jack W. Wilson is Head of the Department of Business Management in the North Carolina State University's College of Management. His research concentrates on financial markets, with a focus on market volatility and market panics. Dr. Wilson's academic career has included appointments at Duke and Princeton Universities as well as the Universities of Maryland, Oklahoma, and Bowling Green. He earned a bachelor's degree in finance, as well as MA and PhD degrees in economics, from the University of Oklahoma.

Stanley C. Wisniewksi is a Senior Professional Associate at the National Education Association where he specializes in pension, health care, and other benefits policy. His research interests include public pension plans with a special focus on teacher pensions, compensation policy, labor market trends and collective bargaining, and healthcare issues. He previously served on the faculty at American University and Howard University; was research director for the Service Employees International Union; held the position of President of Workplace Economics Inc.; and has been a practicing attorney and expert witness. Dr. Wisniewski earned a bachelor's degree from Allentown College of St. Francis de Sales, and MA and PhD degrees in economics from the Catholic University of America. He also holds a JD from the University of Maryland School of Law.

Paul Zorn is Director of Governmental Research at Gabriel, Roeder, Smith and Co. in the firm's Southfield, Michigan, office. He specializes in research on public retirement systems and employee benefit plans, and he advises on federal/state accounting standards, benefit policies, and social security. Previously he managed the Research Center at the Government Finance Officers Association where he was instrumental in developing the PENDAT database.

Index

The Pension Research Council

The Pension Research Council of the Wharton School at the University of Pennsylvania is an organization committed to generating debate on key policy issues affecting pensions and other employee benefits. The Council sponsors interdisciplinary research on the entire range of private and social retirement security and related benefit plans in the United States and around the world. It seeks to broaden understanding of these complex arrangements through basic research into their economic, social, legal, actuarial, and financial foundations. Members of the Advisory Board of the Council, appointed by the Dean of the Wharton School, are leaders in the employee benefits field, and they recognize the essential role of social security and other public sector income maintenance programs while sharing a desire to strengthen private sector approaches to economic security.

Executive Director

Olivia S. Mitchell, *International Foundation of Employee Benefit Plans Professor,* Department of Insurance and Risk Management, The Wharton School, University of Pennsylvania, Philadelphia.

Senior Partners

AARP
Actuarial Sciences Associates, Inc.
Buck Consultants, Inc.
Goldman Sachs
Morgan Stanley Dean Witter & Co.
Mutual of America Life Insurance Co.
PricewaterhouseCoopers
SEI Investments, Inc.
State Street Corporation

Richard Prosten, *Director,* Washington Office, Amalgamated Life Insurance/Amalgamated Bank of New York, Washington, D.C.

Anna M. Rappaport, F.S.A., *Managing Director,* William M. Mercer, Inc., Chicago, Illinois

Jerry S. Rosenbloom, *Frederick H. Ecker Professor of Insurance and Risk Management,* The Wharton School, Philadelphia, Pennsylvania

Sylvester J. Schieber, *Vice President and Director of Research and Information Center,* The Wyatt Company, Washington, D.C.

Richard B. Stanger, *National Director,* Employee Benefits Services, Price Waterhouse LLP, New York, New York

Marc M. Twinney, Jr., F.S.A., *Consultant,* Bloomfield Hills, Michigan

Michael Useem, *Professor of Management and Sociology,* The Wharton School, Philadelphia, Pennsylvania

Jack L. VanDerhei, *Associate Professor of Risk and Insurance,* Temple University, Philadelphia, Pennsylvania

Paul H. Wenz, F.S.A., *Second Vice President and Actuary,* The Principal Financial Group, Des Moines, Iowa

Stephen Zeldes, *Benjamin Rosen Professor of Economics and Finance,* Columbia University, New York, New York

Pension Research Council Publications

Demography and Retirement: The Twenty-First Century. Anna M. Rappaport and Sylvester J. Schieber, eds. 1993.

An Economic Appraisal of Pension Tax Policy in the United States. Richard A. Ippolito. 1991.

The Economics of Pension Insurance. Richard A. Ippolito. 1991.

Forecasting Retirement Needs and Retirement Wealth. Olivia S. Mitchell, P. Brett Hammond, and Anna M. Rappaport, eds. 2000.

Fundamentals of Private Pensions. Dan M. McGill, Kyle N. Brown, John J. Haley and Sylvester Schieber. Seventh edition. 1996.

The Future of Pensions in the United States. Ray Schmitt, ed. 1993.

Inflation and Pensions. Susan M. Wachter. 1991.

Living with Defined Contribution Pensions. Olivia S. Mitchell and Sylvester J. Schieber, eds. 1998.

Pension Mathematics with Numerical Illustrations. Howard E. Winklevoss. Second edition. 1993.

Pensions and the Economy: Sources, Uses, and Limitations of Data. Zvi Bodie and Alicia H. Munnell, eds. 1992.

Pensions, Economics and Public Policy. Richard A. Ippolito. 1991.

Positioning Pensions for the Twenty-First Century. Michael S. Gordon, Olivia S. Mitchell, and Marc M. Twinney, eds. 1997.

Prospects for Social Security Reform. Olivia S. Mitchell, Robert J. Myers, and Howard Young, eds. 1999.

Providing Health Care Benefits in Retirement. Judith F. Mazo, Anna M. Rappaport and Sylvester J. Schieber, eds. 1994.

Pensions in the Public Sector. Olivia S. Mitchell and Edwin Hustead, eds. *Forthcoming.*

Retirement Systems in Japan. Robert L. Clark. 1991.

Search for a National Retirement Income Policy. Jack L. VanDerhei, ed. 1987.

Securing Employer-Based Pensions: An International Perspective. Zvi Bodie, Olivia S. Mitchell, and John A. Turner. 1996.

Social Investing. Dan M. McGill, ed. 1984.

Social Security. Robert J. Myers. Fourth edition 1993.

To Retire or Not? Retirement Policy in Higher Education. Robert L. Clark and P. Brett Hammond. 2000.

Available from the University of Pennsylvania Press, telephone: 800/445-9880, fax: 410/516-6998. More information about the Pension Research Council is available at the web site:

http://prc.wharton.upenn.edu/prc/prc.html